Early Christianity

Early Christianity
Theology shaped by Saints

Paul Haffner

GRACEWING

First published in England in 2016
by
Gracewing
2 Southern Avenue
Leominster
Herefordshire HR6 0QF
United Kingdom
www.gracewing.co.uk

ISBN 978 085244 895 3

Cover design by Bernardita Peña Hurtado.
Detail from the apse of the church of St Pudenziana, Rome.

CONTENTS

FOREWORD

Paul Haffner's main theme is the relationship between sanctity and theology within the historical context of the first six centuries after Christ, and how that relationship forged the soul of early Christianity. The pages of this text take the reader on a pilgrimage to the many interesting people, events and places of the early Church. This book is warmly recommended for both theology students as well as for the general public.

Professor Cardinal Prosper Grech, OSA
Rome, 27 August 2016
Feast of St Monica

PREFACE

EARLY CHRISTIANITY EXPLORES how in the first centuries the followers of Jesus Christ lived their faith centred upon Him. It provides a comprehensive introduction, starting from New Testament times, to key figures in the rise of Christianity including Mary, Mother of God, and Saint Peter and Saint Paul, the founders of Christian Rome. The book shows how the theological tradition of the primacy of Rome developed in the Church and with the Papacy. It considers a wide range of issues in the life of the nascent Church, helping us to understand how the early Christians related faith and reason, and were prepared to suffer martyrdom for their belief. Early liturgical and sacramental life is fully described, including a broad examination of the issues surrounding the date of the Easter celebration. It also illustrates how the Church had to face internal conflict and heresy, and examines the work of the first general Councils.

The book throws into bold relief the significant role played by women in early Christianity, and describes the contribution of monks and missionaries in spreading the faith. It illustrates the impact on early Christianity of its leading figures, who exercised the major influence then and are still most important in the Church today. This study is carried out from a Roman perspective, as the Eternal City is the cradle and centre of Christianity. The thorny question of the Fall of Rome is outlined with its consequences for early Christianity.

This text intertwines doctrine and history, tradition and legend, in the hope that the reader will have a colourful ride through the first centuries of the Christian epoch to enable them to emulate what they find there.

I express my gratitude to His Eminence Prosper Cardinal Grech OSA who made some very helpful suggestions and also very kindly supplied the Foreword. My thanks as always go to

Tom Longford at Gracewing, without whose encouragement *Early Christianity* would not have seen the light of day. It is warmly dedicated to my students at the Duquesne University Italian Campus for whom it was written.

Rome, 18 August 2016
Feast of St Helena

ABBREVIATIONS

AAS=
Acta Apostolicae Sedis. Commentarium officiale. Typis Polyglottis Vaticanis, 1909–.

CCC=
Catechism of the Catholic Church. LEV, Città del Vaticano 1992.

CCL =
Corpus Christianorum series latina. Tournai: Brepols, 1954–.

DS=
H. Denzinger. *Enchiridion Symbolorum, Definitionum et Declarationum de rebus fidei et morum*. Edizione bilingue a cura di P. Hünermann. EDB, Bologna 1995.

OR=
L'Osservatore Romano, daily edition.

PG=
J. P. Migne. *Patrologiae cursus completus, series graeca*. 161 voll., Paris 1857–1866.

PL=
J. P. Migne. *Patrologiae cursus completus, series latina*. 221 voll., Paris 1844–1864.

SC=
Sources Chretiennes. Paris: Cerf, 1942–.

SF =
P. F. Palmer. *Sacraments and Forgiveness. History and Doctrinal Development of Penance, Extreme Unction and Indulgences*. Westminster, MD: The Newman Press, 1961.

SW =   P. F. Palmer. *Sacraments and Worship. Liturgy and Doctrinal Development of Baptism, Confirmation and the Eucharist.* Westminster, MD: The Newman Press, 1955.

1 MARY, MOTHER OF GOD

The Gospels are the first fruits of all Scripture and the Gospel of John is the first of the Gospels: no one can grasp its meaning without having leaned his head on Jesus' breast and having received Mary as Mother from Jesus.

Origen, *Commentary on St John's Gospel*

IN OUR TRAVELS through the beginnings of Christianity, the journey starts with Mary, Mother of God. In a very real sense she is the beginning of Christianity, because she bore Christ, her Son, and also because she was His first Disciple. She is also the perfect icon of the Church. We examine the details which Scripture and early Christian tradition furnish about the Mother of God.

1.1 Mary in the New Testament

Although the citations in Scripture referring to Mary may seem be few, they are nevertheless of great importance. At first sight, Holy Scripture seems to offer relatively little detail about Mary. One reason for this may be the focus on Jesus Christ, the Son of God. However, a deeper look at the Scriptures reveals that beneath the surface, beyond the purely literal sense of the Bible, a wealth of indications are to be found concerning the Mother of God. Passages which at first seem rather terse convey a rich tradition. What is important is not the quantity but the quality and depth of the texts. This richness may not be apparent upon a cursory and superficial reading, but becomes clear through a profound analysis which reveals that Mary is present and plays an important part in the decisive moments of the history of salvation.

Scripture presents a series of harmonic images of Mary, which see a certain development in portraying her. First, an historical presentation of Mary features in Matthew and Luke, which speak of her fullness of grace, her virginal maternity and her relationship with Jesus as a disciple. John proposes a mature theological reflection on Mary in which she recognises the messianic transcendence of her Son and receives from Him her maternal mission. Scripture always presents Mary in union to the mystery of Christ. The history of salvation is the context of this presentation in all its stages. Mary appears in the prophecies and prefigurations in the Old Testament, and is then united with Christ in the mysteries of His infancy. She is present at the beginning of the public ministry of her Son. She participates in the Paschal mystery and is attendant at the beginning of the Church. Mary cannot be separated from this economy of salvation and this economy cannot be understood apart from Mary.

1.1.1 Mary fulfils the Old Testament

Mary serves as a link between the two Covenants not just through parallel or prophetic verses but by embodying common themes. She is a bridge between the Old and the New Testaments because Scripture shows her representing both the people of Israel and the Church begun by her Son:

> A very important insight of modern exegesis has brought to light that the mystery of Mary forms in some way the synthesis of all the former revelation about the people of God, and of all that God by his salvific action wishes to realise for his people. In Mary are accomplished all the important aspects of the promises of the Old Testament to the Daughter of Zion, and in her real person there is an anticipation which will be realised for the new people of God, the Church. The history of revelation on the subject of the theme of the Woman Zion, realised in the person of Mary, and continued in the Church, constitutes a doctrinal bastion, an unshakeable structured ensemble for the comprehension of the history of salvation, from its origin up to

its eschatology. A vision of the mystery of Mary, biblically founded, ecclesiologically integrated and structurally developed, gives then a complete image of the concrete realisation of the total mystery of the Covenant.[1]

Various different schemes from biblical theology, which attempt to organise the data contained in Scripture, can be applied to Mary as the fulfilment of the Old Testament. Negative (or *apophatic*) theology considers that, despite having revealed Himself to man, God remains a mystery. According to this approach, characteristic in some ways of Eastern Christendom, God is better understood in silence than in a discourse about him. Within this perspective, Mary appears at the climax of the time of promise, as the convergence of the fulfilment of God's ways. Because God remains hidden despite His revelation, also the way of Mary is shrouded in mystery; it reveals and yet veils God's revelation. Biblical theology can also be organised according to positive (or *kataphatic*) theology. One example of this direction is the thematic approach, characteristic of Western Christendom, where specific topics such as Covenant, the Kingdom of God, the Name of Yahweh, election, and redemption are considered. Our Lady is the woman of the Covenant who is the realisation of the prophecies concerning the Daughter of Sion, in view of the indissoluble union between God and man.

A further approach involves the narrative method. Here, the Old Testament describes an economy of salvation which is brought to fulfilment in the New. The Scriptures trace God's mode of action and discover the principles that guide this. First, the Christ-event is the fundamental principle of the Bible. According to the scheme promise-fulfilment, the Old Testament is intrinsically open to the future and Christ is the final cause of the whole of the Old Covenant. Here, the principle of election-substitution consists in the election of a minority for the redemption of the totality. The history of salvation consists in two movements. One proceeds from plurality to unity: Israel is elected for the salvation of the world; the faithful remnant replaces the people as a whole; this remnant is reduced to one

Man, the servant of Yahweh or the Son of Man; Jesus fulfils this mission becoming the Centre of history. Mary stands alongside her Son as this faithful remnant. The second movement starts with Christ and proceeds from unity to plurality in the Church, applying the salvation which He has won. Here also, Mary collaborates in the distribution of the effects of Christ's salvation within the Church.[2]

A further scheme of biblical theology concerns the event of a dialogue. Biblical revelation is based not only upon concepts such as election, salvation, covenant, but above all upon actions. The theology of the Old Testament as fulfilled in the New, is based on the actions and words of God and man's response. The encounter with God takes the form of an experience of salvation (danger, invocation, God's listening, salvation, answer). The concepts of election and covenant are dependent on this relationship of dialogue, which is not however between two equal partners. The person who partakes of a dialogue with God in an eminent manner is Mary, the woman who experiences God's blessing and salvation. She is, in a way, a "microhistory of salvation", since God's ways converge in her, and again in her the exemplary response to God's economy of salvation can be found. This is seen for example in her response to the Annunciation: "You see before you the Lord's servant, let it happen to me as you have said" (Lk 1:38). The various Old Testament categories which we have discussed are thus brought to fulfilment in the New, in Mary.

1.1.2 Mary in the Synoptic Gospels

The Gospel of Mark

There are three passages in St Mark's Gospel which reveal certain questions for Mariology. These passages are Mark 3:20-21, Mark 3:31–35 and Mark 6:1–6 respectively.[3] The issues are first Jesus' relation with his family; second, the unusual title Son of Mary; and third the question of the brothers of Jesus. As regards this first question, Mark never says explicitly that Mary opposed Jesus, but rather just his fellow citizens, relatives, and family. The passage poses a distinction between the biological family of Jesus and his eschatological family, the Church. This would also imply that Mary always had a growing knowledge of Jesus' salvific mission, even if earlier on that knowledge was partial. Next, the title Son of Mary can be partially explained by St Joseph's death. Nevertheless, its meaning is above all that Mark knew about the virginal conception and wanted to avoid any confusion which would arise by calling him the son of Joseph. Thus, Mark's expression draws specific attention to the Virginal conception and birth of Christ.[4] Third, as regards the question of the brothers of Jesus, these brothers are never called sons of Mary. Also, two of the four sons (James and Joset) are sons of another Mary as can be seen from a later passage of Mark's Gospel: "There were some women watching from a distance. Among them were Mary of Magdala, Mary who was the mother of James the younger and Joset, and Salome" (Mk 15:40, see 15:47). Further, in Semitic languages, brother is the title used to refer to more distant relations like nephews or cousins.[5] Thus, these passages present no problem for the doctrine concerning Mary's virginity. Rather, they witness to her maternal care and her growth in faith, but not from incredulity to faith but rather from a Judaic faith to a faith in Christ.

The Gospel according to Matthew

Even through the first two chapters of St Matthew's Gospel are written in a popular form of the time and not according to the criteria of modern history, their testimony belongs to a mature Christian faith and they transmit historical events. The text reveals a theological development in Judaeo-Christian circles. According to Matthew, Mary forms part of the salvific plan announced in the Old Covenant and fully realised in the New.

Matthew begins his Gospel with the genealogy of Jesus. He does this for three reasons. First, to focus on the identity of Jesus by showing that He belongs to the people of Israel as Son of David and Son of Abraham. Second, he wishes to stress the special status of Jesus as the awaited Davidic Messiah. Third, Matthew desires to present Jesus as the vertex and synthesis of history. This genealogy shows how God works in the history or economy of salvation. Matthew presents the Virginal conception and Birth under the scheme of prophecy-fulfilment:

> 'Joseph son of David, do not be afraid to take Mary home as your wife, because she has conceived what is in her by the Holy Spirit. She will give birth to a Son and you must name Him Jesus, because He is the one who is to save His people from their sins.' Now all this took place to fulfil what the Lord had spoken through the prophet: Look! the virgin is with child and will give birth to a son whom they will call Immanuel, a name which means 'God-is-with-us' (Mt 1:20–23).

In Matthew 1:25, it is stated that Joseph had not had marital relations with Mary when she gave birth to a Son, and named Him Jesus. Some English translations are closer to the Greek, saying that Joseph "knew her not until she had borne a son; and he called His name Jesus." The word "until", in biblical language, negates an action in the past, but does not imply that it will occur in the future.[6] This indicates that Matthew is concerned to emphasise that St Joseph had no part in the conception of Jesus.

In the episodes of the Magi and of the flight into Egypt, St Matthew repeatedly asserts that Christ is the Child of Mary and not of Joseph, and represents Joseph as simply the guardian and protector of them both. In the example of the adoration of the Magi, we read: "and going into the house they saw the child with his mother Mary, and falling to their knees they did him homage. Then, opening their treasures, they offered him gifts of gold and frankincense and myrrh" (Mt 2:11). Later, we find that an angel appeared to St Joseph: "After they had left, suddenly the angel of the Lord appeared to Joseph in a dream and said, 'Get up, take the child and his mother with you, and escape into Egypt, and stay there until I tell you, because Herod intends to search for the child and do away with him.'" (Mt 2:13). St Joseph's response was that he "got up and, taking the child and his mother with him, left that night for Egypt" (Mt 2:14). Later again, an angel encourages St Joseph to return from Egypt: "Get up, take the child and his mother with you and go back to the land of Israel, for those who wanted to kill the child are dead" (Mt 2:20). It is noteworthy that in all these passages the angel who addresses Joseph concerning our Lord, never refers to Him as "your child." According to Matthew, Mary is not only the "Mother of God" but also "the Virgin" who conceives in an extraordinary manner. While the legal adoptive paternity of St Joseph ensures Jesus' Davidic descent, the virginity of Mary guarantees His divine origin. Her virginity, therefore, has a Christological function as it reveals Christ's true identity.

In St Matthew's Gospel, several passages deal with Jesus' relationship with His family, and by that token also with His Mother. However, these passages stress above all the intimate relationship with His new and larger family constituted by His disciples, with ecclesiological connotations. These passages adopt a specific Semitic structure which appears to deny one reality in order to emphasise another one:

> He was still speaking to the crowds when suddenly his mother and his brothers were standing outside and were anxious to have a word with him. But to the man who told him this Jesus replied, 'Who is my mother? Who are my brothers?' And stretching out his hand towards his disciples he said, 'Here are my mother and my brothers. Anyone who does the will of my Father in heaven is my brother and sister and mother' (Mt 12: 46–50).

This passage does not therefore deny in any way that Jesus Christ is the only Son of Mary the Virgin, but rather seeks to extend his human family in an ecclesiological and eschatological sense, as is seen fulfilled when Jesus entrusts his Mother to John at the Crucifixion.

In the following chapter of St Matthew's Gospel, there is a passage which has often been discussed in relation to Mary's virginity:

When Jesus had finished these parables he left the district; and, coming to his home town, he taught the people in the synagogue in such a way that they were astonished and said, 'Where did the man get this wisdom and these miraculous powers? This is the carpenter's son, surely? Is not his mother the woman called Mary, and his brothers James and Joseph and Simon and Jude? His sisters, too, are they not all here with us? So where did the man get it all? And they would not accept him. But Jesus said to them, 'A prophet is despised only in his own country and in his own house,' and he did not work many miracles there because of their lack of faith (Mt 13:53–58).

The passage names the following as "brothers" of Jesus: James, Joseph, Simon and Jude.[7] However, Matthew 27:56 indicates that Mary, the mother of James and Joseph, was at the foot of the Cross. On the other hand, Mark 15:40 states that Mary the mother of James the younger and Joset was there. So, although the proof is not conclusive, it seems that (unless we propose these were others with the same names), the first two, James and Joseph (Joset) had a mother other than the Mother of Jesus. Therefore, the term "brother" was employed for those who were not sons of Mary the Mother of Jesus. So the same use of language could easily have been applied with the other two, Simon and Jude. Further, if Mary had given birth to other natural sons and daughters too at the time of the cross, it would be strange for Jesus to ask John to take care of her, rather than one of His hypothetical blood brothers. In particular, according to St Paul's Letter to the Galatians (Ga 1:19), James the "brother of the Lord" was alive in 49 AD. He should have taken care of Mary, if he were her son. This usage of the expression "brother" or "sister" to denote a close relative who is not a brother or sister according to modern terminology is common in ancient Semitic culture, as can be seen in the Old Testament. One example is Lot, who although the nephew of Abraham (cf. Gn 11:27–31) is called his brother (Gn 13:8 and 14:14-16). The Hebrew and Aramaic expression "ah" was adopted for various types of relations.[8] Hebrew had no word for cousin. They could say "ben-dod" which means son of a paternal uncle, but for other kinds of cousins they would need a complex phrase, such as "the son of the brother of his mother" or, "the son of the sister of his mother."[9]

The Gospel according to Luke and Acts

Luke adopts the scheme "promise-fulfilment" in his Gospel and presents Mary as part of the culmination of the economy of salvation. For Luke, John the Baptist fulfils the time of preparation and Jesus inaugurates the eschatological era.

The Annunciation in Luke 1:26–38 is one of the key Mariological high points of the New Testament, and has been much represented in art and literature.[10] Four different schemes of interpretation can be proposed for the wonder of the Annunciation. First, the consideration of a miraculous birth scheme. The Annunciation shares the same structure as the other miraculous birth scenes in the Old and New Testaments (Gn 18:1–15; Jg 13:3–22; Lk 1:5–25). The scheme runs in this fashion: apparition—perturbation—message—obedience—sign. The miraculous birth is due to the creative action of the Holy Spirit. The second scheme is that of vocation or calling. There are similarities between Mary's calling and that of Gideon (Jg 6:11–24). The structure of this scheme runs as follows: angel's greeting—doubt or perturbation—first message—difficulty—second message—sign—consent. Mary answers a divine call. A third possible scheme is that of apocalyptic whereby everything starts from God above, leading to a new beginning. Finally, the Covenant scheme is also helpful in illustrating the Annunciation. This scheme consists of a discourse concerning a mediator and an answer from the people. By proclaiming herself as the Lord's servant, Mary enters into the work of salvation with total availability. Her "fiat" is a positive and immediate co-operation in the redemptive Incarnation. Without this, the Incarnation would not have taken place.

The salutation of the angel to Mary ("Rejoice, you who enjoy God's favour! The Lord is with you" Lk 1:28), recalls the expressions used of the Daughter of Sion in the Old Testament, who rejoices because the time of the Messiah is near. The angel Gabriel, addressing the Virgin of Nazareth uses the greeting *chaire* (Rejoice in Greek) and then calls her *kecharitomene* (full of grace). The words of the Greek text, chaire and kecharitomene, are essentially interconnected: Mary is invited to rejoice primarily because God loves her and has filled her with grace in view of her divine motherhood.[11] This fullness of grace indicates a condition or state of being, a gift signifying divine favour. It implies a divine choice or election in relation to the Covenant. The expressions "Full of grace" and "you who enjoy God's favour" are renderings of the Greek word *kecharitomene*, which is a passive participle. The verb adopted here by Luke (*charitoun*) is very rare in Greek. It is present only twice in the New Testament: in the text of Luke on the Annunciation (Lk 1:28) as *kecharitomene*, and in the Epistle to the Ephesians (Ep 1:6) as *echaritosen*. These verbs convey the idea of a change of something in the person or the thing affected. Thus, since the root of the verb "charitoo" is "charis" or grace, the idea which is expressed is that of a change brought about by grace. In addition the verb used by Luke is in the past participial form. *Kecharitomene* signifies then, in the person to whom the verb relates, that is, Mary, that the action of the grace of God has already brought about a change. It does not tell us how that came about. What is essential here is that it affirms that Mary has been transformed by the grace of God. The perfect passive participle is used by Luke to indicate that the transformation by grace has already taken place in Mary, well before the moment of the Annunciation.

In what then would this transformation of grace consist? According to the text of the Letter to the Ephesians, Christians have been transformed by grace in the sense that according to the richness of His grace, they find redemption by His blood, the remission of sins (cf. Ep 1:7). This grace, in reality, takes away sin. This sheds light on the case of Mary, who 'transformed by grace', because she has been sanctified by the grace of God. Mary has been transformed by the grace of God in view of the task which she awaits, that of becoming the Mother of the Son of

God, while remaining a virgin. There is a double announcement from the angel: Mary as Mother brings to the world the Son of the Most High (v.33), but that will take place by the 'power of the Most High' (v.35), that is virginally. God had prepared Mary for this by inspiring in her the desire for virginity.[12]

Therefore to convey even more exactly the nuance of the Greek word, one should not say merely "full of grace", but "made full of grace", or even "filled with grace", which would clearly indicate that this was a gift given by God to the Blessed Virgin. This term, in the form of a perfect participle, enhances the image of a perfect and lasting grace which implies fullness. The same verb, in the sense of "to bestow grace", is used in St Paul's Letter to the Ephesians to indicate the abundance of grace granted to us by the Father in his beloved Son (Ep 1:6), and which Mary receives as the first fruits of Redemption.[13] The greeting "the Lord is with you" used by the angel is customary in the context of accounts of callings in the Bible, and highlights Mary's special vocation in God's new covenant. The angel's invitation "Mary, do not be afraid; you have won God's favour", provides reassurance that God is acting. It stresses that Mary is the recipient of a unique favour and privilege in the history of salvation, namely to give birth to the Son of God. The annunciation shows that God chooses the humble. The words of the angel, "You are to conceive in your womb and bear a son, and you must name him Jesus" reflect the structure of the words of the promise in the book of Isaiah: "the young woman is with child and will give birth to a son whom she will call Immanuel" (Is 7:14). Thus the prophetic promise and its fulfilment are intimately linked. Moreover, the expression of the angel to Mary, "He will be great and will be called Son of the Most High" re-echo the prophecy of Nathan to David regarding the Davidic dynastic, and thus the phrase emphasises the fulfilment of the Messianic prophecy. Mary's words of concern "But how can this come about, since I have no knowledge of man?" bear various possible interpretations. The most probable opinion is that she had made a vow of virginity, because when she received the angel's greeting she was already betrothed to Joseph, and therefore, in the ordinary course of events, would be expecting to conceive with him, unless she had already made a vow.[14]

The Annunciation parallels certain biblical accounts that relate the communication of an extraordinary birth to a childless woman. Those cases concerned married women who were naturally sterile, to whom God gave the gift of a child through their typical conjugal life (1 S 1:19–20), in response to their anguished prayers (cf. Gn 15:2, 30:22–23, 1 S 1:10; Lk 1:13). Mary receives the angel's message in a different situation. She is not a married woman with problems of sterility; by a voluntary choice she intends to remain a virgin. Therefore her intention of virginity, the fruit of her love for the Lord, appears to be an obstacle to the motherhood announced to her. At first sight, Mary's words would seem merely to express only her present state of virginity: Mary would affirm that she does not "know" man, that is, that she is a virgin. Nevertheless, the context in which the question is asked: "How can this come about?", and the affirmation that follows: "since I have no knowledge of man", emphasise both Mary's present virginity and her intention to remain a virgin. The expression she uses, with the verb in the present tense, reveals the permanence and continuity of her state.[15]

The angel answered: "The Holy Spirit will come upon you, and the power of the Most High will cover you with its shadow. And so the child will be holy and will be called Son of God" (Lk 1:35). The expression which the angel used is characteristic of a consecration of the temple. Mary's response is one of totally free adherence as consecration to God's will: "Behold the handmaid of the Lord; be it done to me according to your word" (Lk 1:38).

The Magnificat

The Visitation is rich in both Christological and Mariological perspectives. It follows the same structure as the narration of the transportation of the ark to Jerusalem (2S 6:2–15). Both take place in the region of Judah and involve expressions of joy and acclamation. Blessings are received, religious fear is present and a period of three months is significant.[16] Through these parallelisms, Luke expressed the truth that Mary, the Mother of the Lord is God's dwelling place and the Ark of the New Covenant, bringing the old one to fulfilment and perfection. Also, Elizabeth's exclamation "Most blessed are you among women, and blessed is the fruit of your womb" can be compared with two other significant passages, both from the Old Testament. The first is the blessing of Abram by Melchizedek: "Blessed be Abram by God Most High, Creator of heaven and earth. And blessed be God Most High for putting your enemies into your clutches." (Gn 14:19). The second passage reports the blessing imparted by Uzziah upon Judith: "May you be blessed, my daughter, by God Most High, beyond all women on earth; and blessed be the Lord God, Creator of heaven and earth, who guided you to cut off the head of the leader of our enemies!" (Jdt 13:18). These parallels highlight the fact that the blessings imparted by God to Abram, to Judith and to Mary from part of an economy of salvation, in which the person who is blessed is to be a mediator of God's loving kindness. However, in the case of Mary, there is something different: Mary and her Son Jesus are together united in being blessed, which unites them in the culmination of God's economy.

Mary's greeting to Elizabeth causes John, filled with the Holy Spirit, to leap with joy. Elizabeth recognises who Mary is and greets her with three titles: Most blessed among women, the mother of my Lord, and "blessed is she who believed". Mary responds with a special song of thanksgiving. This Canticle, known as the *Magnificat* (Latin) or *Megalynei* (Byzantine), is the song both of the Mother of God and of the Church; the song of the Daughter of Sion and of the new People of God; the song of thanksgiving for the fullness of graces poured out in the economy of salvation and the song of the "poor" or "little ones" (*anawim*) whose hope is met by the fulfilment of the promises made to our ancestors, to Abraham and to his posterity for ever.[17]

Mary's Song of Thanksgiving closely parallels the Song of Hannah, Samuel's mother, in 1 Samuel 2:1–10, with some very specific similarity in detail. For example, Hannah proclaims: "My heart exults in Yahweh, in my God is my strength lifted up" (1 S 2:1). This is very similar to Mary's formulation: "my spirit rejoices in God my Savior…he has routed the arrogant of heart" (Lk 1:47, 51). Hannah portrays herself three times as the Lord's "servant" (1 S 1:11, 16), which Mary does twice (Lk 1:38, 48). The mother of Samuel proclaims: "Yahweh makes poor and rich, He humbles and also exalts. He raises the poor from the dust, He lifts the needy from the dunghill to give them a place with princes, to assign them a seat of honour" (1 S 2:7–8). Mary exclaims: "He has used the power of His arm, He has routed the arrogant of heart. He has pulled down princes from their thrones and raised high the lowly. He has filled the starving with good things, sent the rich away empty" (Lk 1:51–53). Furthermore, the relation between Mary and Hannah continues from the Magnificat into Luke's second chapter. Hannah took her child, Samuel, into the temple of the Lord at Shiloh (1 S 1:24). Similarly, Mary presents her child, Jesus, to the Lord in the temple in Jerusalem (Lk 2:22, 27).

The Magnificat contains, in a sense, the most ancient Mariology. The first part refers to God's action in Mary and the second to God's action in human history. She praises God for having looked upon the humiliation of his servant. This refers to the spiritual attitude of the poor of Yahweh. The praise of Mary is based on both her humility and the great things the Almighty has done for her. The proclamation "The Mighty One has done great things for me, and holy is his name" contains the expression "great things" (*megala* in Greek) which is a technical term signifying all the magnificent actions the Lord has carried out for His chosen people throughout their history, culminating in the coming of Christ through Mary. However, these great things can also include the wonders worked by God in His Church, right from the early moments of its life.

The Presentation of the Lord

When Our Lady fulfilled the demands of the Mosaic Law and presented Jesus in the Temple, Simeon proclaimed: "Now,

Master, You are letting your servant go in peace as You promised; for my eyes have seen the salvation which You have made ready in the sight of the nations; a light of revelation for the gentiles and glory for your people Israel" (Lk 2:29–32). Simeon also said to Mary His mother, "Look, He is destined for the fall and for the rise of many in Israel, destined to be a sign that is opposed—and a sword will pierce your soul too—so that the secret thoughts of many may be laid bare" (Lk 2:34–35). Simeon's hymn reveals the universality of the redemption. Simeon also announces a prophecy with regards to Mary which complements the angel's message. The "sword" has been interpreted variously the challenge to Mary's faith when faced with the scandal of the cross; the word of God which penetrates the soul; Jesus' passion which will have its impact upon Mary's soul and make her an intimate sharer in it, to the point of earning the palms of martyrdom at the foot of the Cross; the opposition against Jesus which Mary shares.

The Finding in the Temple

In a sense, the "sword" is already present, as a stimulus to a growth in faith for Our Lady, when Jesus goes to Jerusalem for the feast of the Passover, when He was twelve years old. Jesus stayed behind in Jerusalem without His parents knowing it. Three days later, they found Him in the Temple, sitting among the teachers, listening to them, and asking them questions; and all those who heard Him were astounded at His intelligence and His replies. It is certainly no accident that Mary and Joseph found Him three days later, because this episode foreshadows the Death of Christ and His Resurrection on the third day. When Jesus is lost to Mary and Joseph, this prefigures His death, and when He is found, it foreshadows His Resurrection.

> They were overcome when they saw him, and his mother said to him, "My child, why have you done this to us? See how worried your father and I have been, looking for you." He replied, "Why were you looking for me? Did you not know that I must be in my Father's house?" But they did not understand what he meant (Lk 2:48–50).

This moment marks a growth in faith for Mary and maybe also a sense of the sorrow, as well as the joy, which lie in the future.

During the ministry of Jesus, He makes an affirmation which does not undermine the importance of Mary's blood relationship to Him, but rather extends it.

> It happened that as He was speaking, a woman in the crowd raised her voice and said, "Blessed the womb that bore you and the breasts that fed you!" But He replied, "More blessed still are those who hear the word of God and keep it!" (Lk 11:27–28).

This passage highlights the fact that Mary is the first hearer and keeper of the Word of God, she has carried the eternal Word in her womb and kept Him, and she is also Christ's first and foremost disciple.[18]

Mary and the early Christian Community

St Luke also recounts, in his Acts of the Apostles, that with one heart all the Apostles "joined constantly in prayer, together with some women, including Mary the mother of Jesus, and with his brothers" (Ac 1:14). This passage shows that Mary had a special place in the Jewish-Christian community of Palestine due to her union with Christ as Mother. Moreover, she is part of the community and prays, believes and practices the faith with the others. She forms part of the new people of God which receives the Spirit and proclaims the risen Christ but in continuity with the traditions. Mary is called to enter into the divine plan with a special mission of her own. She responds to God's calling with exemplary faith. This faith is the most important aspect of her spiritual life.

1.1.3 Mary in the writings of St John

There is a well-known passage of Origen on the presence of Mary and John on Calvary:

> The Gospels are the first fruits of all Scripture and the Gospel of John is the first of the Gospels: no one can grasp its meaning without having leaned his head on Jesus' breast and having received from Jesus Mary as Mother.[19]

It is most probable that in the years which Mary spent with St John in the house traditionally held to be at Ephesus, Our Lady would have shared with the beloved disciple many of her most profound insights regarding Jesus Christ her Son. In the quiet and humble way that characterised Mary's life on earth, therefore, John's Gospel should be regarded also as a profoundly Marian Gospel. One of the keys to understanding St John's Gospel is the use of the expression "woman", by which Jesus addresses His Mother. Far from being a way of distancing Himself from His blessed Mother, the expression is a term of intimacy and great respect and love all at the same time. "Here," writes de la Potterie, "the Old Testament texts of the 'Daughter of Zion' are applied to a definite woman... This is precisely the reason why, in the Fourth Gospel, both at Cana and at the Cross, Jesus addresses Mary calling her Woman."[20] In this context, the relation between the Wedding Feast at Cana, Mary at the foot of the Cross and the Woman of the Apocalypse is of capital importance.

As regards the wedding at Cana in Galilee, it is highly significant that it takes place on the third day, like the Resurrection. There are links between this passage and the texts dealing with the establishment of the Covenant at Sinai (Ex 19:3–8; 24:3.7). Using the scheme of the Covenant, John shows that Cana is the new Sinai. Jesus takes Yahweh's place and Mary that of Moses. In the Old Testament, the chosen people were often represented by the figure of a woman. The wedding is thus inscribed in a series of theophanic mysteries, which reveal the divinity of Christ and His economy of salvation, of whom the key player next to Christ is His blessed Mother (Jn 2:1–11). The key figures are therefore Christ and His Mother, rather than the couple who had just married. The enormous quantity of wine which Jesus offered, changed from the water in the six stone water jars, each holding twenty or thirty gallons, indicates the divine generosity. The fact that the best wine was kept till last indicates the fulfilment of God's economy in the New Covenant, in which Mary plays a singular part. It is significant also that the servants are not referred to as *douloi*, but *diakonoi*, indicating a liturgical role, rather than a merely functional one. This is all the more interesting given the fact that this miracle also prefigures the far greater wonder in which wine will be changed into His Precious Blood. The miracle of the multiplication of the loaves (Jn 6:1–13) is also a New Testament prefiguration of the Eucharist.[21] At the wedding feast at Cana, water is changed into wine; at the Last Supper, in which wine is changed into Christ's Blood, we have a kind of wedding feast in which the marriage of Christ to His Church is celebrated. This is supported by Christ's own words at the Last Supper "From now on, I tell you, I shall not drink wine until the day I drink the new wine with you in the kingdom of my Father" (Mt 26:29). Jesus' words indicate that the Eucharist is a participation in the definitive Wedding Feast of the Lamb.

Closely linked with the miracle of Cana is the scene of Mary is standing at the foot of Christ's Cross.

> Near the cross of Jesus stood his mother and his mother's sister, Mary the wife of Cleophas, and Mary of Magdala. Seeing his mother and the disciple whom he loved standing near her, Jesus said to His mother, "Woman, this is your son." Then to the disciple he said, "This is your mother." And from that hour the disciple took her into his home (Jn 19:25–27).

This scene is linked to Cana. Both use the term "woman" and talk about Jesus' "hour". Mary becomes the mother of the beloved disciple. She has a role to fulfil in the history of salvation as mother of Jesus' disciples. Mary is the Daughter of Sion, who generates a messianic people. The standing at the foot of the Cross is not merely physical, but also in the context of St John's Gospel refers to the co-operation of Mary in Christ's work of Redemption.[22] The parallelism "this is your son" and "this is your mother" highlights the fact that here we are seeing not only an historical fact, but a spiritual motherhood of Mary within the Church.[23]

Finally, the two passages just considered are linked with a third Mariological passage in St John's Apocalypse. The expression woman,[24] as found in the Wedding at Cana and as addressed by Jesus to Mary at the Foot of the Cross, is also employed in chapter twelve of the book of Revelation, and sheds light on the Mariological import of that chapter. The book of Revelation never mentions Mary by name, and does not speak explicitly of her. The perspective offered is essentially ecclesiological; however the figure of the Woman in chapter twelve, although a personification of the new people of God, cannot be adequately explained unless full account be taken of the historical role of the Mother of Jesus.[25] "Now a great sign appeared in heaven: a woman, robed with the sun, standing on the moon, and on her head a crown of twelve stars. She was pregnant, and in labour, crying aloud in the pangs of childbirth" (Rv 12:1–2). The Woman represents first of all the messianic people who become the Church. However, she also represents Mary, the mother of Jesus and figure of the Church. In Mary, the maternal function of the New Testament community is inaugurated. The figure of the woman is symbolic, but in a polyvalent sense, referring to both Mariological and ecclesiological realities. It would therefore be incorrect to detach this symbol from its concrete historical point of reference, namely Mary. Therefore it is completely one-sided and incomplete to stress solely the ecclesiological interpretation of this passage from the Book of the Apocalypse at the expense of the Mariological one. In St John's writings, Mary is progressively Mother of Jesus, the woman at the service of the faith of the Apostles, and finally mother of the beloved disciple, and Mother in turn of all those "who obey God's commandments and have in themselves the witness of Jesus" (Rv 12:17). It is most likely that St John would have therefore based his ecclesiological symbolism on a Mariological foundation.

One difficulty which could be raised is how the Woman in Revelation could refer to Mary if she suffered the pains of childbirth. This difficulty can be eliminated by the following consideration. In Revelation 5:6, Christ appears in heaven in the form of an immolated lamb (cf. Jn 19:36). The sufferings of the woman who also appears in heaven (Rv 12:2), stands in relation to the immolation of the celestial Lamb (Rv 12:11). Thus, in the twelfth chapter of Apocalypse, the reference is not to the childbirth at Bethlehem, but to the birth pangs of the Redemption, echoed in the words of Christ upon the Cross: "Son, behold your Mother" (Jn 19:27). Thus, here John is speaking about a different type of suffering, which is also found in other parts of the New Testament. For example, speaking to the Galatians, Paul went through the pain of giving birth until Christ was formed within his readers (see Ga 4:19). Also, the Letter to the Romans states: "We are well aware that the whole creation, until this time, has been groaning in labour pains" (Rm 8:22). What is being described is the spiritual motherhood of Mary and the compassion with which the Mother of Jesus shares in the sufferings of the immolated Lamb. The woman of the Crucifixion and the woman of the Apocalypse are closely tied together. In each passage, Mary's motherhood in relation to the disciples entails a context of suffering.[26]

1.1.4 The writings of St Paul

Paul's writings present God's great economy of salvation, in which He offers to all, Jews and Gentiles alike, the gift of eternal life, in Jesus who has died and is risen from the dead. The Christian participates in this gift of salvation, by being united to Christ by faith, dying in Him to sin, and sharing in the power of His Resurrection. This salvation is still being completed in His Body the Church, until He comes again in glory (see Col 1:24). Paul presents Christ's death and resurrection as a expiatory sacrifice, bringing the Jewish sacrifices to fulfilment (Rm 3:24–25; 1 Co 15:3; 2 Co 5:21). Christians participate in this mystery through baptism and the Eucharist. In this context, one finds the only reference to Mary given by Paul but it is very important because of its antiquity and its relation to the history of salvation. Even if the person of Mary remains anonymous, her function is indispensable for the kenotic and salvific Incarnation of the Son of God: "When the completion of the time came, God sent His Son, born of a woman, born a subject of the Law, to redeem the subjects of the Law, so that we could receive adoption as sons" (Ga 4:4–5). In this only direct reference to Mary, Paul refers to her as "woman". Thus, Mary is again referred to as "woman", even outside a Johannine context. This phraseology of "a woman" being tied to Mary has evidently been passed on to Paul, who hands it on to his readers. Here he indicates implicitly the fact of the virginal conception of Jesus. This is highlighted by the expression "born of a woman" in a Semitic society where the usual expression would be "born of Jesse" or whoever the father was. Pointing to Jesus as born of a "woman" instead of a man indicates the uniqueness of Virginal Conception and therefore of the Incarnation.

1.2 Mary's house at Ephesus

The traditional belief that Mary, after Jesus' crucifixion, came to live with and be cared for by John has its roots in a passage from the Gospel of John. In John 19:26–27 Jesus, from the Cross, places His Mother under the protection of His beloved disciple: "When Jesus saw His mother and the disciple whom He loved standing beside her, He said to His mother, 'Woman, here is your son.' Then He said to the disciple, 'Here is your mother.' And from that hour the disciple took her into his own home." To the Christian faithful, it is reasonable to assume that John would have honoured Jesus' request to care for his mother and as Church tradition holds that John's ministry was based in and around Ephesus, it can be concluded that Mary, at the very least, would have spent some time in Ephesus. Church tradition tells us that John and Mary left Jerusalem soon after the martyrdom of St Stephen, but because of the New Testament's silence on their whereabouts during this time, we have to rely on early Church Fathers to expand our knowledge of the travels of John and, by extension, Mary. Early Christian literature and correspondence is peppered with brief mentions that connect John and Mary to Ephesus.

Atop a distant mountain in southwest Turkey, overlooking the ancient city of Ephesus lies a shrine hidden in mystery. Called *Meryem Ana Evi* (Mother Mary's House) by the native Turks, it is believed to be the last home of the Virgin Mary. Unlike the Marian shrines of Lourdes, Fatima, Guadalupe and

Knock, which are held to be the locations of apparitions of Mary,
Our Lady of Ephesus is a shrine connected to her physical
historical presence:

> There is something miraculous which can safely be
> associated with Mary's house: its very existence. Despite
> being repeatedly broken on the rack of time, and eaten
> away by centuries of neglect, it stands today not only as
> a shrine to the Lady who lived there 2,000 years ago, but
> as a monument to all those who refused to let it crumble
> back into the earth. The house itself is the miracle.[27]

An unlettered, invalid German nun named Anne Catherine
Emmerich (1774–1820) received detailed visions of Our Lady's
final years and Assumption. These were dictated to the German
poet, Clemens von Brentano. In her visions Emmerich had seen
the Virgin Mary leaving Jerusalem with St John before the
persecution of Christians had become worse and she had also
seen their arrival in Ephesus; she had also noted that the house
in Ephesus was on a mountain nearby. She detailed furthermore
that the house of the Virgin Mary had been built in stone by St
John, that it was rectangular in plan with a round back wall and
had an apse and a hearth. The room next to the apse was her
bedroom and there was a stream of water running beneath it.

In 1881 a French priest, Fr Julien Gouyet, went to Ephesus
precisely in order to find the house that Catherine Emmerich
described, and the local authority, the archbishop of Smyrna
(about 50 or 60 miles north of Ephesus) encouraged him. He found
the ruins of an ancient house that closely matched the description
in the visions. However, when he returned to Europe we are told,
both in France and in Rome his superiors discouraged him from
making this known to anyone. The uncorroborated witness of one
man seemed to them to deserve no credit. Then, in 1886 Sister
Marie de Mandat-Grancey, a Daughter of Charity, was sent to
Smyrna. While serving in the hospital there, Sister Marie read and
shared with her own Sisters and the local Vincentian priests *The
Life of the Blessed Virgin*, by Anne Catherine Emmerich. Because
of Sister Marie's great devotion to the Blessed Mother, she was

determined to find this sacred spot. Through collaboration with her Vincentian brothers, local Muslim guides, and the people of the area, Our Lady's house was found on *Bubul Dagh* (Nightingale Mountain) as described by the visionary.[28] On Wednesday, 29 July 1891, a group of Vincentian priests led by Fr Henri Jung set out on foot, using Emmerich's writings like a surveyor's map, compass in hand. They were satisfied concerning the identity of the little house they had found and the one Catherine Emmerich had seen. In 1892 they bought the land upon which it stood from its Turkish owner, to the great delight of the archbishop of Smyrna—the same one who had encouraged Gouyet ten years earlier—as he had all along believed the vision was substantially correct. The house became know as Panaghia-Capouli (the gateway to the All-Holy One). Fr Eugène Poulin's diary of the remarkable expedition in 1891 was first translated from his native French into English and published in 1999 by a Turkish publisher.[29]

The local Turks had long held that this was indeed Our Lady's house, where she spent her final earthly days. Pope Leo XIII became a strong defender of the Virgin Mary's house. In 1902 an apparition of our Lady at the house was reported and miraculous cures were claimed. In 1914 Pope St Pius X granted a plenary indulgence to those who visited the shrine. Pope Pius XII reconfirmed this indulgence in 1950 after the definition of the dogma of the Assumption, and Blessed Pope John XXIII reconfirmed it again in 1962. Bishop Roncalli (later Pope St John XXIII) had visited this house, as did his successors to the papal throne. On 26 July 1967, Pope Paul VI visited the house of our Lady. Pope John Paul II travelled to the site on 30 November 1979 to confirm the belief that this was indeed the home of the Mother of God. Pope Benedict XVI celebrated Mass at the House of the Virgin Mary in Ephesus on 29 November 2006. Reflecting on his visit, Pope Benedict remarked:

> The Shrine of Mary's House stands in a pleasant place called the Hill of the Nightingale which overlooks the Aegean Sea. This is a small and ancient chapel, built to contain a cottage which, according to a very old tradition,

the Apostle John had built for the Virgin Mary after taking
her with him to Ephesus... Archaeological research has
shown that from time immemorial the site has been a place
of Marian worship which is also dear to Muslims, who go
there regularly to venerate the One they call "Meryem
Ana", Mother Mary. In the garden in front of the Shrine, I
celebrated Holy Mass for a group of the faithful who came
from the neighbouring city of Izmir, from other parts of
Turkey and from abroad. At *Mary's House* we truly felt at
home, and in that atmosphere of peace we prayed for peace
in the Holy Land and throughout the world.[30]

This little home served as a powerhouse of prayer to the infant
Church. Though little is written of it, we do know that St Paul
wrote in the final lines of his first Letter to the Corinthians that
he would "remain at Ephesus until Pentecost" (1 Co 16:8); he
was there for two years. His stay occurred as a decisive moment
in the formative years of the Church. When he wrote his Letter
to the Ephesians, he addressed them as the "fellow citizens of
the saints of God," (Ep 2:19) and that, in all probability, he visited
the Mother of God to receive encouragement and strength as he
went out again on fire to spread the Word of God. Most scripture
scholars agree that St Luke, also venerated at Ephesus, must
have received the pre-Infancy and Infancy narratives first-hand
from Our Lady. Since the Evangelist was baptized by Paul after
the Apostles had fled Jerusalem, it must be deduced that he,
also, sought her out at Ephesus, perhaps en route to his See at
Antioch. Independent of the "eyewitness account theory," many
other Scripture scholars have projected the Gospel's authorship
as having been undertaken within the ancient city.

It is also significant that the third Ecumenical Council of 431
AD was held in Ephesus and more specifically in the Church of
St Mary. It was at this Council that Mary was proclaimed
Theotokos, the Mother of God. It is of some importance that the
Bishops would choose this site to proclaim Mary's position in
the Church. The house of Virgin Mary is reached by the road
leading from the Magnesia Gate to Mount Solmissos (Aladag).
A round cistern that can be seen today in the small square 100

metres away from the house and an arched wall on the side facing the hill were the first remains to be discovered. The steps on the west side of the cistern are completely destroyed, only a part resembling a section of a pool is extant. At the end of the road that goes on from the cistern, there is a small, domed church with a cross-shaped plan. This is the building known as the House of the Virgin Mary. What guided the archaeologists was the finding that a part of the foundations of the chapel and some pieces of coal revealed in the excavations dated from the first century AD. The interior of the house decorated with various gifts with great care but, at the same time, in a very simple and modest way, seems to reflect the Virgin Mary's personality. It seems to awake in the visitor deep feeling of tranquillity. Coming out of the house, one feels moved by the depth and mystic beauty of the nature unrolling before one's eyes.

1.3 Mary and Mount Athos

Mount Athos or *Agion Oros*, as it is locally known, is the oldest surviving monastic community in the world. It dates back more than a thousand years, to Byzantine times. It is a unique monastic republic, which, although part of Greece, it is governed by its own local administration. It occupies the best part of the Athos peninsula in Halkidiki. It consists of a range which runs south-east for thirty miles from Xerxes' Canal, where Xerxes the Persian King cut a canal across the peninsula for his ships to pass. A rugged, sea-battered peninsula 56 kilometers long. Two kilometers wide at the canal, it broadens to eight, with a long back-bone rising into peaks of roughly five hundred, six hundred, six hundred and fifty, eight hundred and fifty and a thousand meters. Finally the imposing marble summit of Athos itself, 2,039 meters high, 6,670 feet of grey-white crystalline limestone. Its snow cupped peak is usually crowned by white clouds, an awesome sight to see. Because of its isolation Mount Athos has remained one of the most unspoiled parts of Greece.

The landscape is stunning and wild, with small green valleys and gorges, well wooded peaks interspersed with precipitous ravines and an inaccessible coastline. Small streams of crystal clear water run free under the deep shade of the chestnut trees. Here and there in this wilderness are the fortified walls of the monasteries, with small vegetable plots around them, encircled by a silver-green sea of the olive groves. Hidden among the greenery and the impassable gorges, perched in the most unexpected positions is the white speckle of a little hut were a hermit spends his days in solitude and contemplation. It is a land where myth is entwined with history, miracles mingle with reality. Savage mountain scenery reflecting on the dark blue sea create that essential framework of isolation in a peaceful, solitary world, chosen by the hermits for their monastic state. The tradition of Mount Athos is linked with the Mother of God.

Returning from Ephesus and Antioch, the Mother of God then remained in Jerusalem for a considerable period. During this time, St Lazarus, (whom the Lord had raised from the dead on the fourth day of his repose according to John 11:14–44), was living on the island of Cyprus. The Apostle Barnabas had consecrated him as bishop. Now St Lazarus had a great longing to behold the Theotokos who he had not seen in a long while. However, he dared not enter Jerusalem for fear of the Jews, who still sought him. The Theotokos learned of this and wrote to St Lazarus, the true friend of her Son, a letter wherein she comforted him. She asked him to send a ship to her that she might visit him in Cyprus, for she would never demand of him to come to Jerusalem for her sake. When the holy Lazarus read her letter, he was filled with tremendous joy and, at the same time, he wondered at her great humility.

Without a moment's delay, he sent a ship for her together with a letter of reply. Whereupon, the Theotokos together with Christ's beloved deciple, John, and others, who reverently accompanied them, set sail. It is said that she had sewn St Lazarus an *omophorion* (a bishop's stole, pall) with *epimanikia* (cuffs) and that she wished to present them to him personally. The year was 52 A.D. The

Virgin Mary and her company set sail from the Holy Land on a bright and glorious day. As the ship parted from the shore, the Virgin prayed to her almighty Son that He pilot their vessel, according to his will. It happened that, after a time at sea, a violent sea storm raged and the sailing vessel was forced off course. By divine intervention, as the storm abated, they found themselves outside the port of Clemes (*Clementos*) on Athos.

At that time, Athos was inhabited by pagan tribes. In ancient times, the citizens of that region were mostly young virgins dedicated to the goddess Diana and destined to become priestesses to serve in the idolatrous temples of Greece. To this purpose, young girls were sent there from all parts of Greece. It was forbidden, under penalty of death, for men to enter. When the ship carrying the Virgin Mary approached Athos, Jupiter's statue, at the top of the mountain fell and shattered to pieces in a thunderous noise. The presence of this statue is mentioned in ancient history. Plutarch and Anaximander and others also mention that at the top of Athos there was a great gold-ivory statue of Jupiter which, instead of eyes, bore two large gems, reflecting the starlight. Emitting flashes by night, they served as lighthouses to the seaman sailing around Athos.

It is said that Our Lady's group came ashore close to the present Monastery of Iveron which is situated above a picturesque inlet on the northeastern side of the peninsula. There, the holy Virgin rested for a while, overwhelmed by the beauty of the place, she asked her Son to give her the Mountain, despite the fact that the inhabitants were pagans. A voice was then heard saying: "Let this place be your inheritance and garden, a paradise and a haven of salvation for those seeking to be saved." The Virgin then brought to mind the words of the Archangel Gabriel, who told her some twenty years earlier, after Pentecost, that her lot would be a Macedonian peninsula, Mount Athos. Thus it was consecrated as the inheritance and garden of the Mother of God, and immediately acquired the name Aghion Oros or Holy Mountain, because our Lady the Theotokos chose this Mountain and placed it under her own protection. Upon asking and receiving Athos as a heavenly gift, in that very moment, the ground shook and the pagan statues in all the temples fell prostrate and broke into pieces. Then, even the trees of the peninsula bent forward, as though offering veneration to the Theotokos who had reached the port of Clemes.

On the peninsula there was a pagan temple and shrine of Apollo. Diabolical works such as fortune telling, divination and witchcraft took place there. All the pagans greatly honoured this place as one chosen by the gods. In fact, people from all over the world gathered there to worship. There, they would receive answers to their questions from the diviners. Therefore, when the Mother of God entered port, and all their idols had collapsed, shouting, confusion and uproar were heard from all the idols in Athos. Cries could be heard, saying: "Men of Apollo, go to Clemes harbour and welcome Mary, the Mother of the Great God Jesus!" Thus, all the demons inhabiting the idols, forced against their will, could not resist the power of God and they proclaimed the truth.

Whereupon, all the inhabitants of Athos hastened from all parts to that port. Once there, they welcomed the Theotokos. Meeting her with honour, they took the Theotokos, St John and all their fellow passengers to the common hall, called the *Synagogeion* (meeting house or assembly room).They then asked her, "What God did you bear and what is His name?" Opening her divine lips, Mary explained, in detail, to the people everything about Christ. The natives diligently posed questions concerning the mystery of providence in the divine Incarnation. They even wondered at how she, a Hebrew woman, explained everything to them in the Greek language. As a result of all the awesome and supernatural occurrences coinciding with her arrival, they believed. Upon being catechised by her teaching, they accepted the Christian faith. They then fell down to the ground and worshipped the God Who was born of her and showed great respect to the Virgin who bore Him in the flesh. The Mother of God also worked many miracles on the Holy Mountain. After their baptism, she appointed a leader and teacher for the newly-illumined from among them.[31]

1.4 The Assumption of Our Lady

Where Mary passed the last years of her life on earth has been often a matter for discussion, although various traditions propose Ephesus or near Jerusalem as possibilities. Some apocryphal works dating from the second to the fourth century are all favourable to the Jerusalem tradition. The letter of Dionysius the Areopagite to the Bishop Titus (363), as well as the *Joannis liber de Dormitione Mariae* (third to fourth century), locate her tomb at Gethsemane. Historically these works have some value despite being apocryphal, since they echo a belief from earlier centuries. The indication of a tomb of the Virgin in the valley of Josaphat dates from about the fifth century, and this tomb became the object of pilgrimage and devotion.[32] St John Damascene bears witness to a tradition that Our Lady passed from this world from Jerusalem: "Sion is the mother of churches in the whole world, who offered a resting-place to the Mother of God after her Son's Resurrection from the dead. In it, lastly, the Blessed Virgin was stretched on a small bed."[33] He indicated Gethsemane as the place of her Assumption: "Then they reached the most sacred Gethsemane, and once more there were embraces and prayers and panegyrics, hymns and tears, poured forth by sorrowful and loving hearts. They mingled a flood of weeping and sweating. And thus the immaculate body was laid in the tomb. Then it was assumed after three days to the heavenly mansions".[34] Within this tradition, then, there are various opinions as to whether Mary's tomb was in the Garden of Olives or in the Valley of Josaphat. A pointer towards placing the tomb of Mary in Gethsemane is the basilica erected above the sacred spot, about the end of the fourth or the beginning of the fifth century. The present church was built in the same place in which the old edifice had stood.[35]

Another tradition posits the place of Mary's transition as being in Ephesus. Since St John had lived in Ephesus and had been buried there,[36] it has been inferred that since he took Our Lady into his care after the death of the Lord, she could have lived there after Christ's Ascension, and then passed from this life in that town. Pope Benedict XIV states that Mary followed St John to Ephesus and died there. He intended also to remove from the Breviary those lessons which mention Mary's death in Jerusalem, but died before carrying out his intention.[37] Various private revelations indicate Ephesus as the place of Mary's passage from this life.[38]

Many Fathers attest the pious tradition that at least some of the Apostles were present at Our Lady's passing from this world. In the East, St John Damascene wrote:

> When the Ark of God [Mary], departing from Mount Sion for the heavenly country, was borne on the shoulders of the Apostles, it was placed on the way in the tomb. First it was taken through the city, as a bride dazzling with spiritual radiance, and then carried to the sacred place of Gethsemane, angels overshadowing it with their wings, going before, accompanying, and following it, together with the whole assembly of the Church.[39]

In the West, St Gregory of Tours (d.593) observed:

> When finally the Blessed Virgin had fulfilled the course of this life, and was now to be called out of this world, all the Apostles were gathered together from each region to her house… and behold the Lord Jesus came with His angels and, receiving her soul, entrusted it to the Archangel Michael and departed. At the break of day the Apostles lifted the body with the couch and laid it in the sepulchre, and they guarded it awaiting the coming of the Lord. And behold the Lord again stood by them, and commanded that the holy body be taken up and borne on a cloud into Paradise, where now, reunited with (her) soul and rejoicing with the elect, it enjoys the good things of eternity which shall never come to an end.[40]

That nothing is found explicitly in the New Testament about Our Lady's Assumption is not surprising, since it is possible that much of it may have been composed before the event. This is clearly a matter of conjecture, especially if many of the Apostles were present at her Dormition, as many Fathers propose. No isolated text of the New Testament explicitly affirms the doctrine of the Assumption. However, the Church does not read the Word of God as segmented texts of Scripture alone, but in its fullness in relation to the whole deposit of Revelation as it is also expressed in Tradition.[41] The Church's Tradition shows that Mary's Assumption was at least implicitly revealed. It is false to maintain, along with the rationalists that the later tradition of the Church expressing belief in the Assumption is an outgrowth of the Apocrypha.[42] A concrete indication of belief in the Assumption of Mary, is found in the fact that the Church has never looked for the bodily relics of the Blessed Virgin nor proposed them for veneration.[43] It is probable that the revelation made to the Apostles, or to one of them, was even explicit, since otherwise it is difficult to explain the universal tradition of Mary's Assumption in the East and the West from the seventh century at the latest, which is also expressed in the liturgical celebration of the Feast.[44] Nevertheless, "the liturgy of the Church does not engender the Catholic faith, but rather springs from it, in such a way that the practices of the sacred worship proceed from the faith as the fruit comes from the tree".[45]

The feast of the Assumption began its life in the East as did many of the older Marian feasts. At first, Mary was implicitly honoured in her Assumption by a celebration known as The Memory of Mary, the celebration of which began in the East around the fourth century. Honour was given to Mary's Assumption here because the Church intended to celebrate the "birthday" of Mary, or her entrance into heaven. Later, The Memory of Mary liturgy was changed and became the feast of the *Dormitio*, or the "Falling asleep" of the Blessed Mother. The feast of the *Dormitio* or *Koimesis* celebrated as its object the death, resurrection, and Assumption of the Blessed Mother, and was widely established in the East by the end of the fourth century.

The development of the doctrine of the Assumption of Mary, involved various elements which can be summarised in this way. A common Patristic theme is that the doctrine of the Second Eve implies assumption as the final and complete victory of the woman. Next, Mary in her predestination is always associated with her Son. Further, Mary's Immaculate conception and sinlessness imply exemption from corruption in the grave, and so lead to her immediate resurrection and glory. Another theme is that the perpetual virginity of Our Lady, as fleshly incorruption, involved exemption from physical corruption after death. A further argument is that the filial piety of the divine Son implied that He would grant her the favour of the Assumption, if it were otherwise possible and fitting. Mary at her death was more exalted in dignity than other creatures will ever be. If, then, other Christians are destined to he bodily with Christ in heaven, this must have applied to Mary straight-away after her death. Finally, the woman of the Apocalypse is already seen in her glory, after being taken by eagle's wings.[46]

The definition of the dogma of the Assumption was prepared for and preceded by a period of discussion which included a consideration of how the dogma was founded in the Scriptures and in Tradition. In 1950, after many requests, Pope Pius XII solemnly defined the dogma which had been believed by the Church for well over a thousand years:

> After we have poured forth prayers of supplication again and again to God, and have invoked the light of the Spirit of Truth, for the glory of Almighty God who has lavished his special affection upon the Virgin Mary, for the honour of her Son, the immortal King of the Ages and the Victor over sin and death, for the increase of the glory of that same august Mother, and for the joy and exultation of the entire Church; by the authority of our Lord Jesus Christ, of the Blessed Apostles Peter and Paul, and by our own authority, we pronounce, declare, and define it to be a divinely revealed dogma: that the Immaculate Mother of God, the ever Virgin Mary, having completed the course of her earthly life, was assumed body and soul into heavenly glory.[47]

Notes

1 I. de la Potterie, *Mary in the Mystery of the Covenant* (New York: Alba House, 1992), p. 262.

2 For the collaboration of Mary with Christ's act of Redemption and then with the distribution of the effects of this act, see P. Haffner, *The Mystery of Mary* (Leominster/Chicago: Gracewing/Liturgy Training Publications, 2004), chapter 7, pp. 187–201 and chapter 9, pp. 254–266 respectively.

3 For the convenience of the reader, we set out the three passages here.

1) "He went home again, and once more such a crowd collected that they could not even have a meal. When his relations heard of this, they set out to take charge of him; they said, 'He is out of his mind'" (Mk 3:20–21).

2) "Now his mother and his brothers arrived and, standing outside, sent in a message asking for him. A crowd was sitting round him at the time the message was passed to him, 'Look, your mother and brothers and sisters are outside asking for you.' He replied, 'Who are my mother and my brothers?' And looking at those sitting in a circle round him, he said, 'Here are my mother and my brothers. Anyone who does the will of God, that person is my brother and sister and mother'" (Mk 3:31–35).

3) "Leaving that district, he went to his home town, and his disciples accompanied him. With the coming of the Sabbath he began teaching in the synagogue, and most of them were astonished when they heard him. They said, 'Where did the man get all of this? What is this wisdom that has been granted him, and these miracles that are worked through him? This is the carpenter, surely, the son of Mary, the brother of James and Joset and Jude and Simon? His sisters, too, are they not here with us?' And they would not accept him. And Jesus said to them, 'A prophet is despised only in his own country, among his own relations and in his own house'; and he could work no miracle there, except that he cured a few sick people by laying his hands on them. He was amazed at their lack of faith" (Mk 6:1–6).

4 See R. Laurentin, *La Vergine Maria* (Roma: Edizioni Paoline, ³1983), p. 22, note 4.

5 See Haffner, *The Mystery of Mary*, pp. 159–166.

6 The Greek expression is ἕως To confirm this usage see Ps 110:1 and 2 S 6:23.

7 The manuscripts vary on the spelling of at least one of these, namely Joseph, who in Mark 6:3 is put as Joset: "This is the carpenter, surely, the son of Mary, the brother of James and Joset and Jude and Simon? His sisters, too, are they not here with us?' And they would not accept him."

8 Cf. M. Sokoloff, *A Dictionary of Jewish Palestinian Aramaic of the Byzantine*

period (Ramat-Gan, Israel: Bar Ilan University Press, 1990), p. 45.

9   See *ibid.*, p. 111 and 139.

10   Among the famous artists who have painted the Annunciation are Leonardo da Vinci, Carolo Crivelli, Fra Angelico and Sandro Botticelli. Paul Claudel wrote *L'annonce faite a Marie* (Paris: Gallimard, 1950). The passage in question runs: "In the sixth month the angel Gabriel was sent by God to a town in Galilee called Nazareth, to a virgin betrothed to a man named Joseph, of the House of David; and the virgin's name was Mary. He went in and said to her, 'Rejoice, you who enjoy God's favour! The Lord is with you.' She was deeply disturbed by these words and asked herself what this greeting could mean, but the angel said to her, 'Mary, do not be afraid; you have won God's favour. Look! You are to conceive in your womb and bear a son, and you must name him Jesus. He will be great and will be called Son of the Most High. The Lord God will give him the throne of his ancestor David; he will rule over the House of Jacob for ever and his reign will have no end.' Mary said to the angel, 'But how can this come about, since I have no knowledge of man?' The angel answered, 'The Holy Spirit will come upon you, and the power of the Most High will cover you with its shadow. And so the child will be holy and will be called the Son of God. And I tell you this too: your cousin Elizabeth also, in her old age, has conceived a son, and she whom people called barren is now in her sixth month, for nothing is impossible to God.' Mary said, 'You see before you the Lord's servant, let it happen to me as you have said.' And the angel left her" (Lk 1:38).

11   See Pope John Paul II, *Discourse at General Audience* (8 January 1986), 1.

12   See I. de la Potterie, *Mary in the Mystery of the Covenant* (New York: Alba House, 1992), pp. 17–20.

13   See Pope John Paul II, *Discourse at General Audience* (8 January 1986), 2

14   See St Augustine, *De sancta virginitate*, I, 4, in PL 40, 398: "Her virginity also itself was on this account more pleasing and accepted, in that it was not that Christ being conceived in her, rescued it beforehand from a husband who would violate it, so as to preserve it Himself; but, before He was conceived, chose it, already dedicated to God, as that from which to be born. This is shown by the words which Mary spoke in answer to the Angel announcing her conception. She said: "But how can this come about, since I have no knowledge of man?" Which assuredly she would not say, unless she had before vowed herself unto God as a virgin. But, because the habits of the Israelites as yet refused this, she was espoused to a just man, who would not take from her by violence, but rather guard against violent persons, what she had already vowed."

15   See Pope John Paul II, *Discourse at General Audience* (24 July 1996), 1.

16   See Haffner, *The Mystery of Mary*, pp. 30–31, where these parallels are dealt with in detail.

[17]   See CCC 2619.

[18]   For a development of the various aspects of Mary's discipleship, see Haffner, *The Mystery of Mary*, chapter 7.

[19]   Origen, *Commentary on St John's Gospel* I, 6 in PG 14, 31. See Saint Ambrose, Exposition on the Gospel according to St Luke, X, 129–131 in CSEL 32/4, 504f.

[20]   I. de la Potterie, *Mary in the Mystery of the Covenant* (New York: Alba House, 1992), p. 48.

[21]   See P. Haffner, *The Sacramental Mystery* (Leominster: Gracewing, 2008), p. 91.

[22]   See Haffner, *The Mystery of Mary*, pp. 187–201.

[23]   For the theme of the spiritual motherhood of Mary within the Church, see Haffner, *The Mystery of Mary*, chapter 9.

[24]   In Greek the expression used is γυνή.

[25]   A. Valentini, "Il grande segno di Apocalisse 12. Una Chiesa ad immagine della Madre di Gesù" in *Marianum* 59 (1997), p.62.

[26]   See Jn 19:25 and Rv 12:2 and also S. Manelli, *All Generations Shall Call Me Blessed* (New Bedford, Massachusetts: Academy of the Immaculate, 1995), pp. 359–360.

[27]   D. Carroll, *Mary's House: The Extraordinary Story Behind the Discovery of the House Where the Virgin Mary Lived and Died* (Texas: Christian Classics, 2000), p. 89.

[28]   See C. G. Schukte, *The Life of Sr. Marie de Mandat-Grancey & Mary's House in Ephesus* (Charlotte, NC: Tan Books, 2011).

[29]   See E. Poulin, *The Holy Virgin's House, The True Story of its Discovery* (Istanbul: Arikan Yayinlari Tic., 1999).

[30]   Pope Benedict XVI, *Discourse at General Audience* (6 December 2006).

[31]   See Mother Mariam, *The Life of The Theotokos* (Holy Apostles Convent and Dormition Skete: 1989).

[32]   This tradition can be seen for example in the Venerable Bede, *Liber de locis sacris* 2, 5 in CSEL 39, 309f.

[33]   St John Damascene, *Homily 2 on the Dormition of the Blessed Virgin*, 4 in PG 96, 730. St Gregory of Tours, St Sophronius, Patriarch of Jerusalem, St Germanus, Patriarch of Constantinople, St Andrew, bishop of Crete, and the Venerable Bede indicate this same tradition, common to East and West.

[34]   St John Damascene, *Homily 2 on the Dormition of the Blessed Virgin*, 14 in PG 96, 739.

[35]   See E.–P. Le Camus, *Notre voyage aux pays bibliques*, (Paris: 1894), I, p. 253.

[36]   See Eusebius, *Historia Ecclesiastica*, III, 31; V, 24, in PG 20, 280; 493.

[37]   Cf. D. Arnaldi, *Super transitu Beatae Mariae Virginis Deiparae expertis omni labe culpae originalis dubia proposita* (Genuae: Montaldi, 1879), I, c. I.

[38] According to the meditations of Blessed Catherine Emmerich (d. 1824), compiled and published in 1852, the Blessed Virgin died and was buried a few miles south of Ephesus. In Panaghia Kapoli, on a hill about nine or ten miles distant from Ephesus, the remains of a house were discovered, in which Mary is supposed to have lived, according to the indications given by Blessed Catherine Emmerich in her life of the Blessed Virgin.

[39] St John Damascene, *Homily 2 on the Dormition of the Blessed Virgin*, 12 in *PG* 96, 738.

[40] St Gregory of Tours, *De gloria beatorum martyrum*, 4 in *PL* 71, 708.

[41] See Vatican II, *Dei Verbum*, 9: "For Sacred Scripture is the word of God inasmuch as it is consigned to writing under the inspiration of the divine Spirit, while sacred tradition takes the word of God entrusted by Christ the Lord and the Holy Spirit to the Apostles, and hands it on to their successors in its full purity, so that led by the light of the Spirit of truth, they may in proclaiming it preserve this word of God faithfully, explain it, and make it more widely known. Consequently it is not from Sacred Scripture alone that the Church draws her certainty about everything which has been revealed. Therefore both sacred tradition and Sacred Scripture are to be accepted and venerated with the same sense of loyalty and reverence." See also Council of Trent, session IV, *Decree on Scriptural Canons* in DS 1501.

[42] E. Renan, *L'Eglise Chrétienne*, in *Histoire des origines du Christianisme*, Vol. 6 (Paris: 1879) p. 513; C. Tischendorf, *Apocalypses Apocryphae* (Leipzig: 1866), p. 34.

[43] See St Bernardine of Siena, *In Assumptione B. Mariae Virginis*, Sermo 11.

[44] See R. Garrigou-Lagrange, *The Mother of the Savour and Our Interior Life* (Dublin: Golden Eagle Books, 1948), pp. 164–165.

[45] Pope Pius XII, Apostolic Constitution *Munificentissimus Deus*, 20.

[46] See Rv 12:14 and also p. 19 above, where it was stated that the figure of the woman in the book of Revelation "is symbolic, but in a polyvalent sense, referring to both Mariological and ecclesiological realities".

[47] Pope Pius XII, *Munificentissimus Deus*, 44.

2 ST PETER AND ST PAUL

What fairer light is this than time itself doth own,
The golden day with beams more radiant brightening?
The princes of God's Church this feast day doth enthrone,
To sinners heavenward bound their burden lightening.
One taught mankind its creed, one guards the heavenly gate,
Founders of Rome, they bind the world in loyalty;
One by the sword achieved, one by the cross his fate;
With laurelled brows they hold eternal royalty.

Elpis, *Decora lux*

S T PETER AND ST PAUL were the two most significant Apostles. The Church is founded on the Apostles, and the notion of apostle starts with Christ's choice of the Twelve:

> Now the names of the twelve apostles are these: The first, Simon, who is called Peter, and Andrew his brother; and James the son of Zebedee, and John his brother; Philip and Bartholomew; Thomas and Matthew the tax-gatherer; James the son of Alphaeus, and Thaddaeus; Simon the Zealot, and Judas Iscariot, the one who betrayed Him (Mt 10:2–4).

The title of apostle was gradually extended beyond those who constituted the group of the Twelve. Matthias was elected to fill the place left by Judas, and so was listed as one of the twelve Apostles (Ac 1:15–26). James, mentioned in the Letter to the Galatians, is no longer considered to be James the son of Alphaeus, but rather one who had known Jesus and who had a certain prominence in the primitive Church. He is regarded as enjoying apostolic power (Ga 1:19; 2:9). The title of apostle was also assigned to Paul and Barnabas (Ac 14:4, 14). The progression in the use of this title is seen in St Paul's description of the appearances of the risen Christ:

> First He appeared to Cephas and secondly to the Twelve. Next He appeared to more than five hundred of the brothers at the same time, most of whom are still alive, though some have died; then He appeared to James, and then to all the apostles; and last of all He appeared to me too (1 Co 15:5–8).

The office of being an apostle involved an investiture which consisted of the laying–on of hands and a prayer, as can be seen in the case of Paul and Barnabas (Ac 13:3). Those who were apostles, but not numbered among the Twelve shared in common with the Twelve an episcopal power and also the privilege of having seen the risen Christ; they participated in the foundational quality of the experience of the early Church. However, being part of the Twelve involves more: it means having been present the whole time the Lord Jesus was exercising His ministry, and sharing the experience of the Paschal Mystery (Ac 1:21–22). A disciple is a follower of Jesus; an apostle is one who is sent by Jesus. Most of the New Testament was written by eyewitnesses of Jesus or their disciples.

2.1 St Peter

After Jesus Christ, Peter is the figure best known and most frequently cited in the New Testament writing. Peter's name is mentioned more often than all the other disciples put together: 191 times. John is next in frequency with 48 appearances, and Peter is present 50% of the times that John appears in the Bible. In effect, Peter is named a remarkable 60% of the times any disciple is referred to. He is mentioned 154 times with the special name of Pétros, "rock", which is the Greek translation of the Aramaic name Jesus gave him directly: *Kephas*, attested to nine times, especially in St Paul's Letters. The frequently-occurring name Simon (75 times) is a hellenization of his original Hebrew name "Symeon" (this occurs twice: in Ac 15: 14; and in 2 Pt 1: 1). Simon was the son of Jonah and was born in Bethsaida (Jn 1:42, 44), a little town to the east of the Sea of Galilee (also know as

Gennesaret). The Apostle Andrew was his brother, and the Apostle Philip came from the same town. Simon pursued in Capernaum the profitable occupation of fisherman on Lake Galilee, possessing his own boat (Lk 5:3). Simon settled in Capernaum, where he was living with his mother-in-law in his own house (Mt 8:14; Lk 4:38) at the beginning of Christ's public ministry, around AD 26–28. Recent archaeological excavations have brought to light, beneath the octagonal mosaic paving of a small Byzantine church, the remains of a more ancient church built in that house, as the graffiti with invocations to Peter testify.[1] Simon was thus married, and, according to Clement of Alexandria, had children.[2] The same writer relates the tradition that Peter's wife suffered martyrdom.[3]

Like so many of his Jewish contemporaries, Simon was attracted by John the Baptist's preaching of penance and was, with his brother Andrew, among John's associates in Bethania on the eastern bank of the Jordan. John the Baptist pointed to Jesus who was passing, saying, "Behold, the Lamb of God" (Jn 1:36), and Andrew and another disciple followed the Saviour to His residence and remained with Him that day. Later, meeting his brother, Simon, Andrew said "We have found the Messiah", and brought him to Jesus, who, looking upon him, said: "You are Simon the son of John; you will be called Kephas" (Jn 1:42). Already, at this first meeting, the Saviour foretold the change of Simon's name to *Kephas*, the Aramaic for rock, which is translated *Pétros* in Greek (in Latin *Petrus*) a proof that Christ had already special plans with regard to Simon. Later, probably at the time of his definitive call to the Apostolate with the eleven other Apostles, Jesus actually gave Simon the name of *Kephas*, after which he was usually called Peter, especially on the solemn occasion after Peter's profession of faith (Mt 16:18). The Evangelists often combine the two names, while St Paul uses the name *Kephas*.

After this first meeting, Peter with the other early disciples remained with Jesus for some time, accompanying Him to Galilee (for the Marriage at Cana), to Judaea, and to Jerusalem, and through Samaria back to Galilee (Jn 2–4). Here Peter resumed his occupation of fisherman for a short time, but soon received the definitive call of the Saviour to become one of His permanent disciples. Peter and Andrew were engaged at their work when Jesus met and addressed them: "Come after me, and I will make you fishers of men" (Mt 4:19). On the same occasion, the sons of Zebedee were called (Mt 4:18–22; Mk 1:16–20; Lk 5:1–11; it is assumed here that Luke refers to the same occasion as the other Evangelists). Thereafter, Peter remained always in the immediate neighbourhood of Our Lord. After preaching the Sermon on the Mount and curing the son of the centurion in Capernaum, Jesus came to Peter's house and cured his wife's mother, who was sick with a fever (Mt 8:14–15; Mk 1:29–31). A little later, Christ chose His Twelve Apostles as His constant associates in preaching the kingdom of God.

The New Testament notes the growing prominence of Peter among the Twelve. Though of irresolute character, he clings with the greatest fidelity, firmness of faith, and inward love to the Saviour; rash alike in word and act, he is full of zeal and enthusiasm, though momentarily easily accessible to external influences and intimidated by difficulties. The more prominent the Apostles become in the Gospel narrative, the more conspicuous does Peter appear as the first among them. In the list of the Twelve on the occasion of their solemn call to the Apostolate, not only does Peter stand always at their head, but the name given him by Christ is especially emphasized. For example in the list of the Apostles we read:

> The names of the twelve apostles are these: first, Simon called Peter, and his brother Andrew; James, the son of Zebedee, and his brother John; Philip and Bartholomew, Thomas and Matthew the tax collector; James, the son of Alphaeus, and Thaddaeus; Simon the Cananean, and Judas Iscariot who betrayed him (Mt 10:2–4).[4]

On various occasions Peter speaks in the name of the other Apostles (Mt 15:15; 19:27; Lk 12:41). When Christ's words are addressed to all the Apostles, Peter answers in their name (see, for example Mt 16:16). Frequently the Saviour turns specially to Peter (Mt 26:40; Lk 22:31).

Peter's name occurs first in all lists of apostles (Mt 10:2; Mk 3:16; Lk 6:14; Ac 1:13). Matthew even calls him the "first' (πρῶτος in Greek, see Mt 10:2). The name of Judas Iscariot, however, is invariably mentioned last. Peter is almost without exception named first whenever he appears with anyone else. Peter's name is always the first listed of the "inner circle' of the disciples (Peter, James and John—Mt 17:1; 26:37,40; Mk 5:37; 14:37). In one example to the contrary, Galatians 2:9, where he ("Cephas") is listed after James and before John, he is clearly pre-eminent in the entire context (Gal 1:18–19; 2:7–8). Peter is often the central figure relating to Jesus in dramatic Gospel scenes, such as walking on the water (Mt 14:28–32; Lk 5:1 ff., Mk 10:28; Mt 17:24 ff.). Peter first confesses Christ's divinity (Mt 16:16). Peter alone among the apostles receives a new name, *Rock*, solemnly conferred by Jesus Christ (Jn 1:42; Mt 16:18). Likewise, Peter is regarded by Jesus as the Chief Shepherd after Himself (Jn 21:15–17), by name in the singular, and over the universal Church, even though others have a similar but subordinate role (Ac 20:28; 1 Pt 5:2).

Peter alone among the apostles is mentioned by name as having been prayed for by Jesus Christ in order that his "faith may not fail" (Lk 22:32). Peter alone among the apostles is exhorted by Jesus to "strengthen his brethren" (Lk 22:32). Peter alone is told that he has received divine knowledge by a special revelation (Mt 16:17). Peter is regarded by the Jews (Ac 4:1–13) as the leader and spokesman of Christianity, and is regarded by the common people in the same way (Ac 2:37–41; 5:15). Jesus Christ uniquely associates Himself and Peter in the miracle of the tribute-money (Mt 17:24–27). Christ teaches from Peter's boat, and the miraculous catch of fish follows (Lk 5:1–11): perhaps a metaphor for the Pope as a "fisher of men" (cf. Mt 4:19). Peter was the first apostle to set out for, and enter the empty tomb (Lk 24:12; Jn 20:6). Peter is specified by an angel as the leader and representative of the apostles (Mk 16:7). Peter leads the apostles in fishing (Jn 21:2–3,11). The barque of Peter is regarded as a figure of the Church, with Peter at the helm. Peter alone casts himself into the sea to come to Jesus (Jn 21:7). Peter's words are the first recorded and most important in the upper room before Pentecost (Ac 1:15–22).

Very characteristic is the expression of true fidelity to Jesus, which Peter addressed to Him in the name of the other Apostles. Christ, after He had spoken of the mystery of the reception of His Body and Blood (Jn 6:22 ff.) and many of His disciples had left Him, asked the Twelve if they too would leave Him. Peter's answer comes immediately: "Master, to whom shall we go? You have the words of eternal life. We have come to believe and are convinced that you are the Holy One of God" (Jn 6:68–69). Christ Himself unmistakably accords Peter a special precedence and the first place among the Apostles, and designates him as such on various occasions. Peter was one of the three Apostles (with James and John) who were with Christ on certain special occasions like the raising from the dead of the daughter of Jairus (Mk 5:37; Lk 8:51); the Transfiguration of the Lord (Mt 17:1; Mk 9:1; Lk 9:28), the Agony in the Garden of Gethsemane (Mt 26:37; Mk 14:33). On several occasions, Christ also favoured him above all the others. For example, Jesus enters Peter's boat on Lake Gennesaret to preach to the multitude on the shore (Lk 5:3). When He was miraculously walking upon the waters, He called Peter to come to Him across the lake (Mt 14:28 ff). Moreover, Jesus sent him to the lake to catch the fish in whose mouth Peter found the coin to pay as tax (Mt 17:24 ff.).

St Peter's profession of faith took place at Caesarea Philippi. This place was so named because it had been rebuilt by the tetrarch Philip in honour of Caesar Augustus. It was the summer before the Crucifixion, with Jesus filled with presentiments of His Death. Perhaps Jesus withdrew here because it is a pleasant place to escape in summertime the torrid heat of the Lake of Galilee. However, the area has other associations which make it a suitable site for this scene. Hermon is traditionally a holy mountain, a meeting place of God and man, a suitable background to this episode of revelation and solemn mission. They walked a while up the mountain road to Mount Hermon. The Jordan had its source in these mysterious ravines; the spring of the Jordan is, in Jewish legend, the opening to hell.[5] The precipitous southern end of one of the foothills of Mount Hermon forms a wall of bare rock about 200 feet high and 500 feet wide, which formed the backdrop for Peter's profession of faith.[6] Here, Jesus asked His disciples: "Who do people say that the Son of Man is?" (Mt 16:13). Some of them had heard that people took Him for the risen John the Baptist, others for Elijah or one of the prophets. "But who do you say that I am?", continued Jesus. Quicker than any of the others, came Peter's confession of faith: "You are the Christ, the Son of the living God" (Mt 16:16). Jesus responded with the words: "Blessed are you, Simon son of Jonah. For flesh and blood has not revealed this to you, but my heavenly Father." Then Jesus added:

> And so I say to you, you are Peter, and upon this rock I will build my Church, and the gates of hell shall not prevail against it. I will give you the keys to the kingdom of heaven. Whatever you bind on earth shall be bound in heaven; and whatever you loose on earth shall be loosed in heaven (Mt 16:18–19).

These words of the Lord, written down in the latter half of the first century are inscribed in Latin, in golden letters, within the dome of St Peter's Basilica in Rome.

In Hebrew thought, a person's name expresses the reality concerning that person. St Peter's new name encapsulates his mission as bedrock of the Church and foundation of its unity in Christ. By the word "rock" the Saviour cannot have meant Himself, but only Peter, as is so much more apparent in Aramaic in which the same word (*Kipha*) is used for "Peter" and "rock". Christ's statement means that He wishes to make Peter the head of the whole community of those who believed in Him as the true Messiah; that through this foundation (Peter) the Kingdom of Christ would be unconquerable; that the guidance of the faithful was placed in the hands of Peter, as the special representative, or Vicar, of Christ. Moreover, *Rock* also embodies a metaphor applied to him by Christ in a sense analogous to the suffering and despised Messiah (1 Pt 2:4–8; cf. Mt 21:42). Without a solid foundation a house falls. St Peter is the foundation, but not the founder of the Church; the administrator, but not the Lord of the Church.

Christ says to St Peter "I will give you the keys of the kingdom of heaven" (Mt 16:19). This "power of the keys" concerns ecclesiastical discipline and administrative authority with regard to the requirements of the faith, as prefigured in Isaiah 22:22 (cf. Is 9:6; Jb 12:14; Rev 3:7). From this power flows the use of censures, excommunication, absolution, baptismal discipline, the imposition of penances, and legislative powers. In the Old Testament a steward, or prime minister, is a man who is set "over a house" (Gen 41:40; 43:19; 44:4; 1 Ki 4:6; 16:9; 18:3; 2 Ki 10:5; 15:5; 18:18; Is 22:15,20–21). Jesus adds "whatever you bind on earth shall be bound in heaven, and whatever you loose on earth shall be loosed in heaven" (Mt 16:19). The words "bind" and "loose" are not merely metaphorical, but are concrete Jewish juridical rabbinical terms, which meant to "forbid" and "permit" with reference to the interpretation of the law, and secondarily to "condemn" or "place under the ban" or "acquit". Thus, St Peter and the Popes are given the authority to determine the rules for doctrine and life, by virtue of revelation and the Spirit's leading (Jn 16:13), and to demand obedience from the Church. "Binding and loosing" represent the legislative and judicial powers of the Papacy and the bishops (Mt 18:17–18; Jn 20:23). St Peter, however, is the only apostle who receives these powers by name and in the singular, making him pre-eminent. The close link between Christ and St Peter after his profession of faith is illustrated by the episode in which Jesus sent him to the lake to catch the fish in whose mouth Peter found the coin to pay as tax for both of them (Mt 17:24 ff.).

The position of Peter among the other Apostles and in the Christian community was the basis for the Kingdom of God on earth, that is, the Church of Christ. Peter was personally installed as Head of the Apostles by Christ Himself. This foundation created for the Church by its Founder could not disappear with the person of Peter, but was intended to continue and did in fact continue (as actual history shows) in the primacy of the Roman Church and its Popes.

In spite of his firm faith in Jesus, Peter had thus far no complete knowledge of the mission and work of the Saviour. The sufferings of Christ especially, challenged his worldly conception of the Messiah, and were inconceivable to him. Peter's incomplete conception occasionally elicited a sharp reproof from Jesus (Mt 16:21–23, Mk 8:31–33). During the Passion, Peter's weakness was manifested. The Saviour had already told him that Satan had desired to sift him as wheat. However, Christ had prayed for Peter that his faith may not fail, and, after being converted, he would confirm his brothers (Lk 22:31–32). Peter's assurance that he was ready to accompany his Master to prison and to death, elicited Christ's prediction that Peter would deny Him (Mt 26:30–35; Mk 14:26–31; Lk 22:31–34; Jn 13:33–38). When Christ proceeded to wash the feet of His disciples before the Last Supper, and came first to Peter, the latter at first protested, but, on Christ's declaring that otherwise he should have no part with Him, immediately said: "Lord, not only my feet, but also my hands and my head" (Jn 13:1–10). In the Garden of Gethsemane, Peter had to submit to the Saviour's reproach that he had slept like the others, while his Master suffered deadly anguish (Mk 14:37). At the seizing of Jesus, Peter in an outburst of anger wished to defend his Master by force, but was forbidden to do so. At first he fled with the other Apostles (Jn 18:10–11; Mt 26:56); then turning he followed his captured Lord to the courtyard of the High Priest, and there denied Christ three times, asserting explicitly and swearing that he did not know Him (Mt 26:58–75; Mk 14:54–72; Lk 22:54–62; Jn 18:15–27). This denial did not constitute a lapse of interior faith in Christ, but was an expression of exterior fear and cowardice. His sorrow was thus so much the greater, when, after his Master had turned His gaze towards him, he clearly recognized the wrong he had done.

In spite of this weakness, Peter's position as head of the Apostles was later confirmed by Jesus, and his precedence was at least as clear after the Resurrection as before. The women, who were the first to find Christ's tomb empty, received from the angel a special message for Peter (Mk 16:7). To him alone of the Apostles did Christ appear on the first day after the Resurrection (Lk 24:34; 1 Co 15:5). Moreover, most important of all, when He appeared at the Lake of Galilee, Christ renewed to Peter His special commission to feed and defend His flock, after Peter had thrice affirmed his special love for his Master (Jn 21:15–17). The encounter involves a very significant play on words. In Greek, the word *"fileo"* means the love of friendship, which is limited and not all-encompassing; instead, the word *"agapao"* means total and unconditional love without reserve. Jesus asks Peter the first time: "Simon... do you love me *(agapas-me)"* with this total and unconditional love (Jn 21:15)? Prior to the experience of betrayal, the Apostle Peter certainly would have said: "I love you *(agapo-se)* unconditionally". Now that he has known the bitter sadness of infidelity, the drama of his own weakness, he says with humility: "Lord; you know that I love you *(filo-se)"*, that is, "I love you with my poor human love". Christ insists: "Simon, do you love me with this total love that I want?" And Peter repeats the response of his humble human love: *"Kyrie, filo-se"*, "Lord, I love you as I am able to love you". The third time Jesus only says to Simon: *"Fileis-me?"*, "Do you love me?" Simon Peter understands that his poor love is enough for Jesus, it is the only one of which he is capable, nonetheless he is grieved that the Lord spoke to him in this way. He thus replies: "Lord, you know everything; you know that I love you *(filo-se)"*.[7] Finally, Christ foretold the violent death Peter would have to suffer, and thus invited him to follow Him in a special manner (Jn 21:20–23). In this manner, Peter was called and prepared to exercise the primacy of the Apostles, which he carried out with courage after Christ's Ascension into Heaven.

Among the crowd of Apostles and disciples who, after Christ's Ascension into Heaven from the Mount of Olives, returned to

Jerusalem to await the fulfilment of His promise to send the Holy Spirit, Peter clearly stands out as the leader of all, and is henceforth constantly recognized as the head of the original Christian community in Jerusalem. He takes the initiative in the appointment to the Apostolic College of another witness of the life, death and resurrection of Christ to replace Judas (Ac 1:15–26). After the descent of the Holy Spirit on the first feast of Pentecost, Peter stands at the head of the Apostles and delivers the first public sermon to proclaim the life, Death, and Resurrection of Jesus, and wins a large number of Jews as converts to the Christian community (Ac 2:14–41). As the first among the Apostles he worked a public miracle, when with John he went up into the temple and cured the lame man at the Beautiful Gate. To the people crowding in amazement about the two Apostles, he preaches a long sermon in the Porch of Solomon, and brings new members to the flock of believers (Ac 3:1–4:4).

In the subsequent examinations of the two Apostles before the Jewish High Council, Peter defends in courageous fashion the cause of Jesus and the obligation and liberty of the Apostles to preach the Gospel (Ac 4:5–21). When Ananias and Sapphira attempt to deceive the Apostles and the people, Peter appears as judge of their action, and God executes the sentence of punishment passed by the Apostle by causing the sudden death of the two guilty parties (Ac 5:1–11). By numerous miracles, God confirms the Apostolic activity of Christ's witnesses, and here also special mention is made of Peter, since it is recorded that the inhabitants of Jerusalem and neighbouring towns carried their sick on their beds into the streets so that the shadow of Peter might fall on them and they might thereby be healed (Ac 5:12–16). The ever-increasing number of the faithful caused the Sanhedrin to adopt new measures against the Apostles, but Peter and the Apostles answer that they "ought to obey God rather than men" (Ac 5:29 ff.). Not only in Jerusalem itself did Peter labour in fulfilling the mission entrusted to him by his Master. He also connected with the other Christian communities in Palestine, and preached the Gospel both there and in the lands situated farther north. When Philip the Deacon had won a large number of believers in Samaria, Peter and John were deputed to travel there from Jerusalem to organize the community and to invoke the Holy Spirit to descend upon the faithful. Peter appears a second time as judge, in the case of the magician Simon, who had wished to purchase from the Apostles the power to invoke the Holy Spirit (Ac 8: 14–25). On their way back to Jerusalem, the two Apostles preached the joyous tidings of the Kingdom of God. Subsequently, after Paul's departure from Jerusalem and conversion on the road to Damascus, the Christian communities in Palestine were left in peace by the Jewish council.

Peter then undertook an extensive missionary tour, which brought him to the maritime cities, Lydda, Joppe, and Caesarea. In Lydda he cured the paralyzed Aeneas, in Joppe he raised Tabitha (Dorcas) from the dead; and at Caesarea, instructed by a vision which he had in Joppe, he baptized and received into the Church the first non-Jewish Christians, the centurion Cornelius and his kinsmen (Ac 9:32–10:48). On Peter's return to Jerusalem a little later, the strict Jewish Christians, who regarded the complete observance of the Jewish law as binding on all, asked him why he had entered and eaten in the house of the uncircumcised. Peter tells of his vision and defends his action, which was ratified by the Apostles and the faithful in Jerusalem (Ac 11:1–18).

A confirmation of the position accorded to Peter by Luke, in the Acts, is afforded by the testimony of St Paul (Ga 1:18–20). After his conversion and three years' residence in Arabia, Paul came to Jerusalem "to see Peter". Here the Apostle of the Gentiles clearly designates Peter as the authorized head of the Apostles and of the early Christian Church. Peter's long residence in Jerusalem and Palestine soon came to an end. Herod Agrippa I began (AD 42–44) a new persecution of the Church in Jerusalem; after the execution of James, the son of Zebedee, this ruler had Peter cast into prison, intending to have him also executed after the Jewish Passover was ended. However, Peter was freed in a miraculous manner, and, proceeding to the house of the mother of John Mark, where many of the faithful were assembled for prayer, informed them of his liberation from the hands of Herod, commissioned them to communicate the fact to James and the brethren, and then left Jerusalem to go to "another place" (Ac 12:1–18). Concerning St Peter's subsequent activity we receive no further comprehensive information from Scriptural sources, although we possess short notices of certain individual episodes of his later life.

It is certain that St Peter remained for a time at Antioch; he may even have returned there several times. The Christian community of Antioch was founded by Christianized Jews who had been driven from Jerusalem by the persecution (Ac 11:19ff.). Peter's residence among them is proved by the episode concerning the observance of the Jewish ceremonial law even by Christianized pagans, related by St Paul (Ga 2:11–21). The chief Apostles in Jerusalem, the "pillars", Peter, James, and John, had unreservedly approved St Paul's apostolate to the Gentiles, while they themselves intended to labour principally among the Jews. While Paul was dwelling in Antioch (the date cannot be accurately determined), St Peter came there and mingled freely with the non-Jewish Christians of the community, frequenting their houses and sharing their meals. However, when the Christianized Jews arrived from Jerusalem, Peter, fearing lest these rigid observers of the Jewish ceremonial law should be scandalized, and his influence with the Jewish Christians be endangered, afterwards avoided eating with the uncircumcised. His conduct made a great impression on the other Jewish Christians at Antioch, so that even Barnabas, St Paul's companion, now avoided eating with the Christianized pagans. As this action was entirely opposed to the principles and practice of Paul, and might lead to confusion among the converted pagans, this Apostle addressed a public reproach to St Peter, because his conduct seemed to indicate a wish to compel the pagan converts to become Jews and accept circumcision and the Jewish law. The whole incident is another proof of the authoritative position of St Peter in the early Church, since his example and conduct was regarded as decisive. Tradition makes Peter the first bishop of

Antioch, and thus its first Patriarch. Some scholars interpret Paul's mention of Peter in 1 Corinthians 1:12 as evidence that Peter had also visited Corinth.

Peter returned occasionally to the original Christian Church of Jerusalem, the guidance of which was entrusted to St James, the relative of Jesus, after the departure of the Prince of the Apostles (AD 42–44). The last mention of St Peter in the Acts (15:1–29; see Ga 2:1–10) occurs in the report of the Council of the Apostles on the occasion of such a passing visit. Between Peter and Paul there was no dogmatic difference in their conception of salvation for Jewish and Gentile Christians. The recognition of Paul as the Apostle of the Gentiles (Ga 2:1–9) was entirely sincere, and excludes all question of a fundamental divergence of views. St Peter and the other Apostles recognized the converts from paganism as Christian brothers on an equal footing.

It is an established historical fact that St Peter laboured in Rome during the last portion of his life, and there ended his earthly course by martyrdom. As to the duration of his Apostolic activity in the Roman capital, the continuity or otherwise of his residence there, the details and success of his labours, and the chronology of his arrival and death, all these questions are uncertain, and can be solved only on more or less well-founded hypotheses. The essential fact is that Peter died at Rome, which is linked to the historical foundation of the claim of the Bishops of Rome to the Apostolic Primacy of Peter. The manner, and therefore the place of his death, must have been known in widely extended Christian circles at the end of the first century. This is clear from Christ's prophecy in the Gospel of St John that Peter would be led where he do not want to go, indicating the type of death with which he would glorify God (Jn 21:18–19).

St Peter's First Letter was written almost undoubtedly from Rome, since the salutation at the end reads: "The chosen one at Babylon sends you greeting, as does Mark, my son" (1 Pt 5:13). Babylon must here be identified with the Roman capital; since Babylon on the Euphrates, which lay in ruins, or New Babylon (Seleucia) on the Tigris, or the Egyptian Babylon near Memphis, or Jerusalem cannot be meant, the reference must be to Rome, the only city which is called Babylon elsewhere in ancient Christian literature (Rev 17:5; 18:10). From Bishop Papias of Hierapolis and Clement of Alexandria, who both appeal to the testimony of the old disciples of the Apostles, we learn that Mark wrote his Gospel in Rome at the request of the Roman Christians, who desired a written memorial of the doctrine preached to them by St Peter and his disciples, and this fact is confirmed by St Irenaeus.[8]

2.1.1 The sufferings and martyrdom of St Peter

St Peter was imprisoned on two separate occasions during his 25 year reign as the Vicar of Christ. To please the enemies of the Christians, Herod Agrippa had put St James to death, and then he planned to do the same to St Peter, the Head of the Church. Once he had him in prison, he set a heavy guard about him to make sure he would not escape. However, all the Christians of Jerusalem begged the Lord to save St Peter, and their prayers were answered. The night before he was to be condemned, St Peter was peacefully sleeping in his prison cell between his two guards bound tightly by two chains. He was unafraid of death and ready to do God's will. Suddenly an angel appeared and tapped him on the side to awaken him. He told him to get up at once, put on his cloak and sandals and follow him. According to the Acts of the Apostles (12:7), the angel caused the chains to fall from Peter's hands and led him past slumbering guards to freedom. The pious Eudocia, wife of Emperor Theodosius II, journeyed to Jerusalem to fulfil a vow, and while there she was honoured with many gifts, the greatest of which was an iron chain adorned with gold and precious stones, and affirmed to be that with which the Apostle Peter had been bound by Herod. Eudocia piously venerated this chain, and then sent it to Rome to her daughter Eudoxia. The chain was eventually given as a gift to Pope St Leo the Great (440–461). In Rome there was already a chain that was greatly prized which had bound the saint during his nine month imprisonment by Nero in the Mamertine Prison near the Forum. When the pope compared the two chains, they miraculously fused together into one unbreakable series of links. Because of this miracle, Empress Eudocia had built the Basilica of Saint Peter in Chains, and dedicated it to St Peter in the year 442. The relic is now kept in a golden urn beneath the high altar, close to the famous statue of Michelangelo's Moses. The Feast of St Peter's Chains is kept on August 1.

A testimony concerning the martyrdom of Peter and Paul is supplied by Pope Clement I around AD 95–97:

> Through zeal and cunning the greatest and most right-
> eous supports of the Church have suffered persecution
> and been put to death. Let us place before our eyes the
> good Apostles, like St Peter, who in consequence of unjust
> zeal, suffered not one or two, but numerous miseries, and,
> having thus given testimony, has entered the merited
> place of glory.[9]

He then mentions Paul and a number of elect, who were assembled with the others and suffered martyrdom "among us" (namely among the Romans). He is speaking undoubtedly of the persecution under Nero, and thus fixes the martyrdom of Peter and Paul to that epoch.

St Irenaeus of Lyons, a native of Asia Minor and a disciple of Polycarp of Smyrna (himself a disciple of St John the Apostle), passed a considerable time in Rome shortly after the middle of the second century, and then proceeded to Lyons, where he became bishop in AD 177. Irenaeus described the Roman Church as the most prominent and chief preserver of the Apostolic tradition:

> However, since it would be too long to enumerate in such
> a volume as this the succession of all the churches, we
> shall confound all those who, in whatever manner,
> whether through self-satisfaction or vainglory, or through
> blindness and wicked opinion, assemble other than where
> it is proper, by pointing out here the successions of the
> bishops of the greatest and most ancient church known
> to all, founded and organized at Rome by the two most
> glorious apostles, Peter and Paul, that church which has
> the tradition and the faith which comes down to us after
> having been announced to men by the apostles. With that

church, because of its superior origin, all the churches must agree, that is, all the faithful in the whole world, and it is in her that the faithful everywhere have maintained the apostolic tradition.[10]

He thus cites the universally known and recognized fact of the Apostolic activity of Peter and Paul in Rome. Irenaeus also outlines the Papal succession:

The blessed apostles [Peter and Paul], having founded and built up the church [of Rome], then handed over the office of the episcopate to Linus. Paul makes mention of this Linus in the letter to Timothy. To him succeeded Anacletus, and after him, in the third place from the apostles, Clement was chosen for the episcopate. He had seen the blessed apostles and was acquainted with them. It might be said that he still heard the echoes of the preaching of the apostles and had their traditions before his eyes. And not only he, for there were many still remaining who had been instructed by the apostles... To this Clement, Evaristus succeeded... and now, in the twelfth place after the apostles, the lot of the episcopate [of Rome] has fallen to Eleuterus. In this order, and by the teaching of the apostles handed down in the Church, the preaching of the truth has come down to us.[11]

Eusebius records that Paul was beheaded in Rome itself, and Peter, likewise, was crucified, during the reign of the Emperor Nero:

The account is confirmed by the names of Peter and Paul over the cemeteries there, which remain to the present time. And it is confirmed also by a stalwart man of the Church, Caius by name, who lived in the time of Zephyrinus, Bishop of Rome (198–217 AD). This Caius speaks of the places in which the remains of the aforementioned apostles were deposited: "I can point out the trophies of the apostles. For if you are willing to go to the Vatican or to the Ostian Way, you will find the trophies of those who founded this Church".[12]

Around 210 AD, Tertullian supplies a further testimony to the martyrdom of St Peter and St Paul and its importance for Rome:

> But if you are near Italy, you have Rome, where authority
> is at hand for us too. What a happy Church that is, on
> which the apostles poured out their whole doctrine with
> their blood; where Peter had a passion like that of the
> Lord, where Paul was crowned with the death of John the
> Baptist, by being beheaded.[13]

Tradition has it that St Peter suffered martyrdom under Nero in
the year 67, having arrived in Rome under the Emperor Claudius, according to Jerome, in 42 AD. He would thus have
completed in Rome twenty-five years of Papacy. Eusebius also
records the manner of St Peter's crucifixion, from a theologian
named Origen (who wrote about AD 230): "Peter appears to
have preached through Pontus, Galatia, Bithynia, Cappadocia,
and Asia, to the Jews that were scattered abroad; who also,
finally coming to Rome, was crucified with his head downward,
having himself requested to suffer in this way."[14] These facts are
borne out also by St Jerome:

> Simon Peter, the son of Jonah, from the village of Bethsa-
> ida in the province of Galilee, brother of Andrew the
> apostle, and himself chief of the apostles, after having
> been bishop of the church of Antioch and having
> preached to the Dispersion... pushed on to Rome in the
> second year of Claudius to over-throw Simon Magus, and
> held the sacerdotal chair there for twenty-five years until
> the last, that is the fourteenth, year of Nero. At his hands,
> he received the crown of martyrdom being nailed to the
> cross with his head towards the ground and his feet raised
> on high, asserting that he was unworthy to be crucified
> in the same manner as his Lord.[15]

In art, St Peter is featured with the keys, based on Christ giving
to him the keys of the kingdom of heaven (Mt 16:19), these keys
are of silver and gold, referring to the episode in Acts 3:6.

2.2 St Paul

Paul's biographical details are to be found respectively in the Letter
to Philemon, in which he says he is "an old man" (Phm 9: *presbytes*)

and in the Acts of the Apostles in which, at the time of the stoning of Stephen, he is described as "a young man" (Ac 7:58: *neanís*). Both these expressions are obviously generic but, according to ancient calculations, a man of about 30 was described as "young" whereas he would be called "old" by the time he had reached the age of about 60. The date of Paul's birth depends largely on the dating of the Letter to Philemon. He is traditionally supposed to have written it during his imprisonment in Rome in the mid-60s. Paul would have been born in approximately the year 8. He would therefore have been about 30 at the time of the stoning of Stephen. In any case, Paul was born in Tarsus, Cilicia (cf. Ac 22:3).

Tarsus was the capital of Cilicia, and was of Greek language, but Roman in its political persuasion, through the favour of Caesar. The city was distinguished for its commercial accomplishments and its literary achievements. In 51 BC, it had as Proconsul no less than Marcus Tullius Cicero himself, while 10 years later, in 41 BC, Tarsus was the place where Mark Anthony and Cleopatra met for the first time.[16] Like most trading centres in the Graeco-Roman world, it had a Jewish colony into which the future Apostle was born. It appears that the boy was given two names after birth: Saul, an honoured name in the tribe of Benjamin to which he belonged (Ph 3:5), and Paul, in token of the Roman citizenship which he inherited, for his father was a Roman citizen (Ac 22:26–28; cf. 16:37). The Latin term *paulus* also means small or little, an allusion perhaps to his small stature which is recorded in the apocrypha of the New Testament.

A Jew from the Diaspora, Saul spoke Greek although his name was of Latin origin. Moreover, it derived by assonance from the original Jewish Saul or Saulos, and he was a Roman citizen (cf. Ac 22:25–28). Paul thus appears to be at the intersection between three different cultures—Roman, Greek and Jewish—and perhaps partly because of this was disposed for fruitful universalistic openness, for a mediation between cultures, for true universality. He also learned a manual trade, perhaps from his father, that of "tentmaker" (Ac 18:3: *skenopoios*). This should probably be understood as a worker of uncarded goat wool or linen fibres who made

them into mats or tents (cf. Ac 20:33–35). At about the age of 12
to 13, the age at which a Jewish boy becomes a *bar mitzvah* ("son
of the commandment"), Paul left Tarsus and moved to Jerusalem
to be educated at the feet of Rabbi Gamaliel the Elder, a nephew
of the great Rabbi Hillel, in accordance with the strictest Pharisaic
norms and acquiring great zeal for the Mosaic Torah (cf. Ga 1:14;
Ph 3:5–6; Acts 22:3; 23:6; 26:5).[17] On the basis of this profound
Orthodoxy that he learned at the school of Hillel in Jerusalem, he
saw the new movement that referred to Jesus of Nazareth as a
risk, a threat to the Jewish identity, to the true Orthodoxy of the
fathers. This explains the fact that he proudly "persecuted the
Church of God" as he was to admit three times in his Letters (1
Co 15:9; Ga 1:13; Ph 3:6).

Although at first he persecuted Christians to the death, Paul
later embraced the belief against which he had fought. Two types
of source describe his conversion. The first kind, the best known,
flows from the pen of Luke. In the Acts of the Apostles there are
three accounts of the conversion of St Paul (Ac 9:1–19; 22:3–21;
26:9–23) presenting some slight differences, which can be
harmonized and which do not affect the basis of the narrative,
which is perfectly identical in substance. Acts 9:1–9 clearly
describes the vision Paul had of Jesus on the road to Damascus,
a vision that led him to turn to Christ.[18] The accounts contain
clear concrete details, such as the light in the sky, falling to the
ground, the voice that called him, his new condition of blindness,
his healing like scales falling from his eyes and the fast that he
made. All these details converge on the heart of the event: the
Risen Christ appears as a brilliant light and speaks to Saul,
transforms his thinking and his entire life. The dazzling radiance
of the Risen Christ blinds him; thus what was his inner reality
is also outwardly apparent, his blindness to the truth, to the
Light that is Christ. Then his definitive "yes" to Christ in Baptism
restores his sight and makes him really see.[19]

The second type of source concerning his conversion consists
in St Paul's actual Letters. He never spoke of this event in detail,
because he presumed that everyone knew the essentials of his

story: everyone knew that from being a persecutor he had been transformed into a fervent apostle of Christ. This had not happened after his own reflection, but after a powerful event, an encounter with the Risen One. Even without going into detail, he speaks on various occasions of this most important episode, that, in other words he too is a witness of the Resurrection of Jesus, the revelation of which he received directly from Jesus, together with his apostolic mission. The clearest text is found in his narrative of what constitutes the centre of salvation history: the death and Resurrection of Jesus and his appearances to witnesses (cf. 1 Co 15). In the words of the ancient tradition, which he too received from the Church of Jerusalem, he says that Jesus died on the Cross, was buried and after the Resurrection appeared risen first to Cephas, that is Peter, then to the Twelve, then to 500 brethren, most of whom were still alive at Paul's time, then to James and then to all the Apostles. To this account handed down by tradition, Paul adds: "Last of all... He appeared also to me" (1 Co 15:8). Thus he makes it clear that this is the foundation of his apostolate and of his new life. There are also other texts in which the same concept appears: "Jesus Christ our Lord, through whom we have received grace and apostleship" (cf. Rm 1:4–5); and further: "Have I not seen Jesus Our Lord?" (1 Co 9:1), words with which he alludes to something that everyone knows. Lastly, the most widely known text is found in his letter to the Galatians:

> But when He who had set me apart before I was born, and had called me through His grace, was pleased to reveal His Son to me, in order that I might preach Him among the Gentiles, I did not confer with flesh and blood, nor did I go up to Jerusalem to those who were Apostles before me, but I went away into Arabia; and again I returned to Damascus (Ga 1:15–17).

He definitely stresses that he is a true witness of the Risen One, that he has received his own mission directly from the Risen One. He frequently claimed that his authority as Apostle to the Gentiles came directly from God (Ga 1:13–16), and not from man.

The only adequate explanation for Paul's conversion is found in this vision. This turning point in his life, this transformation of his whole being was not the fruit of a psychological process, of a maturation or intellectual and moral development. Rather it came from the outside: it was not the fruit of his thought but of his encounter with Jesus Christ. In this sense it was not simply a development of his "ego", but rather a death and a resurrection for Paul himself. One existence died and another, new one was born with the Risen Christ. There is no other way in which to explain this renewal of Paul. None of the psychological analyses can clarify or solve the problem. This event alone, this powerful encounter with Christ, is the key to understanding what had happened: death and resurrection, renewal on the part of the One who had shown Himself and had spoken to him. In this deeper sense we can and we must speak of conversion. This encounter is a real renewal that changed all his parameters. Now he could say that what had been essential and fundamental for him earlier had become "refuse" for him; it was no longer "gain" but loss, because henceforth the only thing that counted for him was life in Christ.[20]

Thus the two sources, the Acts of the Apostles and the Letters of St Paul, converge and agree on the fundamental point: the Risen One spoke to Paul, called him to the apostolate and made him a true Apostle, a witness of the Resurrection, with the specific task of proclaiming the Gospel to the Gentiles, to the Greco-Roman world. At the same time, Paul learned that despite the immediacy of his relationship with the Risen One, he had to enter into communion with the Church, he himself had to be baptized, he had to live in harmony with the other Apostles. Only in such communion with everyone could he have been a true apostle, as he wrote explicitly in the First Letter to the Corinthians: "whether it was they or I, this is what we preach and what you believed" (1 Co 15:11). There is only one proclamation of the Risen One, because Christ is only one.[21]

Following his stay in Damascus after conversion, Paul first went to live in the Nabataean kingdom (which he called "Arabia") for an unknown period, which may have constituted a type of retreat for him. He then came back to Damascus, which by this time was under Nabataean rule. After three more years (Ga 1:17–18) he was forced to flee from that city under the cover of night (Ac 9:23; 25; 2 Co 11:32ff.) because of the explosive reaction of some of the strict Jews to his preaching. He went to Jerusalem to see Peter (Ga 1:18), but remained only fifteen days, for the snares of the Greeks threatened his life. He then left for Tarsus and was lost to sight for five or six years (Ac 9:29–30; Ga 1:21). Barnabas went in search of him and brought him to Antioch where for a year they worked together and their apostolate was most fruitful (Ac 11:25–26). Together also they were sent to Jerusalem to carry alms to the brethren on the occasion of the famine predicted by Agabus (Ac 11:27–30). They do not seem to have found the Apostles there; these had been scattered by the persecution of Herod.

The period of twelve years encompassing 45–57 was the most active and fruitful of St Paul's life. It comprises three great Apostolic expeditions of which Antioch was in each instance the starting-point, and which invariably ended in a visit to Jerusalem. St Paul's first missionary journey is described in Acts 13:1–14:27, his second missionary journey in Acts 15:36–18:22 and his third in Acts 18:23–21:26.

The First Missionary Journey of Paul took place from 46–48 AD. Paul, Barnabas and John Mark started this first missionary journey from Syrian Antioch in the year 47 AD.[22] They went to the harbour town of Seleucia and sailed first to Salamis in Cyprus, the place of origin of Barnabas. The group arrived at Salamis (Acts 13:4–5), one of the great commercial harbours of Cyprus. There, they proclaimed the word of God in the Jewish synagogues. They crossed the island from east to west and arrived in the city of Paphos, the centre of Roman rule and the cult of Aphrodite; that city had an evil reputation for the moral laxity of its inhabitants. Paul and companions met the Roman Proconsul, Sergius Paulus and a sorcerer called Elymas who was blinded by Paul (Ac 13:11). The Proconsul became a believer and from this point on Saul started using his Roman name, Paul.

From Paphos they sailed to the southern coast of Anatolia, today Turkey, to Perga in Pamphylia. Young John Mark then left the party to return to Jerusalem (Ac 13:13). Paul and Barnabas journeyed towards Pisidian Antioch, located 100 miles to the north of Perga. In Pisidian Antioch Paul uttered his famous words: "Now we turn to the Gentiles" (Ac 13:46). After Pisidian Antioch, Paul and Barnabas moved to Lystra where people thought that Paul and Barnabas were gods. Then some Jews arrived from Antioch and Iconium and turned the people against them (Ac 14:19). Paul was stoned and beaten to such an extent that people thought he had died (Ac 14:19). The next city they arrived in was Derbe where the apostles made many disciples (Ac 14:21), and one of them was Gaius (Ac 20:4) who accompanied Paul during his last missionary journey. When they finished preaching the Gospel in Derbe, Paul and his companions retraced their steps through Lystra, Iconium, Pisidian Antioch and Perga to strengthen and teach the brethren (Ac 14:21-25). From Attalia they sailed back to Antioch (Ac 14:25-26), their starting point.

Thus the Church of the Gentiles was born. Paul and Barnabas stayed and preached in Antioch from autumn 46 AD to 49 AD (Ac 14:26–28). Certain men from Jerusalem travelled to Antioch and began teaching that the Gentiles must be circumcised in order to receive salvation (Ac 15:1,5). After Paul and Barnabas discussed and disputed this teaching with those promoting it, they and other Church members went to Jerusalem to confer about the issue with the apostles and elders (Ac 15:2, Ga 2:1–2). To resolve this fundamental problem for the Church, the so-called Council of the Apostles met in Jerusalem to settle on a solution, on which the life of the universal Church depended. It was decided that the observance of Mosaic Law should not be imposed upon converted pagans (cf. Ac 15:6–30): that is, they were not to be bound by the rules of Judaism; the only thing necessary was to belong to Christ, to live with Christ and to abide by His words. Thus, in belonging to Christ, they also belonged to Abraham and to God, and were sharers in all the promises.

After this decisive event Paul separated from Barnabas, chose Silas and set out on his Second Missionary Journey (Ac 15:36–18:22). This journey lasted from AD 49–51, and again started from Syrian Antioch. In late 49 AD Paul and Silas left Antioch for Tarsus. From there they travelled to Derbe and Lystra. It is in Lystra that Paul met Timothy, a very important figure in the nascent Church, the son of a Jewish woman and a pagan, who would become his frequent travelling companion and fellow labourer in spreading the Gospel (Ac 16:1; 1 Tm 1:2, 4:14). Paul had Timothy circumcised (Ac 16:3). Paul, Silas and Timothy travelled to Iconium, Antioch in Pisidia, and then to the Asia Minor port city of Troas, on the northern coast of the Aegean Sea. Here another important event occurred: in a dream he saw a Macedonian from the other side of the sea, that is from Europe, who was saying: "Come and help us!" (Ac 16:9). It was the Europe of the future that was asking for the light and help of the Gospel. On the impetus of this vision he set sail for Macedonia and thus entered Europe. Paul takes the vision as a sign from God and the three men immediately set sail for Neapolis (Ac 16:10–11).[23]

Having disembarked at Neapolis, they made for Philippi, where Paul founded a beautiful community. In Philippi a woman named Lydia heard Paul's preaching and was baptized along with her entire household (Ac 16:12–15). While in Philippi, Paul cast out a demon from a female slave (Ac 16:16–18). Her masters, angry that they had lost the ability to make more money from the slave's demonic divination, aroused the city against Paul and Silas. The two were arrested, beaten and put in prison (Ac 16:19–24). An earthquake, coupled with a miraculous loosening of bonds and opening of all prison doors, freed Paul and Silas (Ac 16:25–40). When the jailer woke and saw the doors wide open he drew his sword and was about to commit suicide, presuming that the prisoners had escaped. However, Paul reassured him and baptised him then and there with all his household (Ac 16:33).

Paul, Silas and Timothy passed through the cities of Amphipolis and Apollonia, then travelled to Thessalonica (Ac 17:1). In that latter city Paul visited a Jewish synagogue and for three consecutive Sabbaths (Saturdays) explained that Jesus is the Saviour of Mankind, as the Old Testament prophesied (Ac 17:2–4). Although many believed him, certain Jews, envious of the success of the Gospel, formed a mob and started a riot (Ac 17:4–5). The riotous crowd went to the house of Jason seeking Paul and Silas. As they were not found, the crowd dragged Jason and some brethren to the local civil magistrates and accused them of wrongdoing (Ac 17:5–8). In a short time, however, Jason and the brethren were freed. Paul, Silas and Timothy soon left the city for Berea.

Paul and Silas visited and preached in a synagogue in Berea. The Bereans, unlike those in Thessalonica, were not only willing to listen to what Paul had to say, but they also became believers (Ac 17:11–12). Unfortunately, Jews from Thessalonica arrived in the city seeking to cause more trouble for Paul (Ac 17:13). He immediately left for the coast and set sail for Athens while Silas and Timothy remained in Berea (Ac 17:14). Once in Athens, Paul wrote to Silas and Timothy requesting they come to him as soon as possible (Ac 17:15). As he waited for their arrival, he was troubled by how pervasive among the Athenians was the worship of false gods (Ac 17:16). His preaching led to an invitation by several Athenians to elaborate on the Gospel. In this capital of ancient Greek culture, he preached to pagans and Greeks, first in the Agora and then on the Areopagus. The discourse of the Areopagus, mentioned in the Acts of the Apostles, is the model of how to translate the Gospel into Greek culture, of how to help Greeks understand that this God of the Christians and Jews was not a God foreign to their culture but was the unknown God they were awaiting, the true answer to the deepest questions of their culture.[24] Paul was taken to the Areopagus, also known as Mars Hill (where the supreme judges of Athens assembled) where he used the existence of an altar dedicated "To the Unknown God" to reveal the existence of the Creator God who alone is worthy of worship (Ac 17:22–32).

Then from Athens he arrived in Corinth, where he stayed for a year and a half. Here we have an event that is chronologically very reliable. It is the most reliable date in the whole of his biography because, during this first stay in Corinth he was obliged to appear before the Governor of the Senatorial Province of Achaia, the Proconsul Gallio, who accused him of illegitimate worship. In Corinth there is an ancient inscription, found in Delphi, which mentions this Gallio and that epoch. It says that Gallio was Proconsul in Corinth between the years 51 and 53. Thus we have one absolutely certain date. Paul stayed in Corinth in those years. We may therefore suppose that he arrived there in about the year 50 and stayed until 52.[25] Then from Corinth, passing through Cenchreae, the port on the eastern side of the city, he set sail for Palestine and arrived in Caesarea Marittima. From here he sailed for Jerusalem, before returning to Antioch on the Orontes.

St Paul's Third Missionary Journey lasted from AD 53–57, and when he started, the city in his mind was Ephesus and that was the main aim of his third trip. The third missionary journey (cf. Ac 18:23–21:16), began, like all his journeys, in Antioch, which had become the original core of the Church of the Gentiles, of the mission to the Gentiles, and was also the place where the term "Christian" was coined. It was here, St Luke tells us, that Jesus' followers were called "Christians" for the first time (Ac 11:26). From Antioch Paul started out for Ephesus, the capital of the Province of Asia where he stayed two years (Ac 19:10), carrying out a ministry whose fruitful effects were felt throughout the region. It was from Ephesus that Paul wrote the Letters to the Thessalonians and to the Corinthians. The population of the town, however, was set against him by the local silversmiths, who saw their income diminishing with the reduction in the number of those who worshipped Artemis; the temple dedicated to her in Ephesus, the *Artemysion,* was one of the seven wonders of the ancient world (Ac 19:24–29); Paul was thus forced to flee north. He crossed Macedonia once again and went back to Greece, probably to Corinth, where he remained for three months and wrote his famous Letter to the Romans.

Paul then retraced his steps: he went back through Macedonia, reaching Troas by boat, and then, staying very briefly on the islands of Mitylene, Chios and Samos, arrived at Miletus where he delivered an important discourse to the elders of the Church of Ephesus, outlining a portrait of a true Pastor of the Church (see Ac 20). From here he set sail for Tyre from whence he came to Caesarea Marittima, on his return journey to Jerusalem. Here he was arrested on the basis of a misunderstanding. Certain Jews had mistaken other Jews of Greek origin for Gentiles, whom Paul had taken into the temple precinct reserved for Israelites. He was spared the inevitable death sentence by the intervention of the Roman tribune on guard in the Temple area (see Ac 21:27–36); this happened while the imperial Procurator in Judea was Antonius Felix. After a spell in prison (the duration of which is debated), and since Paul as a Roman citizen was an appellee of Caesar (at that time Nero), the subsequent Procurator, Porcius Festus, sent him to Rome under military escort: "You have appealed to Caesar; to Caesar you shall go" (Ac 25:12).

The journey of the captive Paul from Caesarea to Rome is described by St Luke with exactness and vividness; it constituted his Fourth Missionary Journey. The centurion Julius (Ac 27:1) had shipped Paul and his fellow-prisoners on a merchant vessel, taking also on board Luke and Aristarchus. As the season was advanced, the voyage was slow and difficult. They skirted the coasts of Syria, Cilicia, and Pamphylia. At Myra in Lycia the prisoners were transferred to an Alexandrian vessel bound for Italy, but with contrary winds they reached with difficulty a place in Crete called Fair Havens, near the town of Lasea (Ac 27:8). Paul advised that they should spend the winter there, but his advice was not followed, and the vessel driven by the tempest drifted aimlessly for fourteen whole days, before being finally wrecked on the coast of Malta. In Malta, Paul and his companions were treated with great kindness, he was not hurt by a poisonous snake, and he healed several people, including the father of Publius, the chief of the island (Ac 28:1–9). The three months during which navigation was considered most dangerous were spent there, but with the first days of spring all haste was made to resume the voyage:

> We put in at Syracuse and stayed there three days, and from there we sailed round the coast and arrived at Rhegium. After a day, a south wind came up and in two days we reached Puteoli. There we found some brothers and were urged to stay with them for seven days. And thus we came to Rome. The brothers from there heard about us and came as far as the Forum of Appius and Three Taverns to meet us. On seeing them, Paul gave thanks to God and took courage (Ac 28:12–15).

Paul must have reached Rome some time in March. There, "he remained for two full years in his lodgings. He received all who came to him, and with complete assurance and without hindrance he proclaimed the kingdom of God and taught about the Lord Jesus Christ" (Ac 28:30–31). With these words the Acts of the Apostles conclude.

2.2.1 The martyrdom of St Paul

The life of this great man ended in Rome after the great fire which ravaged the city. Paul was condemned and executed in 67 AD, just a year before the death of Emperor Nero. Since he was a Roman citizen, he was beheaded just outside the city wall, near the Ostian Gate at the Salvian Springs.

The last period of St Paul's life is wrapped in deep obscurity since we have no guide save an often uncertain tradition and the brief references of the Pastoral epistles. Luke mentions neither a sentence of Caesar (Nero) nor, even less, the death of the accused. Later traditions speak of his liberation which would have been propitious for either a missionary journey to Spain or a subsequent episode in the East, and specifically in Crete, Ephesus and Nicopolis in Epirus. Paul was released from prison around 63 AD and travelled to the island of Crete (Titus 1:5). He then went to Nicopolis in Macedonia (Titus 3:12). From 64 to 67 AD Paul perhaps fulfilled his goal of visiting Spain (Romans 15:24, 28) and maybe even Britain. Tradition renders probable Paul's journey to

Spain. In any case he cannot have remained there long, for he was in haste to revisit his Churches in the East. He may have returned from Spain through southern Gaul if it was there, as some Fathers have thought, and not to Galatia, that Crescens was sent later (2 Tm 4:10).When towards the end of his captivity he announces his coming to Philemon (Phm 22) and to the Philippians (Ph 2:23–24), he does not seem to regard this visit as immediate since he promises the Philippians to send them a messenger as soon as he learns the outcome of his trial; he therefore plans another journey before his return to the East. We may readily believe that afterwards he kept the promise made to his friend Philemon and that on this occasion he visited the churches of the valley of Lycus, Laodicea, Colossus, and Hierapolis.

The itinerary now becomes very uncertain, but the following facts seem indicated by the Pastoral Letters: Paul remained in Crete exactly long enough to found there new churches, the care and organization of which he confided to his fellow-worker Titus (Tt 1:5). He then went to Ephesus, and besought Timothy, who was already there, to remain until his return while he proceeded to Macedonia (1 Tm 1:3). On this occasion he paid his promised visit to the Philippians (Ph 2:24), and naturally also saw the Thessalonians. The Letter to Titus and the First Letter to Timothy must date from this period; they seem to have been written about the same time and shortly after the departure from Ephesus. The question is whether they were sent from Macedonia or, more probably, from Corinth. The Apostle instructs Titus to join him at Nicopolis of Epirus where he intends to spend the winter (Tt 3:12). In the following spring he must have carried out his plan to return to Asia (1 Tm 3:14–15). Here occurred the obscure episode of his arrest, which probably took place at Troas; this would explain his having left with Carpus a cloak and books which he needed (2 Tm 4:13). He was taken from there to Ephesus, capital of the Province of Asia, where he was deserted by all those on whom he thought he could rely (2 Tm 1:15). Still on a hypothetical basis, another arrest is conjectured and a second imprisonment in Rome (where he is supposed to have written the three so-called Pastoral Letters, that is, the two to Timothy and the Letter to Titus), with a second trial that would have proven unfavourable to him. Being sent to Rome for trial, he left Trophimus sick at Miletus, and Erastus, another of his companions, remained at Corinth, for a reason which is unclear (2 Tm 4:20). When Paul wrote his Second Letter to Timothy from Rome he felt that all human hope was lost (2 Tm 4:6); he begs his disciple to rejoin him as quickly as possible, for he is alone with Luke. We do not know if Timothy was able to reach Rome before the death of the Apostle.

Only in the Second Letter to Timothy do we find these premonitory words: "For I am already on the point of being sacrificed"; the time to set sail had come (2 Tm 4:6; cf. Ph 2:17). Two images are used here, the religious image of sacrifice that he had used previously in the Letter to the Philippians, interpreting martyrdom as a part of Christ's sacrifice, and the nautical image of casting off: two images which together discreetly allude to the event of death and of a brutal death.

His martyrdom is recounted for the first time in the *Acts of Paul*, written towards the end of the second century. They say that Nero condemned him to death by beheading, an order which was carried out immediately.[26] The date of his death already varies in the ancient sources which set it between the persecution unleashed by Nero himself after the burning of Rome in July 64 and the last year of his reign, that is, the year 68.[27] The calculation heavily depends on the chronology of Paul's arrival in Rome. Later traditions specify two other elements. One is that his martyrdom occurred at the *Aquae Salviae,* on the Via Laurentina, and that his head rebounded three times, giving rise to a source of water each time that it touched the ground, which is why, to this day, the place is called the *Tre Fontane* (three fountains).[28] The second version, in harmony with the ancient account of the priest Gaius, is that his burial not only took place "outside the city... at the second mile on the Ostian Way", but more precisely "on the estate of Lucina", who was a Christian matron.[29] It was here, in the fourth century, that the Emperor Constantine built a first church. Then, between the fourth and fifth centuries it was considerably enlarged by the Emperors Valentinian II, Theodosius and Arcadius. The present-day Basilica of Saint Paul Outside the Walls was built here after the fire in 1800.

Ancient tradition thus makes it possible to establish the following points. First, Paul suffered martyrdom near Rome at a place called *Aquae Salviae* (now known as *Tre Fontane*), somewhat east of the Ostian Way, about two miles from the Basilica of St Paul's Outside the Walls (*San Paolo fuori le mura*), which marks his burial place. St Paul was beheaded, and where his head fell, three fountains sprang up miraculously. Second, the martyrdom took place towards the end of the reign of Nero, in the fourteenth year, according to St Jerome. Third, according to the most common opinion, Paul suffered in the same year (67 AD) and on the same day as Peter. Fourth, from time immemorial the solemnity of the Apostles Peter and Paul has been celebrated on 29 June, which is the anniversary either of their death or of the translation of their relics. Formerly the Pope, after having pontificated in the Basilica of St Peter, went with his attendants to that of St Paul, but the distance between the two basilicas (about five miles) rendered the double ceremony too exhausting, especially at that season of the year. Thus arose the custom of transferring to the next day (30 June) the Commemoration of St Paul. The feast of the Conversion of St Paul (25 January) is of more recent origin. In art, St Paul is represented with the sword, symbolizing the Word of God (see Heb 4:12).

Notes

1   See P. Haffner, *New Testament Theology. An Introduction* (Leominster: Gracewing, 2008), pp. 65–67.
2   Clement of Alexandria, *Stromata*, 3, 6.
3   *Ibid.*, 7, 11.
4   See also the parallels in Mark 3:14–19, and Luke 6:13–16.
5   See *Revue Biblique* 62 (1955), p. 405. See also Mt 16:18.
6   See S. L. Jaki, *And on this Rock. The Witness of One Land and Two Covenants* (Manassas, VA: Trinity Communications, 1987²), p. 16.
7   See Pope Benedict XVI, *Discourse at General Audience* (24 May 2006).
8   See Eusebius, *Ecclesiastical History*, 2, 15; 3, 40; 6, 14. See also St Irenaeus, *Adversus haereses*, 3, 1. Clement of Alexandria stated: "After Peter had announced the Word of God in Rome and preached the Gospel in the spirit of God, the multitude of hearers requested Mark, who had long accompanied Peter on all his journeys, to write down what the Apostles had preached to them." From Eusebius, *Ecclesiastical History*, 4, 14.
9   Pope Clement I, *Letter to the Corinthians*, 5.
10 See St Irenaeus, *Adversus haereses*, 3, 3, 2.
11 *Ibid.*, 3, 3, 3.
12 Eusebius, *Ecclesiastical History*, 2, 25. He quotes Caius, *Disputation with Proclus*.
13 Tertullian, *On the prescription of heretics*, 36.
14 Eusebius, *Ecclesiastical History*, 3,1.
15 St Jerome, *Lives of Illustrious Men*, 1.
16 See Pope Benedict XVI, *Address at General Audience* (27 August 2008).
17 See *ibid.*
18 Damascus is the capital of modern Syria. It was known as the "Pearl of the East", an ancient and important city of Syria, standing at over 2,000 feet in a large oasis. It was one of the city-states of the Decapolis, and a great centre of trade.
19 See Pope Benedict XVI, *Address at General Audience* (3 September 2008).
20 See *ibid.*
21 See Pope Benedict XVI, *Address at General Audience* (27 August 2008).
22 Syrian Antioch is present-day Antakya in southern Turkey. This Antioch was known as "Queen of the East", capital of the province of Syria, and the third largest city in the Roman Empire after Rome and Alexandria. With a population of over half a million people, it was located on the River Orontes, and a junction of trade routes between East and West. It should not to be confused with Pisidian Antioch, a Phrygian town in the Roman province of Galatia.
23 See Pope Benedict XVI, *Address at General Audience* (27 August 2008).

24 See *ibid*.
25 See *ibid*.
26 Cf. *Acts of Paul* 9:5.
27 Cf. St Jerome, *De viris illustribus* 5, 8.
28 See Pseudo-Marcellus, *Acts of Peter and Paul*.
29 See Pseudo-Abdias, *Passion of Paul*.

3 THE EARLY POPES

We point out here the successions of the bishops of the greatest and most ancient Church known to all, founded and organized at Rome by the two most glorious apostles, Peter and Paul, that Church which has the tradition and the faith which comes down to us after having been announced to men by the apostles. With that Church, because of its superior origin, all the churches must agree, that is, all the faithful in the whole world, and it is in her that the faithful everywhere have maintained the apostolic tradition.

St Irenaeus, *Against the Heresies*, 3:3:2

THE EARLY POPES were very influential in the formative years of Christianity, as indeed they have been thereafter. A look at the first twenty Popes will convey concretely their impact.

3.1 The first twenty Popes and one antipope

3.1.1 Saint Peter

In the preceding chapter, we have already described St Peter's life in detail. Here a brief survey of his Papacy will be offered. Blessed Peter, son of Jonah, of the province of Galilee and the town of Bethsaida, brother of Andrew and chief of the apostles, first occupied the seat of the bishop in Antioch for seven years. Peter entered the city of Rome when Nero was Cæsar and there occupied the bishop's chair for 25 years, 1 month and 8 days. He was bishop in the time of Tiberius Cæsar and of Caligula and of Tiberius Claudius and of Nero. He wrote two epistles which are called Catholic, and effectively the Gospel of Mark, for Mark was his disciple and son by baptism; this was afterwards the source of the other Synoptic gospels.

He ordained two bishops, Linus and Cletus, who in person fulfilled the priestly ministry in the city of Rome for the inhabitants and for pilgrims; then the blessed Peter gave himself to prayer and preaching, instructing the people. He disputed many times with Simon Magus both before Nero, the emperor, and before the people, since by magic arts and trickery Simon was drawing away those whom the blessed Peter was gathering into the faith of Christ. While they debated once at great length Simon Magus was struck dead by the will of God.

The Acts of Peter is thought to be the source for the tradition about the famous phrase "*Quo vadis, Domine?*" (or "*Pou Hupageis, Kurios?*" which means, "Where are You going, Master?"), a question that, according to this tradition, Peter, fleeing Rome to avoid execution, asked a vision of Jesus, and to which Jesus responded that He was "going to Rome, to be crucified again", causing Peter to decide to return to the city and accept martyrdom. This story is commemorated in an Annibale Carracci painting. The Church of Quo Vadis, near the Catacombs of Saint Callixtus, contains a stone in which Jesus' footprints from this event are supposedly preserved. The presence of the Apostle Peter in this area, where he is supposed to have lived, appears to be confirmed in an epigraph in the Catacombs of Saint Sebastian that reads *Domus Petri* (House of Peter). An epigram by Pope Damasus I (366–384) in honour of Peter and Paul reads: "You that are looking for the names of Peter and Paul, you must know that the saints have lived here."

Clement of Rome, in his Letter to the Corinthians, written during the last twenty years of the first century AD, describes Peter's martyrdom in the following terms:

> Let us take the noble examples of our own generation. The greatest and most just pillars of the Church were persecuted, and came even unto death... Peter... endured not one or two but many trials, and at last, having delivered his testimony, departed unto the place of glory due to him.[1]

St Peter was crucified upside down near the palace of Nero, in the Vatican, on June 29, in the year 64 or the year 67. Vaticanus was the ancient name of the hill forming the prolongation of the Janiculum toward the north, and the Campus or Ager Vaticanus was the space between the foot of the hill and the Janiculum and the Tiber.[2]

3.1.2 Saint Linus

St Linus was the first successor of St Peter, according to Irenaeus, Jerome, Eusebius, John Chrysostom, the Liberian Catalogue and the *Liber Pontificalis*. He reigned from 67 to around 76 AD. St Irenaeus identifies him with the Linus mentioned in 2 Timothy 4:21: "Greetings to you from Eubulus, Pudens, Linus, Claudia and all the brothers." Irenaeus observed: "The blessed apostles, then, having founded and built up the Church, committed into the hands of Linus the office of the episcopate. Of this Linus, Paul makes mention in the Epistles to Timothy."[3] According to the *Liber Pontificalis*, Linus was an Italian from Tuscany (though his name is Greek), and his father's name was Herculanus. The Apostolic Constitutions name his mother as Claudia. Pope Linus was considered to have decreed that women should enter a church with their heads covered.[4] The *Liber Pontificalis* also states that he died a martyr and was buried on the Vatican Hill next to Peter. It gives the date of his death as 23 September, the date on which his feast is still celebrated.[5] His name is included in the Roman Canon of the Mass.

3.1.3 Saint Cletus

St Cletus is also known as St Anacletus, and reigned from about 76 to 88 AD. The name "Cletus" in ancient Greek means "one who has been called", and "Anacletus" means "one who has been called back". St Cletus is traditionally said to have been a Roman, son of Emilianus, from the precinct Vicus Patricius.[6] He was Pope in the time of Vespasian and Titus from the seventh consulship of Vespasian and the fifth of Domitian until the year when Domitian was consul for the ninth time and Rufus was consul with him. Tradition also has it that this Pope divided Rome into twenty-five parishes. One of the few surviving records concerning his papacy mentions that he ordained twenty-five priests.[7] He was buried next to his predecessor, Saint Linus, in St Peter's Basilica. His name (as Cletus) is included in the Roman Canon of the Mass. He was crowned with martyrdom, and was also buried near the body of the blessed Peter in the Vatican, on 26 April, which is now his feast day.

3.1.4 Saint Clement I

Pope Saint Clement I, was the fourth Pope and Bishop of Rome and is considered the first Apostolic Father of the early Christian Church. He was a native Roman, from the district of the Coelian Hill, son of Faustinus.[8] Origen identifies Pope Clement with St Paul's fellow-labourer (Philippians 4:3), and so do Eusebius, Epiphanius, and Jerome—but this Clement was probably a Philippian. In the middle of the nineteenth century it was the custom to identity this pope with the consul of 95, Titus Flavius Clemens, who was martyred by his first cousin, the Emperor Domitian, at the end of his consulship. However, this was never suggested in ancient times, and Pope Clement is said to have lived on till the reign of Trajan. It is unlikely that he was a member of the imperial family. The continual use of the Old Testament in his Epistle has suggested that he was of Jewish origin. Probably he was a freedman or son of a freedman of the emperor's household, which included thousands or tens of thousands. He reigned from 88 to 97 AD. According to Tertullian, writing around 199 AD, the Roman Church claimed that Clement was ordained by St Peter.[9]

Clement's letter to the Corinthian church (First Epistle of Clement) was widely read and is one of the oldest Christian documents still in existence outside the New Testament. This important work is the first to manifest Rome's primacy. The epistle is cited as Clement's by Irenaeus,[10] several times by Clement of Alexandria, who in one place gives his namesake the title of Apostle,[11] and by Origen;[12] and in fact on this subject the testimony of antiquity is unanimous. An ancient homily by an anonymous author has come down to us in the same two Greek manuscripts as the First Epistle of Clement, and is called the Second Epistle of Clement to the Corinthians. It is first mentioned by Eusebius, who considered it spurious, as being unknown to the ancients;[13] he is followed (perhaps not independently) by Rufinus and Jerome. Its inclusion as a letter of Clement in the *Codex Alexandrinus* of the whole Bible in the fifth century is the earliest testimony to a belief in its authenticity

Among the most authentic proofs of the prominence of Clement in the Roman Church is the mention of his name in its liturgy. On the death of a bishop, the early Christians did not discontinue the mention of his name in their public prayers. Now the Roman Canon of the Mass to this day, next after the names of the apostles, recites the names of Linus, Cletus, Clement; and there is some evidence that the liturgy contained the same names in the same order from as early as the second century. Probably, then, this commemoration dates from Clement's own time. An independent proof that Clement held high position in the Church of Rome is afforded by the *Shepherd of Hermas*, a work not later than the episcopate of Pope Pius I (140–155 AD), the writer of which claims to have been contemporary with Clement. He represents himself as commissioned to write for Clement the book of his Visions in order that Clement might send it to foreign cities, that being his function; while Hermas himself was to read the Vision at Rome with the elders who presided over the Church.[14] Thus Clement is recognized as the organ by which the Church of Rome communicated with foreign churches.[15]

St Irenaeus indicates that Clement was the fourth Pope: "In the third place from the apostles, Clement was allotted the bishopric."[16] Pope Clement created seven districts and assigned them to faithful notaries of the Church that they might make diligent and careful inquiry, each in his own district, regarding the acts of the martyrs. He held two ordinations in the month of December, and consecrated 10 priests, 2 deacons and 15 bishops;

the priests and deacons were to serve in the city, the bishops in the dioceses around the city.[17]

According to traditions dating to around the fourth century, Clement was banished from Rome to the Chersonesus during the reign of the Emperor Trajan and was set to work in a stone quarry.[18] Finding on his arrival that the prisoners were suffering from lack of water, he knelt down in prayer. Looking up, he saw a lamb on a hill, went to where the lamb had stood and struck the ground with his pickaxe, releasing a gushing stream of clear water. This miracle resulted in the conversion of large numbers of the local pagans and his fellow prisoners to Christianity. As punishment, Saint Clement was martyred by being tied to an anchor and thrown from a boat into the Black Sea. The tradition recounts that every year a miraculous ebbing of the sea revealed a divinely-built shrine containing his bones.

The Inkerman Cave Monastery marks the supposed place of Clement's burial in the Crimea. A year or two before his own death in 869, Saint Cyril brought to Rome what he believed to be the bones of Saint Clement, which he had found in the Crimea buried with an anchor on dry land. They are now enshrined in the Basilica of San Clemente in Rome. This church lies in the valley between the Esquiline and Coelian hills, on the direct road from the Coliseum to the Lateran. It is now in the hands of the Irish Province of Dominicans. With its atrium, its choir enclosed by a wall, its ambos, it is the most perfect model of an early basilica in Rome. Other relics of Saint Clement, including his head, are claimed by the Kiev Monastery of the Caves in Ukraine. St Clement is commemorated on November 23 as Pope and martyr.

3.1.5 Saint Evaristus

Little is known about Evaristus. According to the *Liber Pontificalis*, he came from a family of Hellenic Jewish origin, son of a Jew named Judah, from the city of Bethlehem. He was elected during the reign of the Roman Emperor Domitian, the time of the second general persecution. He reigned from 97 to 105 AD. Eusebius stated that Evaristus died in the twelfth year of the reign of the

Roman Emperor Trajan, after holding the office of bishop of the Romans for eight years.[19] The two decretals attributed to Evaristus, one of which was addressed to the bishops of Africa, and the other to all the faithful in Egypt, are now considered to be apocryphal.[20] When he became sovereign pontiff, he ordered, according to the apostolic tradition, that marriages should be celebrated publicly and with the priestly benediction, and that no bishop should preach without the assistance of seven deacons. This latter order was given to prevent their rivals from imputing error to them; but it could also be so that those deacons should learn the truth in the ministry of preaching. Evaristus distributed to the priests the titles of the churches of Rome, which forms the basis of the later Roman titular churches for cardinals. To the rite of the consecration of churches, passed from the Old to the New Testament, Evaristus added some ceremonies. In three or four ordinations he created five bishops, six, or according to some authors seventeen, priests, and two deacons.

Under his pontificate the Church was attacked from outside by the persecution of Trajan, and torn within by various heresies. Nevertheless, one of the consolations of this pontiff was the courage in martyrdom of Saint Ignatius of Antioch, a disciple of Saint Peter and of Saint John. Evaristus had maintained his correspondence with Palestine and Syria. He knew that Saint Ignatius, named Theophorus, or God-bearer, had been ordained Bishop of Antioch in the year 68, after Saint Evodius, the immediate successor to Saint Peter.[21] It was once supposed that all the early Popes were martyrs. However, the martyrdom of Evaristus, though traditional, is not historically proven. Pope Evaristus, who is listed without the title of Martyr in the Roman Martyrology, has his feast day on 26 October.

3.1.6 Saint Alexander I

Alexander was by nationality a Roman, son of Alexander, from the region of *Caput Tauri*.[22] It is said that this pontiff pursued his studies under the direction and advice of Pliny the Younger and Plutarch. There are attributed to him two decrees and three decretal letters; the first addressed to all the orthodox, the second to the bishops, and the third to all the priests. Modern critics have decided those pieces to be apocryphal. They find in them no trace of the system of composition of the two great writers above mentioned. In all probability Plutarch could not give lessons in Latin literature to Alexander; but the painter of the virtue of the Greeks, who was born in 66 AD, in the little town of Chaeronea, in Boeotia, could instruct the Christian in the art of meditating upon Greek literature. This a pontiff could not neglect, as he necessarily had to maintain correspondence with so many illustrious cities which spoke the language of Homer and Herodotus. It is unfortunate that we have no letter or other document from the pen of Alexander containing any expression of a feeling of gratitude towards such masters, as it might have enabled us to learn something as to the various sentiments of Pliny and Plutarch upon the great question of religion which at that period divided the pagans. The letter that Pliny wrote in favour of the Christians is justly famous, and does credit to his enlightened tolerance. The virtues of that friend of Trajan, who was then proconsul and governor of Bithynia, induced, it is said, some persons to reckon him among them, and to assign him a place in their diptychs.

Alexander was still young when he arrived at the papacy. Some say that he was only twenty, and others that he was thirty, when he became pope. On that point one commentator says: "Alexander was young in years; but in morals, knowledge, and virtue, he was a veteran." Alexander is cited as having seen a vision of the Infant Jesus.[23] It was he who ordered that the priests should celebrate only one Mass daily, and this rule was observed until the papacy of Saint Deodatus, in 615. Pope Alexander I is also said to have introduced the tradition of blessing water mixed with salt for the purification of Christian homes from evil influences, and the custom of mixing water into the chalice during the Offertory at Mass.

Alexander converted to the faith Hermes, prefect of Rome, and his wife, and numerous illustrious citizens. He was then thrown into prison for those glorious efforts where he converted the tribune Quirinus and his daughter Balbina. Alexander, in three ordinations, consecrated five bishops, six priests, and two or three deacons. He suffered martyrdom by beheading under Hadrian, on the Via Nomentana along with Eventius, the priest, and Theodulus, the deacon. The persecution in which Pope Saint Alexander perished had not been expressly ordered by the emperor, but the sycophantic governors, hoping to please him, and often without any orders, or under misinterpreted orders, sent Christians to execution. Saint Alexander had governed the Church from 105–119 AD; he has the title of martyr in the Sacramentary of Pope Gregory the Great, and in all the martyrologies. Pope Saint Alexander was buried on the Via Nomentana, where he had been beheaded, on 3 May 119.[24] After several centuries his body was removed to Saint Sabina, and placed beneath the high altar erected by Sixtus V. Pope Saint Alexander I is commemorated liturgically on 3 May.

3.1.7 Saint Sixtus I

Born of the Roman senatorial family of the Colonnas, Sixtus (sometimes spelled Xystus) son of Pastor was elected pontiff on 29 May 119. During the reign of Saint Sixtus Christians suffered less persecution. A proconsul still more courageous than Pliny represented to the Emperor Hadrian how unjust it was to inflict cruel tortures, without examination and trial, from mere prejudice against a class whose only fault, in the estimation of all reasonable Romans, consisted in the name of Christian. That proconsul was Serenius Granianus. History should display in letters of gold the name of that minister who ventured to expose himself to the hatred of the emperor in defence of truth and justice. The emperor was moved, and the Apologies which were presented to him by Quadratus and Aristides completely appeased him. Hadrian wrote a memorable letter in favour of the Christians, strictly forbade denunciations of them, and ordered that those who offended in that way should be punished. This showed that if he had not already learned to worship

Jesus, he had at least learned to venerate him. Before long, however, the inconsistent emperor enabled persecution to begin again. Sixtus was its victim.

Full of generous and considerate ideas, Sixtus had ordered that no bishop having been summoned to Rome, and subsequently returning to his bishopric, should be received there, except on his presenting to his people apostolic letters called *formatae*.[25] These recommended the unity of the faith, and a mutual love between the head of the Church and the children of Jesus Christ. Besides the letters called *formatae* there were others termed canonicals, which were delivered to the bishops when they were about to return to their dioceses. Still more explicit than the *formatae*, the canonicals tended to strengthen and render unalterable the unity of the faith, obedience to the Holy See, the charity of the pope, and that of the members of the Church. The word canonicals well explains the sense of those letters. To prevent all system of fraud, those letters were later sanctioned by the first Council of Nicea, which prescribed their tenor, and in some way even the cipher in which they should be written; for their language was not intelligible to all. There were also letters called *communicatives*. These were given to pilgrims, and testified to their Catholic faith and to their communion with the church in which they lived. *Letters commendatory* served pilgrims in their travelling expenses. Sixtus was also the first to direct that the chalice and the paten should be touched only by the sacred ministers.[26] He also decreed that, after the Preface in the Mass, the priest should recite the Sanctus with the people.[27] Saint Alexander and Saint Sixtus, successively, in accordance with the Christian spirit, laboured to render more venerable the most august of all the sacraments, the Mass.

Saint Sixtus consecrated four bishops, eleven priests, and four deacons, and governed the Holy See during a period of nearly six years, from from about 119–125 AD.[28] The Felician Catalogue of popes and the various martyrologies style him a martyr. St Irenaeus of Lyons, writing in the second century, says nothing of his martyrdom; his successor Telesphorus is the first pope after St Peter whom Irenaeus designates a martyr. He was buried in the Vatican, beside the tomb of St Peter, and his feast is celebrated on April 6.

3.1.8 Saint Telesphorus

Saint Telesphorus was a Greek by birth, though some authors maintain that he was born in Terranova, in Calabria. Others affirmed that his father was an anchorite, and that Telesphorus himself was Roman by birth.[29] He reigned from 125–136 AD, during the periods of Roman Emperors Hadrian and Antoninus Pius. The tradition of Christmas Midnight Masses, the celebration of Easter on Sundays, the keeping of a seven-week Lent before Easter and the singing of the *Gloria* are often attributed to his pontificate. In his four ordinations Telesphorus created thirteen bishops, twelve priests, and eight deacons.[30] Saint Telesphorus presided over the Holy See during eleven years, eight months, and eighteen days. The Carmelites venerate Telesphorus as a patron saint of the order since some sources depict him as a hermit living on Mount Carmel. The writer St Irenaeus of Lyons said that St Telesphorus suffered martyrdom. Some pious Christians removed his body after execution, and placed it near that of Saint Peter, in the Vatican. In the Roman Martyrology his feast is celebrated on 2 January. The Greek Church celebrates it on 22 February.

3.1.9 Saint Hyginus

Saint Hyginus was born at Athens, and was elected to the papacy by the Roman clergy and the people in 136 AD. He carried further the organization of the clergy into definite ranks with the assignment of special tasks and functions., which led much later to the foundation of the College of Cardinals. The custom of having a godfather and a godmother at baptism has been attributed to Hyginus. He also decreed that all churches be consecrated. He excommunicated the Syrian Gnostic Cerdo, a precursor of that heresy which afterwards was known as the

Marcionism. This heresy taught that there were two gods, one good and the other cruel. Cerdo denied that Jesus Christ had ever lived in the flesh, averring that he was only a shadow.[31] Another heretic who came to Rome at about this time was Valentinus, a leading exponent of Gnosticism.[32]

Some affirm that this pope suffered martyrdom under the persecution of Roman Emperor Marcus Aurelius, but Eusebius and Saint Cyprian say that, though he endured much for the sake of the Church, he did not, strictly speaking, suffer martyrdom. He governed the Holy See during three years, eleven months, and twenty-nine days and reigned from 136–140 AD. Saint Hyginus was buried at the Vatican, and his feast day is 11 January.

3.1.10 Saint Pius I

Pius I was born at Aquileia, in Northern Italy, during the late first century. His father was called Rufinus. It is stated in the second-century Muratorian Canon, and in the Liberian Catalogue, that he was the brother of Hermas, author of the text known as *The Shepherd of Hermas*.[33] The writer of the latter text identifies himself as a former slave. This has led to speculation that both Hermas and Pius were freedmen. He was created pontiff in 140 AD. Like Saint Hyginus, he condemned the followers of Cerdo and also Marcion. The latter heretic recognized two principles, the good and the evil. Marcion repudiated the Old Testament, as having been given by the evil principle, and he composed a work which he entitled *Antitheses*, or the Contradictions between the Old Law and the New Testament. His followers abstained from animal food, and used only water in holy communion. They carried their abhorrence of flesh-meat even to accepting death for this cause. This heresy had a great number of believers, not only in many places, but also during many centuries. The condemnation pronounced by Saint Pius I added weight to the excommunication already pronounced against this heresy by Saint Hyginus. Pius I also had to combat the Gnostic heresy of Valentinus, which had already surfaced during the pontificate of Hyginus.[34]

In 150 AD, during the papacy of Pius I, Justin Martyr composed an *Apology* for the Christians. Justin Martyr, in his *First Apology*, explained Christian doctrine, teaching the adoration of the eternal God, the author of all things, of His Son Jesus Christ, who was crucified under Pontius Pilate; and the honour of the prophetic Holy Spirit. Saint Justin proceeded to say that Jesus Christ is the sovereign Reason who entirely changes the heart of His worshippers. The discourses of Jesus were the word of God, brief and exact, which have convinced us. The Christians are the only people who are punished for their creed and worship, while all other religions are tolerated. Some adore trees, flowers, cats, rats, and crocodiles, and generally animals. Moreover, all do not adore the same things, and so the worship is different, in accordance with their gods; therefore each sect is impious in the estimation of all the others.

To Saint Pius I is attributed a decree establishing the celebration of Easter on a Sunday. He ordered the publication of the *Liber Pontificalis*. The same pontiff directed that converts to the Catholic faith from Judaism and from the sect of Cerinthus should be received and baptized.[35] At the request of Saint Praxedes, daughter of the Christian senator Pudens, Pius erected a church in the palace belonging to the latter, where Saint Peter had lodged and celebrated Mass. On this site there is now the church of Saint Pudentiana, sister of Saint Praxedes. In five ordinations, Saint Pius I created twelve bishops, nineteen priests, and twenty-one deacons.[36] He governed the Church about fifteen years and is said to have died a martyr; his feast day is 11 July.

3.1.11 Saint Anicetus

His name is Greek for 'unconquered' and he was a Syrian, son of John, from the city of Emesa (modern-day Homs), northern Syria. He reigned from 155–166 AD. According to Saint Irenaeus, it was during his pontificate that the aged Saint Polycarp of Smyrna, a disciple of Saint John the Evangelist, visited the Pope. Between Saint Anicetus and Saint Polycarp, Bishop of Smyrna, there was a great controversy, which divided them in opinion, but did not disturb their friendship. It was upon the subject of the celebration of Easter. Anicetus followed the tradition of Saint Peter, in celebrating Easter on the Sunday following the fourteenth day of the moon of the vernal equinox. Saint Polycarp, on the contrary, preferred the tradition of the Apostle Saint John, celebrating on the day of that full moon, which sometimes fell on a weekday. While the two did not agree on a common date, Pope Anicetus conceded to St Polycarp and the Church of Smyrna the faculty to retain the date to which they were accustomed. The controversy was to boil up again in the course of the following centuries. That question was subsequently decided, as we shall relate in the life of Saint Victor I.[37]

The Christian historian Hegesippus also visited Rome during Anicetus' pontificate. This visit is often cited as a sign of the early importance of the Roman See. Anicetus had the ability to preserve his flock from the poison of error, and to keep the great trust of the faith in all its purity; he condemned the heresies of Gnosticism, Marcionism and Montanism.[38] According to the *Liber Pontificalis*, Anicetus decreed that priests were not allowed to have long hair, perhaps because the Gnostics were long-haired, perhaps also following the precept of St Paul (1 Co 11:14).[39] In five ordinations he created nine bishops, seventeen priests, and four deacons.[40]

St Anicetus is reported to have suffered martyrdom during the reign of the Roman Co-Emperor Lucius Verus. His remains, which for fourteen hundred and twenty-nine years had rested in the cemetery of Callixtus, are at present venerated in the chapel of the Altemps palace at Rome, where they were deposited on the 28 October 1504. This favour was granted, by Pope Clement VIII, to prince John Angelo, Duke of Altemps. 16, 17 and 20 April are all cited as the date of his death, but 17 April is celebrated as his memorial or feast day.

3.1.12 Saint Soter

Fondi, near Naples in Campania, was the birth place of Saint Soter; his name derives from the Greek (σωτήρ) meaning a saviour, or a deliverer. He was elected pontiff in 166 AD and reigned until 175 AD. Although little else is known about Soter, a letter from Bishop Dionysius of Corinth testifies to him as a man of significant charity. In his letter, preserved by Eusebius, Dionysius praises Soter and the Roman church for their generosity, saying:

> From the beginning it has been your custom to do good to all the brethren in many ways, and to send alms to many churches in every city, relieving the poverty of those who sent requests, or giving aid to the brethren in the mines, by the alms which you have had the habit of giving from old, Romans keeping up the traditional custom of the Romans; which your blessed Bishop Soter has not only preserved, but has even increased, by providing the abundance which he has sent to the saints, and by further consoling with blessed words the brethren who came to him, as a loving father his children.[41]

At the same time, this pontiff opposed the heresies which gnawed away at Christianity. He is said to have declared that marriage was only valid as a sacrament if blessed by a priest, and he inaugurated Easter as an annual festival in Rome.

The zeal of the sovereign pontiff obtained the important concession that Christians should not be condemned for their religion—that unless charged with some distinct crime against the state, their Christian creed should not be imputed to them as a crime. In five ordinations Saint Soter created eleven bishops, eighteen priests, and nine deacons.[42] He governed the Church nine years and a few months. To this period belongs the miracle of the Thunder Legion.

> In an extreme scarcity of water that was endured by the army of Marcus Aurelius in Germany, a Christian legion obtained rain sufficient to quench the thirst of all the troops, accompanied by thunder that terrified the enemy. This miracle caused the legion to receive, or to have confirmed to it, the title of the Thunder Legion. The emperor was touched by that miracle, and wrote to the senate in favour of the Christians. Subsequently his false

> priests persuaded him to attribute to their prayers and to
> their false gods the miracle for which the pagans had not
> even presumed to express a wish.

Evidence of this miracle is to be seen in the bas-reliefs of the Antonine column. The Romans are there represented with weapons in hand against the barbarians, who are seen extended upon the ground with their horses, while a torrent of rain is pouring upon them, and they seem to be prostrated by the thunderbolts. On that occasion, in fact, Marcus Aurelius, in his letter to the senate, declared that his army had been saved by the prayers of the Christian soldiers.

It has often been supposed that all the earliest Popes suffered martyrdom; but the Roman Martyrology does not give Pope Soter the title of Martyr, simply stating: "Saint Soter, Pope, whom Dionysius of Corinth praises for his outstanding charity towards needy exiled Christians who came to him, and towards those who had been condemned to the mines." From the cemetery of Saint Callixtus, where his body was at first buried, it was removed by Sergius II, in 845, to the Church of Saints Sylvester and Martin *ai Monti*, and then to the Appian Way, to the Church of Saint Sixtus, belonging to the Dominican Fathers. Saint Soter's feast day is on 22 April.

3.1.13 Saint Eleuterus

According to several writers, Saint Eleuterus (or Eleutherus) was a Greek, his name is Greek for "frank, honest, free-spirited" and he was born at Nicopolis, now called Prevesa. According to his contemporary Hegesippus, Eleuterus was earlier a deacon of the Roman Church under Pope Anicetus, and remained so under Pope Soter, the following pope, whom he succeeded in about 175.

Eleuterus' most important contribution to Church history seems to have been his manner of dealing the Montanist heresy. At first disposed to tolerate the movement, he was eventually persuaded to condemn it. The Montanist movement, which originated in Asia Minor, made its way to Rome and Gaul in the second half of the second century, around the reign of Eleuterus; its peculiar nature made it difficult for Christians to take a decisive stand against it.[43] During the violent persecution of Christians by imperial authorities at Lyon in 177, local confessors wrote from their prison concerning Montanism to the Asiatic and Phrygian communities, and also to Eleuterus as the bishop of Rome. The bearer of the letter to Eleuterus was the priest St Irenaeus, soon to become bishop of Lyon. It appears from statements of Eusebius concerning these letters that the Christians of Lyon, though opposed to the Montanist movement, advocated patience and pleaded for the preservation of ecclesiastical unity rather than the expulsion of the alleged heretics.

Meanwhile, at Rome, the Gnostics and Marcionites continued to preach against the Catholic faith. The *Liber Pontificalis* ascribes to Pope Eleuterus a decree that no kind of food should be despised by Christians: "No kind of food in common use should be rejected, especially by the Christian faithful, inasmuch as God created it; provided, however, it be rational food and fit for humankind."[44] Some believe the decree was directed against the Montanists, who often abstained from rich foods. It would also fit with the Church's position against those forms of Christian Gnosticism which practiced vegetarianism, as well as teaching Christians, still under the Old Testament dispensation, who refused to eat non-kosher foods.

The *Liber Pontificalis* also provides a remarkable assertion concerning the early missionary activity of the Roman Church.[45] Eleuterus, says this writer, received from the British king Lucius a letter in which he declared his desire to become a Christian. At the end of the second century the Roman administration was securely established in Britain, and it is indeed likely that local rulers could have been introduced to the Christian message by Roman officials who had privately adopted the faith. The venerable Bede alludes to this as follows:

> In their time, whilst the holy Eleuterus presided over the Roman Church, Lucius, king of Britain, sent a letter to him, entreating that by a mandate from him he might be

made a Christian. He soon obtained his pious request,
and the Britons preserved the faith, which they had
received, uncorrupted and entire, in peace and tranquillity until the time of the Emperor Diocletian.[46]

Thirteenth-century chronicles add other details. The *Liber Lan-davensis*, for example, gives the names of the envoys sent by Lucius to the pope as Elfan and Medwy. The ninth-century *Historia Brittonum* sees in Lucius a translation of the Celtic name *Llever Maur* (Great Light). At the request of Lucius, this pope sent Fugacius and Damian into England, to endeavour to convert it to the Catholic faith. It must be remembered that previously some Christians were present in England, but this was the first organized missionary effort.

Marcus Aurelius was succeeded in the empire by Commodus, and, by a strange but welcome contradiction, the Church, which had been persecuted during the reign of a good prince, was left in peace by a monstrous one. Eleuterus died in 189 AD, and governed the Church for fourteen years. In three ordinations he created fifteen bishops, twelve priests, and eight deacons.[47] At first, he was buried in the Vatican. Later tradition holds that St Eleuterus' body was eventually moved to the church of San Giovanni della Pigna, near the pantheon. In 1591, his remains were again moved to the church of Santa Susanna at the request of Camilla Peretti, the sister of Pope Sixtus V. Venerated in the western Church as a saint, his feast is celebrated on 26 May.

3.1.14 Saint Victor I

Pope Saint Victor I was bishop of Rome from about 189 to 199 AD. Having been born in the Roman Province of Africa, he was the first African pope. During the closing years of the reign of Commodus (180–192) and the early years of Septimius Severus (from 193), the Roman Church enjoyed, in general, a time of external peace, from which Pope Victor and his flock benefited in comparison to earlier times of persecution. The favourable opinion of the Christians held by Commodus is ascribed to the influence of a woman named Marcia, reportedly the emperor's mistress and later one of his assassins. According to the testimony of Hippolytus, Marcia had been brought up by the presbyter Hyacinthus, and was very positively inclined toward the Christians, perhaps even a Christian herself.[48] One day she summoned Pope Victor to the imperial palace and volunteered to help gain the freedom of the Roman Christians who had been previously condemned to forced labour in the mines of Sardinia. The pope provided her a list of these sufferers, and Marcia, after receiving the required document of pardon from the emperor, sent Hyacinthus to Sardinia with an order of release. The future Pope Callixtus was among those released, although he did not return to Rome but remained at Antium, where he received a monthly pension from the Roman Christians.

Victor is best known for his role in the Easter controversy, in which he attempted to require that all Christians celebrate the Resurrection of Jesus on Sunday, rather than on the exact date of Passover. Before his elevation to the Papacy, a difference in dating the celebration of the Christian Passover (Easter) between Rome and the bishops of Asia Minor had been tolerated by both the Roman and Eastern churches. The churches in Asia Minor celebrated it on the fourteenth day of the Jewish month of Nisan, the day before Jewish Passover, regardless of what day of the week it fell on, as the Crucifixion had occurred on the Friday before Passover. The Latins called them *Quartodecimans*. Rome and the West celebrated Easter on the Sunday following the fourteenth of Nisan.

Pope Victor decided to bring about unity in the observance of the Easter festival and to persuade the Quartodecimans to join in the practice of the Roman Church. He wrote, therefore, to Bishop Polycrates of Ephesus and persuaded him to call together the bishops of the province of Asia in order to discuss the matter with them. This was done, but the result was not to the pope's liking. In the letter sent to Victor by Polycrates in reply, he declared that he firmly held to the Quartodeciman custom as did the majority of the many other bishops of that region.

Victor then called a meeting of Italian bishops at Rome, which is the earliest known Roman synod. He also wrote to the leading bishops of the various districts, urging them to call together the bishops of their sections of the country and to take counsel with them on the question of the Easter festival. Letters came from all sides: From the synod in Palestine, at which Theophilus of Caesarea and Narcissus of Jerusalem presided; from the synod of Pontus over which the venerable Palmas presided; from the communities in Gaul whose bishop was Irenaeus of Lyons; from the bishops of the Kingdom of Osrhoene;[49] and also from individual bishops, such as Bakchylus of Corinth. These letters unanimously agreed with Victor that Easter was to be observed on Sunday.

Pope Victor, as the head of Catholic Christendom, now ordered the bishops of the province of Asia to abandon their custom and to accept the practice of always celebrating Easter on Sunday. Some excitable persons wanted Saint Victor to excommunicate the Asiatic bishops; but, at the persuasion of Saint Irenaeus, Victor did not pronounce the decree of separation. Irenaeus reminded him that even though his predecessors had maintained the Sunday observance of Easter, they had never broken off friendly relations and communion with bishops because they followed another custom. Under this influence, Victor lifted the threat of excommunication against the Asiatic churches.[50]

Victor also had difficulties with a Roman priest named Florinus. As an official of the imperial court, Florinus had become acquainted in Asia Minor with Saint Polycarp, and later became a presbyter of the Roman Church. He allegedly fell into the Gnostic heresy and defended the views of the Gnostic leader Valentinus. Irenaeus wrote two treatises against Florinus' opinions: *On the Monarchy of God and that God is not the Author of Evil*, and *On the Ogdoad*.[51] Irenaeus called Victor's attention to the writings of Florinus, and Victor forbade him to practice his priestly functions and may have expelled him from the Church altogether.[52] Pope Victor faced another challenge when a rich Christian called Theodotus the Tanner (who came from Constantinople to Rome) taught that Christ, rather than being the

Incarnation of God from His birth, was only endowed by the Holy Spirit with divine power when He was baptized by John the Baptist. Victor condemned this teaching as heresy and excluded Theodotus from the Church. Theodotus, however, would not submit. Together with his adherents, he formed a separate congregation, which maintained itself for several years at Rome. This heretical sect became known as the Theodotians, and later would develop into Adoptionism.[53] Pope Victor condemned Praxeas, who maintained that the Father and not the Son had suffered on the Cross, and also denied the three Persons of the Most Holy Trinity.

Until Victor's time, Rome celebrated the Mass in Greek. Pope Victor changed the liturgical language to Latin, which was used in his native North Africa. According to Jerome, he was the first Christian author to write theological works in Latin.[54] As the first Latin writer of the Catholic Church, Victor left an important legacy, as Latin would eventually become the official language of the Western Church. He also ordained that, during a time of necessity, any pagan who came to be baptised, wherever it might be, whether in a river or in the sea or in a spring or in a marsh, if only he pronounced the Christian confession of faith, should be thereafter a Christian in full standing. He celebrated two ordinations in which he consecrated four priests, seven deacons, and twelve bishops.[55] It may have been during Victor's administration that the Canon of scripture used at Rome, and which has been partially preserved in the Muratorian Fragment, was drawn up.[56] Although he is traditionally venerated as a martyr, there is no evidence of Victor's martyrdom in the historical records. Indeed, he seems to have been the first pope to have enjoyed close connections to the imperial household. His reign was marked by improved and peaceful relations with the Roman state. Saint Victor I was buried in the Vatican. His feast day is kept on 28 July.

3.1.15 Saint Zephyrinus

Zephyrinus, a Roman, was elected pontiff in 199 AD. During his long papacy, the fortunes of the Roman Church in relation to the state at first worsened when Emperor Septimius Severus turned hostile, but began to improve under Caracalla. The position of the Christians, which had remained favourable in the first years of the government of Emperor Septimius Severus (193–211), grew constantly worse. Partly this was because, three years into Zephyrinus' pontificate, Septimius held a celebration to mark his tenth anniversary as emperor, which prominent Christians generally boycotted due to its pagan character. Zephyrinus is described by Hippolytus as a simple man without education.[57] Although Hippolytus was hardly an objective reporter, it may be true that Zephyrinus had not engaged in higher theological studies, but devoted himself instead to the practical administration of the Church throughout his time as a churchman. Immediately after his elevation to the Roman See, Zephyrinus called to Rome the confessor Callixtus, who had been freed from servitude in the mines under Pope Victor's administration. Zephyrinus placed Callixtus in charge of the Christian cemetery on the Via Appia which now bears his name. Callixtus was Zephyrinus' deacon and close advisor, and his influence over the pope would soon become a bone of contention in Zephyrinus' troubles, particularly with Hippolytus.

Internally, during Zephyrinus' long reign, serious disputes arose within the Roman Church. The Montanists were especially active in Rome during this period. Moreover, the Adoptionist movement originally led by Theodotus the Tanner grew in stature. Zephyrinus' greatest problem, however came in the form of a conflict over the doctrine of the Trinity in which his inaction led to harsh criticism from the future Saint Hippolytus and became part of the basis for a major schism in which Hippolytus would act as antipope after Zephyrinus' death. Also, the teacher Theodotus the Tanner, formerly of Byzantium, who had been excommunicated by Pope Victor, formed an independent community in Rome with his adherents. The sect came to be led by a formerly orthodox Christian of substantial repute, Natalis, a confessor who had clung to his faith without wavering and had suffered torture. After a series of nightmares, Natalis became fearful of his salvation and determined to repent of his heresy. He reportedly put on a penitential garment, covered himself with ashes, and threw himself with tears at the feet of Zephyrinus. He confessed his wrong-doing and begged to be received back into communion with the Church. Zephyrinus, following the precedent of his predecessors who held that lapsed Christians could be forgiven after due penance, eventually admitted him back into the fold.[58]

The most prolific source of information about Zephyrinus was his harshest critic, Hippolytus of Rome. A prolific writer, Hippolytus was the most important theologian among the Roman priests of this era. He was a strong adherent of the theology which taught that the Divine Logos, who became man in Christ, was a distinct person from God the Father. An opposing school of theological thought was represented at Rome by Cleomenes and particularly by Sabellius. These men themselves were strong opponents of the Theodotians, but they disagreed with Hippolytus in that they were not willing to acknowledge the Logos as a distinct person from the Father. They emphasized above all the absolute unity (*monarchia*) of God. Thus they explained the Incarnation as a modality of the unified Godhead—a way in which God manifested Himself only as a unity—rather than considering the Son as a diistinct Person from the Father. Consequently they were called Modalists or Monarchians.[59]

Since the Christian populace held firmly to the unity of God and at the same time to the true Godhead of Christ, at first no distrust of this doctrine was felt among them. Moreover, Pope Zephyrinus himself did not speak out authoritatively in the dispute between the two schools, preferring to hope for Christian unity among the learned brethren in their theological speculations. Hippolytus, however, insisted that the pope should promulgate a definite doctrine affirming that the Person of Christ is actually distinct from that of the Father and condemning the opposing view of the Monarchians. However, Zephyrinus would not consent to this.

The result was that Hippolytus grew increasingly irritated with the pope, and particularly with his deacon Callixtus, whom Hippolytus blamed for the pope's inaction. Hippolytus went so far as to accuse the pope of favouring the heretics and of subverting the discipline of the Church by receiving back into the Church sinners such as Natalis, who had been found guilty of grave spiritual offences. Meanwhile, in 212, the persecution of Jews and Christians was lifted when Emperor Caracalla issued an edict which granted full citizenship for all free people of the Roman Empire regardless of their religion. While the situation of Christians with regard to the state thus began to improve, Zephyrinus' papacy continued to be plagued by bitter internal strife until his death.

Saint Zephyrinus condemned the Montanists and the Encratites.[60] Tertullian, priest of Carthage, died towards the close of the reign of Saint Zephyrinus. Unhappily, Tertullian did not persist in the Catholic faith. He became a Montanist; and he left that sect and then became the founder of a new heresy. His works are of two kinds—those which he wrote before and after his separation from Rome. Tertullian was excommunicated, and endeavoured to avenge himself by sarcasm, unworthy of so lofty a genius, which pride rendered heretical. It was under Saint Zephyrinus that the famous Origen went to Rome to visit the first and most celebrated of all the Christian churches.

According to Anastasius, who wrote the life of this pope, he ordered that all the priests living with a bishop should be present whenever he should officiate; that no patriarch, primate, or archbishop should pass sentence upon a bishop without the authority of the pope; that all Christians should communicate at Easter; that the patens and chalices should not be of wood, as till then they had been, but of glass, gold or silver.[61] He also decreed that ordination ceremonies should be public.[62] Saint Zephyrinus, in four ordinations, created thirteen bishops, fourteen priests, and seven deacons.[63] He governed the Church for seventeen years. Zephyrinus was buried in a separate sepulchral chamber in the cemetery on the Appian Way named after Callixtus, his immediate successor. The feast of St Zephyrinus, Pope and Martyr, is celebrated on 20 December, the day of his death.

3.1.16 Saint Callixtus I

Pope Saint Callixtus I, also written Callistus I, was pope from 217–222 AD, during the reigns of the Roman emperors Heliogabalus and Alexander Severus. He was by nationality a Roman, son of Domitius, from the district *Urbs Ravennantium*.[64] Prior to becoming pope, Callixtus had suffered hard labour in the mines of Sardinia before being freed through the efforts of Pope Victor I during the reign of Emperor Commodus. He remained outside of Rome after his liberation until he was summoned by his predecessor, Pope Zephyrinus, to serve as his deacon. Callixtus was placed in charge of the famous Christian burial chambers along the Appian Way which bear his name. As Zephyrinus' closest adviser, Callixtus earned the lasting enmity of the future Saint Hippolytus of Rome, so much so that Hippolytus refused to recognize Callixtus' election as pope and formed a rival congregation with himself as antipope. Hippolytus and Tertullian were both upset by the Callixtus' admitting to communion those who had repented for murder and adultery. Hippolytus also accused him of theological error and toleration of heresy.

Callixtus' pontificate was only one-fourth as long as that of his predecessor, and for the most part he continued the policies he had helped Zephyrinus to develop and implement. He was apparently more of a conciliator than a judge, but his tendency to forgive brought him into conflict with the two of the most significant and unbending writers in Hippolytus and Tertullian. However, since he left no writings of his own, we are thus forced to rely on his critics for information about his views. Doubtless Hippolytus and Tertullian were upholding the stricter moral tradition of earlier times. However, granting absolution to those guilty of grave crimes was an outrage to Montanists like Tertullian: "As to your decision," he complained, "I ask, how do you usurp this right of the Church? The power of loosing and of binding committed to Peter had nothing to do with the capital sins of believers."[65] Other complaints of Hippolytus are that Callixtus did not submit converts from heresy to the humiliation of public penance for their sins before absolution; that he had received into the Church those whom Hippolytus had excommunicated; and that he declared that a mortal sin was not always a sufficient reason for deposing a bishop. Callixtus also allowed the lower orders of the clergy to marry and permitted noble ladies to marry commoners and slaves. Although Paul had insisted that "in Christ there is neither slave no free," such unions were forbidden by Roman law. Interestingly, neither Tertullian nor Hippolytus criticized Callixtus' moral behaviour after his promotion to the papacy, nor do they argue against the validity of his election, even if Hippolytus did accuse him of bribery.

Hippolytus did indeed regard Callixtus as a heretic. He accused him both of Ditheism and a type of Modalism called Sabellianism.[66] In fact, however, Zephyrinus and Callixtus had been critical of the theologies of both Sabellius and Hippolytus, and the latter had never forgiven Callixtus for refusing to influence Zephyrinus to support Hippolytus and condemn Sabellius. Although Pope Callixtus eventually condemned Sabellianism, it became popular among the African churches in the mid-third century, where it was opposed by Bishop Dionysius of Alexandria.

It is related that this pope expressly ordered that priests, on receiving holy orders, should make a vow of continence, and should never contract marriage; that marriage should not be contracted between relatives, and that the fast of the ember days of the year, which in some countries was neglected, should be strictly observed.[67] In five ordinations this pontiff created eight bishops, sixteen priests, and four deacons.[68]

It is not easy to explain Callixtus' martyrdom, since his reign took place in a time of peace for the Roman Church under Alexander Severus, whose mother was a Christian. His death took place during a period of civil unrest in 222, which is confirmed elsewhere in the historical records. This pontiff perished during a popular insurrection, and ecclesiastical memoirs state that he was thrown from a window and into a well. He did not die on the spot, and men daily went down to maltreat the glorious martyr, who made no complaint. The well is still to be seen in the Church of Saint Callixtus, near that of Santa Maria in Trastevere.[69] He was buried in the cemetery of Calepodius on the Aurelian Way, and the date of his death, given by the *Depositio Martyrum* and subsequent martyrologies, is 14 October, which is now his feast day. Since the ninth century his relics have been kept in the Church of Santa Maria in Trastevere.

3.1.17 The antipope Saint Hippolytus

Hippolytus was the first antipope in the history of the Church, and, as far as I know, the only one who was also a saint! It is uncertain when or where he was born, but as a priest of the church at Rome under Bishop Zephyrinus (199–217), Hippolytus was distinguished for his learning and eloquence. Origen, then a young man, heard him preach.[70] However, questions of theology and church discipline soon brought Hippolytus into direct and bitter conflict with Pope Zephyrinus, who had declined to condemn certain doctrines regarding the nature of the Trinity which Hippolytus considered heretical. For this Hippolytus gravely censured him, representing him as an incompetent man, unworthy to rule the Church of Rome. He characterized the pope as a tool in the hands of the allegedly ambitious and intriguing deacon Callixtus, whose early life Hippolytus maliciously depicted in his *Philosophumena*.[71]

At the beginning of the third century Hippolytus was unquestionably the most learned member of the Roman Church, and a man of very considerable literary activity; his works were very numerous, and their circulation spread from Italy to the East, some having been translated into Syriac, Arabic, Armenian, Ethiopian, and perhaps other languages. His learning and erudition made him a logical candidate to succeed Zephyrinus, but his divisiveness and unwillingness to forgive sinners argued against him. Consequently, when Callixtus was elected pope in 217 on the death of Zephyrinus, Hippolytus immediately left the communion of the Roman Church. He accused the new pope

of favouring the Christological heresies of the Monarchians—
who emphasized the oneness of God as opposed to the Trinitarian notion of God being three distinct Persons in one substance.
Further, Hippolytus accused Callixtus of subverting the discipline of the Church by receiving back into the Church those
guilty of gross offences, including adultery, thus establishing
the tradition of eventual absolution for all repented sins. The
result was a schism, and for perhaps over ten years Hippolytus
stood at the head of a separate congregation, giving him the
distinction of being the first antipope, as well as later a martyr
and saint. His reign in opposition to Callixtus continued through
the succeeding pontificates of Urban I (222–230) and at least part
of that of Pontian (230–235).

Hippolytus' voluminous writings embrace the spheres of
exegesis, homiletics, apologetics and polemic, chronography,
and ecclesiastical law. His works have come down to us in such
a fragmentary condition that it is difficult to obtain from them
any very exact notion of his intellectual and literary importance.
Of his exegetical works the best preserved are the *Commentary
on the Prophet Daniel* and the *Commentary on the Song of Songs*. Of
the dogmatic works, that on Christ and Antichrist survives in a
complete state. Among other things it includes a vivid account
of the events preceding the end of the world, and it was probably
written at the time of the persecution under Septimius Severus,
around 202. The liturgical treatise known as the *Apostolic
Tradition* is now generally attributed to him, and is a valuable
source of information concerning the rites and liturgies of the
Roman Church in the early third century.

During or shortly after the pontificate of Pontian, the schism
apparently came to an end. Under the persecution by Emperor
Maximinus the Thracian, Pontian and other church leaders,
among them Hippolytus, were exiled in 235 by the emperor to
Sardinia, where both of them died. The tradition that he was
dragged to death by wild horses may be apparently legendary.[72]
It is more likely that he, like Pontian, died as a result of forced
mine labour. An entry in the Liberian Catalogue of bishops of

Rome for the year 235 AD records that Hippolytus the presbyter was transported as an exile to the island of Sardinia where he gained the title of martyr by dying in the mines on 13 August 235. The Liberian Catalogue further records that the body of Hippolytus was brought back to Rome from Sardinia and interred in the cemetery on Via Tiburtina. His memory was henceforth celebrated in the Church as that of a saint and martyr, and his feast day, along with St Pontian is 13 August. Because of the tradition that he was dragged to death by wild horses, Hippolytus thus became the patron saint of horses.

3.1.18 Saint Urban I

Urban, the successor of Callixtus in the Roman see, is said to have been the son of Pontian, a powerful Roman noble. He was elected in the year 222, and died in 230 AD. The *Liber Pontificalis* portrays Urban as an effective preacher who converted many by his preaching. He baptized many persons belonging to the Roman nobility, among others Saint Cecilia and her husband Valerian.[73] He also ordered that all the vessels used in the sacred mysteries should be of silver.[74] Urban specified that confirmation was to be administered only by a bishop. In four ordinations Saint Urban I created thirteen bishops, fourteen priests, and seven deacons.[75] Pope Urban left no known personal writings. However, the following decree was attributed to him, concerning the donations of the faithful at Mass:

> The gifts of the faithful that are offered to the Lord can only be used for ecclesiastical purposes, for the common good of the Christian community, and for the poor; for they are the consecrated gifts of the faithful, the atonement offering of sinners, and the patrimony of the needy.

The dissension produced in the Roman Church by Hippolytus, the bitter opponent of Pope Callixtus I, persisted during Urban's pontificate. Hippolytus and his adherents continued in this schism, with Hippolytus as their antipope. It was probably during the reign of Urban that Hippolytus wrote his *Philosophu-*

mena, in which he criticized heresy of all types but also severely attacked Callixtus, as well as his predecessor Zephyrinus. Urban maintained the same attitude toward the schismatic party and its leader that his predecessor had adopted. Later, during or shortly after the papacy of Pontian (230–235), Hippolytus would be reconciled to the main body of the Church and would eventually be recognized himself as a saint. The historical sources give no specific details concerning the other factions troubling the life of the Roman Church during this specific era, but it is certain that they existed. Gnosticism, Montanism, Sabellianism, and Novatianism, for example, all continued to challenge the Church both before and after Urban's papacy.

In 222, shortly before Urban's election, Alexander Severus became Roman emperor. He favoured a religious eclecticism and also protected Christianity. His mother, Julia Mammaea, was reputed to be a Christian, and was clearly a friend of the Alexandrian Christian teacher Origen, whom she summoned to Antioch. Hippolytus dedicated his work on the Resurrection to her. The result of the favourable opinion of Christianity held by the emperor and his mother was such that Christians enjoyed almost complete peace and were not persecuted, although their legal status was not really improved. The major exception to this, if historically accurate, is the story which explains why Urban's election became necessary: the martyrdom of his predecessor Callixtus in an act of mob violence.

Pope Urban I probably died a confessor, not a martyr.[76] Two different possibilities exist as to his grave. In the *Acts of Saint Cecilia* and the *Liber Pontificalis*, it is said that Urban was buried in the Catacomb of Praetextatus on the Via Appia. Furthermore, the itineraries of the graves of the Roman martyrs in the seventh century all mention the grave of a person named Urban who is among those buried in that catacomb. These itineraries give this Urban the title *Bishop and Confessor*. Consequently Roman tradition venerated the pope of this name as the Bishop Urban of the Catacomb of Praetextatus. The second possibility results from later evidence indicating that Pope Urban may have been buried in the nearby cemetery of Saint Callixtus while the Urban buried at Saint Praetextatus was the bishop of another see who died at Rome. The head of this pontiff is venerated in the Church of Santa Maria in Trastevere, in the chapel of the Madonna di Strada Cupa, which was richly ornamented and consecrated by Henry Benedict, Cardinal Duke of York, commendatory of that basilica.[77] The burial ceremony took place on the 14 November 1762. Urban I's feast day is celebrated on 19 May. Saint Urban is invoked against storm and lightning. He is represented in art by a vine and grapes, a fallen idol beneath a broken column, a stake at which he is scourged and his severed head.

3.1.19 St Pontian

Pope Saint Pontian or Pontianus, was pope from 230 to 235. Sentenced to exile during a persecution, he was the first pope to abdicate the office. He is best known, however, for his death in the mines together with his adversary, the antipope Hippolytus, who, along with Pontian, was later declared both saint and martyr. Pontian was not directly criticized by Hippolytus, who had condemned his predecessor, Callixtus I, as a heretic, but it is not known whether Pontian and Hippolytus ever reached the point of holding communion with each other. According to the *Liber Pontificalis* Pontian was born in Rome, and his father was named Calpurnius. The *Liberian Catalogue* of the popes is able to add several specific details not available in the biographies of earlier bishops of Rome. According to this account Pontian was made pope 21 July 230, and reigned until 235.

Some learned men think that it was this pope who ordered the singing of the psalms in the Church, both by day and by night; but other writers maintain that this custom is older. It is possible that Saint Pontianus published a decree on this subject, for the better regulation of the ecclesiastical practice. In two ordinations Saint Pontianus created six bishops, six priests, and five deacons.[78]

During Pontian's pontificate a Roman synod condemned certain teachings of the Alexandrian Christian writer Origen. It is likely that Pontian presided at this council, which, according to Jerome, upheld the decisions of an Alexandrian synod against Origen in 231–232.[79] Although it is not known exactly what the Roman synod in Pontian's time decreed regarding Origen, one of Origen's heterodox ideas was of the pre-existence of souls. Origen proposed that human souls exist prior to their connection to earthly forms, in the spiritual world with God. He also doubted the resurrection of the physical body, speculated about the life of the stars, and wondered whether heavenly bodies possessed souls. Origen's most widely condemned doctrine, however, was his teaching of universal restoration (*apokatastasis*). He likened the Creator to a divine teacher, who could not fail, in the long run, in properly instructing His students. He thus concluded that, in time, all humans would be restored to their former sinless status, becoming perfect and living in the presence of God. In his view, this restoration included all souls, not just humanity, but fallen angels, and even Satan.

In 235, during the reign of Maximinus the Thracian, the Roman Church again suffered persecution. The policy was directed chiefly against the heads of the Christian community, rather than against the rank and file. Its first victims were both Pontian and Hippolytus, a fact which argues for Hippolytus still serving as bishop of his own congregation. They were banished to the island of Sardinia, where they were probably forced to do hard labour in the mines. To make the election of a new pope possible, Pontian resigned 28 September 235, according to the *Liberian Catalogue*. Pope Fabian (236–250) had the remains of Pontian and Hippolytus both brought back to Rome at a later date. Pontian was buried in the papal crypt of the Catacomb of Callixtus. His feast day is celebrated jointly with that of Hippolytus on August 13. The reconciliation of the rival congregations of Rome, effected by the joint martyrdoms of pope and antipope, is Pontian's most lasting legacy.

3.1.20 Saint Anterus

The *Liber Pontificalis* indicates that Anterus was a Greek and that his father's name was Romulus. He became pope after his predecessor, Pontian, was sentenced to exile in the Sardinian mines under the persecution of Emperor Maximinus I, known as the Thracian. Pope Saint Anterus was bishop of Rome from 21 November 235 to 3 January 236, succeeding Pope Pontian, who had been deported from Rome, along with the antipope Hippolytus, to Sardinia. His reign was a very short one, lasting only 40 days. Tradition holds that he collected and stored various Acts of the martyrs. He created one bishop, for the city of Fondi.[80]

The idea of his martyrdom is supported by the fact that his predecessor died in the mines after being exiled under persecution, but more telling is the report in the Liberian Catalogue of the popes that he "fell asleep", a euphemism for a natural death. A later tradition holds that Anterus was martyred for having caused the Acts of the martyrs to be collected by notaries and deposited in the archives of the Roman Church.[81] The Church celebrates his feast as that of a martyr on 3 January.

3.1.21 St Fabian

According the Liber Pontificalis, Fabian was a Roman by birth, and his father's name was Fabius. Nothing more is known about his background. The legend concerning the circumstances of his election on 13 January 236 is preserved by the fourth century writer Eusebius of Caesarea.[82] After the short reign of Pope Anterus, Fabian had come to Rome from the countryside when the new election began. Although present, Fabian was in the mind of nobody; he was an unknown quantity. While the names of several illustrious and noble churchmen were being considered, a dove suddenly descended upon the head of Fabian. To the assembled electors, this strange sight recalled the Gospel scene of the descent of the Holy Spirit on Jesus Christ at the time of His Baptism by John the Baptist. Believing the current dove's flight to be divinely inspired, they unanimously chose Fabian to be the next pope.

During Fabian's reign of 14 years, there was a lull in the storm of persecution which had resulted in the exile of both Anterus' predecessor Pontian and the antipope (and later saint) Hippolytus. Fabian had enough influence at court to effect the return of the bodies of both of these martyrs from Sardinia, where they had died at hard labour in the mines. The report that he baptized the emperor Philip the Arab and his son, however, is probably a legend, although he did seem to enjoy some connections at court, since the bodies of Pontian and Anterus could not have been exhumed without the emperor's approval.

It was probably during Fabian's reign that the congregation of Hippolytus was fully brought back into full communion with the main body of the Roman Church. The underlying issues of the schism, however, were not completely resolved. These involved the issue of the purity of the Church, especially the integrity of the clergy during the persecution and the forgiveness of serious sins like adultery. One of the bishops apparently consecrated by Fabian, namely Novatian, would go on to become the next antipope and form a long-lasting and widespread schism, based in part on these very issues.

The *Liber Pontificalis* states that Fabian divided Rome into seven *Rioni*—quarters or districts—as Augustus had divided it into fourteen, each supervised by a deacon.[83] Eusebius adds that he appointed seven subdeacons to help collect the Acts of the Martyrs—the reports of the court proceedings on the occasion of their trials.[84] Fabian had found the ancient civil division inadequate; whereas the division he had adopted enabled the seven deacons who were charged to oversee the seven other deacons, as well as the seven subdeacons, to take care of the poor in the seven churches. In this ecclesiastical division originated the titles of the Cardinal-deacons, who at first were entitled *Regionari*. There is also a tradition that he instituted the four minor clerical orders: porter, lector, exorcist, and acolyte. The *Liberian Catalogue* of the popes adds that Fabian initiated considerable work on the catacombs, where honoured Christians were buried, and where he also caused the body of Pope Pontian to be entombed at the catacomb of St Callixtus. Fabian also gave orders that on Holy Thursday the old oil of the holy chrism from the previous year should be burned. It has also been stated that Fabian decreed that no one should be ordained priest at an earlier age than thirty years; that, in civil judgment, no priest could be either accuser, or judge, or witness; that the faithful should receive Holy Communion three times in every year; that priests who had lost their mental faculties as the result of illness should no longer be allowed to celebrate the Holy Sacrifice of the Mass; and that marriage should be prohibited to the faithful up to the fourth degree of consanguinity.

Later accounts attribute to Fabian the consecration (around 245) of seven bishops as missionaries to Gaul: Gatien to Tours, Trophimus to Arles, Paul to Narbonne, Saturnin to Toulouse, Denis to Paris, Austromoine to Clermont, and Martial to Limoges. In five ordinations Fabian created either eleven bishops, twenty-two priests, and seven deacons.[85]

The famous Christian teacher and scholar Origen wrote to Fabian, as well as to many other bishops, defending the orthodoxy of his teaching, which had been condemned both at Alexandria and later in Rome, in a synod over which Anterus had probably presided.[86] Saint Cyprian, speaking of Saint Fabian, calls him an excellent man, and says that the glory of his death was conformable to the purity, the holiness, and the integrity of his life. He had the glory to banish from the Church a new heretic, Privatus of Lambaesa, an African bishop, who had been previously condemned by a synod for grave faults, and who endeavoured by an insidious false humility to impose upon the candour of the pope.[87]

With the advent of Emperor Decius, the Roman government's tolerant policy toward Christianity temporarily ended. Decius ordered leading Christians to demonstrate their loyalty to Rome by offering incense to the icons of deities which represented the Roman state. This, of course, was unacceptable to most Christians, who, while no longer holding most of the laws of the Old Testament to apply to them, took the commandment against idolatry with deadly seriousness. Fabian was thus one of the earliest victims of Decius, dying as a martyr on 20 January 250, at the beginning of the Decian persecution, probably in prison rather than by execution. He was buried in the crypt of the popes in the Catacomb of St Callixtus which he himself had helped to improve. In modern times the Italian archaeologist Giovanni Battista de Rossi discovered his epitaph: "Fabian, bishop and martyr".[88] The tradition of Fabian's martyrdom is thus accepted as historical. In art, he is often pictured with Saint Sebastian, whose feast day he shares on 20 January.

3.2 The early Papal election

The earliest bishops appear to have been chosen for Christian communities by the apostles and their immediate successors who founded the Church in that area. As these communities became more fully established, bishops were chosen by the clergy and laity of the community with the assistance of the bishops of neighbouring dioceses. St Cyprian says that Pope Cornelius was chosen Bishop of Rome

> by the judgment of God and of His Christ, by the testimony of almost all the clergy, by the suffrage of the people who were then present, and by the assembly of ancient priests and good men, when no one had been made so before him, when the place of Fabian, that is, when the place of Peter and the degree of the sacerdotal throne was vacant.[89]

As was true for bishops of other dioceses, the clergy of the Diocese of Rome constituted the electoral body for the Bishop of Rome, but they did not cast votes, instead selecting the bishop by general consensus or by acclamation. The candidate would then be submitted to the people for their general approval or disapproval. This lack of lucidity in the election procedures sometimes gave rise to rival Popes or antipopes, and, to avoid factions, the Roman Emperor sometimes confirmed the selection.

As regards the question whether the Pope can select his own successor, it is possible that Peter, the first Pope chose his own immediate successor, St Linus. History records the case of Felix IV who in 530, on his deathbed, chose his successor, Boniface II. Felix even handed him his *pallium*. However the question then arises whether the latter become Pope in virtue of this election or in virtue of the later ratification by the Roman clergy. Nevertheless, the fact that the Senate published an edict forbidding discussion of Papal succession during a reigning Pontiff's lifetime, indicates that this was indeed an example of a Pope naming his successor. Boniface II, in his turn, made the Roman clergy promise to maintain after his death the choice he had made of Vigilius as his successor: but fearing, later on, for the consequences of such an act, he publicly retracted it.[90] For certain theologians, like Cajetan, the direct election of a successor by the reigning Pope would be invalid. According to Cajetan, the power to elect a successor resides in the Pope not in a formal manner, apt to pass into act (as the builder's craft is in the builder), but in an eminent manner, inapt for immediate exercise (as the builder's craft is in the architect).[91] This is an extreme position, and other theologians would simply point out that it is not fitting, since the act of electing a Pope precedes, strictly speaking, any exercise of the papal power; and so it is fittingly assigned to the Church and not to the Pope.[92] For many other theologians, however, it would be simply contra-indicated in the present state of things. It could well be proposed that as the Pope can appoint a coadjutor bishop with right of succession to any other see, he could do the same to his own See of Rome.[93]

The Lateran Synod held in 769 officially abolished the theoretical suffrage held by the Roman people, though in 862, a Synod of Rome restored it to Roman noblemen. Early on, the Pope took oaths of loyalty to the Holy Roman Emperor, whose task it was to provide security and public peace in Rome. A major change was introduced in 1059, when Pope Nicholas II decreed in his document *In Nomine Domini* that the cardinals were to elect a candidate, who would take office after receiving the assent of the clergy and laity. The most senior cardinals, the cardinal bishops, were to meet first and discuss the candidates before summoning the cardinal priests and cardinal deacons for the actual vote. Imperial confirmation was dropped. The Second Council of the Lateran in 1139 removed the requirement that the assent of the lower clergy and the laity be obtained.

In 1587, Sixtus V fixed the number of cardinals at 70: six cardinal bishops, 50 cardinal priests, and 14 cardinal deacons. Beginning with Pope John XXIII's attempts to broaden the backgrounds of the cardinals, that number has increased to 120. In 1970 Pope Paul VI limited the electors to cardinals under 80 years of age. The Pope may change the procedures for electing his successor by issuing an apostolic constitution; the current procedures were established by Pope St John Paul II in his constitution *Universi Dominici Gregis*.[94] The procedure was slightly amended by a *Motu Proprio* of Pope Benedict XVI dated 11 June 2007.

Electors formerly made choices by three methods: by acclamation, compromise or scrutiny. If voting by acclamation, the cardinals would unanimously declare the new pope *quasi afflati Spiritu Sancto* (as if inspired by the Holy Spirit). If voting by compromise, the deadlocked College would select a committee of cardinals to conduct an election. In reality voting was done by scrutiny with the electors casting secret ballots. The last election by compromise is thought to be that of John XXII (1316), and the last election by acclamation that of Gregory XV (1621). New rules introduced by Pope John Paul II have formally abolished these long-unused systems and election is always by totally secret ballot.

Until 1179, a simple majority sufficed for an election, when the Third Lateran Council increased the required majority to two-thirds. Cardinals were not allowed to vote for themselves; an elaborate procedure was adopted to ensure secrecy while at the same time preventing self-voting. In 1945, Pius XII increased the requisite majority to two-thirds plus one. In 1996, Pope John Paul's Constitution allowed election by absolute majority if deadlock prevailed after seven ballots. In 2006 Pope Benedict XVI rescinded Pope John Paul's change (as there could have been a problem effectively abolishing the two-thirds majority requirement, since then any majority would suffice to block the election until a simple majority was enough to elect the next pope). Pope Benedict has reaffirmed the requirement of a two-thirds majority. Cardinals formerly used these intricate ballot papers, one of which is shown folded below. Currently, the ballots are simple cards, folded once (like a note card), with the words "I elect as Supreme Pontiff ..." printed on them.

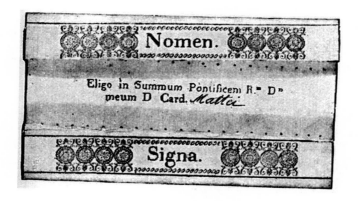

The Papacy is attached to the See of Rome for ever. Peter was prompted by the Holy Spirit to come to Rome, the same Holy Spirit who assisted the Apostles in founding the Church. Peter was expressly led by the divine will to unite the Papacy to the See of Rome for all future time. The Church of Christ, the Church of Peter, the Church of the successors of Peter, is Roman for ever. The title "Roman" is more than a merely historical one reminding us that after twenty centuries the primacy of jurisdiction remains attached to the Roman See; it is a prophetic title signifying that for all ages to come the primacy of jurisdiction will be tied to the See of Rome. The See of Rome is to be distinguished from residence in Rome. The Pope can leave Italy, and go to Avignon. In ecclesiastical law, which is always revocable, he could even annex the episcopate of Avignon to the universal episcopate. He remains however, by divine right, the Roman Pontiff; and there can be no other legitimate Bishop of

Rome. If Rome one day should be utterly destroyed, we should then have to say that the exclusive authority of the Pope over it would have become in fact without object, though continuing to exist in right. The See associated with the Petrine authority cannot be detached or changed by any human authority. No matter where he lives, the true successor of St Peter will necessarily remain the Bishop of Rome.[95]

3.2.1 The new Papal name

After the counting of the ballots produces a consensus candidate, the new pope is asked, "By which name will you be known?" The new pope then simply states what his name will be. Occasionally, he may offer an explanation for his choice; sometimes, he may offer an explanation later. The first pope who chose a different name instead of using his birth name was Pope John II, whose birth name was Mercurius, after the pagan god Mercury; he was elected as the 56th pope on 31 December 532, and reigned until 27 May 535.[96] He did not want to use the name of a pagan god, so he selected John II as his papal name, becoming the first pope to change his name. The idea caught on, but it wasn't until the tenth century that it became routine. In that period, clerics from beyond the Alps, especially Germany and France, were elected to the papacy and replaced their foreign-sounding names with more traditional Roman-sounding ones. Pope Marcellus II in 1555 was the last pope to use his own Christian name.

The practice has even more ancient roots. Old Testament figures were invested with new names after times of great spiritual transition. For instance, God changed Abram's (high father) name to "Abraham" meaning father of a multitude (Gn 17:5) and his wife's name from "Sarai" (my princess) to "Sarah" signifying "mother of nations" (Gn 17:15). After a vision of an angel wrestling with him, Old Testament character Jacob was renamed Israel, which means "contended with God" (Gn 32:38). Thus the new name corresponds to a new mission which God gives.

3.3 Church and State

The question of Church and State and the problems to which their relation has given rise, are as old as Christianity. In a true sense there was no problem of Church and State before the advent of Christ when, for all practical purposes, the public authority was regarded equally competent in the field of religion as in the secular domain. With the coming of the Catholic Church, however, an essential change was introduced by her Founder, who transferred to her the sphere of religion and the whole moral direction of mankind, independent of the power of the State.

The classic statement of Christ on the relation of His kingdom to the civil authority was provoked by officials of religion who had no sympathy with the secular power to which they were subject. The Pharisees sought to trap Jesus by asking Him if it was lawful to render tribute to Caesar; the word tribute comprised all kinds of taxes payable to state officials. The Pharisees and Herodians had long since adjusted their conscience to the payment. However, they now hoped to force Christ to compromise Himself no matter how He answered. If He advised non-payment, as they expected, He would have become liable to Roman punishment. The pseudo-Messiah, Judas the Galilean, had perished for this very cause some twenty years before. Should He have advised payment, He would have lost His Messianic hold on the people for whom Messianism meant complete independence from foreign domination. Instead of falling into the trap set for Him, Jesus asked for a coin with Caesar's image on it, declaring that, since the coin had come from Caesar, justice requires that it be returned to him. "Pay to Caesar," He replied, "what belongs to Caesar, and to God what belongs to God" (Mt 22:21). In other words, civil transactions like the payment of taxes lie on one plane, but the rights of God are on another. There is no inevitable clash provided, as was the case in the relationship of Rome to the Jewish people, that the civil demands did not hinder the exercise of man's duties to God.

One aspect of Christ's reply to the Pharisees that is easy to overlook is His recognition of the rights of civil authority, as distinct from those of the Church. The emperor to whom Christ declared that tribute could be lawfully paid was officially a god. From the first beginnings of the Empire, the deification of Roman rulers became an established practice of the nation. Julius Caesar was proclaimed to be a god. *Divus* was the expression adopted; this title had been given him by senatorial decree, and his worship was put on a full ceremonial basis, with temple, priests, and ritual. The same thing was done for Augustus, Claudius, Vespasian, and Titus. As time went on, this phase of Roman religion grew spontaneously and accounted in great measure for the hostility of Rome to Christianity. The last of the *Divi*, deified in 307 AD, was Romulus, the son of Maxentius, whom Constantine defeated at the Milvian bridge. When Christ, therefore, granted the right of rulers to demand obedience in temporal and secular affairs, He made the most drastic distinction possible between legitimate civil authority and its illegitimate pretensions. Insofar as the Emperor commanded what was due to him as a ruler of state, all the citizens, including Christians, were bound to obey, notwithstanding his abuse of power and even the blasphemous claim to divinity.

In the apostolic Church, Peter implemented Christ's teaching by urging Christians to accept the established form of government and submit to those in authority "for the sake of the Lord", in order not to bring discredit on His followers: "Accept the authority of every human institution: the emperor, as the supreme authority, and the governors as commissioned by him to punish criminals and praise those who do good. It is God's will that by your good deeds you should silence the ignorant talk of fools" (1 Pt 2:13–15). St Peter concluded, "fear God and honour the emperor" (1 Pt 2:17). As with the case of Christ, so here the injunction to be subject to the emperor, takes on added significance when this emperor is identified as Nero, and the motive indicated is the will of God.

The most elaborate exponent of Church and State relations in early Christianity was St Paul. His exhortation to the Romans remains to this day an epitome of the obedience that a Christian owes to the civil rulers:

> Everyone is to obey the governing authorities, because there is no authority except from God and so whatever authorities exist have been appointed by God. So anyone who disobeys an authority is rebelling against God's ordinance; and rebels must expect to receive the condemnation they deserve. Magistrates bring fear not to those who do good, but to those who do evil (Rm 13:1–3).

Yet the ultimate reason for submission is not the physical punishment caused by disobedience. Rather, one "must be obedient, therefore, not only because of this retribution, but also for conscience's sake" (Rm 13:5). This is also why one should pay taxes, "because the authorities are all serving God as His agents, even while they are busily occupied with that particular task" (Rm 13:6).

In the first three centuries of the Christian era, the relation of Church and State was one of incessant conflict, in which the Roman Empire reacted against the Church as its mortal enemy, conscious on the one hand of the latter's inherent power over the hearts and minds of men, but blind to the fact that Christianity was not a political rival and still less a threat to civil authority. Pliny's letter to Trajan (112 AD) describing how he dealt with the Christians in Bithynia furnishes an insight into motives behind the pagan persecution. "I ask them if they are Christian," wrote Pliny. "If they admit it, I repeat the question a second and a third time, threatening capital punishment; if they persist, I sentence them to death. For I do not doubt that, whatever kind of crime it may be to which they have confessed, their pertinacity and inflexible obstinacy should certainly be punished."[97] The crime for which the Christians were punished was nothing more or less than "obstinacy" in professing their religious belief against the mandates of civil power.

Nevertheless, all the time they were being persecuted, the Christians protested their loyalty to the government and only pleaded for justice, not to be punished for crimes they did not commit or, as Christ Himself had demanded, to be shown where they had done wrong (cf. Jn 18:23). "If it is certain," Tertullian asked, "that we are the most guilty of men, why do you trust us differently from our fellows, that is, from other criminals?... Christians alone are not allowed to say anything to clear themselves, to defend truth, to save a judge from injustice. That alone is looked for, which public hatred requires: the confession of the name, not the investigation of the charge." In spite of this manifest injustice, however, "We call upon God for the welfare of the Emperor, upon God the eternal... whose favour, beyond all others, the Emperor desires." If this seems incredible to the pagan mind, let them "examine God's words, our scriptures [and] learn from them that a superfluity of benevolence is enjoined upon us, even so far as to pray for our enemies and to entreat blessings for our persecutors."[98] Evidently the early Christians distinguished between the spiritual allegiance they owed the Church and the civic loyalty that was due to the State. Where the latter encroached on the former, it could not be obeyed; but within the limits of due authority, the State had a right to obedience and a claim on Christian prayer, that the Lord might direct the rulers in their government and assist their temporal reign.

When, after three centuries of cruel persecution, the State finally gave freedom to the Christian religion, it recognized what the Church had always been teaching, that Christianity is not an enemy of the State but its most powerful ally. The edict of liberation ran:

> When we, Constantine and Licinius, Emperors, met at Milan in conference concerning the welfare and security of the realm, we decided that of the things that are of profit to all mankind, the worship of God ought rightly to be our first and most important care... We therefore announce that, notwithstanding any provisions concerning the Christians in our former instructions, all who choose that religion should be allowed to continue in practising it, without any let or hindrance, and are not to be troubled or molested in any way.[99]

At the same time that Christianity was being legalized, all others are to be allowed the free and unrestricted practice of their religions; "for it accords with the good order of the realm and the peacefulness of our times that each should have freedom to worship God after his own choice."[100] The Edict of Milan was thus a political compromise between Licinius, an avowed pagan, and Constantine, who was already a Christian at heart, although he did not immediately profess the faith. Prescinding from its motive, the decree was a practical necessity, a *modus vivendi* for two strong opposing forces. Soon after the edict, Licinius started a pagan reaction, which Constantine repulsed by defeating his rival in 324. Despite being at an advantage as a result, Constantine was still obliged to make concessions to the pagan nobility. However, later proclamations became even more favourable to the Christians, like the prohibition of soothsaying and fortune-telling, the grant of a regular subsidy to the Catholic clergy, their exemption from military and other civil duties, and the state recognition of Sunday as a feast day with civil effects. However, paganism was not yet entirely suppressed.

Within less than a century of the Edict of Milan, Catholicism had become so widely recognized that the civil authorities found in religious unity their strongest support for political stability. With the fall of paganism, Catholic Christianity might have become the religion of the Empire without State intervention, except for the Arian crisis of the fourth century. After its condemnation at the Councils of Nicea and Constantinople, Arianism was finally crushed by a composite decree of the Emperors Gratian, Valentinian II and Theodosius, who made acknowledgment of the Most Holy Trinity a condition of civil liberty:

> We desire all people, whom the benign influence of our clemency rules, to turn to the religion which tradition from Peter to the present day declares to have been delivered to the Romans by blessed Peter the Apostle... This faith is that we should believe that there is one Godhead, Father, Son and Holy Spirit, in an equal Majesty and a holy Trinity. We order those who follow this

> doctrine to receive the title of Catholic Christians, but
> others we judge to be mad and raving and worthy of
> incurring the disgrace of heretical teaching, nor are their
> assemblies to receive the name of churches. They are to
> be punished not only by divine retribution but also by
> our own measures, which we have decided in accordance
> with divine inspiration.[101]

This imperial edict did more than introduce Catholic orthodoxy as the established religion of the Roman world. It is the first recorded instance when the civil power contemplated the use of physical force in the service of Christianity with consequences that critics of the Church have exploited beyond the objective facts. There is no evidence that the threat of punishment radically "converted" the heretics against whom the decree was aimed; on the other hand, there is ample evidence that, even without civil intervention, orthodox Christianity would have continued (as it had begun) its conquest of the Mediterranean world simply by preaching the word of God.

More significant from the viewpoint of Church-State relations was another imperial decree in the following century (445 AD) when Valentinian III and Theodosius II recognized the Pope as Head of the Catholic Church. Aside from its value as an early witness of the Petrine primacy, the document shows how carefully even the rulers of the Roman Empire distinguished between the spiritual autonomy of the Papacy and their own function as aids to the Pope in those material forces which he did not enjoy. The emperors stated:

> It is clear that for us and our Empire the only support is in
> the favour of the Supreme Godhead; to merit this we must
> assist in the first place the Christian faith and venerable
> religion. Since therefore the merit of St Peter... the dignity
> of the City of Rome and the authority of a holy synod have
> established the primacy of the Apostolic See, let not
> presumption attempt to carry out anything contrary to the
> authority of that See. But let whatever the Apostolic See
> decrees or shall decree, be accepted as law by all.[102]

The emperors intervened to protect papal authority against an episcopal rebel, the Bishop of Arles, who challenged the right of Pope Leo I to decide against him.

In the latter part of the fifth century, the Holy See stated its concept of the relative status of ecclesiastical and civil power which to this day is the most succinct expression of the Church's mind on the subject. It was occasioned by the attitude of the Eastern Emperor, Anastasius I, who presumed to favour the schismatic patriarchs of Constantinople, particularly with regard to the Monophysite heresy condemned by Rome. Pope Gelasius I (492–496), wrote to the Emperor, to point out to him the illegality of his interference in Church affairs. His letter included an exposition of the Gelasian thesis that the spiritual and secular authorities are each independent in their own sphere, with which the other must not interfere:

> There are two powers by which this world is chiefly ruled: the sacred authority of the Popes and the royal power. Of these, the priestly power is much more important, because it has to render account for the kinds of men themselves at the divine tribunal. For you know that although you have the highest place in dignity over the human race, yet you must submit yourself faithfully to those who have charge of divine things, and look to them for the means of your salvation... For if in matters pertaining to the administration of public discipline, the bishops of the Church, knowing that the Empire has been conferred on you by divine instrumentality, are themselves obedient to your laws, lest in purely material affairs contrary opinions may seem to be voiced, with what willingness, I ask you, should you obey those to whom is assigned the administration of divine mysteries?[103]

Here, for the first time, a papal document of universal application spells out the Church's new status in reference to the political power. Until the Edict of Milan, the problem was almost unilateral, how the Church's rights could be protected in the atmosphere of a totalitarian State. A period of flux followed for a century or so after Constantine, in which the hitherto pagan civil authority gradually became Christian and, while emancipating the Church, also assumed (often without being asked) the responsibility of assisting the Church with the might of its secular arm. Depending on their ambition, the emperors sometimes went beyond their legitimate function of auxiliaries to interfere in the internal affairs of ecclesiastical policy, with consequent harm to the Church's spiritual welfare. Gelasius' reprimand of Anastasius was chronologically the beginning of a long line of similar papal reactions. Basically the attitude is not different from Peter's during the persecution of Nero, except that now the Church is in a position to protest against political intrusion, instead of merely exhorting the Christians to bear the injustice with patience. However, as in Peter, so in Gelasius, the sovereign rights of the State are forcefully recognized, even to the point of obedience on the part of ecclesiastics when purely secular interests are involved.

Notes

1   Clement of Rome, *Letter to the Corinthians*, Chapter 5.
2   See *The Book of the Popes* (*Liber Pontificalis*) I, *To the pontificate of Gregory I*. Translated with an Introduction by L. Ropes Loomis (New York: Columbia University Press, 1916), pp. 4–5.
3   St Irenaeus, *Against the Heresies*, Part 3, Book 3, chapter 3.
4   See J. S. Brusher, *Popes Through the Ages* (Princeton, NJ: D. Van Nostrand Company, 1959).
5   *Liber Pontificalis*, p. 6.
6   Near the modern Via Urbana, a region extending from the Viminal to the Esquiline hills.
7   *Liber Pontificalis*, p. 6.
8   *Ibid.*, p. 7. The author probably deduced the location of Clement's house from the situation of the church of San Clemente which stands between the Coelian and the Esquiline hills.
9   Tertullian, *On the Prescription of Heretics*, 32.
10   St Irenaeus, *Against the Heresies*, Part 3, Book 3, chapter 3.
11   Clement of Alexandria, *Stromata*, i. 7, iv. 17, v. 12, vi. 8.
12   Origen, *De Principiis*, ii. 3; *Commentary on Ezekiel*, 8; *Commentary on John*, i. 29.

13   See Eusebius, *Church History*, III, 37.

14   Hermas, *The Shepherd*, Vision II, 4, 3.

15   H. Wace, *A Dictionary of Christian Biography and Literature to the End of the Sixth Century AD, with an Account of the Principal Sects and Heresies* (Grand Rapids, MI: Christian Classics Ethereal Library, 2000), p. 281.

16   St Irenaeus, *Against the Heresies*, Part 3, Book 3, chapter 3.

17   *Liber Pontificalis*, p. 8.

18   The Chersonesus Taurica (Greek: Χερσόνησος; Latin: Chersonesus; Byzantine Greek: Χερσών) is an ancient Greek colony founded approximately 2,500 years ago in the southwestern part of the Crimea, known then as Taurica.

19   See Eusebius, *Ecclesiastical History* IV, I,

20   See Pope St Evaristus, Letters *De Ordine Diaconorum et Legitimo Ac Regulari Coniugio atque de Fide* and *Epistola Supra Quod Christus Sit Caput et Sponsus Ecclesiae* as found in *PG* 5, 1047–1056.

21   For St Ignatius of Antioch, see chapter 4, subsection 4.2.3 below.

22   The district is said to be in the Fifth Region, which, if the reference be to the regions of Augustus, comprised a large part of the Esquiline Hill along the city wall. See *Liber Pontificalis*, p. 10, note 3.

23   See P. H. Wiebe, *Visions of Jesus: Direct Encounters from the New Testament to Today* (Oxford: Oxford University Press, 1998), p. 20.

24   The "tomb of Alexander" is mentioned in an itinerary attributed to William of Malmesbury. The site of it, near the Via Nomentana, was rediscovered in 1855. But it is probable that there were two Alexanders and that the martyr has been erroneously identified with the pope. See *Liber Pontificalis*, p. 11, note 2.

25   The *formatae* were so named on account of the seal or of the special form used in writing them.

26   See *Liber Pontificalis*, p. 11.

27   See *Liber Pontificalis*, p. 12.

28   See *Liber Pontificalis*, p. 12.

29   An anchorite was usually a person who lived an eremitic religious life in a small cell which was attached, or "anchored", to a church or oratory. See chapter 11, section 11.5 below for more on this topic.

30   See *Liber Pontificalis*, p. 13.

31   For more on Marcionism see chapter 7, subsection 7.2.2 below.

32   For more on Gnosticism see chapter 7, subsection 7.2.1 below.

33   See *Liber Pontificalis*, p. 14, note 2.

34   Valentinus had at first preached the Catholic faith in Egypt, where he is said to have been born, and afterwards in Rome, but it was in the isle of Cyprus that he departed from the faith. Possessing both ability and eloquence, he hoped for a bishopric, but being disappointed, in his anger

he undertook to combat the doctrine of the Church. He had studied the writings of the Greeks, and especially Platonic philosophy.

35 See *Liber Pontificalis*, p. 15.

36 See *Liber Pontificalis*, p. 15.

37 On the question of the date of Easter see chapter 4, section 4.10 below.

38 For brief descriptions of these heresies see see chapter 7, subsections 7.2.1, 7.2.2 and 7.2.6 below.

39 See *Liber Pontificalis*, p. 15. St Jerome alludes to a prohibition of this sort; see St Jerome, *In Ezechiele*, 14, 20.

40 *Liber Pontificalis*, p. 15.

41 Eusebius, *Church History*, IV, 24.

42 See *Liber Pontificalis*, p. 16.

43 For more on Montanism see chapter 7, subsection 7.2.6 below.

44 See *Liber Pontificalis*, p. 17. In the Latin it states: "Et hoc iterum firmavit ut nulla esca a Christianis repudiaretur, maxime fidelibus, quod Deus creavit, quæ tamen rationalis et humana est."

45 See *Liber Pontificalis*, p. 17.

46 St Bede, *Ecclesiastical History*, Book I, chapter IV.

47 See *Liber Pontificalis*, p. 17.

48 Hippolytus, *Philosophumena*, IX, 12.

49 Osroene, also spelled Osrohene and Osrhoene (Ancient Greek: Ὀσροηνή) and sometimes known by the name of its capital city, Edessa (modern Şanlıurfa, Turkey), was a Syriac-speaking kingdom located in upper Mesopotamia, which enjoyed semi-autonomy to complete independence from the years of 132 BC to 244 AD.

50 On the question of the date of Easter see chapter 4, section 4.10 below.

51 In Egyptian mythology, the Ogdoad (Greek ογδοάς, the eightfold) were eight deities worshipped in Hermopolis during what is called the Old Kingdom, the third through sixth dynasties, dated between 2686 to 2134 BC. The concept of an Ogdoad also appears in Gnostic systems of the early Christian era, and was further developed by the theologian Valentinus (around 160 AD).

52 Eusebius, *Church History*, V, 15.

53 For more on Adoptionism see chapter 7, subsection 7.2.5 below.

54 St Jerome calls Pope Victor the first Latin writer in the Church. See *De Viris Illustribus*, XXXIV: "Victor, thirteenth bishop of the Roman city, the writer of certain opuscula on the Paschal question and others, ruled the Church ten years under Severus." See also Idem, *Chronicle*, Ad anno, 193: "Victor receives the thirteenth episcopate of Rome for 10 years, whose modest volumes *On Religion* are extant."

55 See *Liber Pontificalis*, p. 18.

56 For more on the Canon of the New Testament see chapter 8 below.

[57] Hippolytus, *Philosophumena*, IX, 11.

[58] Eusebius, *Church History*, V, 32.

[59] For more on Modalism see chapter 7, subsection 7.2.7 below.

[60] The Encratites ("self-controlled") were an ascetic second-century Gnostic sect who forbade marriage and counselled abstinence from meat. Eusebius (*Church History*, IV, 28–29) says that Tatian was the author of this heresy. It has been supposed that it was these Gnostic Encratites who were chastised by St Paul in 1 Timothy 4:1–4.

[61] See *Liber Pontificalis*, p. 19–20.

[62] See *Liber Pontificalis*, p. 19.

[63] See *Liber Pontificalis*, p. 20.

[64] A district beyond the Tiber peopled by settlers from Ravenna, the modern Trastevere.

[65] Tertullian, *On Modesty*, 21.

[66] Sabellianism is the error that God the Father, God the Son and the Holy Spirit are only three modes or aspects of God. Once popular but later declared heretical, Sabellianism and similar theologies developed out of the earlier view known as Modalistic Monarchianism, with which it is often identified. Its proponent, Sabellius, lived in the early third century AD and was probably a Roman presbyter. For more on Sabellianism see chapter 7, subsection 7.2.7 below.

[67] In the liturgical calendar of the Western Christian churches, Ember days are four separate sets of three days within the same week—specifically, the Wednesday, Friday, and Saturday—roughly equidistant in the circuit of the year, that were formerly set aside for fasting and prayer. These days set apart for special prayer and fasting were considered especially suitable for the ordination of clergy. The Ember Days are known in Latin as the *quattuor anni tempora* (the "four seasons of the year"), or formerly as the *jejunia quattuor temporum* ("fasts of the four seasons"). The Ember Weeks—the weeks in which the Ember Days occur—are the week between the third and fourth Sundays of Advent, between the first and second Sundays of Lent, the week between Pentecost and Trinity Sunday, and the week beginning on the Sunday after Holy Cross Day (September 14), the liturgical Third Week of September.

[68] See *Liber Pontificalis*, p. 20.

[69] The *Historiae Augustae* relates that a spot on which Callixtus had built an oratory was later claimed by the tavern-keepers of Rome, but the emperor decided that the worship of any god, even the god of the Christians, was better than a tavern. This is said to have been the origin of the Church of Santa Maria in Trastevere. The Church of St Callixtus is close by, containing the well into which legend says his body was thrown.

[70] See St Jerome, *De Viris Illustribus*, 61; Eusebius, *Church History*, VI, 14, 10.

[71] Hippolytus, *Philosophumena*, IX, 10–11.

[72] See the account by Prudentius, *Liber Peristephanon*, 11, who says Hippolytus was torn in pieces at Ostia by wild horses, like the Hippolytus of mythology. Thus the pagan myth of Hippolytus the son of Theseus was apparently transferred to Hippolytus of Rome. The mythological Hippolytus, whose name means "loose horse" in Greek, had been dragged to death by wild horses. This death, according to legend, was the very method by which the historical Hippolytus became martyred. Prudentius describes the subterranean tomb of the saint and states that he saw on the spot a picture representing this execution, and that this martyrdom was commemorated on August 13. He gives an account of the crowds who flocked to the commemoration and a description of a stately church, with a double row of pillars.

[73] See *Liber Pontificalis*, p. 21.

[74] *Ibid.*.

[75] See *Liber Pontificalis*, p. 22.

[76] See *Liber Pontificalis*, p. 21.

[77] A commendatory is an ecclesiastic, or sometimes a layman, who holds a basilica or abbey *in commendam*, that is, who draws its revenues and, if an ecclesiastic, may also have some jurisdiction, but does not exercise any authority over its inner monastic discipline. The chapel of the Madonna di Strada Cupa had been given by the chapter to Henry Benedict, Cardinal Duke of York, the brother of Prince Charles Edward. Henry Benedict was the last of the Stuarts, and died in 1788. He had on his medals the title of Henry IX, King of England.

[78] See *Liber Pontificalis*, p. 23.

[79] St Jerome, *Epistle 33*, to Paula.

[80] See *Liber Pontificalis*, p. 24.

[81] See *Liber Pontificalis*, p. 23.

[82] Eusebius, *Church History*, VI, 29.

[83] See *Liber Pontificalis*, p. 24.

[84] See Eusebius, *Church History*, VI, 43.

[85] See *Liber Pontificalis*, p. 25.

[86] See Eusebius, *Church History*, VI, 34.

[87] See St Cyprian, *Letter 54*.

[88] See *Roma Sotterranea* II, 59.

[89] St Cyprian, *Epistle 51: To Antonianus about Cornelius and Novatian*, 8.

[90] See J. N. D. Kelly, *The Oxford Dictionary of Popes* (Oxford: University Press, 1987), pp. 56–57.

[91] Cajetan, *Apologia de Comparata Auctoritate Papae et Concilii*, cap. xiii, no. 736.

[92] See C. Journet, *The Church of the Word Incarnate* (London: Sheed and Ward, 1955), Chapter 8, excursus 8, 2.

93   See P. Haffner, *Mystery of the Church* (Leominster: Gracewing, 2014), p. 168, where I outline this idea.

94   See Pope St John Paul II, Apostolic Constitution *Universi Dominici Gregis* (22 February 1996).

95   See Journet, *The Church of the Word Incarnate*, Chapter 8, 5, B, 3.

96   See H. Wace, *A dictionary of Christian biography and literature to the end of the sixth century AD: With an account of the principal sects and heresies* (Grand Rapids, MI: Christian Classics Ethereal Library, 2000), pp. 901–902.

97   C. Plinius Secundus Minor, *Epistola ad Trajanum*, n.96. See also J. Hardon, manuscript *Christ to Catholicism*, chapter XII "Principles of Church and State in Historical Perspective" which provided material for some of the following points.

98   Tertullian, *Apologeticus adversus gentes pro christianis*, chapter 2, 1 and 3; chapter 30, 1; chapter 31, 1–2 in *CCL* 1, 87; 1, 141–142.

99   *Edict of Milan* in Lactantius, *De Mortibus Persecutorum*, in *PL* 7, 267–270.

100 *Ibid.*

101 T. Mommsen, *Codex Theodosianus* (Berlin: 1905), Vol. I, part 2, p. 833.

102 Valentinian III, *Novella* 17 (July 8, 445), in *PL* 54, 636–637.

103 Pope Gelasius I, *Epistula ad Anastasium*, in *PL* 56, 633.

4 SACRAMENTAL LIFE

On the Lord's Day, gather yourselves together and break bread, give thanks, but first confess your sins so that your sacrifice may be pure.

Didaché 14,1

4.1 House Churches

AUL'S LETTERS OFFER some important glimpses into the inner workings of ancient Christian churches. These groups did not own church buildings but met in homes, no doubt due in part to the fact that Christianity was not legal in the Roman world of its day. These homes were a domain in which women played key roles. The first "house churches" were private homes that were converted into Christian churches (or meeting houses) after the fact. These churches fully emerged in third-century Rome and became known in Latin as *domus ecclesiae*. These structures are closely tied to domestic Roman architecture of this period, specifically to the peristyle house, in which the rooms were arranged around a central courtyard.[1] These house churches had a central courtyard surrounded on three sides by a number of rooms. The rooms were often adjoined to create a larger gathering space that could accommodate small crowds of around fifty people. Other rooms were used for different religious and ceremonial purposes, including the celebration of the Mass, the baptism of Christian converts, storage of charitable items, private prayer and education. In the early Christian Church, catechumens were only permitted to partake in certain portions of Church liturgy, until they were baptized. For the remainder of their worship time, they were required to listen from a separate room. This necessitated the building of rooms situated directly outside but audibly proximal to the main worship rooms.[2] As a result, the

Roman peristyle home was extensively remodelled when it was converted into a Christian church.

When Christianity was legalized in the fourth century, Christians were no longer forced to use their homes as their churches and meeting places. Instead, they began to construct church buildings of their own. Even then, Christian churches often purposefully featured unassuming—even plain—exteriors, but they tended to be much larger, as the rise in the popularity of the Christian faith meant that churches needed to accommodate an increasing number of people.

4.2 The concept of sacrament

Certain sacred signs in the Old Covenant foreshadowed the sacramental economy brought about by Christ. In the New Testament, salvation and eternal life are transmitted through matter and the word, as is seen in St Paul's bridal imagery for the Church: "He made her clean by washing her with water with a form of words" (Ep 5:26). This divine life communicated by the sacraments of the new law is the fulfilment of the Old Testament promises: "How much more effectively the Blood of Christ, who offered himself as a perfect sacrifice to God through the eternal Spirit, can purify our inner self from dead actions so that we can do our service to the living God" (Heb 9:14).

St Paul's reference to the bridal imagery of Christ and His Church involved the expression "mystery", a term which is capable of various interpretations (See Ep 5:32). The Greek word *mystérion* which denotes mystery here, derives from the expression *muo* meaning "to shut the mouth". The expression *mystérion* in biblical terms refers to a hidden thing, a secret or a mystery, and in rabbinic writings denoted the mystic or hidden sense of an Old Testament saying or of an image seen in a vision. In its turn, the Latin word *sacramentum* renders the equivalent of *mysterion* in the Vulgate. The English word *sacrament* is a translation of the Latin word, which for the early Christians had the sense of something sacred, secret, involving initiation to some type of service. Among the Romans the expression was used specifically for the oath which soldiers took on entering the service of the emperor.[3] Tertullian (steeped in the Roman legal tradition) was one of the first to apply the word in the context of Christian rites, especially those of initiation.

Before the Church arrived at a unified vision of the sacraments it took nearly eleven centuries. During this time, it became necessary to distinguish the sacraments from other sacred realities in the life of the Church. The Greeks, following the Alexandrian school in the works of Clement of Alexandria and Origen, adopted the word *mystérion* or its plural *mystéria*. They thought in Platonic categories, according to which the world of the senses is a world of images and symbols, above which lies the true world of divine ideas. Origen employed the expression *mystérion* to refer to baptism and the Eucharist, and by the beginning of the fourth century this usage seems to be common. At the end of the fourth century, St John Chrysostom used the formulation "the mysteries" to refer to the Holy Eucharist. Unfortunately, among certain pagan rites such as those of Mithras, the cult was also described in terms of *mystéria*. As the pagan religions faded away, the word *mystéria* was used increasingly also in the West so that two words evolved into use for the idea of sacrament in the Latin West, *sacramentum* and *mysterium*.[4] Gradually, in the West, the word *sacramentum* became more favoured to describe the rites, while *mysterium* was used to denote the realities of the faith and salvation in themselves, like the mystery of the Holy Trinity.

Thereafter, in the West, controversies took place which refined the usage of the expression *sacramentum*. St Augustine forged the important distinction between sign (*signum*) and content (*res*). This distinction was used in the struggle against the Donatists. The Donatists arose from a development of the dispute between the See of Rome and that of Carthage concerning the re-baptism of apostates and heretics. St Cyprian and the Church in Carthage maintained that an apostate needed to be re-baptized. Pope Stephen I objected to this, because it was a departure from the Tradition of the Church. In the year 256, Pope Stephen wrote to Cyprian stating that, in accordance with Tradition, heretics should be reconciled by the sacrament of penance, and not by re-baptism.[5] Later, in the fourth and fifth centuries, the Donatists emerged in North Africa, denying the truth that Baptism is once and for all. The Donatists, while believing that re-baptism was necessary, twisted the doctrine of baptism to their own end, maintaining that as they really had the sacrament of baptism (and this could not be denied after Stephen I had spoken), then they were the Church of Christ. In this context, St Augustine gave the word *sacramentum* the refinements which have remained with it ever since. He distinguished between the sacramental sign (*signum*) and the grace content (*res*). In this formulation, the Donatists received the sacrament validly, but not the grace, as they put an obstacle in the way by opposing the true Church of Christ.

St Augustine stressed the visible sign aspect of the sacrament, and its relation to the spiritual reality which it signifies. Further steps in sacramental theology led to the medieval picture. Isidore of Seville (d. 636) distinguished more sharply than Augustine between sign and reality; although he employed the word sacrament in many senses, he was the first to offer the idea of sacrament to a unified picture of baptism, confirmation and the Eucharist.[6] St Isidore was therefore a bridge in sacramental theology linking St Augustine with medieval thought.

4.3 Baptism

Several early Christian texts bear witness to the existence of Baptism in the early Church. The *Didaché*, which dates from around 100 AD, speaks of a rite of immersion in running water, but also of a triple pouring of water on the head of the candidate.[7] St Hippolytus, writing around the year 215 gave a very detailed description of baptism as it was celebrated at Rome. A period of catechumenate, even as long as two or three years, prepared for the sacrament. The rite bore a remarkable resemblance to the ceremony as performed today, with the pre-baptismal anointings and exorcism, the profession of faith, the baptism by immersion and then a post-baptismal anointing. Account was taken also of infant baptism, in which the parents answered on behalf of their children. The whole of Tertullian's treatise on Baptism which is the oldest monograph on this sacrament, dating from the late second century, tacitly assumes that Christ instituted the sacrament.[8]

St Augustine clearly affirmed that Christ instituted the sacrament: "Baptism does not derive its value from the merits of the one who is baptized nor from the merits of the one who baptizes, but possesses its own holiness and power, by the merits of Him who instituted it."[9] Christ's institution of baptism was envisaged in terms of a gift by St Gregory Nazianzen who highlighted the various aspects of this sacrament:

> Baptism is God's most beautiful and magnificent gift...
> We call it gift, grace, anointing, enlightenment, garment of immortality, bath of rebirth, seal and most precious gift. It is called gift because it is conferred on those who bring nothing of their own; grace since it is given even to the guilty; Baptism because sin is buried in the water; anointing for it is priestly and royal as are those who are anointed; enlightenment because it radiates light; clothing since it veils our shame; bath because it washes; and seal as it is our guard and the sign of God's Lordship.[10]

The fifth century inscription by Pope Sixtus III on the marble work in the baptistery of the basilica of St John Lateran in Rome also indicates the divine origin of Baptism:

> With virginal generation the Church conceives her children by the power of the Holy Spirit and gives birth to them in water. If you wish to be innocent, be purified in this bath, whether you are burdened by personal or original sin. This is the font which bathes the whole world, and which takes the wounds of Christ for its origin. Hope in the Kingdom of Heaven, all you who are regenerated in this font.[11]

Ancient illustrated baptisteries as that of the Duomo in Florence, which depicts salvation history culminating in Christ, implicitly affirm the divine institution of baptism.

4.4 Confirmation

The very early Christian liturgies of initiation included a post-baptismal laying-on of hands and anointing, but it is not always clear whether this was a sacrament separate from Baptism. Even today in the current rite of Baptism of children, there is an anointing with chrism after Baptism, and this foreshadows the later Confirmation of the child. This anointing is a vestige of Confirmation from the rite of initiation of adults when all three sacraments of initiation were given together, and is applied with the following prayer:

> God the Father of Our Lord Jesus Christ has freed you from sin, given you a new birth by water and the Holy Spirit, and welcomed you into His holy people. He now anoints you with the chrism of salvation. As Christ was anointed Priest, Prophet, and King, so may you live always as members of His body, sharing everlasting life.

However, the distinction between the two sacraments became clear by the time St Hippolytus in his Treatise on the Apostolic Tradition, dating from about 215 A.D., referred to the Roman rite of initiation, in which two post-baptismal anointings took place. After baptism, the candidates came out of the font and were immediately anointed with the oil of thanksgiving by the priests who used the following words: "I anoint you with holy oil in the Name of Jesus Christ."[12] Then, afterwards, the second anointing which followed with consecrated oil, clearly seems to be Confirmation. After everyone had been dried and dressed, all went into the church, where the Bishop laid hands upon the candidates, and prayed over them. He then poured the conse-crated oil on each candidate and laid his hand on the head of each one, reciting the formula: "I anoint you with holy oil in God the Father Almighty and Christ Jesus and the Holy Spirit."[13] The bishop then sealed every candidate on the forehead and gave him a kiss of peace. This very early description of Confirmation is very similar to what occurs today. Tertullian referred to three distinct phases in the rite of Christian initiation, so that Confirmation was seen as a sacrament in its own right:

> The flesh is washed that the soul may be made spotless; the flesh is anointed so that the soul may be consecrated; the flesh is signed with the cross that the soul may also be protected; the flesh is overshadowed by the imposition of the hand that the soul also may be enlightened by the Spirit; the flesh feeds on the Body and Blood of Christ so that the soul as well may be replete with God.[14]

In the Christian East, around the middle of the fourth century, St Cyril of Jerusalem treated of the sacrament of Confirmation in his catechetical lectures:

> Now just as Christ was truly crucified, and buried, and raised again, and through Baptism, in virtue of a kind of likeness, you were accounted worthy of being crucified, and buried, and raised again, so too it is with the unction. He was anointed with the spiritual oil of gladness, that is with the Holy Spirit, who is the Oil of gladness since He is the Author of spiritual joy. But you were anointed with ointment, having been made partakers and associates of Christ.[15]

In the West, at the end of the fourth century, St Ambrose dealt with all the sacraments of initiation including Confirmation:

> Now after Baptism you went up to the bishop. Consider the anointing that followed. As David says: "It is like precious oil upon the head, running down upon the beard, running down upon Aaron's beard." You have received the spiritual seal. God the Father has sealed you, Christ has confirmed you, and the Spirit has given you the pledge in your heart.[16]

Thereafter, the theological development of Confirmation was greatly influenced by the thought of a certain Faustus who was Abbot of Lérins and then bishop of Riez in Southern France during the second part of the fifth century. One of his homilies had a great impact on the later medieval sacramental theology of Confirmation. His idea was that Confirmation equipped the Christian to be a soldier of Christ:

> Military proceedings require that when a commander receives a man into the number of his soldiers, he should not only put his mark upon him, but also equip him with arms suitable for fighting... So the Holy Spirit, who descended upon the baptismal waters bearing salvation, gave at the font all that is needed for innocence: at Confirmation He gives an increase of grace, for in this world those who survive through the different stages of life, must walk among dangers and invisible enemies. In Baptism we are born again to life, after Baptism we are confirmed for battle.[17]

4.5 The Holy Eucharist

4.5.1 Presence

In continuity with the realism concerning the Eucharist professed in the New Testament, the early Fathers expressed their faith in the real and substantial presence of Christ in this sacrament. In the first centuries, St Ignatius of Antioch, St Justin and St Irenaeus argued the real presence of Christ in the Eucharist against the Docetists, who did not believe in the reality of the Incarnation. It is highly significant also for the later history of theology that belief in the doctrine of God made Man is closely connected with Eucharistic faith. For when the Reformers denied the substantial presence of Christ in the Eucharist, that error was but a step away from denying the very dogma of the Incarnation. At the beginning of the second century, St Ignatius of Antioch taught that the Eucharist is the Flesh of our Saviour Jesus Christ, which suffered for our sins and which the Father raised from the dead.[18] About fifty years later, St Justin Martyr also affirmed, against the Docetists, the reality of Christ's presence in the Eucharist:

> We call this food the Eucharist... Not as ordinary food and drink do we partake of them, but just as, through the

word of God, our Saviour Jesus Christ became incarnate and took upon Himself Flesh and Blood for our salvation, so, we have been taught, the food which has become the Eucharist by the prayer of His word, and which nourishes our flesh and blood by assimilation, is both the Flesh and Blood of that Jesus who was made flesh.[19]

About thirty years later, St Irenaeus took for granted the reality of Christ's presence in the Eucharist:

Just as a cutting from a vine, planted in the earth, bears fruit in due season, and a grain of wheat, falling on the ground therein dissolves, and rises again with large increase by the Spirit of God who sustains all things, and thereafter, by the Wisdom of God, becomes fit for man's food, and at last receives the Word of God and becomes a Eucharist, which is Christ's Body and Blood, so too our bodies, nourished by the Eucharist, and laid in the earth there to suffer dissolution, will in due season rise again.[20]

In the middle of the fourth century, St Cyril of Jerusalem clearly taught that the bread and wine are changed into the Body and Blood of Christ. Nevertheless he was unclear as to when this change took place, linking it rather with the *epiclesis*.[21] St Gregory of Nyssa on the other hand, towards the end of the fourth century, taught the doctrine of the change in the elements of bread and wine and also indicated that the moment of consecration was linked with the words of institution: "Rightly then do we believe that now also the bread which is consecrated by the word of God is made over into the Body of God the Word."[22] During the same period, St John Chrysostom wrote about the Eucharistic change, which in some of his works he associated with the epiclesis, and in others with the words of institution:

Christ is present, and He who arranged that table (of the Last Supper) the very same even now arranges this table. For it is not man who brings about that the gifts which are set forth become the Body and Blood of Christ, but Christ Himself who was crucified for us.[23]

In the early part of the fifth century, St Cyril of Alexandria also taught the reality of the Eucharistic change, and moreover furnished reasons why the appearances of bread and wine remain:

> For lest we be stunned with horror on seeing flesh and blood set out on the holy tables of the churches, God condescends to our weakness and sends the power of life into the elements and transforms them into the power of His own flesh, that we may have and partake of them as a means of life, and that the Body of life may become in us a life-giving seed.[24]

In St Augustine's writings on the Eucharist, two tendencies are to be found. One of these highlighted the realism of continuity between Christ's flesh which hung upon the Cross and the Eucharistic Christ:

> From Mary's flesh He took flesh. And because in His very flesh He walked on earth, and because His very flesh He gave us to eat for our salvation—and no one eats that flesh unless he has first adored it—we find how ... not only do we not sin by adoring, but we sin by not adoring.[25]

On the other hand, St Augustine also emphasized the spiritual and sacramental manner in which Christ's flesh is to be eaten.: "Then it shall come to pass that the Body and Blood of Christ will be life to each one, when that which is received visibly in the sacrament is in very truth spiritually eaten, spiritually drunk."[26] Both aspects of St Augustine's thought are necessary to make up the full Catholic vision of the Holy Eucharist. The danger was that, in the later development, some thinkers exaggerated the spiritual aspect of the Eucharist, so drifting into mere symbolism.

There were then two tendencies in both Western and Eastern thought, the realist and the symbolist approaches. While St John Chrysostom and St Ambrose stressed the identity between the Christ of history, born of the Virgin Mary and the Eucharist, Origen highlighted the more symbolic side. So long as the tendencies were held together, as in St Augustine, the integrity of the faith was maintained.

4.5.2 Sacrifice

The teaching of the Letter to the Hebrews on the Priesthood and on Sacrifice of Christ stimulated Christian thought on the Eucharist as a Sacrifice.[27] From human religious experience, from the Scriptures and from Christian reflection, it can be seen that there are many elements contained in the idea of Sacrifice. The basic theme is that of making something or someone holy, and this comes from the Latin root of the words sacrifice and consecration. This action of making holy involves an offering to God, in terms of a sacrificial victim. However, someone must offer the victim and that person is the priest. The priest offers upon an altar of sacrifice, which is located in a holy place or a temple. The appropriate response in the sacrificial action is worship and adoration of God, in a context of commemoration and memorial, involving forgiveness of sins, expiation and atonement. The sacrifice is concluded with participation, union and communion.

Already in the *Didaché* (Teaching of the Twelve Apostles) which dates from around the year 100, the idea of the Sacrifice of the Mass can be found, though not of course in its fully developed form: "On the Lord's own day, assemble in common to break bread and offer thanks; but first confess your sins so that your sacrifice may be pure."[28] In his dialogue with Trypho around the year 150, St Justin Martyr regarded the Sacrifice of the Eucharist as the fulfilment of the prophecy of the prophet Malachi (Ml 1:10–12):

> God has therefore announced in advance that all the sacrifices offered in His name, which Jesus Christ commanded to be offered, that is, in the Eucharist of the Bread and of the Chalice, which are offered by us Christians in every part of the world, are pleasing to Him.[29]

St Irenaeus also referred to the Eucharist as the fulfilment of Malachi's prophecy: "Therefore the oblation of the Church, which the Lord taught was to be offered in the whole world, has been regarded by God as a pure sacrifice, and is acceptable to Him."[30] Tertullian, in his Catholic phase, referred to the Eucharist as a

Sacrifice, and is one of the oldest witnesses, around the beginning of the third century, to the offering of Mass for the dead.[31]

In the East, St Gregory Nazianzen developed the connection between the Sacrifice of the Mass and the spiritual sacrifice of the participant: "No-one is worthy of the great sacrifice and of the great High Priest of God, unless first he has made of himself a living and holy offering pleasing to God and offered to God a sacrifice of praise and a contrite heart."[32] St John Chrysostom expressed the link between the Sacrifice of Calvary and the Sacrifice of the Mass:

> For Christ is everywhere one complete Body. Just as He is one Body and not many bodies even though He is offered in many places, so too there is but one sacrifice. It is our High Priest who offered the sacrifice which cleanses us. So we offer now that which was then offered, and which cannot be exhausted.[33]

St Cyprian referred to the Eucharist as the memorial of the Lord's Passion:

> If our Lord and God, Jesus Christ, is Himself the High Priest of God the Father, and offered Himself as a Sacrifice to the Father, and commanded this to be done for a memorial of Himself, certainly that priest truly performs his office in the place of Christ who imitates that which Christ did, and then offers in the Church to God the Father a real and complete sacrifice.[34]

St Augustine maintained that Christ was mystically offered in the Mass:

> The whole redeemed city, that is to say, the congregation and community of the saints, is offered as a corporate sacrifice through the great Priest, who also offered Himself in His Passion for us, in the form of a servant, that we might be the body of so glorious a Head... This is the sacrifice which the Church continually celebrates in the sacrament of the altar.[35]

In his many writings, Augustine developed both the spiritual-dynamic and realist-objective ideas of the Sacrifice of the

Eucharist. Sometimes he emphasized one aspect and sometimes the other, so that at times he has been misinterpreted especially by those who over stress the spiritual aspect at the expense of the objective element.

Pope St Leo the Great clearly indicated that it was our Saviour's wish to found the Mass as a Sacrifice: "Christ instituted the Sacrament of His Body and Blood and taught that this sacrifice must be offered to God."[36] Faustus of Riez deepened further this theme that the Lord instituted the sacrament of His Sacrifice:

> And since Christ wished to remove His Body from our eyes and ascend to the heavens, it was necessary that He consecrate... the Sacrament of His Body and Blood, so that what was sacrificed once and for all as our Ransom, may be constantly worshipped in the mystery constantly renewed.[37]

Pope St Gregory the Great stressed the fact that the sacrifice of the Mass renews the Paschal Mystery in a salvific way: "Every time that we present to Him the sacrifice of His Passion, we renew His Passion for our redemption."[38]

The Greek Fathers highlighted the relationship between the Incarnation and the Eucharist. The school of Antioch identified the real Body of Christ, born of the Virgin Mary, crucified and risen with the Eucharistic Christ and thus put more stress on the Redemption, the saving action of Christ. On the other hand, the school of Alexandria saw the dignity of the Eucharist in terms of the Body and Blood of the Word which create union with Him and hence put more stress on the Incarnation.

In general, in the first Millennium of the Church the stress was on the event-character of the Eucharist, while in the Second Millennium the emphasis has been more on the objective content aspect. Both the aspects of being and of action have always been present in the Mass. Sometimes the Fathers adopted the expressions spiritual sacrifice or memorial for the Eucharistic Sacrifice, but this does not mean that they thought that the Eucharist was not the real Sacrifice of Calvary; it was only later, especially with the Reformers that there was a denial of the Sacrifice of the Mass.

4.6 Penance

On the basis of the well-known Gospel texts (Mt 13:16–19; 18:15–20 and Jn 20:21–23) as well as of the practice of the primitive community in excluding and re-admitting the sinner, there developed the Catholic doctrine of the sacrament of Penance. In the post-apostolic age as in the apostolic one, there was a clear distinction between everyday sins and grave ones. Perhaps in the early Church very grave sins were not that common, and it is in this context that the severe penitential practice of early Christianity must be evaluated. Theologically, according to ecclesial and theological tradition, for a Christian who is in a state of grace and participates in the normal sacramental life of the Church, the power of grace is such that he is not easily exposed to grave sin and this does not normally enter into Christian life.[39]

In the early Church, for serious sins, the penitential practice involved an exclusion from the Church community and a readmission; this period of exclusion can be seen as fostering a 'nostalgia' for the Church. Hence the sacrament of Penance was applied to those sins which we would call mortal or grave. There was no obligation to sacramental Penance in the case of venial sins. It was held by the Church that every sin, without exception, could be forgiven if the sinner was repentant. The question was how often could one be forgiven. Certain rigorist heretics opposed this position of the Church.

An early second century document, the *Didaché* or Teaching of the Twelve Apostles, taught that everyday or venial sins could be expiated by prayer, fasting, and almsgiving. All serious sins could be forgiven, by a process which seemed to have involved confession and also a period of separation from the community of the Church until repentance took place.[40] St Ignatius of Antioch drew attention to the same process, in which the bishop with his priests determined the penance which the penitent must perform: "The Lord forgives all those who mend their ways and return to union with God and to communion with their bishop."[41] The

Shepherd, written by Hermas (around the year 180), furnished the clearest description of the penitential practice of the Roman Church in the second century. The Church did not wish to publicise too readily the existence of a second chance of obtaining forgiveness for serious sins committed after baptism as this might have been seen as a loophole allowing people to sin. However, if Christians did go astray, all sins could be forgiven, even apostasy and adultery. In the *Shepherd*, Hermas stated that only one chance of repentance should be allowed to a Christian who has fallen into mortal sin; the fact that he opposed the offering of many chances, seems to imply that the Roman practice at that time was to allow more than one chance.[42] Hermas' reason for allowing only one chance of repentance after baptism was also connected with his belief that Christ would soon come again. St Irenaeus described confession for serious sins in which the sinner went to the bishop or a priest, who possess a type of judicial power. They must bring the sinner to conversion, inflicting a penance which could involve excommunication in certain cases. Public confession also included a public penance.

In the third century Christian East, the work known as the *Didascalia Apostolorum* maintained that all sins could be forgiven. A period of penance (a fast of two to seven weeks) was imposed after excommunication, followed by a reconciliation conveyed by the imposition of hands by the bishop.[43] Clement of Alexandria (who died before 215) explained that the difference between Baptism and later reconciliation lies in the fact that, in Baptism, God forgives sins through His pure divine mercy, while the baptized person who becomes a sinner again must make expiation for his sins before God will forgive him. In brief, in the East, the tendency was to follow Origen (of the Alexandrine school) for whom Penance had a pastoral and educational aspect, as a healing from sin. Nevertheless, the period of penance was longer than the baptismal catechumenate.[44]

In the Western Church of the third century, Tertullian (who died after 220) contributed writings which can be divided into two periods, one as a Catholic and the other as a Montanist.

During his Catholic phase, Tertullian traced a clear description of the penitential life of the Church. For him and for other Fathers the sacrament of Penance was the "second plank after the shipwreck of the loss of grace".[45] It is not clear from Tertullian's writings whether the confession of sins was public (namely, in front of the whole community) or only in front of the priests. However, the penance was always public, so that it was clear who was performing it. Tertullian in his period as a Montanist (from the year 205 onwards) became very severe, and considered that the three sins of murder, apostasy and adultery could not be forgiven. The Catholic bishops, on the other hand, admitted that serious sins as murder and apostasy could only be forgiven on the sinner's death bed after lifelong penance.

A great crisis which also led to clarification concerning penitential discipline was provided by the Novatian schism. The Roman priest Novatian joined forces with a rigorist minority in Rome and became the second anti-Pope. He maintained that the Church could not pardon certain sins even at the moment of death, but this error was condemned by the First General Council of Nicaea in the year 325, which also stated how reconciliation was to be offered to the Novatians. The Council also insisted that reconciliation was not to be denied to the dying.[46] The Novatian schism continued to plague Christendom for at least three centuries. St Cyprian (who died in 258) was one of many bishops who opposed the heresy of Novatian. In one of his letters, he stated that "the Church flourishes, crowned with so many virgins, and chastity and modesty keep the glorious tenor of their way, nor has the vitality of continence been destroyed because penance and pardon are allowed the adulterer."[47] More than any other Church Father of this period, St Cyprian taught the sacramentality of Penance, which involved three stages. The first part started with a private confession made to the bishop. A period of penance was then imposed upon the contrite sinner, which would include prayer, fasting, acts of charity and other renunciations. The second stage involved the request by the sinner to the bishop, clergy and the community to be readmitted to communion with the Church.

The third and final phase consisted of the reconciliation which occurs through the laying-on of the hands by the bishop. Those who were gravely ill could enjoy a less strict penitential discipline.[48] In the West, following St Cyprian, there followed a tendency to see Penance as expiation, satisfaction and ecclesiastical reconciliation.

Donatism, a further rigorist heresy, was opposed by St Augustine in the fifth century. The Donatist heresy included the false notion that the Church was only for the perfect so that if a Christian sinned gravely, he could not return to the Church. On the other hand, St Augustine maintained that a grave sinner need not be excommunicated in every case, but only if his sin aroused scandal. Nevertheless, every grave fault excluded the sinner from the Eucharist. Against the Donatist heresy, St Augustine also asserted that any bishop could forgive sins, not just a holy one, because the bishop does so in virtue of the power of orders. It is considered that St Augustine introduced private confession or at least paved the way for it. Further progress against rigorist tendencies came about during the same period when Pope Celestine I insisted that all those who so requested should have easy access to reconciliation at the moment of death.[49]

In the fifth century, St Leo the Great did not introduce private confession, but rather confirmed this existing practice for private sins:

> I order that all measures be taken to eradicate the presumptuous deviation from the apostolic rule through an illicit abuse of which I have learned of late. In the procedure of Penance... there should be no public confession of sins in kind and number read from a written list, since it is enough that the guilt of conscience be revealed to the priests alone in secret confession.[50]

From this declaration, it is clear that the safeguarding of the reputation of the penitent is of Apostolic tradition. However, Pope Leo did not say that penance had to be private; he was advocating private confession with a public penance in cases of sins which were not generally known. Even if people knew that someone was expiating a sin, they did not know what the offence was. Leo the Great also insisted on the necessary role of the priest in confession acting on behalf of Christ. Already in Leo's thought can be found the idea that confession, contrition and satisfaction are necessary components of the sacrament of Penance.[51]

In the East, a development away from public confession also took place, but for different reasons. At the end of the fourth century, the public confession of a lady of the upper classes who had been involved in a sexual relationship with a deacon gave great scandal to the populace, so that Bishop Nectarius of Constantinople suppressed the office of priest penitentiary (who had previously supervised the procedure for public penance) and decreed that each member of the faithful had to decide whether they were worthy to come to communion or not. Other local churches followed suit, and so the penitential apparatus of the primitive Church was gradually dismantled.

In conclusion, the penitential practice of the first six centuries can be summarized in the following terms. The first stage generally involved confession of the sin or sins which could be public or private. The general tendency was that confession became increasingly private in the West after St Leo the Great and in the East after Bishop Nectarius of Constantinople. The second phase consisted of a period of separation from the Church of varying length, during which the penitent was required to perform acts of mortification. The length of this period of penance depended on the gravity of the offence. St Basil stipulated twenty years penance for wilful murder, fifteen for adultery, seven years for fornication, two years for theft and lifelong penance for apostasy. The bishop enjoyed a certain discretion in reducing these penances especially for the fervent.[52] The special penitential practices which took place during the penitential period could involve prayers (especially the penitential psalms), fasting from meat or wine, the wearing of red clothes, almsgiving to the poor and abstinence from marital relations. The final stage involved the reconciliation of the penitents and this was often carried out on Holy Thursday. Generally this absolution took place after the period of penance, though it sometimes took place beforehand. In either case, the penance had to be completed before Holy Communion was received.

By the early part of the sixth century, a new penitential discipline had arrived from Ireland and England to France and thence to Spain. This new concept permitted reconciliation to penitents as often as they asked for it. The Third Council of Toledo reacted severely against the new approach, but it was only a regional council and the new way prevailed.[53] The new approach solved the problem of many Christians, who having fallen into grave sin, because of the heavy and disabling public penance, felt that they must wait until there was a danger of death before being reconciled. As a matter of fact, in the English and Irish Churches, the practice of "once-only" reconciliation and public penance never really became established.

In the penitential book of Bishop Theodore of Tarsus who was made Archbishop of Canterbury in 668, there was no ceremony of public reconciliation in the English Church because there was no public penance. Either Theodore imported into England the more lenient practices of his Greek Church of origin or he simply developed his system according to the Celtic approach which was already in force.[54] Hence, since there was no public exclusion and no obligation to perform humiliating public penances over a long period, and moreover since the sacrament could be often repeated, then logically it could also apply to small offences. Therefore, from the seventh and eighth centuries onwards, the practice of confessing venial sins developed. Monks from the British Isles brought this system over to the continent from the sixth century onwards, so that by the eighth century repeated confession had spread all over Europe. Penance books (or *penitentials*) also fixed the amount of satisfaction which sinners had to perform, thus taking this right away from the priest or the bishop. They contained some bizarre elements, and although penance was less severe than in the early Church, it was still rigorous by modern standards.

4.7 Anointing of the Sick

In the early centuries, relatively little was written concerning the Anointing of the Sick. One reason for this may be that while the sacrament of Penance was carried out publicly, Anointing was administered privately. Therefore the latter rite attracted less attention and required less explanation than the sacraments of Christian initiation and of Penance. Nevertheless, even in the very early centuries, there is evidence that the sacrament of the Anointing of the Sick took place.

In the *Apostolic Tradition*, dating from around the year 215 and attributed to Hippolytus, a rite for the blessing of the oil of the sick by the bishop was indicated at the end of the Eucharistic prayer.[55] Tertullian, during his Montanist phase, in the early part of the third century referred in an obscure passage to the fact that the Christian Proculus had healed Septimius Severus "with oil".[56] A letter written in the year 416 by Pope Innocent I to the Bishop of Gubbio indicated the understanding of Anointing of the Sick at that time. The Pope affirmed the continuity of this sacrament with the rite mentioned by the Apostle St James, and stated that the oil had to be blessed by the bishop; however, priests could also perform the anointing. Moreover, Innocent spoke of anointing carried out by lay people, but this must be considered as a sacramental rather than a sacrament, even though the distinction was not clear at that time. Nevertheless, the Anointing of the Sick was regarded as 'of the nature of a sacrament' since it could not be administered to someone undergoing Penance, and who was therefore excluded from the Eucharist.[57] Also in the fifth century, but in the East, St Cyril of Alexandria insisted on "calling in the presbyters" after the manner of the Letter of St James in the case of sickness.[58] Victor of Antioch described the significance of oil in the sacrament of Anointing:

> Now oil is both a remedy against fatigue and a source of
> light and gladness. And so the anointing with oil signifies

the mercy of God, a remedy for sickness and enlightenment of the heart.[59]

In the sixth century, St Caesarius of Arles exhorted the faithful,
in time of illness, to rely on the Eucharist and on the Anointing
of the Sick, rather than be tempted to invoke pagan rites:

> How much more correct and salutary it would be to hurry
> to the church, to receive the Body and Blood of Christ,
> and with oil that is blessed to anoint in all faith themselves
> and their dear ones; for according to what James the
> Apostle says, not only would they receive health of body,
> but also remission of sins.[60]

It is notable that Caesarius encourages lay anointing, and also
that Anointing was not restricted to those in danger of death. In
the eighth century, the Venerable Bede wrote the first extant
commentary on the Letter of St James. St Bede's references to
the Sacrament of the Sick indicate that anointing was carried out
by the presbyters, but also that lay people could make use of the
oil blessed by the bishop. He also seems to regard forgiveness
of sins as exclusively caused by the sacrament of Penance.[61] In
the early centuries, the oil which had been blessed by the bishop
was also employed by lay persons to anoint the sick and the sick
person could even anoint himself or herself with the oil. As time
went on, the distinction between this application of blessed oil
as a sacramental and its employment as the sacrament became
progressively clearer. By the Middle Ages, the oil was always
exclusively reserved to the priest or bishop in the context of the
sacrament of Anointing of the Sick.

4.8 Holy Orders

It is evident that the Apostles shared with others the sacrament
of Order which they possessed in its fullness. What remains less
clear is the concrete way in which they handed on their power
of Orders in the primitive Church. Not all scholars agree that
those who were designated with the title of overseer (*episcopos*)
in the apostolic era were in fact endowed with the fullness of

the priesthood.[62] Nevertheless, it is commonly held that at least Timothy and Titus, whom St Paul set over the churches of Ephesus and Crete, enjoyed episcopal orders. Titus was given the power of organizing the church in Crete and of appointing elders (*presbyteroi*) in the various towns (Tt 1:5).Timothy was reminded about the gift which he received in episcopal ordination: "You have in you a spiritual gift which was given to you when the prophets spoke and when the body of elders laid their hands on you; do not let it lie unused" (1 Tm 4:14). This text can be taken to indicate the laying-on of hands as a central rite in ordination, its collegial quality and also the sacramental character imparted thereby.

As regards the delineation of a second rank of the sacrament of order, there is a problem, namely that the Greek New Testament expressions elder (*presbyteros*) and overseer or presiding elder (*episcopos*), in the earliest times did not univocally correspond to the later terms priest and bishop.[63] Indeed in some passages, the overseers seem to be identified with the elders (Tt 1:5, 7; Ac 20:17, 28). What seems clear however, is that both in the Jewish-Christian communities and among the Gentiles, the primitive Christian communities were governed by a body of elders. It is probable that these elders were endowed with the fullness of the priesthood, so as to be able to confer the power of orders to other elders. In this primitive era, a high concentration of men of episcopal rank would have been necessary to ensure a rapid expansion of the Church. The spread of the Church would have required the convenient ordination of men to celebrate the Holy Eucharist. This rapidity of expansion and corresponding ordination is borne out by St Paul's prudent injunction to Timothy: "Do not be too quick to lay hands on any man" (1 Tm 5:22). The overseers and elders were appointed by the apostles (Ac 14:23) or their representatives (Tt 1:5) by the laying-on of hands (1 Tm 5:22), and their powers were of divine institution (Ac 20:28).

The body of elders gradually developed into communities ruled by one bishop and a college of priests; a system involving a monarchical episcopate would have been in place by about

100 AD. There may have also been some intermediate development but this is subject to a certain amount of speculation. In
other words, within a relatively short period, those with episcopal powers were regularly ordaining men of the second rank,
who enjoyed sacramental orders corresponding to the priesthood which we know today.

A further question regards the diaconate. The ordination of
the Seven described in the Acts of the Apostles (Ac 6:1–6), the
earliest existing account of an ordination, is accepted by many
theologians, right from the time of St Irenaeus, to refer to that
of deacons.[64] Nevertheless, there is another school of thought,
dating back to St John Chrysostom, which does not make this
rapid identification.[65] More recently some scholars consider that
the Seven were ordained presbyters.[66] However, the presence
of a diaconal office elsewhere in the New Testament (1 Tm
3:8–13) indicates that a lower rank of orders existed which was
associated with service (they should "carry out their duties
well") and preaching ("conscientious believers in the mystery
of faith"). It is possible that the *diaconos* mentioned in the New
Testament is also not yet the deacon known by the later Church,
but a figure endowed with a higher power of orders; however
he was entrusted with a specific role of service.

In conclusion, it can be proposed that the Apostles had all the
power of orders which they shared in different ways with those
whom they subsequently ordained. It is also accepted that in the
generation succeeding the Apostles a hierarchy of bishops, priests
and deacons was established everywhere in the early rapidly-
growing Church of Christ. At the beginning of the second century,
around 100 AD, St Ignatius of Antioch wrote about the threefold
sacrament of order: "Let everyone revere the deacons as Jesus
Christ, the bishop as image of the Father, and the presbyters as
the senate of God and the assembly of the apostles. For without
them, one cannot speak of the Church."[67] St Ignatius bore witness
to the monarchical episcopate at Antioch, in his letter to the
Ephesians: "Your justly respected clergy, who are a credit to God,
are attuned to their bishop like the strings of a harp, and the result

is a hymn of praise to Jesus Christ from minds that are in unison, and affections that are in harmony."[68]

4.9 Holy Matrimony

At the very beginning there was no specifically Christian form of Marriage, but Christians celebrated it like other people, in a ceremony presided over by the father of the family, employing simple rites and gestures like linking the hands of the man and woman. A Christian rite gradually developed. St Ignatius of Antioch remarked that the faithful should obtain the bishop's permission before contracting Marriage.[69] The aim of this injunction was to dissuade Christians from marrying non-Christians. Tertullian also bore witness to the fact that Marriage was contracted before the Church:

> How shall I be able to describe the happiness of a Marriage which the Church performs, the offering of the sacrifice ratifies, and the blessing seals, to which the angels assent, and which the heavenly Father recognizes.[70]

By the fourth century, there is evidence of a priestly prayer and blessing for the rite of Matrimony. In the Roman Church, the first examples of a nuptial Mass for the celebration of weddings date from the fourth and fifth centuries. The rite of veiling (*velatio*) received a liturgical significance early on: "Like the virgin who is betrothed to Christ, her only Spouse, a Christian woman who is being joined to a Christian man in Marriage received a veil from the hands of the Church as a sign of her new state."[71]

In the West, the Christian vision of Matrimony was bound up with ideas derived from Roman law. Within this perspective arose a problem as regards establishing the essential element from the juridical viewpoint. It became established that the consent of the couple was the determining factor. For this reason, until the time of the Council of Trent, so-called *clandestine* marriages were considered valid in the West. In Eastern Christendom, on the other hand, right from ancient times, priests and bishops actively participated in the celebration of Marriage, along with the parents of the couple or even replacing them. This procedure took place at the request of the families and with the approval of the state authorities. Gradually, some of the rites which were originally used in the family sphere were absorbed into the liturgical rites. Thus, in the East, it became accepted that the ministers of the mystery of Holy Matrimony were not only the couple, but essentially the priest or bishop.

The Tradition of the Church concerning Matrimony gradually but surely unfolded. From the third to the fifth centuries, three concepts were often repeated by the Fathers. One of these was that Christian marriage is a symbol of Christ and His Church, and this idea is found, for instance in the writings of St John Chrysostom and St Ambrose. A second notable theme is that marriage confers grace, as Tertullian and Origen did not hesitate to point out. Third, the elevation of Marriage to the order of grace occurred at the Marriage Feast at Cana, according to St Cyril of Alexandria and St Maximus of Turin.

Furthermore, St John Chrysostom stressed the complementary nature of marriage and virginity:

> Whoever denigrates marriage also diminishes the glory of virginity. Whoever praises it makes virginity more admirable and resplendent. What appears good only in comparison with evil would not be truly good. The most excellent good is something even better than what is admitted to be good.[72]

St Augustine stressed the goodness of marriage against the Manichaeans, who taught that matter in general and Marriage in particular were evil; he firmly stated that the three goods of Marriage were fidelity, children and a sacrament.[73] According to Augustine, the essential content (*res*) of Marriage is indissolubility, which reflects the indissoluble mystical union between Christ and His Church: "The essence of this Sacrament is that the man and the woman, united in marriage as long as they live, remain unseparated."[74] He also stressed the concept of Marriage as a remedy for concupiscence, in continuity with the Pauline idea that "if they cannot control the sexual urges, they should get married, since it is better to be married than to be tortured" (1 Co 7:9).

The Augustinian formulation was refined and broadened into a synthesis by St Isidore of Seville and this body of doctrine concerning Matrimony from a sacramental perspective was passed on to the medieval theologians.[75]

4.10 The date of Easter

The feast of Easter is the central celebration of Christian redemption in the life of the faithful. Two factors are especially responsible for this development: first of all the unfolding of the Easter festival itself, by increasing the duration of preparation and celebration; and, second, the administration of the sacrament of Christian initiation within the Paschal liturgy. The beginnings of this double movement extend back probably into the second century, since they are already apparent in an advanced stage early in the third. The sources which show this development most clearly, such as the Syrian *Didascalia*, some writings of Tertullian and the *Apostolic Tradition* of Hippolytus, belong in all instances to the third century. The homilies on the Psalms by Asterius the Sophist were in fact written in the early fourth century, but often reflect a state of liturgical development which can be ascribed to the late third century. Despite differences of emphasis in detail, considerable similarity of view concerning the root idea of the celebration of the Easter festival can be assumed in both the East and West. It commemorated the fundamental truths and facts of Christian redemption, which were conferred upon mankind by the death and triumphant Resurrection of the Lord.

Ecclesiastical history preserves the memory of three distinct phases of a dispute regarding the correct time of observing Easter. The essence of the Paschal controversy was, whether the Jewish Passover (be it a Friday or not), or the Christian Sunday, should determine the idea and time of the entire festival. The Johannine practice of Asia represented here the spirit of adhesion to historical precedent, and had the advantage of an immovable Easter, involving the Jewish tradition of the observance of a fixed day of the month. The Roman custom represented the principle of freedom and discretionary change, and the independence of the Christian festival system. Dogmatically stated, the difference would be, that in the former case the chief stress was laid on the Lord's Death; in the latter, on His Resurrection. However, the leading interest of the question for the early Church was not the astronomical aspect, nor the dogmatic one, but the liturgical one. The main object was to secure uniformity of observance, and to assert the originality of the Christian festive cycle, and its independence from Judaism; for both reasons the Roman usage at last triumphed even in the East. Thus Easter became a movable festival whose date varies from the end of March to the latter part of April.

4.10.1 First phase

The first phase was mainly concerned with the lawfulness of celebrating Easter on a weekday.

The Christians of Asia Minor, following the Jewish chronology, and appealing to the authority of the apostles John and Philip, celebrated the Christian Passover uniformly on the fourteenth of Nisan (which might fall on any of the seven days of the week) by a solemn fast; they fixed the close of the fast accordingly, and seem to have partaken on the evening of this day, as the close of the fast, of the Eucharist, as the Christian Passover and the festival of the redemption completed by the death of Christ. The Eucharist on the evening of the 14th (or, according to the Jewish mode of reckoning, the day from sunset to sunset, on the beginning of the 15th) of Nisan was celebrated in memory of the Last Supper of Christ. This observance did not exclude the idea that Christ died as the true paschal Lamb. For we find among the Fathers both this idea and the other that Christ ate the regular Jewish Passover with his disciples, which took place on the 14th.[76] From the day of observance, the Asiatic Christians were afterwards called *Quartadecimans* (fourteenthers).[77] Hippolytus of Rome speaks of them contemptuously as a sect of contentious and ignorant persons, who maintain that "the pascha should be observed on the fourteenth day of the first month according to the law, no matter on what day of the week it might fall".[78] Nevertheless the Quartadeciman observance was probably the oldest and in accordance with the Synoptic tradition of the last Passover of our Lord, which it commemorated.

The Roman Church, on the other hand, likewise appealing to early custom, celebrated the death of Jesus always on a Friday, the day of the week on which it actually occurred, and His Resurrection always on a Sunday after the March full moon, and extended the paschal fast to the latter day; considering it improper to terminate the fast at an earlier date, and to celebrate the communion before the festival of the Resurrection. Nearly all the other churches agreed with the Roman tradition in this observance, and laid the main stress on the resurrection-festival on Sunday. This Roman practice created an entire holy week of solemn fasting and commemoration of the Lord's Passion, while the Asiatic practice ended the fast on the 14th of Nisan, which may fall sometimes several days before Sunday.

The difference came to a head first on a visit of Polycarp, bishop of Smyrna, to Pope Anicetus, between 150 and 155 AD. It was not settled; yet the Pope and the bishop parted in peace, after the Pope had charged his venerable guest to celebrate the Mass in his church. There exists a brief, but interesting account of this dispute by Irenaeus, a pupil of Polycarp, which runs as follows:

> When the blessed Polycarp sojourned at Rome in the days of Anicetus, and they had some little difference of opinion likewise with regard to other points, they forthwith came to a peaceable understanding on this issue [the observance of Easter], having no love for mutual disputes. For neither could Anicetus persuade Polycarp not to observe inasmuch as he had always observed with John, the disciple of our Lord, and the other apostles, with whom he had associated; nor did Polycarp persuade Anicetus to observe his custom who said that he was bound to maintain the custom of the presbyters (bishops) before

him. These things being so, they communed together; and in the church Anicetus yielded to Polycarp, out of respect no doubt, the celebration of the Eucharist, and they separated from each other in peace, all the church being at peace, both those that observed and those that did not observe [the fourteenth of Nisan], maintaining peace.[79]

A few years later, about 170 AD, the controversy broke out in Laodicea, but was confined to Asia, where a difference had arisen either among the Quartadecimans themselves, or rather among these and the adherents of the Western observance. The accounts on this interim dispute are incomplete and obscure. Eusebius merely mentions that at that time Melito of Sardis wrote two works on the Passover. But these are lost, as also that of Clement of Alexandria on the same topic. The chief source of information is Claudius Apollinarius, bishop of Hierapolis, in Phrygia, in two fragments of his writings upon the subject, which have been preserved in the *Chronicon Paschale*. These are as follows:

There are some now who, from ignorance, love to raise strife about these things, being guilty in this of a pardonable offence; for ignorance does not so much deserve blame as need instruction. And they say that on the fourteenth [of Nisan] the Lord ate the paschal lamb (τὸ πρόβατον ἔφαγε) with his disciples, but that He himself suffered on the great day of unleavened bread [i.e. the fifteenth of Nisan]; and they interpret Matthew as favouring their view from which it appears that their view does not agree with the law, and that the Gospels seem, according to them, to be at variance. The Fourteenth is the true Passover of the Lord, the great sacrifice, of the Son of God in the place of the lamb... and who was buried on the day of the Passover, the stone having been placed upon his tomb.[80]

Here Apollinarius evidently protests against the Quartadeciman practice, yet simply as one arising from ignorance, and not as a blameworthy heresy. He opposes it as a chronological and exegetical error, and seems to hold that the fourteenth, and not the fifteenth, is the great day of the death of Christ as the true

Lamb of God, on the false assumption that this truth depends upon the chronological coincidence of the crucifixion and the Jewish Passover.

The controversy arose again, in a more vehement way, between 190 and 194, and extended over the whole Church, occasioning many synods and synodical letters. Pope Victor I, a very different man from his predecessor Anicetus, required the Asiatics, in a stronger tone, to abandon their Quartadeciman practice. Against this Polycrates, bishop of Ephesus, solemnly protested in the name of a synod held by him, and appealed to an imposing array of authorities for their primitive custom. Eusebius has preserved his letter, which is quite characteristic:

> As for us, then, we scrupulously observe the exact day, neither adding nor taking away. For in Asia great luminaries have gone to their rest, who shall rise again in the day of the coming of the Lord, when He comes with glory from heaven and shall raise again all the saints. I speak of Philip, one of the twelve apostles, who is laid to rest at Hierapolis; and his two daughters, who arrived at old age unmarried; his other daughter also, who passed her life under the influence of the Holy Spirit, and reposes at Ephesus; John, moreover, who reclined on the Lord's bosom, and who became a priest wearing the mitre, and a witness and a teacher-he rests at Ephesus. Then there is Polycarp, both bishop and martyr at Smyrna; ... and Melito the eunuch, who performed all his actions under the influence of the Holy Spirit, and lies at Sardis, awaiting the visitation from heaven, when he shall rise again from the dead? These all kept the passover on the fourteenth day of the month, in accordance with the Gospel, without ever deviating from it, but keeping to the rule of faith. Moreover I also, Polycrates, who am the least of you all, in accordance with the tradition of my relatives, ... I say, who am sixty-five years old in the Lord, and have fallen in with the brethren in all parts of the world, and have read through all Holy Scripture, am not frightened at the things which are said to terrify us. For those who are greater than I have said, "We ought to obey God rather than men." (Ac 5:29)[81]

Victor turned a deaf ear to this remonstrance, branded the Asiatics as heretics, and threatened to excommunicate them. However, many of the Eastern bishops, and even Irenaeus, in the name of the Gallic Christians, though he agreed with Victor on the disputed point, earnestly reproved him, and reminded him of the more brotherly conduct of his predecessors Anicetus, Pius, Hyginus, Telesphorus, and Sixtus. He dwelt especially on the fraternal conduct of Anicetus to Polycarp. Irenaeus proved himself on this occasion, a true peacemaker, and his vigorous protest seems to have prevented the schism. The Quartodeciman minority remained faithful to their previous practice throughout the whole of the third century, and the Novatians in Asia Minor followed them in this. The first canon of the Synod of Aries in 314 imposed the Sunday celebration of Easter. The Syriac Christians always held their Easter festival on the Sunday after the Jews kept their Pesach. On the other hand, at Alexandria, and seemingly throughout the rest of the Roman Empire, the Christians calculated the time of Easter for themselves, paying no attention to the Jews. In this way the date of Easter as kept at Alexandria and Antioch did not always agree. The Jewish communities in some places, possibly including Antioch, used methods of fixing their month of Nisan that sometimes put the 14th day of Nisan before the spring equinox. The Alexandrians, on the other hand, accepted it as a first principle that the Sunday to be kept as Easter Day must necessarily occur after the equinox.

4.10.2 Second phase

The second stage in the Easter controversy centres round the Council of Nicaea (AD 325). Granted that the great Easter festival was always to be held on a Sunday, and was not to coincide with a particular phase of the moon, which might occur on any day of the week, a new dispute arose as to the determination of the Sunday itself. The Council of Nicaea seems to have extended further the principle here laid down. We do not have its exact words, but we may safely infer from scattered notices that the council ruled:

1. that Easter must be celebrated by all throughout the world on the same Sunday;

2. that this Sunday must follow the fourteenth day of the paschal moon;

3. that that moon was to be accounted the paschal moon whose fourteenth day followed the spring equinox; that some provision should be made, probably by the Church of Alexandria as best skilled in astronomical calculations, for determining the proper date of Easter and communicating it to the rest of the world.[82]

This ruling of the Council of Nicaea did not remove all difficulties nor at once win universal acceptance among the Syrians. But to judge from the strongly worded canon I of the Council of Antioch, as also from the language of the Apostolic Constitutions and Canons, the Syrian bishops loyally co-operated in carrying into effect the decision of the Council of Nicaea. In Rome and Alexandria the lunar cycles by which the occurrence of Easter was determined was not uniform. Rome, after the hundred-and-twelve year cycle of Hippolytus, adopted an eighty-four year cycle, but neither gave satisfactory results. Alexandria adhered to the more accurate nineteen-year cycle of Meton. However, it seems to be clearly established that the lunar cycles were only considered to be aids towards ascertaining the correct date of Easter; also that where the calculations of Rome and Alexandria led to divergent results, compromises were made upon both sides and that the final decision always lay with accepted ecclesiastical authority.[83]

The Council of Nicaea had ruled that all churches should follow a single date for Easter, which should be computed independently of the Jewish calendar, as at Alexandria. However, it did not make any explicit ruling about the details of the computation, and it was several decades before the Alexandrine computations stabilized into their final form, and several centuries beyond that before they became normative throughout Christendom.

4.10.3 Third phase

The divergent cycles which Rome had successively adopted and rejected in its attempt to determine Easter more accurately led to the third stage in the Paschal controversy. The Roman missionaries coming to England at the time of Pope St Gregory the Great found the British Christians, the representatives of that Christianity which had been introduced into Britain during the period of the Roman occupation, still adhering to an ancient system of Easter computation which Rome itself had by then abandoned. The British and Irish Christians were not Quartadecimans, as some unwarrantably accused them of being, for they kept the Easter festival upon a Sunday. They are supposed to have observed an eight-four year cycle and not the 532 year cycle of Victorius which was adopted in Gaul, but it is quite difficult to determine what system they followed; possibly they derived their rule for determining Easter direct from Asia Minor. The story of this controversy, which together with the difference in the shape of the tonsure, seems to have prevented all fraternization between the British Christians and the Roman missionaries, is told at length in the pages of St Bede.[84]

The Roman missionaries coming to Britain in the time of Pope Gregory I (590–604) found the British Christians, who had been evangelized by Irish missionaries from the north, adhering to a different system of Easter computation from that used in the Mediterranean basin. This system, on the evidence of Bede, fixed Easter to the Sunday falling in the seven-day period from the 14th to the 20th of its lunar month, according to an 84-year cycle.[85] The limits of Nisan 14–Nisan 20 are corroborated by Columbanus.[86] The method used by the Roman Church had the limits of Easter between Nisan 15–Nisan 21. The 84-year cycle, the lunar limits, and an equinox of March 25 could have led to occasional discrepancies from the date of Easter as celebrated in the Alexandrine system.[87]

This 84-year cycle (called the *latercus*) gave way to the Alexandrine computus in stages. The Alexandrine computus may have been adopted in parts of the south of Ireland in the first half of the seventh century. In 630 Pope Honorius wrote to the Irish threatening excommunication if they did not conform to the Roman way of calculating Easter. As a result of this letter, the southern Church in Ireland held a synod in 632 at Magh Lene, or Old Leighlin as it is known today, in County Carlow. The synod probably took place at the site of Old Leighlin Cathedral which is built upon the ruins of an early monastic site founded by St Gobban in the early seventh century. At the time of the synod, St Laserian, the successor of Gobban, was the leader of the religious community there. The synod decided to send a delegation to Rome, including St Laserian. Upon their return, the southern Church decided to conform to the Roman Easter; however the northern Church did not conform until it was accepted by the archbishop of Armagh in the third quarter of the seventh century. Among the northern English, the use of the Alexandrine computus over the British and Irish cycle was decided at the Synod of Whitby in 664 AD.[88] The Alexandrine computus was finally adopted by the Irish colonies in northern Britain in the early eighth century.

Notes

[1] One of the oldest known house churches was built in Dura Europos in Syria, the far eastern edge of the Roman empire. The house was constructed by the first third of the third century and was converted for use as a Christian church at some point between 240 AD and 250 AD. The space could hold fifty to sixty Christian worshippers.

[2] See R. Krautheimer, *Early Christian and Byzantine Architecture* (Harmondsworth and New York: Penguin Books, 1979), p. 28.

[3] See, for example, A. Holbrook, *Loyalty and the Sacramentum in the Roman Republican Army* (Hamilton, Ontario: McMaster University, 2003).

[4] This fact is illustrated by the fact that St Ambrose wrote works involving both expressions, namely *De Mysteriis* and *De Sacramentis*. See St Ambrose, *De Mysteriis* in *PL* 16, 389–410; see Idem, *De Sacramentis* in *PL* 16, 409–462.

[5] Pope Stephen I, *Letter to Cyprian, Bishop of Carthage* in ND 1401.

[6] See A. Miralles, "Il tragitto patristico-medievale fino alla definizione classica di sacramento" in *Annales theologici* 10(1996), p. 337.

7   See *Didaché*, 7.

8   Tertullian, *De Baptismo* in CCL 1, 275–295.

9   St Augustine,*Contra Cresconium* 4, 19 in PL 43, 559.

10   St Gregory Nazianzen, *Oratio* 40, 3–4, in PG 36, 361.

11   The full inscription reads:
Gens sacranda polis hic semine nascitur almo,
quam foecundatis Spiritus edit aquis.
Virgineo foetu genitrix Ecclesia natosquos,
spirante Deo, concipit, mane parit.
Coelorum regnum sperate, hoc fonte renati:
non recipit felix vita semel genitos.
Fons hic est vitae, qui totum diluit orbem,
sumens de Christi vulnere principium.
Mergere, peccator, sacro purgande fluento;
quem veterem accipiet proferet unda novum.
Insons esse volens, isto mundare lavacro,
seu patrio premeris crimine, seu proprio.
Nulla renascentum est distantia, quos facit unum
unus fons, unus Spiritus, una fides.
Nec numerus quemquam scelerum, nec forma suorum terreat,
hoc natus flumine sanctus erit.
See also M. Schmaus, *Dogmatica Cattolica*. IV/1 *I Sacramenti* (Casale: Marietti, 1966), pp. 133–134.

12   St Hippolytus, *The Apostolic Tradition* 21, 19 as in *SW*, p. 8.

13   St Hippolytus, *The Apostolic Tradition* 22, 2 as in *SW*, p. 8.

14   Tertullian, *De Resurrectione Carnis*, cap. 8, 3 in CCL 2, 931.

15   St Cyril of Jerusalem, *Mystagogical Catecheses* 3, 2; in PG 33, 1089–1090.

16   St Ambrose, *De Mysteriis*, 6, 29; 7, 42; in PL 16, 398, 402–403. See Ps 133:2.

17   St Faustus of Riez, *Homily for Pentecost*. English translation from L. G. Walsh, *The Sacraments of Initiation* (London: Geoffrey Chapman, 1988), p. 141. Latin text from *Eusebius 'Gallicanus' Collectio homiliarum. De qua critice disseruit Iohannes Leroy* in CCL 101, 337–338: 'Ergo Spiritus Sanctus, qui super aquas baptismi salutifero descendit illapsu; in fonte plenitudinem tribuit ad innocentiam; in confirmatione augmentum praestat ad gratiam, quia in hoc mundo tota aetate uicturis inter inuisibiles hostes et pericula gradiendum est. In baptismo regeneramur ad uitam, post haptismum confirmamur ad pugnam; in baptismo abluimur post baptismum roboramur. Ac sic continuo transituris sufficiunt regeneration is beneficia, uicturis autem necessaria sunt confirmationis auxilia. Regeneratio per se saluat mox in pace beati saeculi recipiendos, confirmatio armat et instruit ad agones mundi huius et proelia reseruandos.'

18   St Ignatius, *To the Smyrnaeans*, 7 in *SW* p. 133.

19   St Justin, *The First Apology* as found in *SW* p. 133.

20   St Irenaeus, *Against the Heresies* Lib. 5, cap. 2, 3 in *PG* 7, 1127.

21   See St Cyril of Jerusalem, *On the Mysteries* 1,7 in *SW* p. 137.

22   St Gregory of Nyssa, *Catechetical Oration*, 37 in *PG* 45, 95–96. See also St Gregory Nazianzen, *Letter to Amphilochius*, 171 in *PG* 37, 279–282: "Cease not to pray and plead for me when you draw down the Word by your word, when in an unbloody cutting you cut the Body and Blood of the Lord, using your voice for a sword."

23   St John Chrysostom, *Homily 1 on the Betrayal of Judas*, 6 in *PG* 49, 380.

24   St Cyril of Alexandria, *Commentary on Luke 22:19* in *PG* 72, 911–912.

25   St Augustine, *Commentary on Psalm 98*, 9 in *PL* 37, 1264.

26   St Augustine, *Sermon 131*, cap. 1 in *PL* 38, 729.

27   See Heb 8:6–13 which deals with the themes of covenant and sacrifice and Heb 10:11–18 which treats of sacrifice, purification from sins and sanctification.

28   The *Didache* 14,1 as found in *SW*, p. 39.

29   St Justin Martyr, *Dialogue with Trypho*, 117 as found in *SW* 117.

30   St Irenaeus, *Adversus haereses* Lib. 4, cap. 18, 1 in *PG* 7, 1024.

31   See Tertullian, *On the Crown* in cap. 3, 3 in *CCL* 2, 1043.

32   St Gregory Nazianzen, *Oratio* 2, 95 in *PG* 35, 498.

33   St John Chrysostom, *Homily 17 on Hebrews*, 3 in *PG* 63, 131.

34   St Cyprian, *Epistle* 63, 14 in *SW* p. 186.

35   St Augustine, *The City of God* Lib. 10, cap. 6 in *PL* 41, 284.

36   Pope St Leo the Great, *Sermon* 58, cap. 3 in *PL* 54, 333.

37   St Faustus of Riez, *Sermon on the Body and Blood of Christ* in *PL* 30, 272.

38   Pope St Gregory the Great, *Homilia 37 in Evangelia*, 7 in *PL* 76, 1279.

39   See Pontifical Theological Commission, *La riconciliazione e la penitenza* (1982) C III.4 in Commissione Teologica Internazionale, *Documenti* (Vatican City: LEV, 1988), p. 415. See also St Thomas, *De Veritate* 27,1, ad.9.

40   See *Didaché*, 4:6,14; 8:1–3; 11:7, 14:1; 15:3 in *SC* 248, pp. 160–161, 164–165, 172–175, 184–185, 192–193, 194–195.

41   St Ignatius of Antioch, *Letter to the Philadelphians*, 8 in *PG* 5, 703–704.

42   Hermas, *The Shepherd* in *SC* 53, 158–163.

43   See *Didascalia Apostolorum*, 6 in *SF* pp. 61–62.

44   See *SF* p. 59.

45   See Tertullian, *De paenitentia* 4, 2 in *CCL* 1, 326. See also St Jerome, *Epistola 84 ad Pammachium et Oceanum*, 6 in *PL* 22, 748.

46   See Nicaea I, canons 8 and 13 in *ND* 1601–1602.

47   St Cyprian, *Epistle 55*, 20 in *SF* p. 52.

48   See St Cyprian, *On the Lapsed* in *PL* 4, 447–510.

49   Pope Celestine I, *Letter to the bishops of Narbonne and Vienne* in *ND* 1604.

50 Pope St Leo I, *Letter to the Bishops of the Roman rural districts* (459) in ND 1606.

51 See Pope St Leo I, *Letter to Theodore, Bishop of Frejus* (452) in ND 1605.

52 See St Basil, *Epistle 217 To Amphilochius* in SF pp. 75–76.

53 See Third Council of Toledo as found in ND 1607.

54 See SF pp. 147–148 for some extracts from the Penitential of Theodore. From this it can be seen that the period of penance for fornication was one year, for adultery four years, for homosexual acts ten years. Theft and manslaughter were punished with seven years of penance.

55 See Hippolytus, *Apostolic Tradition* V, 2 in SF p. 277.

56 Tertullian, *Ad Scapulam* 4, 5 in CCL 2, 1130.

57 See Pope Innocent I, *Letter to Decentius, Bishop of Gubbio* (416) in ND 1603.

58 See St Cyril of Alexandria, *On Adoration in Spirit and in Truth*, 6 in SF pp. 281–282.

59 Victor of Antioch, *Commentary on Mark 6:13* in SF p. 282.

60 St Caesarius of Arles, *Sermon 279*, 5 in SF p. 285.

61 See St Bede the Venerable, *On the Epistle of James*, 5 in SF, pp. 286–287.

62 See A. Piolanti, *I sacramenti* (Città del Vaticano: Libreria Editrice Vaticana, 1990), pp. 480–481.

63 See M. Schmaus, *I sacramenti* (Casale: Marietti, 1966), p. 665.

64 See St Irenaeus, *Against the heresies* Lib. 3, cap. 12, 10; Lib. 4, cap. 15, 1 in PG 7, 904–905, 1013.

65 See St John Chrysostom, *Homilia 14 in Acta Apostolorum*, 3 in PG 60, 116.

66 See J. Galot, *Theology of the Priesthood* (San Francisco: Ignatius Press, 1985), pp. 160–164.

67 St Ignatius of Antioch, *Letter to the Trallians*, 3 in PG 5, 677–678.

68 St Ignatius of Antioch, *Letter to the Ephesians*, 4 in PG 5, 735–736.

69 See St Ignatius of Antioch, *Letter to Polycarp*, 5 in PG 5, 723–724.

70 Tertullian, *Ad uxorem*, Lib. 2, 8, 6 in CCL 1, 393.

71 J. McAreavey, *The Canon Law of Marriage and the Family* (Dublin: Four Courts Press, 1997), p. 148.

72 St John Chrysostom, *De virginate*, 10 in PG 48, 540.

73 See St Augustine, *De nuptiis et concupiscentiis*, Lib. 1, cap. 11, 13 in PL 44, 421; Idem, *De bono coniugali*, 24, 32 in PL 40, 394.

74 St Augustine, *De nuptiis et concupiscentiis*, Lib. 1, cap. 11, 10 in PL 44, 420.

75 See St Isidore of Seville, *De ecclesiasticis officiis*, Lib. 2, cap. 20 in PL 83, 809–814.

76 See, for example, St Irenaeus, *Against the Heresies*, II, 22, 3; Tertullian, *On Baptism*, 19. St Paul first declared Christ to be our Passover (1 Co 5:7), and yet his companion Luke, with whom his own account of the institution of the Lord's Supper agrees, represents Christ's Passover meal as taking place on the 14th.

77   See Ex 12:6; Lv 23:5, where this day is prescribed for the celebration of the Passover. Hence Τεσσαρεσκαιδεκατῖται in Greek, in Latin, Quartadecimani.

78   St Hippolytus, *Refutation of all Heresies*, VIII, 18.

79   St Irenaeus, *Letter to Pope Victor*, cited by Eusebius of Caesarea, *Church History*, V, xxiv.

80   L. A. Dindorf, *Chronicon Paschale* (Bonn: Weber, 1832), I, 13 in *Corpus Scriptorum Historiae Byzantinae*.

81   Polycrates of Ephesus, *Letter to Pope Victor and the Roman Church*, as found in Eusebius, *Ecclesiastical History*, V, 24.

82   See Pope St Leo, *Letter to the Emperor Marcian* in *PL* 54, 1055.

83   H. Thurston, "Easter Controversy" in *The Catholic Encyclopedia* (New York: Robert Appleton Company, 1909). Retrieved 8 February 2016 from New Advent: http://www.newadvent.org /cathen/05228a.htm.

84   The *tonsure* is the shaving of the head or of some part of it as a religious practice or rite, especially in preparation for entering the priesthood or a monastic order.

85   St Bede, *Church History of the English People*, 2,2.

86   St Columbanus, *Letter to Pope Gregory*, in *A Select Library of Nicene and Post-Nicene Fathers of the Christian Church*, Second Series, Volume 13, p. 40.

87   D. McCarthy, "Easter Principles and a Fifth-Century Lunar Cycle used in the British Isles" in *Journal for the History of Astronomy* 24 (1993), pp. 204–224.

88   St Bede, *Church History*, 3,25.

5 EARLY CHRISTIAN MARTYRS

The blood of the martyrs is the seed of the Church.

Tertullian, *Apologeticus*, Chapter 50

The long and bloody war of heathen Rome against the Church, which is built upon a rock, utterly failed. It began in Rome under Nero, it ended near Rome at the Milvian bridge, under Constantine. Aiming to exterminate, it purified. It called forth the virtues of Christian heroism, and resulted in the consolidation and triumph of the new religion.

Philip Schaff, *Church History*

THE CHRISTIAN FAITH developed rapidly in Rome and all over the world from the first century, owing to its being original and suitable for all mankind; but this was also due to the testimony of fervour, of brotherly love and of charity shown by the Christians towards everybody.

The Roman authorities were at first indifferent to the new religion, yet very soon they became hostile, also because the Christians refused to worship the ancient pagan deities of Rome, as well as the emperor. The Christians were falsely accused of disloyalty to their fatherland, of atheism, of hatred towards mankind, of hidden crimes, such as incest, infanticide and ritual cannibalism; likewise they were held responsible for many natural calamities, such as plagues, floods, famines.

The first three centuries constitute the age of Martyrs, which ended in 313 AD with the edict of Milan, by which the emperors Constantine and Licinius gave freedom to the Church. The persecution was not always continuous and universal, nor equally cruel and bloody. Periods of martyrdom were followed by times of relative peace. Christians faced persecution with courage, a very large percentage with heroism, but they did not submit to it without opposition. They defended themselves with great strength by confuting the accusations of those crimes as being false and groundless and by outlining the contents of their faith (*What we believe*) and describing their identity (*Who we are*).

It will be helpful to see what was the prevalent attitude towards Christianity and Judaism, prior to the persecution of the Church. First, Judaism, despite being monotheistic, had been recognised as a *religio licita* (legitimate religion) by Julius Caesar and had been awarded privileges by him and by subsequent rulers. The Jews were permitted to have civil jurisdiction over their own territory; thus making them almost a state within the larger Roman state. The destruction of the Temple at Jerusalem in 70 AD did not have a devastating effect on Judaism in general. The Jews continued to be protected by the State, mainly because of their usefulness to the economy. There were, however, times when they were not in favour with the populace and frequently bore the brunt of cruel taunts and wicked insinuations denigrating their faith. On occasion, they even suffered physical violence at the hands of illegal mobs. Judaism, despite occasional opposition, continued to thrive. At one time in Rome—due to the decline of the pagan religions—it became fashionable to convert to Judaism. This trend ended with the edicts issued by Hadrian and Septimius Severus which banned proselytism.

The early Christian Church was, from its beginning until the persecution by Nero in 64 AD, tolerated by the Roman authorities who regarded it as merely another Jewish sect. Thus, Christianity received the same protection and privileges from Roman law that Judaism did. However, the relationship between the Church and Judaism was far more tempestuous—as can be seen within the Acts of the Apostles. It was from the Jews that the early Church was to suffer persecution. The Roman authorities ignored this; viewing it as an insignificant argument between two factious groups of Jews. Comparing the Synoptics with John's Gospel a change of emphasis may be seen. Within the Synoptics the Scribes and Pharisees were the primary persecutors of the Christians. However, in John's Gospel the Jews, as a whole, are spoken of as being the sole persecutors. In none of the Gospels are the Romans referred to as persecuting the Christian Church.

To this Jewish period belong the Holy Innocents as early martyrs for Christ. The Massacre of the Innocents is an episode of infanticide by Herod that appears in the Gospel of Matthew (Matthew 2:16–18). Matthew relates that King Herod ordered the execution of all young male children in the village of Bethlehem, so as to avoid the loss of his throne to the newborn King of the Jews whose birth had been announced to him by the Magi. The Feast of the Holy Innocents is kept on 28 December.

Saint Stephen is known as the first martyr of Christianity. The Acts of the Apostles recount how Stephen was tried by the Sanhedrin for blasphemy against Moses and God (Acts 6:11) and speaking against the Temple and the Law (Acts 6:13–14) and he was then stoned to death (c. 34–35 AD) by an infuriated mob encouraged by Saul of Tarsus, the future Saint Paul: "Saul entirely approved of putting him to death" (Ac 8:1). Stephen's final speech charged the Jews with continuing to persecute the prophets who spoke out against their sins: "Which one of the Prophets did your fathers not persecute, and they killed the ones who prophesied the coming of the Just One, of whom now, too, you have become betrayers and murderers" (Ac 7:52). The feast day of St Stephen is kept on 26 December.

5.1 Motives for persecution

We now discuss the motives behind the violent hatred displayed by the Romans towards Christianity. Seven possible motives can be proposed. The first is that of the exclusive and separatist nature of Christianity as viewed by the pagan world. The Christians were regarded by both the common people and the authorities as being separatists. The Christian lifestyle seemed distanced from that of the pagan world. Nevertheless, Christians did not distance themselves so far from the world, as a contemporary description of the Christian community shows: "They pass their lives in whatever township—Greek or foreign—each man's lot has determined: and conform to ordinary local usage in their clothing, diet, and other habits." The letter goes on to describe the uniqueness of the Christian in his attitude to persecution, generosity, and so forth.[1]

Second, believers looked to the immediate needs of their fellow Christians and exhorted one another to be gainfully employed, not idle.[2] The believer did, however, exclude himself from certain professions, such as acting, gladiatorial fighting and, in some cases, even teaching. The most significant problem appertaining to employment was whether or not a Christian could serve in the army. Tertullian, for example, urged that believers should not: Origen and Lactantius also shared this belief. There was a particular dilemma that faced the Christian soldier, especially those of rank. For example, a centurion was duty-bound to participate in and to witness pagan sacrificial ceremonies. If he did not comply he would lose his office and, most probably, his life.[3] The army was a prime target whenever persecution was to break out; many Christian soldiers lost their lives rather than deny their faith.[4] Indeed it was the questionable loyalty of some sections of the army that was one of the contributory factors in the Great Persecution under Diocletian and Maximian.

The third area to be examined is that of the pagan misunderstanding of the rites and ceremonies of the Christian Church. Christians were singled out as being a "gang of ignorant men and credulous women".[5] They were noted for their stubbornness or "mere contumacy",[6] and were persecuted and hated for their "name".[7] A regular accusation propagated against Christianity was that of atheism. Christianity, because of its monotheistic faith, would not offer the customary sacrifices and worship to other gods: a duty of Roman subjects. Justin Martyr wrote: "Hence are we called atheists. And we confess that we are atheists, so far as gods of this sort are concerned, but not with respect to the most true God."[8] The necessary secrecy surrounding the believer's meetings then aroused suspicion; the rites and ceremonies were interpreted as immoral. The *agape*, or love feast, a name for the Eucharist was regarded as an orgy and as Athenagoras records: "Three things are alleged against us: atheism, Thyestean feasts [cannibalism], Oedipodean intercourse [incest]."[9] Thus even the Eucharistic rite was believed to be an act of cannibalism. The Christian *kiss of charity* was also misunderstood.[10]

Other religions, such as Mithraism, the worship of Isis and other pagan gods endeavoured to take precautions against persecution. The Church, however, did not conform nor compromise to avoid danger; indeed Christians were observed to adopt a deliberately aggressive attitude towards the State, inciting and deliberately seeking martyrdom. Often Christians were punished for when misfortune took place, like natural disasters and defeat in battle; the logic behind this was that the pagan gods had been offended by the Christian's atheism and were making the people suffer as a result. Christianity was reported as being a "foreign superstition"[11] possessing a "new and mischievous religious belief".[12]

The fourth factor that induced anger from the populace was the Church's eschatology by which they believed that the Lord would come again in glory as Judge and King, to judge the living and the dead. This belief deeply challenged the pagan, who, according to Christian teaching, was doomed. The Church taught that upon the fall of the sinful world the reign of the saints would begin.[13] It is worth noting that the instructions concerning the Eucharist, contained within the *Didaché*, close with the word *Maranatha*, meaning "come O Lord".[14] This shows the early Church's expectation and desire for Christ's return.

A fifth aspect that aroused concern for the Roman authorities was the Christian attitude to wealth and property. It is possible that the Christian community had gradually begun to acquire some wealth. This was perhaps gained by abstention from the excesses of the pagan world, which for the Christian led to a more frugal existence than that of his contemporaries in Roman

society. Of prime concern was the Church's radical view concerning the position and treatment of slaves. The slave was
considered by pagans to be a mere chattel: a possession with no
rights or liberties. The teaching of the Church, however, was that
slaves were no longer to be regarded in such a way. The slave
was to be accepted as a brother and an equal.[15] As Chadwick
writes: "In the Church masters and slaves were brethren."[16] It
was not unusual for emancipated slaves to rise to positions of
importance within the Church, some being appointed as deacons, priests and even bishops or popes, like Pope Callixtus.
Such people became highly respected members of the Church.

The Christian attitude towards wealth and property ran
contrary to the materialistic position held by many pagans.
Indeed, wealth was considered to be a hindrance to those who
held high office within the Church. Many advocated that
poverty was a prerequisite for those of rank within the faith.
This appeared to the State to be nothing less that anarchy.

The threat to the established pattern of family life was a sixth
sphere of Christian influence that challenged many unbelievers.
Some felt that Christian teaching, such as St Paul's, actively
discouraged marriage.[17] Any inter-marriage between Christian
and pagan was forbidden and in some cases Christians
attempted to divorce their unbelieving partners.[18] Those who
remained with their partners were a source of much concern and
consternation. The pagan Apollo, in reply to a question of how
to recall a wife from Christianity said that one would more
"probably find it easier to write lasting characters on the water,
or lightly fly like a bird through the air, than to restore right
feeling in your impious wife once she has polluted herself".[19]
Another problem was that of burial rites. A decision had to be
made as to whether the deceased would be given a Christian or
a pagan funeral. Many families were split because of this, for
those who had both pagans and Christian believers within them
it was impossible to satisfy both parties.

In the seventh place, the political threat posed by the Church
will be considered. Throughout the whole period of persecution

there hung continually a question mark over the loyalty of Christians to the State. The Roman authorities were sensitive to unrest, as the expulsion of the Jews from Rome under Claudius reveals. Complete submission and obedience was a pre-requisite for peaceful relations with the authorities; Christians gave neither to the State, for their allegiance lay with God. The Church was looking "forward to the day of God" (2 Pt 3:12) and had made its own laws—described, for example, in the *Didaché*—and would not countenance any secular law that contradicted its own. Celsus, a notable opponent of Christianity, pointed out this failure to comply with the required homage demanded by the State.[20] This refusal was to be a major issue, leading to the martyrdom of many faithful believers who resolutely refused to participate in Roman civic and national ceremonies. The Christian would not offer worship to either throne or State and this was interpreted as treason and disloyalty. The problem increased for the State since the Church, despite policies of persecution against it, continued to flourish in wealth, influence and number.[21] It was partly because of this rapid growth that the second period of more general persecutions was instigated in which the State endeavoured to crush and eradicate the growing Church.

5.2 *Periods of persecution*

From the fifth century it has been customary to reckon ten great persecutions: under Nero, Domitian, Trajan, Marcus Aurelius, Septimius Severus, Maximinus, Decius, Valerian, Aurelian, and Diocletian.[22] This number was suggested by the ten plagues of Egypt taken as types, and by the ten horns of the Roman beast making war with the Lamb, taken for so many emperors.[23] Only two imperial persecutions—those, of Decius and Diocletian—extended over the empire; but Christianity was always an illegal religion from Trajan to Constantine, and was subject to persecution and violence everywhere.

In this text, we aim to ouline twelve periods of Roman persecution. Within these periods, we can identify two distinct eras. The first era stretched from Nero in 64 to the end of the reign of Maximinus in 238. The second era extended from the Decian persecution of 249 through to the signing of the *Edict of Milan* in 313. The first era, in comparison with the second, was neither as systematic nor as relentless, being more sporadic and localised: the result of transient animosity rather than clearly defined legislation against Christianity. The persecutions during this period were, although at times ferocious, less severe and had less effect upon the Church than did the period that followed. The second period began with the emperor Decius, who had inherited an Empire in which the Christian Church had grown significantly in size and influence. Decius started a campaign in which he hoped that Christianity would be eradicated. Thus began a policy of general persecution against the Church that was to be continued by later emperors. It was during this period that many were to be martyred; shedding their blood in defiance of the Roman State. During this period, as with the first, there were seasons of apparent tranquillity which were broken by renewed hostility that was savage in its intensity, if not, at times, in its extent.

5.2.1 First period: Nero and Vespasian

The first period extended during the reign of the emperor Nero (64–68 AD). In this late New Testament period, the number of Christians grew, and the separation from Judaism became more apparent. The first documented case of imperial persecution of the Christians in the Roman Empire begins with Nero (37–68). A six-day fire burned much of Rome in July 64 AD, destroying portions of the city and economically devastating the Roman population. Nero was rumoured at the time of having intentionally started the fire himself, in order to remodel Rome. After a good start to his reign Nero had become unpopular and much feared; as much by his family as by the people. He led a life of excess and had carelessly drained the treasury. He then resorted to subterfuge, extortion and many dubious devices to replenish his much depleted funds.[24] In his *Annales*, Tacitus states that "to get rid of the report, Nero fastened the guilt and inflicted the most exquisite tortures on a class hated for their abominations, called Christians by the populace".[25] The apostles Saint Peter and Saint Paul were martyred in Rome during this persecution. Gruesome forms of execution used by the Romans included burning, systematic murder, crucifixion, and the feeding of Christians to dogs and other wild beasts. Tacitus' *Annales* record how

> a vast multitude, were convicted, not so much of the crime of arson as of hatred of the human race. And in their deaths they were made the subjects of sport; for they were wrapped in the hides of wild beasts and torn to pieces by dogs, or nailed to crosses, or set on fire, and when day declined, were burned to serve for nocturnal lights.[26]

While Vespasian was preparing to besiege the city of Jerusalem, emperor Nero committed suicide, plunging the empire into a year of civil war known as the Year of the Four Emperors. After the emperors Galba and Otho perished in quick succession, Vitellius became emperor in April 69 AD. In response, the armies in Egypt and Judaea declared Vespasian emperor on 1 July. On 20 December, Vitellius was defeated, and the following day Vespasian was declared emperor by the Roman Senate.

To Vespasian's reign is ascribed the martyrdom of Saint Apollinaris. The Roman Martyrology describes him as a bishop who spread among the nations the profound riches of Christ, led his flock as a good shepherd and honoured the Church of Classis near Ravenna by a glorious martyrdom.

According to tradition, Saint Apollinaris was a native of Antioch in Roman Province of Syria. As the first Bishop of Ravenna, he faced nearly constant persecution. He and his flock were exiled from Ravenna during the persecutions of Emperor Vespasian (or Nero, depending on the source). He was made Bishop of Ravenna by Saint Peter himself. It is not certain that he was one of the seventy-two disciples of Christ, as has been suggested. The precise date of his consecration cannot be ascertained, but he was believed to have been Bishop of Ravenna for twenty-six years.

The miracles he wrought there soon attracted official attention, for they and his preaching won many converts to the Faith, while at the same time bringing upon him the fury of the idolaters, who beat him cruelly and drove him from the city. He was found half-dead on the seashore, and kept in concealment by the Christians, but was captured again and compelled to walk on burning coals and a second time expelled. Nevertheless, he remained in the vicinity, and continued his work of evangelization. He then journeyed in the Roman province of Aemilia (now Emilia in Italy). A third time he returned to Ravenna. Again he was captured, hacked with knives, had scalding water poured over his wounds, was beaten in the mouth with stones because he persisted in preaching, and was flung into a horrible dungeon, loaded with chains, to starve to death; but after four days he was put on board a ship and sent to Greece.

There the same course of preachings, miracles and sufferings continued; and when his very presence caused the oracles to be silent, he was, after a cruel beating, sent back to Italy. All this continued for three years, and a fourth time he returned to Ravenna. The emperor Vespasian, in answer to the complaints of the pagans, issued a decree of banishment against the Christians. Apollinaris was kept concealed for some time, but as he was passing out of the gates of the city, was set upon and savagely beaten, probably at Classis, a suburb, but he lived on for seven days, foretelling meantime that the persecutions would increase, but that the Church would ultimately triumph.

5.2.2 Second period: Domitian

The second period of persecution occurred under Domitian (81–96 AD). According to many historians, Jews and Christians were heavily persecuted toward the end of Domitian's reign. The Book of Revelation is thought by many scholars to have been written during this period; here St John urges faithful endurance and assures of God's victory (Rv 3:10–12).

Domitian was a suspicious and blasphemous tyrant, accustomed to call himself and to be called "Lord and God", treated the embracing of Christianity a crime against the state, and condemned to death many Christians, even his own cousin, the consul Flavius Clemens, on the charge of atheism; or confiscated their property, and sent them, as in the case of Domitilia, the wife of the Clemens just mentioned, into exile. His jealousy also led him to destroy the surviving descendants of David; and he brought from Palestine to Rome two kinsmen of Jesus, grand-sons of Jude, the "brother of the Lord", but seeing their poverty and rustic simplicity, and hearing their explanation of the kingdom of Christ as not earthly, but heavenly, to be established by the Lord at the end of the world, when He should come to judge the living and the dead, he let them go. Tradition (in St Irenaeus, Eusebius, St Jerome) assigns to the reign of Domitian the banishment of John to Patmos. Tertullian and Jerome attest St John was brought to Rome during the reign of the emperor Domitian, and was thrown in a vat of boiling oil near the Latin Gate, from which he was miraculously preserved unharmed.[27]

Domitian's humane and justice-loving successor, Nerva (96–98), recalled the banished, and refused to treat the confession of Christianity as a political crime, though he did not recognise the new religion as a *religio licita*.

5.2.3 Third period: Trajan

The third period of persecution came about under the emperor Trajan (98–117). Trajan, one of the best and most praiseworthy emperors, honoured as the "father of his country", but, like his friends, Tacitus and Pliny, wholly ignorant of the nature of Christianity, was the first to pronounce it a *proscribed religion*, as it had been all along in fact. He revived the rigid laws against all secret societies, and the provincial officers applied them to the Christians, on account of their frequent meetings for wor-ship. His decision regulated the governmental treatment of the Christians for more than a century. It is embodied in his correspondence with the younger Pliny, who was governor of Bithynia in Asia Minor from 110 to 113. Pliny came in official contact with the Christians. He himself saw in that religion only a "depraved and immoderate superstition", and could hardly account for its popularity. He reported to the emperor that this superstition was constantly spreading, not only in the cities, but also in the villages of Asia Minor, and captivated people of every age, rank, and sex, so that the temples were almost forsaken, and the sacrificial victims found no sale. To stop this progress, he condemned many Christians to death, and sent others, who were Roman citizens, to the imperial tribunal. But he requested of the emperor further instructions, whether, in these efforts, he should have respect to age; whether he should treat the mere bearing of the Christian name as a crime, if there were no other offence. Pliny wrote to Trajan as follows:

> Meanwhile, in the case of those who were denounced to me as Christians, I have observed the following proce-
> dure: I interrogated these as to whether they were Chris-
> tians; those who confessed I interrogated a second and a
> third time, threatening them with punishment; those who
> persisted I ordered executed. For I had no doubt that,
> whatever the nature of their creed, stubbornness and
> inflexible obstinacy surely deserve to be punished. There
> were others possessed of the same folly; but because they
> were Roman citizens, I signed an order for them to be
> transferred to Rome.[28]

To these inquiries Trajan replied:

> You have adopted the right course, my friend, with regard
> to the Christians; for no universal rule, to be applied to
> all cases, can be laid down in this matter. They should not
> be searched for; but when accused and convicted, they
> should be punished; yet if any one denies that be has been
> a Christian, and proves it by action, namely, by worship-
> ping our gods, he is to be pardoned upon his repentance,
> even though suspicion may still cleave to him from his
> antecedents. But anonymous accusations must not be
> admitted in any criminal process; it sets a bad example,
> and is contrary to our age.[29]

This decision seemed much milder than might have been expected from a heathen emperor of the Roman type. Tertullian charges it with self-contradiction, as both cruel and lenient, forbidding the search for Christians and yet commanding their punishment, thus declaring them innocent and guilty at the same time. However the emperor evidently proceeded on political principles, and thought that a transient and contagious enthusiasm, as Christianity in his judgment was, could be suppressed sooner by leaving it unnoticed, than by openly assailing it. He wished to ignore it as much as possible; but every day it forced itself more and more upon public attention, as it spread with the irresistible power of truth.

During this period, St Ignatius of Antioch was martyred. St Ignatius, also called Theophorus (the Greek Θεοφόρος means "God-bearer"), according to tradition succeeded Evodius, the first bishop of Antioch after St Peter.[30] Nothing is known for certain of his youth or even of his episcopate. It is surmised that he was born a pagan and became converted to the faith later in life. He was bishop of Antioch when a persecution, the cause of which is unknown to us, broke out. St Ignatius was its noblest and perhaps only victim. Condemned to be exposed to wild beasts, he was led to Rome to undergo martyrdom. He travelled by land and sea and described the journey as follows: "From Syria even to Rome I fight with wild beasts, by land and sea, by night and by day, being bound amidst ten leopards, a company of soldiers, who only grow worse when they are kindly treated."[31]

Passing through Philadelphia, in Lydia, he arrived by land at Smyrna, where he was greeted by its bishop, Polycarp, and received delegations from the neighbouring churches of Ephesus, Magnesia, and Tralles, with their respective bishops, Onesimus, Damasus, and Polybius. It was at Smyrna that he wrote his letters to the Ephesians, to the Magnesians, to the Trallians and to the Romans. From Smyrna he came to Troas, where he wrote his letters to the Churches of Philadelphia and Smyrna and his letter to Polycarp. From there he took ship to Neapolis, where he resumed the land route, passing through Philippi and Thessalonica to Dyrrachium (Durazzo) on the Adriatic Sea. The Philippians received Ignatius with veneration and after his departure wrote to Polycarp, begging him to send by his own courier the letter they dispatched to the Christians of Antioch and asking him at the same time to forward to them (the Philippians) whatever letters of Ignatius he had in his possession. This is the last information we have of the Bishop of Antioch. At Rome he suffered the death he had so earnestly longed for:

> I am writing to all the Churches and I enjoin all, that I am dying willingly for God's sake, if only you do not prevent it. I beg you, do not do me an untimely kindness. Allow me to be eaten by the beasts, which are my way of reaching to God. I am God's wheat, and I am to be ground by the teeth of wild beasts, so that I may become the pure bread of Christ.[32]

5.2.4 Fourth period: Hadrian

The fourth period of persecution occurred under Hadrian (117–138). This emperor, of Spanish descent, a relative of Trajan, and adopted by him on his death-bed, was a man of brilliant talents and fine education, a scholar, an artist, a legislator and administrator, and altogether one of the ablest among the Roman emperors, but of most doubtful morality, governed by changing moods, attracted in opposite directions, and, in the end, lost in self-contradictions and utter disgust of life. His mausoleum (*Moles Hadriani*) still adorns, as the castle of Sant'Angelo, the banks of the Tiber in Rome. He is represented both as a friend and foe of the Church. He was devoted to the religion of the state, bitterly opposed to Judaism, indifferent to Christianity, from ignorance of it. He insulted the Jews and the Christians alike by erecting temples of Jupiter and Venus over the site of the Temple and the supposed spot of the Crucifixion. He is said to have directed the Asiatic proconsul to check the popular fury against the Christians, and to punish only those who should be, by an orderly judicial process, convicted of transgression of the laws.[33] Undoubtedly, however, he regarded, like Trajan, the mere profession of Christianity itself as a transgression.

Tradition assigns to Hadrian's reign the martyrdom of St Eustachius, St Symphorosa and her seven sons, of the Roman Popes Alexander and Telesphorus, and others whose names are scarcely known. Prior to his conversion to Christianity, Eustachius was a Roman general named Placidus, who served the emperor Trajan. While hunting a stag in Tivoli near Rome, Placidus saw a vision of Jesus between the stag's antlers. He was immediately converted, had himself and his family baptized, and changed his name to Eustachius or Eustace (Greek: Ευστάθιος, Eustathios, "good stability" or "fruitful"). A series of calamities followed to test his faith: his wealth was stolen; his servants died of a plague; when the family took a sea voyage, the ship's captain kidnapped Eustace's wife Theopista; and as Eustace crossed a river with his two sons Agapius and Theopistus, the children were taken away by a wolf and a lion. Like Job, Eustace lamented but did not lose his faith. He was then quickly restored to his former prestige and reunited with his family; but when he demonstrated his new faith by refusing to make a pagan sacrifice, the emperor Hadrian condemned Eustace, his wife, and his sons to be roasted to death inside a bronze statue of a bull or an ox, in the year 118 AD. Saint Eustace's feast day in the Catholic Church is 20 September.

Saint Symphorosa (died around 138 AD) was martyred with her seven sons at Tibur (Tivoli) towards the end of the reign of Emperor Hadrian. She was a lady living at Tibur, the widow of the tribune, St Getulius, who had previously been martyred by Emperor Hadrian at Gabii, now Torri, a town of the Sabines. When Hadrian had completed his costly palace at Tibur and began its dedication by offering sacrifices, he received the following supposed response from the gods: "The widow Symphorosa and her sons torment us daily by invoking their God. If she and her sons offer sacrifice, we promise to give you all that you ask for." When all the emperor's attempts to induce Symphorosa and her sons to sacrifice to the gods were unsuccessful, he ordered her to be brought to the Temple of Hercules, where, after various tortures, she was thrown into the river Anio, with a heavy rock fastened to her neck. Her brother Eugenius, who was a member of the council of Tibur, buried her in the outskirts of the city.

The next day, the emperor summoned her seven sons, and being equally unsuccessful in his attempts to make them sacrifice to the gods, he ordered them to be tied to seven stakes erected for the purpose round the Temple of Hercules. Their members were disjointed with windlasses. Then, each of them suffered a different kind of martyrdom. Crescens was pierced through the throat, Julian through the breast, Nemesius through the heart, Primitivus was wounded at the navel, Justinus was pierced through the back, Stracteus was wounded at the side, and Eugenius was cleft in two parts from top to bottom. Their bodies were thrown into a deep ditch at a place the pagan priests afterwards called *Ad septem Biothanatos*.[34] Then the persecution ceased for one year and six months, during which period the bodies of the martyrs were buried on the Via Tiburtina, eight or nine miles (14 km) from Rome.

5.2.5 Fifth period: Antoninus Pius

The fifth wave of persecution arrived under Antoninus Pius (137–161). On the one hand, Antoninus Pius protected the Christians from the tumultuous violence which broke out against them on account of the frequent public calamities. However, the edict ascribed to him, addressed to the deputies of the Asiatic cities, testifying to the innocence of the Christians, and holding them up to the heathen as models of fidelity and zeal in the worship of God, could hardly have come from an emperor, who bore the title of Pius for his conscientious adherence to the religion of his fathers. In any case he could not have controlled the conduct of the provincial governors and the fury of the people against a religion which the empire considered illegal.

The persecution of the Church at Smyrna (now Izmir in Turkey) and the martyrdom of its venerable bishop, which was formerly assigned to the year 167, under the reign of Marcus Aurelius, took place, according to more recent research, under Antoninus in 155, when Statius Quadratus was proconsul in Asia

Minor. Polycarp was a personal friend and pupil of the Apostle John, and bishop of the church at Smyrna, where a plain stone monument still marks his grave. He was the teacher of Irenaeus of Lyons, and thus the connecting link between the apostolic and post-apostolic ages. As he died in 155 AD at an age of eighty-six years or more, he must have been born in 69 AD, a year before the destruction of Jerusalem, and may have enjoyed the friendship of St John for twenty years or more. This gives additional weight to his testimony concerning apostolic traditions and writings. Polycarp steadfastly refused before the proconsul to deny his King and Saviour; he proclaimed: "Eighty-six years have I served Him, and He never did me any injury: how then can I blaspheme my King and my Saviour?"[35] He joyfully went up to the stake, and amidst the flames praised God for having deemed him worthy "to be numbered among his martyrs, to drink the cup of Christ's sufferings, unto the eternal resurrection of the soul and the body in the incorruption of the Holy Spirit".[36] The account in the letter of the church of Smyrna states that the flames avoided the body of the saint, leaving it unharmed, like gold tried in the fire; also the Christian bystanders insisted, that they perceived a sweet odour, as of incense.[37] Then the executioner thrust his sword into the body, and the stream of blood at once extinguished the flame. The corpse was burned after the Roman custom, but the bones were preserved by the Church, and held more precious than gold and diamonds. The death of this last witness of the apostolic age checked the fury of the populace, and the proconsul suspended the persecution.

5.2.6 Sixth period: Marcus Aurelius

The sixth wave of persecution took place under Marcus Aurelius (161–180). Belonging to the later Stoical school, which believed in an immediate absorption after death into the Divine essence, Marcus Aurelius considered the Christian doctrine of the immortality of the soul, with its moral consequences, as dangerous to the welfare of the state. Marcus Aurelius upheld the old Roman ideal of self-reliant Stoic virtue. He had no room in his cosmopolitan philanthropy for the purest and most innocent of his subjects, many of whom served in his own army. He was flooded with apologies of Melito, Miltiades, Athenagoras on behalf of the persecuted Christians, but turned a deaf ear to them. A law was passed under his reign, punishing every one with exile who should endeavour to influence people's minds by fear of the Divinity, and this law was aimed at the Christians.[38]

In 177 AD, the churches of Lyons and Vienne, in the South of France, underwent a severe trial. Heathen slaves were forced by the rack to declare that their Christian masters practised all the unnatural vices which rumour charged them with; and this was made to justify the horrible tortures to which the Christians were subjected. However, the martyrs, strengthened by the fountain of living water from the heart of Christ, displayed extraordinary faith and steadfastness, and felt, that nothing can be fearful, where the love of the Father is, nothing painful, where shines the glory of Christ. The most distinguished victims of this Gallic persecution were the bishop Pothinus, who, at the age of ninety years, and just recovered from a sickness, was subjected to all sorts of abuse, and then thrown into a dismal dungeon, where he died in two days; the virgin Blandina, a slave, who showed almost superhuman strength and constancy under the most cruel tortures, and was at last thrown to a wild beast in a net; Ponticus, a boy of fifteen years, who could be deterred by no sort of cruelty from confessing his Saviour. The corpses of the martyrs, which covered the streets, were shamefully mutilated, then burned, and the ashes cast into the Rhone. At last the people grew weary of slaughter, and a considerable number of Christians survived. The martyrs of Lyons were distinguished by true humility, disclaiming in their prison that title of honour, as due only, they said, to the faithful and true witness, the Firstborn from the dead, the Prince of life (Rev 1:5), and to those of His followers who had already sealed their fidelity to Christ with their blood.[39]

A notable case of martyrdom in this period, was that of Justin Martyr, at Rome, in the year 166; most of what is known about his life derives from his own writings. He was born at Flavia

Neapolis (today Nablus) in Palestine. His parents were pagans. He tells us that he tried first the school of a Stoic philosopher, who was unable to explain God's being to him.[40] He then attended a Peripatetic philosopher but was put off because the philosopher was too eager for his fee. Thereafter he went to hear a Pythagorean philosopher, who demanded that he first learn music, astronomy and geometry, which he did not wish to do. After this he was drawn to Platonism, until meeting an old man on the sea shore who told him about Christianity, and he converted. He was influenced in this by the fearless conduct of the Christians facing execution.[41] This conversion seems to have taken place at Ephesus.

Justin then adopted the dress of a philosopher himself and travelled about teaching. He arrived in Rome in the reign of Antoninus Pius, where he started his own school; Tatian was one of his pupils. In the reign of Marcus Aurelius, after disputing with the cynic philosopher Crescens, he was denounced by the latter to the authorities, according to Tatian and Eusebius.[42] Justin was tried together with six companions by Junius Rusticus who was urban prefect from 163–167, and was beheaded, probably in 165.

The Scillitan Martyrs were a company of twelve North African Christians who were executed for their beliefs on 17 July 180. The martyrs take their name from Scilla (or Scillium), a town in Numidia.[43] The *Acts of the Scillitan Martyrs* are considered to be the earliest documents of the church of Africa and also the earliest specimen of Christian Latin. The Scillitan Martyrs' trial and execution took place in Carthage under the Pro-consul Vigellius Saturninus, whom Tertullian declares to have been the first persecutor of Christians in Africa. The Scillitan sufferers were twelve in all—seven men and five women. Their names are Speratus, Nartzalus, Cittinus, Veturius, Felix, Aquilinus, Laetantius, Januaria, Generosa, Vestia, Donata, and Secunda.

Their trial is also notable among those of early martyrs inasmuch as the accused were not subjected to torture. The dialogue between the Proconsul and the martyrs shows that the former entertained no prejudices against the Christians. He exhorts them simply to comply with the law, and when they decline he suggests that they take time to think on the subject. The Christians quietly assure him that their minds are made up, whereupon he pronounces sentence: "Speratus, Nartzalus, Cittinus, Veturius, Felix, Aquilinus, Laetantius, Januaria, Generosa, Vestia, Donata and Secunda, I have ordered to be executed." The fame of the martyrs led to the building of a basilica in their honour at Carthage, now in Tunisia. This was the concluding scene of the persecution under Marcus Aurelius, who died on 17 March 180, and persecution ceased almost immediately upon the accession of his son Commodus.

Marcus Aurelius was succeeded by his cruel and contemptible son, Commodus (180–192), who wallowed in the mire of every sensual debauchery, and displayed at the same time like Nero the most ridiculous vanity as a dancer and singer; but he was accidentally made to favour the Christians by the influence of a concubine, Marcia, and accordingly did not generally disturb them. Yet under his reign a Roman senator, Apollonius, was put to death for his faith.[44]

5.2.7 Seventh period: Septimius Severus

Another emperor under whom Christians suffered terribly was Septimius Severus who ruled from 193–211, and this was the seventh period of persecution. With Septimius Severus, who was of Punic descent and had a Syrian wife, a line of emperors (Caracalla, Heliogabalus, Alexander Severus) came to the throne, who were more Oriental than Roman in their spirit, and were therefore far less concerned than the Antonines to maintain the old state religion. Yet towards the close of the second century there was no lack of local persecutions, and Clement of Alexandria wrote of those times: "Many martyrs are daily burned, impaled or beheaded, before our eyes."[45] The emperor Severus may not have been personally ill-disposed towards Christians, but the Church was gaining power and making many converts and this led to popular anti-Christian feeling and persecution in Carthage, Alexandria, Rome and Corinth between about 202 and 210.

In 202 Septimius enacted a law prohibiting the spread of Christianity and Judaism. This was the first universal decree forbidding conversion to Christianity. Violent persecutions broke out in Egypt and North Africa. In Alexandria, Leonides, the father of Origen, a Christian apologist, was beheaded. Potamiaena, a virgin of rare beauty of body and spirit, was threatened by beastly passion with treatment worse than death, and, after cruel tortures, slowly burned with her mother in boiling pitch. One of the executioners, Basilides, smitten with sympathy, shielded them somewhat from abuse, and soon after their death embraced Christianity, and was beheaded. He declared that Potamiaena had appeared to him in the night, interceded with Christ for him, and set upon his head the martyr's crown.[46]

The famed Perpetua and Felicity were martyred during this time, as were many students of Origen of Alexandria. Perpetua (born in 181) was a 22-year old married noble, and a nursing mother. Her co-martyr Felicity, an expectant mother, was her slave. The terrors of imprisonment were increased for Perpetua by anxiety for her unweaned child. Two deacons succeeded in gaining admittance by bribing the jailer, and Perpetua's mother brought Perpetua's son in her arms, whom she was permitted to nurse and keep with her, and straightway she became well and was lightened of her labour and care for the child; and suddenly the prison was made a palace for her. A vision assured her of her approaching martyrdom: Perpetua saw herself treading on a dragon's head and ascending a perilous bronze ladder leading to green meadows, where a flock of sheep was grazing. The next day the trial of Christians took place, before the procurator Hilarianus. All resolutely confessed their Christian faith. Perpetua's father, carrying her child in his arms, approached her again and attempted, for the last time, to induce her to apostatise; the procurator also remonstrated with her, but in vain. She refused to sacrifice to the gods. The procurator thereupon had the father removed by force; in the process he was struck with a whip. The

Christians were then condemned to be torn to pieces by wild beasts, for which they gave thanks to God.

Pudens, their gaoler, had come to respect his charges, and he permitted other Christians to visit them. Perpetua's father was also admitted and made another fruitless attempt to dissuade her from her impending martyrdom. Felicity, who was eight months pregnant, was apprehensive that she would not be permitted to suffer martyrdom with the others, since the law forbade the execution of pregnant women, but two days before the games she gave birth to a daughter, who was adopted by a Christian woman. On the day of the games, the Christians were led into the amphitheatre. At the demand of the crowd they were first scourged; then a boar, a bear, and a leopard, were set on the men, and a wild cow on the women. Wounded by the wild animals, they gave each other the kiss of peace and were then put to the sword. But Perpetua, that she might have some taste of pain, was pierced between the bones and shrieked out; and when the swordsman's hand wandered still (for he was a novice), she herself set it upon her own neck. Their bodies were interred at Carthage.

5.2.8 First era of peace

In 211, with the death of Septimius Severus, the first era of peace began. In detail, the same state of affairs continued through the first years of Caracalla (211–217), since this gloomy misanthrope passed no laws against the Christians. The abandoned youth, El-Gabal, or Heliogabalus (218–222), who polluted the imperial throne by the blackest vices and follies, tolerated all the religions in the hope of finally merging them in his favourite Syrian worship of the sun with its abominable excesses. He himself was a priest of the god of the sun, and thence took his name. Heliogabalus was assassinated at the age of 18 and his cousin and successor, Alexander Severus (222–235), was addicted to a kind of religious eclecticism and syncretism, a pantheistic hero-worship. He placed the busts of Abraham and Christ in his domestic chapel with those of Orpheus, Apollonius of Tyana, and the better Roman emperors, and had the golden Gospel rule, "Treat others as you would like them to treat you" (Mt 7:12; Lk 6:31), engraved on the walls of his palace, and on public monuments. His mother, Julia Mammaea, was a patroness of Origen.

5.2.9 Eighth period: Maximinus the Thracian

The eighth period of persecution took place under Maximinus the Thracian (235–238) who assassinated Alexander Severus. Maximinus was first a herdsman and afterwards a soldier; he was the son of a Goth and an Alanic mother. Maximinus was the first emperor never to set foot in Rome. He resorted again to persecution out of mere opposition to his predecessor, and gave free course to the popular fury against the enemies of the gods, which was at that time aroused anew by an earthquake. He was a rude barbarian who plundered also heathen temples. Maximinus the Thracian initiated a persecution in 235 that was directed chiefly against the heads of the Church. One of its first victims was Pope Pontian, who with Hippolytus was banished to the island of Sardinia.

Maximinus marched on Rome, but at Aquileia Maximinus' troops, suffering from famine and disease, bogged down in an unexpected siege of the city, which had closed its gates when they approached, became disaffected. In April 238, soldiers of the II Parthica in his camp assassinated him, his son, and his chief ministers. Their heads were cut off, placed on poles, and carried to Rome by cavalrymen. Pupienus and Balbinus then became undisputed co-emperors.

5.2.10 Second era of peace

Gordian I (159–12 April 238), was Roman Emperor for one month with his son Gordian II in 238, the *Year of the Six Emperors*. Caught up in a rebellion against the Emperor Maximinus the Thracian, he was defeated by forces loyal to Maximinus before committing suicide. Gordian III (20 January 225–11 February 244), was Roman Emperor from 238 to 244 and he left the Church undisturbed.

Philip the Arab (204–249) was Roman Emperor from 244 to 249. He came from Syria, and rose to become a major figure in the empire. Philip's rise to prominence began through the intervention of his brother Priscus, who was an important official under the emperor Gordian III, quickly negotiating peace with the Sassanid Empire. In April of 248 AD, Philip had the honour of leading the celebrations of the one thousandth birthday of Rome, which according to tradition was founded on 21 April 753 BC by Romulus and Remus. Some later traditions, first mentioned in the historian Eusebius in his *Ecclesiastical History*, held that Philip was the first Christian Roman emperor. According to Eusebius, Philip was a Christian, but was not allowed to enter Easter vigil services until he confessed his sins and sat among the penitents, which he did willingly.[47] Nevertheless, to all appearances he continued to follow the state religion. One commentator claims that "Philip was Emperor of all and Christian to himself."[48] Philip was designated by Jerome *primus omnium ex Romanis imperatoribus Christianus* (the first of the Christian Roman emperors), but this is disputed. It is certain that Origen wrote letters to Philip and to his wife, Otacilia Severa.

5.2.11 Ninth period: Decius Trajan

Decius Trajan (249–251), a cruel and energetic emperor, in whom the old Roman spirit once more awoke, resolved to root out the Church as an atheistic and seditious sect, and in the year 250 published an edict to all the governors of the provinces, enjoining return to the pagan state religion under the heaviest penalties. This triggered a persecution which, in extent, consistency, and cruelty, exceeded all those before it. In effect, it was really the first which covered the whole empire, and accordingly produced a far greater number of martyrs than any former persecution. In the execution of the imperial decree confiscation, exile, torture, promises and threats of all kinds, were employed to move the Christians to apostasy. Decius ordered everyone to sacrifice to Roman gods and receive a certificate for doing so. The certificate was known as a *libellus*.[49] The *libelli* were documents notarised by

Roman authorities to certify that someone has offered sacrifice to their idols. In times of persecution these documents were accepted as proof that someone was not a Christian. Many of these *libelli* have been discovered in excavations in Egypt.

The *libellus* was to be obtained from the inferior tribunal constituted by the edict, at a price proportionate to the avarice of the presiding magistrate. It seems that there was a possibility in some cases of going to the magistrate or sending a friend saying that one was a Christian and avoiding actually sacrificing by paying to be allowed to escape sacrificing to the Roman gods. Those who had so bribed the authorities, caused such certificates to be drawn up for them, representing them as having offered sacrifice, without, however, having actually done so, were known as *libellatici*. A two-year sanction was imposed on them as penance, much less severe than that imposed on apostates.

Multitudes of nominal Christians, especially at the beginning, sacrificed to the gods, or procured from the, magistrate a false certificate that they had done so, and were then excommunicated as apostates (*lapsi*); while many also rushed with impetuous zeal to the prisons and the tribunals, to obtain the confessor's or martyr's crown. The confessors of Rome wrote from prison to St Cyprian in Africa:

> For what more glorious, or what more blessed, can happen to any man from the divine condescension, than to confess the Lord God, in death itself, before his very executioners? Than among the raging and varied and exquisite tortures of worldly power, even when the body is racked and torn and cut to pieces, to confess Christ the Son of God with a spirit still free, although departing? Than to have mounted to heaven with the world left behind? Than, having forsaken men, to stand among the angels? Than, all worldly impediments being broken through, already to stand free in the sight of God?[50]

The authorities were specially severe with the bishops and leaders of the churches: Fabian of Rome, Babylas of Antioch, and Alexander of Jerusalem, perished in this persecution. Others withdrew to places of concealment; some from cowardice; some from Christian prudence, in hope of allaying by their absence the fury of the pagans against their flocks, and of saving their own lives for the good of the Church in better times.

A Libellus of the Decian Persecution (250 AD)

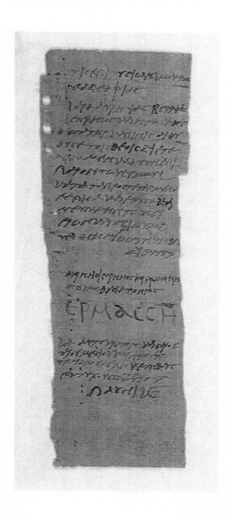

Transcription of the *Libellus of the Decian Persecution*

To those in charge of the sacrifices of the village Theadelphia, from Aurelia Bellias, daughter of Peteres, and her daughter, Kapinis. We have always been constant in sacrificing to the gods, and now too, in your presence, in accordance with the regulations, I have poured libations and sacrificed and tasted the offerings, and I ask you to certify this for us below. May you continue to prosper.

(2nd hand) We, Aurelius Serenus and Aurelius Hermas, saw you sacrificing.

(3rd hand) I, Hermas, certify.

(1st hand) The 1st year of the Emperor Caesar Gaius Messius Quintus Traianus Decius Pius Felix Augustus, Pauni 27.

The *History of the Franks*, written in the decade before 594 by St Gregory of Tours, detailed the persecutions:

> Under the emperor Decius many persecutions arose against the name of Christ, and there was such a slaughter of believers that they could not be numbered. Babylas, bishop of Antioch, with his three little sons, Urban, Prilidan and Epolon... were made perfect by martyrdom because they confessed the name of the Lord.[51]

Pope St Fabian was martyred during the persecution of Christians under Emperor Decius and was one of the first to die on 20 January 250. Also during this period, Origen was tortured on the rack, but survived.

Under the emperor Gallus (251–253) the persecution received a fresh impulse through the incursions of the Goths, and the incidence of pestilence, drought, and famine. Under this emperor the Popes Cornelius and Lucius were banished, and then condemned to death.

5.2.12 Tenth period: Valerian

Valerian (253–260) was at first mild towards the Christians; but in 257 he changed his course, and made an effort to check the progress of their religion without bloodshed, by the banishment of ministers and prominent laymen, the confiscation of their property, and the prohibition of religious assemblies. He brought the death penalty again into play when the early measures proved fruitless. In a 257 edict, the punishment was exile; in 258, the punishment was death. The most distinguished martyrs of this persecution under Valerian are Pope Sixtus II of Rome, and bishop Cyprian of Carthage. Under Valerian, all Christian clergy were required to sacrifice to the gods. Christian senators, knights and ladies were also required to sacrifice under pain of heavy fines, reduction of rank and, later, death. Finally, all Christians were forbidden to visit their cemeteries. According to a letter written by St Dionysius of Alexandria during this time, "men and women, young and old, maidens and matrons, soldiers and civilians, of every age and race, some by scourging and fire, others by the sword, have conquered in the strife and won their crowns".[52]

In Africa, St Cyprian courageously prepared his people for the expected edict of persecution by his *De exhortatione martyrii*, and himself set an example when he was brought before the Roman proconsul Aspasius Paternus in August 257. He refused to sacrifice to the pagan deities and firmly professed Christ. The consul banished him to the desolate Churubis, where he attempted to comfort his flock and his banished clergy to the best of his ability. In a vision, he saw his approaching fate. When a year had passed he was recalled and kept under house arrest in his own villa, in expectation of severer measures after a new and more stringent imperial edict arrived which demanded the execution of all Christian clerics who refused to offer obedience to the state by sacrificing to its gods.

On 13 September 258, he was imprisoned at the behest of the new proconsul, Galerius Maximus. The following day, he was examined for the last time and sentenced to die by the sword. His only answer was "Thanks be to God!" The execution was carried out at once in an open place near the city. A vast multitude followed Cyprian on his last journey. He removed his garments without assistance, knelt down, and prayed. Two of his clergy blindfolded him. He ordered 25 gold pieces to be given to the executioner, who with a trembling hand administered the death-blow.

Cyprian's body was interred by Christian hands near the place of execution, and over it, as well as on the actual scene of his death, churches were afterward erected. These, however, were destroyed by the Vandals. Charlemagne is said to have had the bones transferred to France. Lyons, Arles, Venice, Compiegne, and Roenay in Flanders boast the possession of the martyr's relics. His feast day in the Western and Eastern churches is celebrated on 16 September.

Lawrence of Rome (225–258) was one of the seven deacons of ancient Rome who were martyred during the persecution of Valerian in 258.[53] It had been reported that the Church had amassed great treasures and these were demanded of the deacon. Lawrence then collected a number of the poor of the Church, and presenting them to the prefect, said: "These are our treasures." The prefect felt insulted, and ordered Lawrence to be put to death by a slow fire. By tradition, Lawrence was sentenced at San Lorenzo in Miranda in the Roman Forum, imprisoned in San Lorenzo in Fonte, martyred at San Lorenzo in Panisperna, and buried on the Via Tiburtina in the Catacomb of Cyriaca by Hippolytus and Justinus, a presbyter. Lawrence's feast day is 10 August.

The persecution ended with the capture of Valerian by Shapur I of Persia after the Battle of Edessa: Valerian was tortured, killed and stuffed with straw. He was the only Roman emperor who was captured as a prisoner of war. Valerian's son and successor, Gallienus, revoked the edicts of his father.

5.2.13 Third era of peace

Gallienus (260–268) gave peace to the Church once more, and even acknowledged Christianity as a *religio licita*. This calm continued for forty years; since the edict of persecution, issued by the energetic and warlike Aurelian (270–275), was rendered void by his assassination; and the six emperors who rapidly followed, from 275 to 284, let the Christians alone. During this long season of peace the Church rose rapidly in numbers and outward prosperity. Large and even splendid houses of worship were erected in the chief cities, and provided with collections of sacred books and vessels of gold and silver for the administration of the sacraments. However, in the same proportion discipline relaxed, quarrels, intrigues, and factions increased, and worldliness poured in like a flood.

5.2.14 Eleventh period: Diocletian and Galerius

The forty years' repose was followed by the last and most violent persecution, a struggle for life and death. The accession of the Emperor Diocletian (284–305) is the era from which the Coptic Churches of Egypt and Abyssinia still date, under the name of the *Era of Martyrs*. All former persecutions of the faith were forgotten in the horror with which men looked back upon the last and greatest: the wave of that great storm obliterated all the traces that had been left by others. The fiendish cruelty of Nero, the jealous fears of Domitian, the unimpassioned dislike of Marcus Aurelius, the sweeping purpose of Decius, the clever devices of Valerian, fell into obscurity when compared with the concentrated terrors of that final grapple, which resulted in the destruction of the old Roman Empire and the establishment of the Cross as the symbol of the world's hope.[54]

Diocletian was the son of a slave or at least of obscure parentage, and worked his way up to supreme power. He converted the Roman republican empire into an Oriental despotism. He associated with himself three subordinate co-regents, Maximian (who committed suicide in 310), Galerius (died 311), and Constantius

Chlorus (died 306, the father of Constantine the Great), and divided with them the government of the immense empire; thereby quadrupling the personality of the sovereign, and imparting vigour to provincial administration, but also sowing the seed of discord and civil war.[55] In the first twenty years of his reign Diocletian respected the toleration edict of Gallienus. His own wife Prisca his daughter Valeria, and most of his eunuchs and court officers, besides many of the most prominent public functionaries, were Christians, or at least favourable to the Christian faith. He himself was a superstitious heathen and an oriental despot. Like Aurelian and Domitian before him, he claimed divine honours, as the vicar of Jupiter Capitolinus. He was called, as the Lord and Master of the world, *Sacratissimus Dominus Noster*; he guarded his Sacred Majesty with many circles of soldiers and eunuchs, and allowed no one to approach him except on bended knees, and with the forehead touching the ground, while he was seated on the throne in rich vestments from the far East. Although he long postponed the religious question, he had to face it at last. It could not be expected, in the nature of the case, that paganism should surrender to its dangerous rival without a last desperate struggle to save itself.

The reasons for this persecution are unclear, but Diocletian's actions may have been based on the influence of his junior colleague Galerius (an adherent of Roman religion), Porphyry (an anti-Christian Neoplatonist philosopher), or the usual desire for political unity. However the chief instigator of the renewal of hostility, according to the account of Lactantius, was Diocletian's co-regent and son-in-law, Galerius, a cruel and fanatical heathen.[56] He prevailed at last on Diocletian in his old age to authorize the persecution which gave to his inglorious reign a most disgraceful end.

Diocletian published four edicts during the period 303–304. The emperor ordered the burning of Christian books and churches, but promised not to spill any blood. In actuality, the Diocletian persecution turned out to be extremely violent. This violence did not succeed in annihilating Christianity but caused the faith of the martyrs to blaze forth instead. The persecution began on the twenty-third day of February, 303, the pagan feast of the *Terminalia* (as if to make an end of the Christians), with the destruction of the magnificent church in Nicomedia, and soon spread over the whole Roman empire, except Gaul, Britain, and Spain, where the co-regent Constantius Chlorus, and especially his son, Constantine the Great (from 306), were disposed, as far as possible, to spare the Christians. A fifth edict was issued by co-regent Galerius in 308 ordering that all men, with wives, children, and servants, were to offer sacrifice to the gods, and that all provisions in the markets should be sprinkled with sacrificial wine. As a result, Christians either had to commit apostasy or starve. All the pains which iron and steel, fire and sword, rack and cross, wild beasts and beastly men could inflict, were employed against the Church. Executioners grew tired with all the violence they had to inflict. Christians were expelled from the army; buildings were seized; scriptures destroyed; Christians lost legal rights; many were tortured and executed.

Among those martyred under Diocletian were Saints Cosmas and Damian; they were twins born to Christian parents in Cilicia, part of today's Turkey, in the third century. Saints Cosmas and Damian lived in the region around the border between modern day Turkey and Syria. They practised as physicians in the seaport of Ægea, then in the Roman province of Syria, now Ayas, on the Gulf of İskenderun, and gained a great reputation. They accepted no pay for their services and were, therefore, called *anargyroi*, "the silverless". In this way they brought many to the Catholic Faith. Over 48 miracles were credited to the holy twins, including, amongst others, the development of remedies against plague, scabs, scurvy, kidney stones and bed-wetting. Their most famous miracle involved the miraculous replacement of a diseased leg of a white patient with the leg of a recently-deceased black man. When the persecution of Diocletian began, the Prefect Lysias had Cosmas and Damian arrested in 287, and ordered them to deny their faith in Christ. They refused and underwent a series of tortures, including crucifixion, from which, miraculously, they remained unscathed. The torturers, weary of what they realized was the impossible task of forcing apostasy from their mouths, finally beheaded them both. Their three brothers, Anthimus, Leontius, and Euprepius died as martyrs with them. The execution took place 27 September, probably in the year 287. At a later date, a number of legends grew up about them, connected in part with their relics. The remains of the martyrs were buried in the city of Cyrus in Syria; the Emperor Justinian I (527–565) sumptuously restored the city in their honour. Having been cured of a dangerous illness by the intercession of Cosmas and Damian, Justinian, in gratitude for their aid, rebuilt and adorned their church at Constantinople, and it became a celebrated place of pilgrimage. At Rome Pope Felix IV (526–530) erected a church in their honour, the mosaics of which are still among the most valuable art remains of the city. Their feast is celebrated in the Latin Church on 26 September, and on 17 October in the Greek Church. Cosmas and Damian are regarded as the patrons of physicians and surgeons and are sometimes represented with medical emblems. They are invoked in the Canon of the Mass and in the Litany of the Saints.

Eusebius was a witness of this persecution in Caesarea, Tyre, and Egypt, and saw, with his own eyes, the houses of prayer razed to the ground, the Holy Scriptures committed to the flames in the market places, the pastors hunted, tortured, and torn to pieces in the amphitheatre. Even the wild beasts, he says, at last refused to attack the Christians, as if they had assumed the part of men in place of the heathen Romans; the bloody swords became dull and shattered; the executioners grew weary, and had to relieve each other; but the Christians sang hymns of praise and thanksgiving in honour of Almighty God, even to their last breath. Eusebius himself was imprisoned, but released. In this, as in former persecutions, the number of apostates who preferred the earthly life to the heavenly, was very great. To these was now added also the new class of the *traditores*, who delivered the holy Scriptures to the heathen authorities, to be burned. However as the persecution raged, the zeal and fidelity of the

Christians increased, and martyrdom spread as if by contagion. Even boys and girls showed amazing firmness.[57]

Galerius, the real author of the persecution, brought to reflection by a terrible disease, put an end to the slaughter shortly before his death, by an *Edict of Toleration*, which he issued from Nicomedia in 311, in conjunction with Constantine and Licinius. In that document, he declared that the purpose of reclaiming the Christians from their wilful innovation and the multitude of their sects to the laws and discipline of the Roman state was not accomplished; and that he would now grant them permission to hold their religious assemblies provided they did not disturb the order of the state. To this he added in conclusion the significant instruction that the Christians, after this manifestation of grace, should pray to their God for the welfare of the emperors, of the state, and of themselves, that the state might prosper in every respect, and that they might live quietly in their homes.[58] This edict virtually closed the period of persecution in the Roman empire. For a short time the tyrant Maximinus continued in every way to oppress and vex the church in the East, and the cruel pagan Maxentius (a son of Maximian and son-in-law of Galerius) did the same in Italy.

5.2.15 The Peace of Constantine

However, the young Constantine had already in 306 become emperor of Gaul, Spain, and Britain. He had been raised at the court of Diocletian at Nicomedia and destined to be his successor, but fled from the intrigues of Galerius to Britain, and was appointed by his father and proclaimed by the army as his successor. He crossed the Alps, and under the banner of the Cross, he conquered Maxentius at the Milvian bridge near Rome, and the heathen tyrant perished with his army of veterans in the waters of the Tiber on 27 Oct 312. A few months afterwards Constantine met at Milan with his co-regent and brother-in-law, Licinius, and issued a new edict of toleration (313), to which Maximian also, shortly before his suicide (313), was compelled to give his consent at Nicomedia. The second edict went beyond the first of 311; it was a decisive step from hostile neutrality to friendly neutrality and protection, and prepared the way for the legal recognition of Christianity, as the religion of the empire. It ordered the full restoration of all confiscated church property to the Church, at the expense of the imperial treasury, and directed the provincial magistrates to execute this order at once with all energy, so that peace may be fully established and the continuance of the Divine favour secured to the emperors and their subjects.

Paganism made another spasmodic effort. Licinius fell out with Constantine and renewed the persecution for a short time in the East, but he was finally defeated at the Battle of Chrysopolis in 324, before being executed on the orders of Constantine in 325, and Constantine became sole ruler of the empire. The Forty Martyrs of Sebaste or the Holy Forty (Ancient Greek Ἅγιοι Τεσσεράκοντα, Demotic Ἅγιοι Σαράντα) were a group of Roman soldiers in the *Legio XII Fulminata*, who became martyrs for their Christian faith in 320. They were killed near Sebaste, in Lesser Armenia, victims of the persecutions of Licinius, who, after the year 316, persecuted the Christians of the East. According to St Basil, forty soldiers who had openly confessed themselves Christians were condemned by the prefect to be exposed naked upon a frozen pond near Sebaste on a bitterly cold night, that they might freeze to death.[59] Among the confessors, one yielded and, leaving his companions, sought the warm baths near the lake which had been prepared for any who might prove inconstant. One of the guards set to keep watch over the martyrs beheld at this moment a supernatural brightness overshadowing them and at once proclaimed himself a Christian, threw off his garments, and placed himself beside the thirty-nine soldiers of Christ. Thus the number of forty remained complete. At daybreak, the stiffened bodies of the confessors, which still showed signs of life, were burned and the ashes cast into a river. The Christians, however, collected the precious remains, and the relics were distributed throughout many cities; in this way the veneration paid to the Forty Martyrs became widespread, and numerous churches were erected in their honour. The feast day of the Forty Martyrs falls on 9 March.

Constantine then openly protected and favoured the Church, without forbidding idolatry, and on the whole remained true to his policy of protective toleration until his death (337). This was enough for the success of the Church, which had all the vitality and energy of a victorious power; while heathenism was fast decaying at its root. Large church buildings were built, the clergy acquired civil authority, worship became more formalized, Sunday became a public holiday, and Christian symbols began to appear on coins.

> What a contrast between Nero, the first imperial persecu-
> tor, riding in a chariot among Christian martyrs as
> burning torches in his gardens, and Constantine, seated
> in the Council of Nicaea among three hundred and
> eighteen bishops (some of whom wore the insignia of
> torture on their maimed and crippled bodies), and giving
> the highest sanction of civil authority to the decree of the
> eternal Deity of the once crucified Jesus of Nazareth![60]

5.2.16 Twelfth period: Julian the Apostate

Julian the Apostate (361–363), the last pagan emperor of the Roman Empire, was brought up during a time that paganism was in decline in Rome. Upon being proclaimed emperor in 361 AD, Julian immediately declared his faith in the old Roman gods and began to bring about a pagan revival. However, he was killed in Persia in 363 AD and his attempt to restore paganism ultimately failed. In 364, Libanius stated that Julian was assassinated by a Christian who was one of his own soldiers.[61] Fourteen years later, Libanius said that Julian was killed by a Saracen (Lakhmid) and this may have been confirmed by Julian's doctor Oribasius who, having examined the wound, said that it was from a spear used by a group of Lakhmid auxiliaries in Persian service. Later Christian historians propagated the tradition that Julian was killed by a saint.[62]

Julian used many methods to subtly break the Church. He recalled bishops who had previously been exiled for heretical teachings, stripped clergy of their rights to travel at the expense of the state as they had done previously, and banned Christians from teaching classical works such as the Iliad or the Odyssey. Saints John and Paul were martyred in this era.

Julian was succeeded by the short-lived Emperor Jovian who reestablished Christianity's privileged position throughout the Empire.

5.3 The Issue of Second Repentance

As already mentioned, there was an ebb and flow in the Roman persecution against Christians. It was not unusual for great numbers of believers to "lapse" during times of intense persecution. Some simply backed into the shadows for fear of being associated with the Christians. Others found it easy to go back to riotous living, the life of excessive drink and sexual indiscretions. Once the persecution lifted, bishops would often find themselves faced with literally dozens, and sometimes hundreds, of lapsed believers desiring to be readmitted to the fellowship of the saints. Lapsing during a time of persecution was a serious offence, especially when there were others who stood the test and were tortured or killed. Lapsed believers were not allowed to celebrate the Eucharist or to enter into the main church meeting, but had to sit in an outside room, or even outside the building or house. They could listen, but could not take part. Some never tried to come back, feeling that they were beyond forgiveness, others decided they did not want to come back.

In North Africa, according to Tertullian, lapsed believers would dress in rags to show their penance, lay prostrate in the outer foyer where the elders would enter, and beg for prayer and forgiveness.[63] Following 1 John 5:16,17 the elders were not to speak to or even pray for such "penitents", but were to let them continue in penance until the Lord somehow showed His mercy to them. Some of these lapsed believers would eventually

give up, figuring they had lost their souls. Others would spend
months, maybe years, in this condition, hoping that God would
accept them when they died. Rome was less strict and allowed
the lapsed to be more speedily reconciled.

5.4 The Catacombs

In the first century the Christians of Rome did not have their
own cemeteries. If they owned land, they buried their relatives
there, otherwise they resorted to common cemeteries, where
pagans too were buried. That is how Saint Peter came to be
buried in the great public *necropolis* (city of the dead) on Vatican
Hill, available to everybody. Likewise Saint Paul was buried in
a necropolis along the Via Ostiense.

In the first half of the second century, as a result of various
donations, the Christians started burying their dead underground and that is how the catacombs were founded. Many of
them began and developed around family tombs, whose owners,
newly converted Christians, did not reserve them to the
members of the family, but opened them to their brothers and
sisters in the faith. With the passage of time, these burial areas
grew larger by gifts or by the purchase of new properties,
sometimes on the initiative of the Church itself. Typical is the
case of Saint Callixtus: the Church took up directly the organization and administration of the cemetery, which assumed a
community character.

With the edict of Milan, promulgated by the emperors
Constantine and Licinius in February 313, Christians were no
longer persecuted. They were free to profess their faith, to have
places of worship and to build churches both inside and outside
the city, and to buy plots of land, without fear of confiscation.
Nevertheless, the catacombs continued to function as regular
cemeteries until the beginning of the fifth century, when the
Church resumed to bury exclusively above ground or in the
basilicas dedicated to important martyrs.

The catacombs are made up of underground tunnels in the form of a labyrinth, reaching up to many miles in length. In the tufaceous walls of this intricate system of galleries were cut out rows of rectangular niches, called *loculi*, of various dimensions, which could contain only one body, but not infrequently held the remains of more than one person. The burials of the early Christians were extremely poor and simple. The corpses, in imitation of Christ, were wrapped in a sheet or shroud and placed in the *loculi* without any kind of coffin. The *loculi* were closed with a slab of marble or, in most cases, by tiles sealed with mortar. On the tombstone the name of the deceased was sometimes engraved, along with a Christian symbol or a wish that the person might find peace in heaven. Oil lamps and small vases containing perfumes would often be placed beside the tombs. The structure of the tombs, arranged in rows superimposed one upon another at different levels, gave one the idea of a vast dormitory, called cemetery, a term coming from the Greek expression for "resting place". In this way the Christians affirmed their faith in the resurrection of the body.

5.4.1 Early Christian symbols

In the catacombs, Christians used symbols to distinguish their tombs. Christian symbols were first mentioned in writing by Clement of Alexandria (153–217 AD):

> And let our seals be either a dove, or a fish, or a ship scudding before the wind, or a musical lyre, which Polycrates used, or a ship's anchor, which Seleucus got engraved as a device; and if there be one fishing, he will remember the apostle, and the children drawn out of the water.[64]

The fish was depicted as a Christian symbol in the first decades of the second century. The symbol itself may have been suggested by the miraculous multiplication of the loaves and fishes or the repast of the seven disciples, after the Resurrection, on the shore of the Sea of Galilee (Jn 21:9). Its popularity among Christians was due principally to the famous acrostic consisting of the initial letters of five Greek words forming the word for fish (*Ichthys*), which briefly but clearly describe Christ: *Iesous Christos Theou Yios Soter*, meaning, Jesus Christ, Son of God, Saviour. St Augustine pointed out this meaning:

> If you join the initial letters of these five Greek words, Ἰησοῦς Χριστος Θεοῦ υἱὸς σωτήρ, which mean, "Jesus Christ the Son of God, the Saviour," they will make the word ἰχδὺς, that is, "fish," in which word Christ is mystically understood, because He was able to live, that is, to exist, without sin in the abyss of this mortality as in the depth of waters.[65]

The Cross, which is today one of the most widely recognised symbols in the world, was adopted as a symbol from the earliest times, at least from the second century.[66] By the early third century the Cross had become so closely associated with Christ that Clement of Alexandria, who died between 211 and 216, could, without fear of ambiguity, use the phrase the Lord's sign (τὸ κυριακὸν σημεῖον) to mean the Cross.

5.5 Theological reflection on martyrdom

Derivation of the word martyrdom from the Greek μαρτύριον, meaning witness or testimony. The expression is found in several places in the New Testament.[67] Classically, three conditions are required for martyrdom. First, that physical life has been laid down and real death undergone; second that death has been inflicted in hatred of Christian life and truth; and third that death has been voluntarily accepted in defence of these.[68] The effect of martyrdom is the remission of all sin and temporal punishment due to sin, since it is an act of perfect charity.

On the first count those who ardently desire to die for Christ, or who accept or choose a life of suffering for His sake, are not technically martyrs; nor, on the second count, those who die from disease or in consequence of the accepted risks attendant on the way of life they have chosen for Christ, or from devotion to the cause of scientific research, or for their country, or, however exalted their motives, for error or by suicide; nor, on the third count, those who have not reached the age of reason or who are slain without making a choice. Therefore the following are not genuinely martyrs: those who die by contracting disease in their care of lepers, those who suffer death for natural truths or for heresy, or who indirectly bring about their own death to safeguard their person. Such is the general teaching of theologians, although the final point is not beyond question if it is taken to mean that there must be a conscious act of deliberate choice. Cajetan, characteristically, allows that a man might be martyred in his sleep, and for the same underlying reason he holds that unbaptized babies can be saved in the faith of their parents; thus also is explained why the Church lists the Holy Innocents among the martyrs without crediting them with a miraculous precocity, and by common teaching that the blood that is shed takes the place of the water that flows in Baptism.

The second condition requires some explanation. Many of the martyrs have been killed *in odium fidei*, that is, in direct witness to the truths of faith, but others, such as St John the Baptist and St Maria Goretti, have offered their lives in defence of Christian virtue, and some, such as St Thomas of Canterbury and St John Nepomucene, for the sake of Church order and discipline. What is required is that the cause is the living truth of Christ.

The rule of thumb for the martyr was stipulated by St Augustine: martyrdom derives, not from the punishment inflicted, but the reasons for the punishment (*non poena sed causa*). Although such a rule seems straightforward, it is not always so in actual practice. St Thomas Aquinas, for example, points out that John the Baptist was a martyr because he denounced adultery; hence he was a martyr for the sake of the "truth of faith".[69] Pope Paul VI extended this further in beatifying Maximilian Kolbe (1971) as a "martyr of charity". Kolbe witnessed in the ultimate gesture of love or charity. In that sense, he died for the "defence of the faith" as Aquinas described it. In the canonizations of Maximilian Kolbe (1982) and Edith Stein (1998), Pope St John Paul II manifested an even more nuanced view of martyrdom. Martyrdom may be a public witness unto death for the truth of the Gospel, even when the explicit reason for the martyr's death is not a refusal to apostatise by denying the faith. Neither the sacrifice of a life for the sake of another (Kolbe) nor the death of one out of racial hatred (Stein) is what makes them martyrs. The reason why the Pope sees them as martyrs is that their lives stood in direct and dramatic counterpoint to forces of evil and untruth.[70]

It is disputed whether someone who resists the aggressor is a martyr. St Thomas Aquinas specifies that it would be possible to be considered a martyr fighting as a soldier to defend one's country, the Church or the Pope:

> The good of one's country is paramount among human goods: yet the Divine good, which is the proper cause of martyrdom, is of more account than human good. Nevertheless, since human good may become Divine, for instance when it is referred to God, it follows that any human good in so far as it is referred to God, may be the cause of martyrdom.[71]

The practical tradition of the Church indicates that one who fights back can still be a martyr, as in the case of St Wenceslaus.[72] We might define the characteristics of true martyrs in eight propositions:

- *Real martyrs do not kill themselves*
- *Real martyrs suffer harm but never inflict harm*
- *Real martyrs do not seek death but accept it when it comes*
- *The Christian martyr does not die out of hatred of the enemy, but out of love for Jesus*
- *Real martyrs die bearing witness to truth*
- *Martyrdom properly involves death, not just suffering, however intense*
- *Some people are victims but not martyrs*
- *Some people are heroes but not martyrs*

Martyrdom continues even today: on average, every two weeks at least one Catholic missionary somewhere is put to death.

There were more martyrs for Christ in the twentieth century than in all the previous nineteen centuries put together.[73] These countless deaths have not been without fruit. Now, as earlier, the blood of martyrs is the seed of Christians. Bringing to mind the contemporary Church in Rome which grows because it is "fed by the blood of martyrs", Pope Francis stated that "it is right that our thoughts turn to the many martyrs of today, the many martyrs who give their lives for faith". "It is true that during the times of Nero many Christians were persecuted", Pope Francis observed, "and today there are just as many". Noting how there are "many martyrs today in the Church, many persecuted Christians", the Pope called attention to the Middle East where Christians must flee persecution, where Christians are killed". "Even those Christians who are forced away in an 'elegant' way, with 'white gloves': that too is persecution," he observed, recognizing that "there are more witnesses, more martyrs in the Church today than there were in the first centuries".[74]

Notes

1   *The Epistle to Diognetus,* 5–6.

2   See the *Didaché,* 12, 3–4.

3   Marcellus, a centurion, lost his life by such a refusal. See C. Wordsworth, *A Church History to the Council of Nicea* (London: Rivingtons, 1899), p. 348.

4   In 286 AD, Emperor Maximian ordered the decimation of the Thebaean Legion for their refusal to exterminate fellow Christians. For a detailed account see Wordsworth, *A Church History to the Council of Nicea,* p. 376.

5   Marcus Aurelius, *Meditations* (London: Penguin, 1987), 11.3.

6   *Ibid.*

7   Athenagoras, *Legatio pro Christianis,* 1–3.

8   Justin Martyr, *Apology,* 1, 6.

9   Athenagoras, *Legatio pro Christianis,* 3.

10   Clement of Alexandria gave warnings concerning the misuse of the kiss. See Clement of Alexandria, *Paedagogus,* Book III, chapter 11: "And if we are called to the kingdom of God, let us walk worthy of the kingdom, loving God and our neighbour. But love is not proved by a kiss, but by kindly feeling. But there are those, that do nothing but make the churches

resound with a kiss, not having love itself within. For this very thing, the shameless use of a kiss, which ought to be mystic, occasions foul suspicions and evil reports. The apostle calls the kiss holy (See Rom 16:16). When the kingdom is worthily tested, we dispense the affection of the soul by a chaste and closed mouth, by which chiefly gentle manners are expressed."

11   Tacitus, *Annales*, 13, 32

12   Seutonius, *The Twelve Caesars* (London: Penguin, 1989), p. 221, section 16.

13   *Didaché*, 16, 7.

14   *Didaché*, 10, 6.

15   See Philemon 15–16.

16   H. Chadwick, *The Early Church* (London: Penguin, 1969), p. 60.

17   See 1 Corinthians 7. This was misunderstood and taken as teaching against marriage.

18   This was based on the Pauline Privilege, which is the dissolution of a purely natural (not sacramental) marriage which had been contracted between two non-Christians, one of whom has since become a Christian. The Pauline Privilege is so-named because it is based upon the apostle Paul's words in 1 Co 7:15: "But if the unbeliever chooses to leave, then let the separation take place: in these circumstances, the brother or sister is no longer tied. But God has called you to live in peace."

19   See St Augustine, *The City of God*, Book 19, chapter 23, who quotes Porphyry's concern at advancing Christianity in his *Philosophy from Oracles*.

20   See Origen, *Against Celsus*, VIII, 67–69

21   For example, within Pliny's corresponence to Trajan, Pliny talks of the detrimental effect Christianity was having upon the temple worship and economy of Bithynia. See Pliny the Younger, *Letter* 10, 96.

22   See St Augustine, *De Civitate Dei*, xviii, 52, who mentions Antoninus instead of Marcus Aurelius. Lactantius counts six, Sulpicius Severus nine persecutions.

23   See Ex 5–10; Rev 17:12 ff.

24   Seutonius' account of Nero gives a vivid picture of the depths of depravity and cruelty to which Nero sank. See C. Suetonius Tranquillus, *Life of Nero* in *The Lives of the Twelve Caesars*.

25   Tacitus, *Annales*, 15, 44.

26   *Ibid.*

27   See Tertullian, *De praescriptione haereticorum*, xxxvi.

28   Pliny the Younger, *Letter* 10, 96.

29   Pliny the Younger, *Letter* 10, 97.

30   Eusebius, *Church History*, 3, 22.

31   St Ignatius of Antioch, *Letter to the Romans*, 5.

32   St Ignatius of Antioch, *Letter to the Romans*, 4.

33   The rescript of Hadrian to Minucius Fundanus (124 or 128), preserved by Eusebius in a Greek translation (*Church History*, IV. V. 8, 9), is almost an edict of toleration. Nevertheless, Hadrian was zealously devoted to the worship of the gods.

34   The Greek word *biodanatos*, or rather *biaiodanatos*, was employed for self-murderers and, by the pagans, applied to Christians who suffered martyrdom.

35   The Encyclical Epistle of the Church at Smyrna, *Concerning the Martyrdom of St Polycarp*, 9.

36   *Ibid.*, 14.

37   *Ibid.*, 15.

38   See P. Schaff, *History of the Christian Church*, Volume II: *Ante-Nicene Christianity. A.D. 100–325* (Christian Classics Ethereal Library: 2002), p. 43.

39   *Ibid.*, p. 44.

40   St Justin Martyr, *Dialogues*, 2–8.

41   St Justin Martyr, *Apology*, 2, 12.

42   See Tatian, *Address to the Greeks*, 19 and Eusebius, *Church History*, IV, 16, 7–8.

43   Numidia was an ancient kingdom of the Numidians in what is now Algeria and a smaller part of Tunisia, in North Africa.

44   See Schaff, *History of the Christian Church*, II, p. 44.

45   Clement of Alexandria, *Stromata*, Book 2, chapter 20, 125.

46   Schaff, *History of the Christian Church*, II, p. 45.

47   See Eusebius, *Church History*, 6, 34.

48   Y. Zahran, *Philip the Arab: A Study in Prejudice* London: Stacey, 2001), p. 109.

49   See J. R. Knipfing, "The Libelli of the Decian Persecution" in *The Harvard Theological Review* 16/4 (October 1923), pp. 345–390.

50   St Cyprian, *Epistle 25*.

51   St Gregory of Tours, *History of the Franks*, Book 1, 30.

52   St Dionysius of Alexandria, *Easter Letter to Domitius and Didymus*.

53   His name comes from the Latin *Laurentius*, meaning "laurelled".

54   Schaff, *History of the Christian Church*, II, p. 49–50. Schaff draws on A. J. Mason in his book *The Persecution of Diocletian* (Cambridge: 1976).

55   Maximian (surnamed Herculius) ruled in Italy and Africa, Galerius (Armentarius) on the banks of the Danube, and afterwards in the East, Constantius (Chlorus) in Gaul, Spain, and Britain; while Diocletian reserved to himself Asia, Egypt, and Thrace, and resided in Nicomedia. Galerius married a daughter of Diocletian (the unfortunate Valeria), Constantius a step-daughter of Maximian (Theodora), after repudiating their former wives. Constantine, the son of the divorced Helena, married Fausta, the daughter of Maximian as his second wife (father and son being married to two sisters). He was raised to the dignity of Caesar on 25 July 306.

[56]   Lactantius (*De Mortibus Persecutorum*, c. 9), calls Galerius "a wild beast", in whom dwelt "a native barbarity and a savageness foreign to Roman blood". He died at last of a terrible disease, of which Lactantius gives a minute account (c. 33).

[57]   See Schaff, *History of the Christian Church*, II, p. 52.

[58]   See *ibid.*, p. 54.

[59]   See St Basil, *Homily 19* in *PG* 31, 507 ff.

[60]   Schaff, *History of the Christian Church*, II, p. 56.

[61]   See Libanius, *Orations*, 18, 274.

[62]   Sozomenus, *Historia ecclesiastica*, 6, 2. The saint in question was St Mercurius.

[63]   Tertullian, *On Purity*, 13.

[64]   Clement of Alexandria, *Paedagogus*, 3, 11.

[65]   St Augustine, *De Civitate Dei*, Book 18, chapter 23.

[66]   See Epistle of Barnabas, xi–xii; Justin, *Apologia*, 1, 55–60; Idem, *Dialogue with Trypho* 85–97.

[67]   These include: Matthew 8:4; 10:18; 24:14; Mark 1:44; 6:11; 13:9; Luke 5:14; 9:5; 21:13; Acts 4:33; 1 Corinthians 1:6; 2 Corinthians 1:12; 2 Thessalonians 1:10; 1 Timothy 2:6; 2 Timothy 1:8; Hebrews 3:5; James 5:3.

[68]   See T. Gilby & L. S. Cunningham, "Martyrdom, Theology of" in *New Catholic Encyclopedia*. 2003. (August 31, 2011). http://www.encyclopedia.com/article–1G2–3407707223/martyrdom-theology.html. See also D. Prummer, *Handbook of Moral Theology* (Cork: 1956), §474.

[69]   See St Thomas Aquinas, *Summa Theologiae*, II–II°, q. 124, a. 5.

[70]   See Gilby & Cunningham, "Martyrdom, Theology of".

[71]   St Thomas Aquinas, *Summa Theologiae*, II–II°, q. 124, a. 5, ad. 3. The Angelic Doctor seems to take another position in his Commentary on the Sentences, see *Super Sentiarum*, lib. 4 d. 49 q. 5 a. 3 qc. 2 arg. 11: "Praeterea, bonum commune est potius bono particulari. Sed si aliquis pro conservatione reipublicae moriatur in bello justo, non debetur ei aureola. Ergo etiam si occidatur pro conservatione fidei in seipso; et sic martyrio aureola non debetur."

[72]   See the account of the martyrdom of St Wenceslaus: "The next morning when they rang the bell for matins, Wenceslaus, on hearing the sound, said, 'Praise to you, Lord; you have allowed me to live to this morning.' And so he rose and went to matins. Immediately Boleslaus followed him to the church door. Wenceslaus looked back at him and said, 'Brother, you were a good subject to me yesterday.' But the devil had already blocked the ears of Boleslaus, and perverted his heart. Drawing his sword, Boleslaus replied, 'And now I intend to be a better one!' With these words, he struck his brother's head with his sword. But Wenceslaus turned and said, 'Brother, what are you trying to do?' And with that he seized Boleslaus and threw him to the ground. But one of Boleslaus' counselors ran up and stabbed Wenceslaus in the hand. With his hand wounded, he let go of his brother and took refuge in the church. But two evil men struck him down at the

church door; and then another rushed up and ran him through with a sword."

73   See G. Weigel, "Rediscovering the Martyrology" in *First Things* (26 February 2014).. See also J. L. Allen, *The Global War on Christians: Dispatches from the Front Lines of Anti-Christian Persecution* (New York: Image, 2013).

74   Pope Francis, *Homily at Daily Mass* (30 June 2014).

6 EARLY CHURCH FATHERS

Just as bees can take nectar from flowers, unlike other animals which limit themselves to enjoying their scent and colour, so also from these writings one can draw some benefit for the spirit. We must use these books, following in all things the example of bees. They do not visit every flower without distinction, nor seek to remove all the nectar from the flowers on which they alight, but only draw from them what they need to make honey, and leave the rest. And if we are wise, we will take from those writings what is appropriate for us, and conforms to the truth, ignoring the rest.

St Basil the Great, *Ad Adolescentes*, 4.

THE JEWISH, GREEK, AND ROMAN cultures of the formative first two centuries of the Christian Era had a deep and lasting influence on the new faith of Christianity. Christianity originated in Jewish Palestine, a province of the Roman Empire. The first Christians were Jews who attended the temple, read the Jewish scriptures, kept the Sabbath, and adhered to some Jewish dietary and religious practices. In the decades following the Death and Resurrection of Jesus, Jewish Christians quickly spread to other Mediterranean provinces of Rome and began converting the Gentiles. Jesus, His disciples, and the first Christians were all Jews who kept Jewish laws and customs and studied the Jewish scriptures. Christianity preserves the Jewish scriptures of the Old Testament, incorporating the essential Jewish view of God as the Lord of history. Early Christian missionaries carried the Gospel into the major population centres around the Mediterranean. The message found a receptive audience in the non-Jewish communities of the Roman Empire, including Greek-speaking Gentiles who were trained in classical philosophy. This brought Greek intellectual culture into the heart of Christianity.

6.1 Cultural setting

Christian leaders explored the core beliefs of Christianity in accordance with their intellectual training, launching theological controversies over the use of philosophical terms such as person and substance to refine their understanding of the nature of God. The Christological controversies over the nature of the Incarnation of the Word in Jesus Christ and the Trinitarian discussions over the relationship of the Father, the Son, and the Holy Spirit were particularly sharp and of continuing significance. Both the conclusions formulated and some of the controversies associated with them persist to the present day.

The politics of the Roman Empire had two significant and lasting effects on Christianity. In the first case, the fledgling Christian communities suffered official persecution by the Romans for almost three centuries, leaving a lasting legacy of martyrdom. In the second case, early Christian communities responded to questions of communal organization by adopting the hierarchical model of Roman political organization. This is most apparent in the roles and relationships of clergy, where bishops have authority over priests, and popes have authority over everyone.

When Paul and the other Apostles travelled around the Mediterranean world, they moved within a closely-knit political and cultural unity: the Roman Empire. This Empire embraced many different national groups, often with languages and dialects of their own. However all these groups were governed by the same Emperor; there was a broad Greco-Roman civilization in which educated people throughout the Empire shared; either Greek or Latin was understood almost everywhere in the Empire, and many could speak both languages. These facts greatly assisted the early Church in her missionary work.

However, in the centuries that followed, the unity of the Mediterranean world gradually disappeared. The political unity was the first to go. From the end of the third century the Empire, while still theoretically one, was usually divided into two units, an eastern and a western part, each under its own Emperor. Constantine furthered this process of separation by founding a second imperial capital (Constantinople) in the East, alongside Rome in the West. Then followed the barbarian invasions of the fifth century: apart from Italy, much of which remained within the Empire for some time longer, the West was carved up among barbarian chiefs. The Byzantines never forgot the ideals of Rome under Augustus and Trajan, and still regarded their Empire as in theory universal; but Justinian was the last Emperor who seriously attempted to bridge the gulf between theory and praxis, and his conquests in the West were soon abandoned. The political unity of the Greek East and the Latin West was destroyed by the barbarian invasions, and was never permanently restored.[1]

Into this cultural melting-pot stepped the Fathers of the Church, who often had to dialogue between the Semitic, Roman and Greek cultural visions of the times. The Fathers of the Church are a select group of early Christian teachers, around a hundred in number, depending on the list consulted. The Catholic Church reveres them and gives them a privileged place of doctrinal authority. Many of them are also revered by the Orthodox Churches and other Churches of the East. The Fathers, generally speaking, meet four criteria. First, they are marked by the orthodoxy of their doctrine. Then nearly all the Fathers are marked by holiness of life, and most are revered as saints. Third they are approved by the Church. Finally, they belong to the beginnings of Christianity. The age of the Fathers, sometimes called the Patristic Era, stretched from the middle of the first century until the death of St John Damascene.

The early Church Fathers fall into four basic categories: Apostolic Fathers, ante-Nicene Church Fathers, Nicene and post-Nicene Church Fathers. The Apostolic Church Fathers were contemporaries of the Apostles and were probably taught by them, carrying on the tradition and teaching of the Apostles themselves as their direct successors. Examples of Apostolic Fathers would be Clement and Polycarp. The ante-Nicene Fathers were those who came after the Apostolic Fathers and before the Council of Nicea in 325 AD. Such individuals as Irenaeus and Justin Martyr are ante-Nicene fathers. The Nicene Fathers were those who guided the Church in the fourth century, which was the Golden Age of Doctrine, and includes the Council of Nicaea. These Fathers include Augustine and John Chrysostom. The post-Nicene Church Fathers are such noted men as Jerome, Cyril of Jerusalem, Basil, Ambrose, and Hilary of Poiters.

Knowing that the Fathers were all expected to meet the four criteria of orthodoxy, holiness of life, Church approval, and antiquity we might expect them to be a fairly uniform group. They appear on icons, for example, as long lines of nearly identical men with bald heads and long grey beards; in art, the Fathers seem interchangeable except for the special symbols that artists traditionally place in their hands. However, the Fathers lived in an era that stretched from the middle of the first century AD to the middle of the eighth century. In order to gain perspective, that span is roughly equivalent to the centuries that passed between the time of Marco Polo and the development of the microchip, from Dante's Inferno to the landing on the moon. The Fathers lived in cultures as varied as the high Roman Empire and the first Muslim caliphates, in cosmopolitan cities and in barbarian backwaters, in times of war and in times of peace, though periods of persecution and, finally, through centuries of triumph.

The Fathers would be further distinguished by their works. Some were preachers. Others were popes. Others again were orators and lawyers. Some were academic theologians, others monks and hermits. Some wrote apologies, explaining and defending the Christian faith to the Jews and before hostile or sceptical pagans. Others were exegetes, analysing and expounding the Sacred Scriptures.[2]

The Fathers can also be classified according to the language in which they wrote, be it Latin, Greek or Syriac. Those Fathers who wrote in Latin are generally called the Latin Fathers, those who wrote in Greek, the Greek Fathers, and those who wrote in Syriac, the Syriac Fathers.

6.2 The Latin Fathers

Here is a list of the main Latin Fathers:

St Ambrose of Milan (c. 330–397)
Arnobius (d. 330)
St Augustine of Hippo (354–430)
St Benedict of Nursia (c. 480–543)
St Caesarius of Arles (c. 468–542)
St John Cassian (c. 360–435)
St Celestine I, Pope (reigned 422–432)
St Cornelius, Pope (reigned 251–253)
St Cyprian of Carthage (d. 258)
St Damascus I, Pope (reigned 366–384)
St Dionysius, Pope (reigned 259–268)
St Ennodius of Pavia (473–521)
St Eucherius of Lyons (c. 380–449)
St Fulgentius of Ruspe (464–533)
St Gregory of Elvira (d. after 392)
St Gregory I the Great, Pope (reigned 590–604)
St Hilary of Poitiers (c. 315–368)
St Innocent I, Pope (reigned 401–417)
St Isidore of Seville (560–636)
St Jerome (c. 343–420)
Lactantius (c. 240–323)
St Leo I the Great, Pope (reigned 440–461)
Marius Mercator (c. 390–451)
Marius Victorinus (c. 300–370)
Minucius Felix (2nd century)
St Optatus of Milevis (4th century)
St Pacian of Barcellona (c. 310–390)
St Pamphilus (c. 250–309)

St Paulinus of Nola (c. 353–431)
St Peter Chrysologus (c. 380–450)
St Phoebadius of Agen (d. 395)
Rufinus of Aquileia (c. 345–410)
Salvian (c. 405–495)
St Siricius, Pope (reigned 384–399)
Tertullian (c. 160–223)
St Vincent of Lérins (d. c. 450)

Among the Latin Fathers, we will take a closer look at St Augustine of Hippo.

6.2.1 St Augustine

Augustine was born on 13 November 354, at Thagaste, a Roman *municipium* situated on the Mediterranean side of proconsular Numidia. The ruins of the ancient city lie buried beneath the white buildings of the present-day town of Souk-Ahras in Algeria. His father, whose name was Patricius, a man of generous and impulsive character, a pagan who later became a catechumen, was a small landholder, and a member of the municipal council.[3] His mother, Monica, a Christian richly endowed with human qualities, was educated in modesty and sobriety.[4] The family, which included a brother, Navigius, and a sister whose name we do not know, was of African origin, but the language spoken at home was Latin. The children received a Christian education from Monica. When Augustine, while still a child, was on the verge of dying because of an intestinal blockage, he insistently asked to be baptized but the sacrament was deferred because he recovered.[5] From the first years of his life he showed himself to be "a child of good hope"[6] endowed with a sharp memory and lively intelligence.

When he completed his education at Thagaste in the modest school of a private tutor, he was sent to the Roman colony of Madaura, to continue his studies in grammar and rhetoric. Here, in the homeland of Apuleius, he studied passages from Latin poets and prose-writers, which were commented on and committed to memory. His school experience provided him with a good literary basis, as well as knowledge of elementary notions of mathematics, music and physics. Because of economic difficulties, he was summoned back to Thagaste in 369 by his parents, and there he spent his sixteenth year in idleness, without any scholarly activity, troubled by the feelings of love "What else delighted me then but to love and be loved?"[7]

In the year 371, his father sent him to Carthage to pursue his studies. Thanks to the financial help of a family friend, Romanianus,[8] he was able to enrol there in the School of rhetoric of north Africa, the equivalent of a present-day university, an educational centre for the western part of the Empire and then surpassed in importance only by Rome itself. Here, at seventeen years of age, he continued his studies. At this time he was dominated by three great passions: study, theatrical performances, and the search for sensual pleasure. The following year he decided to live together with a local girl, to whom he seems to have sworn "fidelity as to a legitimate wife". From the union with this unnamed Carthaginian girl, he had a son named Adeodatus.[9] Despite his passion for the performances produced in great numbers in the capital of Numidia, Augustine's commitment to study was steadily growing. "Already I was first in the school of rhetoric, and I found exceptional joy in it."[10]

An excellent training in the knowledge of rhetoric was a requirement, in the fourth century, for a secure career, both in education and in the imperial civil service. The scholastic program for the years 372–373 included the reading of the Cicero's *Hortensius* (a lost work) which contained a ringing exhortation to the study of philosophy and detachment from material goods. The study of this work was to lead Augustine to an unexpected discovery. In the *Confessions* we find his enthusiastic account of this reading:

> At that unstable period of my life, I was studying the books of oratory, in which I was eager to excel, because of a detestable and empty purpose, a joy in human vanity. In the regular course of study, I came upon the book of a

certain Cicero, whose tongue nearly all admire, but not his heart. But that book of his contained an exhortation to philosophy. It was called *Hortensius*. In fact, that book changed my mental attitude (*mutavit affectum meum*). It altered my wishes and my desires. Suddenly, every vain hope became worthless to me and I yearned with unbelievable ardour of heart for the immortality of wisdom. For, it was not to sharpen my tongue (this was the apparent object being bought at my mother's expense, for I was in my nineteenth year and my father had died two years before) it was not, I say, to sharpen my tongue that I used that book. It was not its style of speech which influenced me, but, rather, what it spoke about.[11]

The reading immediately produced an illumination which re-awakened his intelligence and guided his most profound aspirations in a new direction. Augustine became convinced that philosophy is the highest ideal of thought and of life; since it is the search for and love of wisdom, it forms the pre-condition for attaining happiness. The two principal terms of the exhortation to philosophy were, in fact, wisdom and happiness. He embraced this philosophical ideal with a passion which from then onwards was to give a new dimension to all other human ideals in his eyes, ideals of success, pleasure and wealth. The sole disappointment that he felt was the absence in those pages of any mention of the name of Christ.

The only thing to dim my ardour was the fact that the name of Christ was not there, for this name, my youthful heart had drunk in piously with my mother's milk and until that time had retained it in its depths; whatever lacked this name could not completely win me, howsoever well expressed, and polished, and true appearing.[12]

Dominated by a new intellectual interest and persuaded that human existence at its most profound level is defined by the desire for truth and happiness, he decided to open the *Scriptures*. He was disappointed, however, at the obscurity of their content, and at the rough style, not worthy of comparison with Cicero's majestic language.[13] He thought it would be better to entrust himself to those who teach rather than those who order one to believe (*docentibus potiusquam iubentibus esse credendum*).[14] These words explain the long time that Augustine spent far from the Church, whose teaching he initially considered incompatible with rational enquiry.

Having set aside the Scriptures, Augustine did not return to Cicero, but turned rather to the writings of the Manichaeans, in the hope of attaining wisdom through reason alone. Augustine fell into the net of the Manichaeans, who promised a totally rational religion, attracted by two seductive promises: liberation of reason from all forms of conditioning, and the resolution of the problem of evil. His adhesion to the sect, however, was not without reservations: in fact he wrote:

> A childish superstition deterred me from thorough inves-
> tigation, and, as soon as I was more courageous, I cast off
> the darkness and learned to trust more in men who taught
> than in those who ordained obedience, having myself
> encountered persons to whom the very light, seen by their
> eyes, apparently was an object of highest and even divine
> veneration, I did not agree with them, but thought they
> were concealing some important secret which they would
> later divulge.[15]

The faith of Augustine in the sect gradually weakened according to what he tells us in the Confessions[16], mainly because of two factors: the intellectual sterility of the Manichaeans and the weakness of their theory in the field of the physical sciences. While continuing to call himself a Manichaean and to conceive of God and the human soul as material realities and evil as a principle independent of God, his belief in Manichaeism dwindled.

In Augustine's eyes, Rome provided the opportunity for a more serene life and one that would be more brilliant from the professional point of view. In his *Confessions*, Augustine has left us an account of his departure, and his separation from his mother Monica:

> She complained bitterly at the prospect of my leaving,
> and followed me to the seaside. But I deceived her, while

she was urgently trying to get me either to change my
decision or to take her with me. I pretended that I did not
wish to leave a friend until he could set sail with a fair
wind… Yet, when she refused to return without me, I
persuaded her with some difficulty to spend the night in
a place which was near our ship, at a shrine dedicated to
blessed Cyprian. But, on that night, I set out secretly,
while she remained behind in prayer and tears. The wind
blew, filling our sail, and the shore line was lost to our
sight. In the morning, she went wild with sorrow upon
this shore. Yet, after blaming my deceptions and cruelty,
she turned round again to pray to Thee on my behalf. She
went away to her own home and I to Rome.[17]

In Rome he was a guest in the home of a Manichaean *auditor*.
After some time he fell seriously ill.[18] Meanwhile, the doubts
concerning Manichaean teaching became stronger. In the
autumn of 384, his relations with the Manichaeans had definitely
cooled, though he was still unable to overcome their materialism
and dualism, and was attracted more by academic skepticism.
At the end of 384, having followed the Via Flamina and Via
Emilia, Augustine arrived in Milan. In that period he conceived
the created world in this way:

> One great mass, adorned with different kinds of bodies,
> whether the things were in fact bodies, or whether I
> imagined them as such instead of spirits. I made it great,
> not as great as it was, for I could not know this, but as
> great as seemed convenient, and bounded on all sides, of
> course. I imagined embracing it in every part and pene-
> trating it, but remaining everywhere infinite. It was like
> a sea, everywhere and in all directions spreading through
> immense space, simply an infinite sea. And it had in it a
> great sponge, which was finite, however, and this sponge
> was filled, of course, in every part with the immense sea.[19]

In Milan, Monica found her son in a state of total prostration:
"She found me in grievous danger. I was despairing of ever
finding truth."[20] Although he had passed beyond Manichaeism,
Augustine was still assailed by questions and doubts of a

philosophical nature. At that time the Bishop of Milan who had held the see for the last ten years, was Ambrose, son of a high official of the imperial administration. He knew both eastern and western Christian literature, as well as Neoplatonic philosophy. Around Ambrose a group of intellectuals had formed, who united the study of Platonic philosophy with Christian religious practice. From early on in his stay in Milan, Augustine began to attend the Sunday liturgy, with the aim of listening to Ambrose.[21] The preaching of Ambrose helped: on the one hand it caused him to rid himself of two prejudices with which Manichaeanism had infected his mind; the anthropomorphic representation of God[22] and the aversion to the Old Testament[23], on the other hand it clarified in his mind the spiritual notion of God: "For I have noticed frequently in the sermons of our priest, and sometimes in yours, that, when speaking of God, no one should think of Him as something corporal, nor even of the soul, which in the world is the only thing very near to God."[24]

According to recent research,[25] Augustine did not confine himself to reading the Scriptures, nor to listening to the sermons of Bishop Ambrose and conversing with the priest Simplicianus and with Marcus Theodorus, but he also devoted himself to reading Christian writers such as Ambrose, Marius Victorinus and Tertullian, to reflect on the arguments which were particularly dear to them: the doctrine of the Trinity, the meaning of the divine authority of Christ, the problem of the soul and that of evil. In fact in the early dialogues there are already verbal and doctrinal traces of these readings, which show the influence on the new convert not only of pagan literature, but also of a part of Christian literature.

In August 386, Augustine was in the garden of his house. His attention was attracted by a strange and mysterious sing-song voice which repeated "Tolle, lege" ("Take up and read"); perturbed, he went back to pick up the book he had momentarily left aside, and read the first verse in it:

> "Not in revelry and drunkenness, not in debauchery and wantonness, not in strife and jealousy; but put on the Lord

Jesus Christ, and as for the flesh, take no thought for its lusts." No further did I desire to read, nor was there need. Indeed, immediately with the conclusion of this sentence, all the darkness of doubt were dispersed, as if by a light of peace flooding into my heart.[26]

His conversion to Christianity on 15 August 386 therefore came at the end of a long and tormented inner journey and Augustine moved to the countryside north of Milan by Lake Como — with his mother Monica, his son Adeodatus and a small group of friends — to prepare himself for Baptism. So it was that at the age of 32 Augustine was baptized by Ambrose in the Cathedral of Milan on 24 April 387, during the Easter Vigil.

One of Augustine's most beautiful and famous passages describes his conversion:

Late have I loved you, beauty so old and so new: late have I loved you. And see, you were within and I was in the external world and sought you there, and in my unlovely state I plunged into those lovely created things which you made. You were with me, and I was not with you. The lovely things kept me far from you, though if they did not have their existence in you, they had no existence at all. You called and cried aloud and shattered my deafness. You were radiant and resplendent, you put to flight my blindness. You were fragrant, and I drew in my breath and now pant after you. I tasted you, and I feel but hunger and thirst for you. You touched me, and I am set on fire to attain the peace which is yours.[27]

After his Baptism, Augustine decided to return to Africa with his friends, with the idea of living a community life of the monastic kind at the service of God. However, while awaiting their departure in Ostia, his mother fell ill unexpectedly and died shortly afterwards, breaking her son's heart. Having returned to his homeland at last, the convert settled in Hippo for the very purpose of founding a monastery. In this city on the African coast he was ordained a priest in 391, despite his reticence, and with a few companions began the monastic life which had long been in his mind, dividing his time between prayer, study and preaching.[28]

Adapting his life of meditation, Augustine learned, often with difficulty, to make the fruit of his intelligence available to others. He learned to communicate his faith to simple people and thus learned to live for them in what became his hometown, tirelessly carrying out a generous and onerous activity which he describes in one of his most beautiful sermons: "To preach continuously, discuss, reiterate, edify, be at the disposal of everyone—it is an enormous responsibility, a great weight, an immense effort."[29]

He was ordained a Bishop in Hippo four years later, in 395. Augustine continued to deepen his study of Scripture and of the texts of the Christian tradition and was an exemplary bishop in his tireless pastoral commitment: he preached several times a week to his faithful, supported the poor and orphans, supervised the formation of the clergy and the organization of men's and women's monasteries. He was very active in the government of his diocese—with remarkable, even civil, implications—during more than 35 years of episcopate. As bishop of Hippo Augustine exercised a vast influence on the Catholic Church in Roman Africa and, more generally, on early Christianity, coping with religious tendencies and tenacious, disruptive heresies such as Manichaeism, Donatism and Pelagianism, which endangered the Christian faith in the triune God, rich in mercy.

6.3 The Greek Fathers

Here is a list of the main Greek Fathers:

St Anastasius of Sinai (c. 640–700)
St Andrew of Crete (c. 650–726)
Aphraates (c. 270–345)
St Athanasius (c. 296–373)
Athenagoras (c. 133–190)
St Basil the Great (c. 329–379)
St Caesarius of Nazianzus (c. 331–369)

St Clement of Alexandria (c. 150–215)
St Clement I of Rome, Pope (reigned 88–97)
St. Cyril, Patriarch of Alexandria (376–444)
St Cyril of Jerusalem (c. 313–386)
Didymus the Blind, theologian (313–398)
Eusebius of Caesarea (260–340)
St Eustathius of Antioch (c. 270–350)
St Firmillian (d. 268)
Gennadius I of Constantinople (5th century)
St Germanus of Constantinople (634–733)
St Gregory of Nazianzus (329–390)
St Gregory of Nyssa (330–395)
St Gregory Thaumaturgus (213–270)
St Gregory of Pontus (d. 268)
Hermas (2nd century)
St Hippolytus (170–236)
St Ignatius of Antioch (c. 35–107)
St Irenaeus of Lyons (d. c. 202)
St Isidore of Pelusium (c. 360–450)
St John Chrysostom (347–407)
St John Climacus (579–649)
St John Damascene (675–749)
St. Justin Martyr (100–165)
St Leontius of Byzantium (c. 485–555)
St Macarius (c. 300–390)
St Maximus the Confessor (580–662)
St Melito of Sardis (d.c. 180)
St Methodius of Olympus (d.c. 311)
St Nilus the Elder (d.c. 430)
Origen (184–254)
St Polycarp (c. 69–155)
St Proclus of Constantinople (d.c. 446)
Pseudo-Dionysius the Areopagite (6th century)
St Serapion (d.c. 370)
St Sophronius of Jerusalem (560–638)
Tatian the Assyrian, apologist and theologian (120–180)

Theodore of Mopsuestia (350–428)
Theodoret of Cyrrhus (c. 393–458)
St Theophilus of Antioch (late 2nd century)

6.3.1 Theological Schools of Alexandria and Antioch

The inner consolidation of Christianity in the third century is particularly evident and impressive in the domain of early patristic literature. More and more frequently, members of the ruling and educated classes joined the new faith and felt impelled to serve it by word and writing in ways which corresponded with their level of culture. This created an essential condition for the development of a learned theology, relating faith and reason.[30] The earliest attempts of this kind are found as early as the second century, when educated converts such as Justin and his pupil Tatian presented themselves publicly in Rome as teachers of the "new philosophy", and gave a well-grounded introduction to the understanding of the Christian faith to a relatively small circle of pupils. The "schools" of these teachers were not, however, institutions of the Roman Christian community itself, but private undertakings by learned Christians. Out of a sense of missionary obligation, and in the manner of philosophical teachers of the time, these men expounded their religious beliefs to a circle of those who might be interested, and substantiated them by constant comparison with human reflection.[31]

In the Greek East, the Egyptian capital of Alexandria, with its scientific tradition and the interest generally shown by its educated upper classes in religious and philosophical questions, was to prove the most favourable soil for the development of a Christian theology on a learned intellectual basis. Founded in about 180 AD by Pantaenus (a former Stoic philosopher of Sicilian origin), the theological School of Alexandria in Egypt was the first-known organized Christian institution of higher learning. Any interested person, pagan or Christian, could frequent this private school, and the syllabus was entirely a matter for the teacher's judgment. Clement of Alexandria must be considered to have been the second teacher of this kind, but he cannot be regarded as the successor of Pantaenus at the head of any school. He publicly taught the "true gnosis" independently of, and perhaps even simultaneously with Pantaenus. The first phase of Origen's teaching activity still had this private character.[32]

Alexandria became a leading centre of the allegorical method of Scripture interpretation, which was the same exegetical method practiced by Palestinian Rabbinical schools. Allegorical exegesis involves, as St Augustine noted, understanding one passage of Scripture by virtue of example, concept, or another passage. Allegory differs from the parable method in its statement of doctrinal truths rather than practical advice. It also differs from the literal method of Scripture interpretation, in which the basic meaning of a passage is considered. An example of allegory in the Bible is that of the vine, found in Psalm 80:8–16 and Isaiah 5:1–6.

Under such leaders as Clement (c. 150–215) and Origen (c. 185–254), the theological School of Alexandria endorsed a reestablishment of relations between Christian faith and Greek culture (including the Platonic philosophical tradition), and attempted to preserve Orthodox Christianity in the face of heterodox theologies during periods of doctrinal transition. The Alexandrians typically found allegory in most every passage of Scripture. Moreover, in their accounts of the person of Christ, they tended to focus almost exclusively on His divinity.

Some critics have noted that the Alexandrians, in trying to protect against an overemphasis on the humanity of Christ (which they felt led to such heresies as Nestorianism as will be seen in the next chapter),[33] sometimes leaned toward tritheism, into which Origen is said to have drifted. Monophysitism (the view that virtually negates Christ's humanity by claiming Him to be divine only) is considered to have been an extreme form of Alexandrian Christological thinking.

The beginnings of the second theological school in the East are no less obscure than those of the Alexandrian school. It sprang up in the Syrian capital of Antioch, an important centre of the Hellenic world where conditions were similar to those in

Alexandria. Tradition unanimously names the Antiochian priest Lucian (d. 312) as founder of the school, which may have been preceded by undertakings on a smaller scale and more private in character. In the time of Bishop Paul of Samosata, a priest named Malchion enjoyed a considerable reputation in Antioch for wide learning, but he was a teacher in a secular Greek school. He demonstrated his superior theological training in the controversy with Paul of Samosata at the Synod of Antioch (268) which led to the latter's condemnation. Dorotheus, a contemporary of Lucian, another priest of Antioch with praiseworthy biblical interests and knowledge of Hebrew, was also connected with this School, but he is not expressly said to have been a Christian teacher. It is only with Lucian that the records in the sources become more precise. The fact that Lucian was one of the clergy of Antioch permits the assumption that his activity as a Christian teacher was authorized by his bishop. His theological learning, which is praised by Eusebius, did not find expression in extensive publications. His real interest lay in biblical work and more particularly in a new revision of the Septuagint, for which he consulted the Hebrew original. It enjoyed a fine reputation and was widely used in the dioceses of Syria and Asia Minor. Lucian's exegetical method must be gathered from the biblical works of his pupils; mainly it takes into account the literal sense and only employs typological interpretation where the text itself demands it. Similarly, it is only from the works of his pupils that it is possible to form an idea of Lucian's other theological characteristics. He always starts from biblical data, not from theological presuppositions, and attains, among other things, a strict Subordinationism in the doctrine of the Logos.[34] Thus Lucian's strictly theological perspectives were heterodox, and Arius and Eusebius of Nicomedia claimed to be his students, even calling themselves Lucianists.[35] The characteristics of the Antiochene school became fully clear only in the great age of the Fathers, in connection with the Trinitarian and Christological controversies.

The School of Antioch, which emphasized the literal interpretation of the Bible, in some ways contrasted the approaches of the School of Alexandria. Antioch also stressed the completeness of Christ's humanity. This School flourished in the fourth to the sixth centuries, and gave rise to several significant theologians, including Diodore of Tarsus, Theodore of Mopsuestia, Theodoret of Cyrrhus, and St John Chrysostom.

Unlike Theodore of Mopsuestia, St John Chrysostom was foremost a preacher, aptly earning the title *Chrysostomos*, or Golden-Mouthed. The vast majority of Chrysostom's writings were expositions of the Bible, in which he demonstrated himself to be a rigid proponent of Antiochene literalism. His sermons are reflections of the ecclesiastical, cultural, and social status of Constantinople and Antioch in that day. Not hesitant to denounce and condemn heresy, Chrysostom's legacy to Orthodoxy is that of an outstanding rhetorician, writer, homilist, and liturgist.

The final renowned Antiochene bishop, Theodoret of Cyrrhus (c. 393–458), was also a prolific author. His writings were extensive in range, but the most noteworthy are his *Ecclesiastical History*, which continued Eusebius' work to 428, and his *Remedy for Greek Maladies*, which was a series of ancient apologies against paganism. Theodoret also zealously defended Antiochene Christology against Bishop Cyril of Alexandria's theology.

6.3.2 The Cappadocian Fathers

The Cappadocian Fathers (or Cappadocian philosophers) are Basil the Great (330–379), who was bishop of Caesarea; Basil's brother Gregory of Nyssa (c. 330–395), who was bishop of Nyssa; and a close friend, Gregory of Nazianzus (329–389), who became Patriarch of Constantinople. An older sister of Basil and Gregory of Nyssa, St Macrina, became a nun and converted the family's estate into a monastic community. Abbess Macrina there fostered the education and development of the three Cappadocians by providing a peaceful shelter for study and meditation. The Cappadocia region, in modern-day Turkey, was an early site of Christian activity, with several missions by Paul in this region. They, along with St Athanasius the Great, laid the pattern for formulating the doctrines related to the mystery of the Holy

Trinity. The three Cappadocians were characterised by the expression that St Basil was the arm which acted, St Gregory of Nazianzus the mouth which spoke and St Gregory of Nyssa the head which did the thinking.[36]

These three scholars set out to demonstrate that Christians could hold their own in conversations with learned Greek-speaking intellectuals and that Christian faith, while it opposed many of the ideas of Plato and Aristotle (and other Greek philosophers), was an almost scientific and distinctive movement with the healing of the soul of man and his union with God at its centre—one best represented by monasticism. They made major contributions to the definition of the doctrine of the Holy Trinity finalized at the First Council of Constantinople in 381 and the definitive version of the Nicene Creed.

These Fathers made key responses to Arianism, Apollinarianism, and the *Filioque* debate. Subsequent to the First Council of Nicea, Arianism did not simply disappear. The semi-Arians taught that the Son is of like substance with the Father (*homoiousios*) as against the outright Arians who taught that the Son was not like the Father. So the Son was held to be like the Father but not of the same essence as the Father. The Cappadocians worked to bring these semi-Arians back to the orthodox cause. In their writings they made extensive use of the (now orthodox) formula "one substance (*ousia*) in three persons (*hypostaseis*)". The relationship is understandable, argued Basil of Caesarea, in a parallel drawn from Platonism: any three human beings are each individual persons and all share a common universal, their humanity. The formulation explicitly acknowledged a distinction between the Father, the Son and the Holy Spirit, (a distinction that Nicea had been accused of blurring), but at the same time insisting on their essential unity.

Among the Greek Fathers of Cappadocia, we will take a closer look at St Gregory of Nazianzus.

6.3.3 St Gregory of Nazianzus

Gregory was born into a noble family in about 330 AD, and his mother consecrated him to God at birth. After his education at home, he attended the most famous schools of his time: he first went to Caesarea in Cappadocia, where he made friends with Basil, the future Bishop of that city, and went on to stay in other capitals of the ancient world, such as Alexandria, Egypt and in particular Athens, where once again he met Basil. Remembering this friendship, Gregory was later to write: "Then not only did I feel full of veneration for my great Basil because of the seriousness of his morals and the maturity and wisdom of his speeches, but he induced others who did not yet know him to be like him The same eagerness for knowledge motivated us. This was our competition: not who was first but who allowed the other to be first."[37]

On his return home, Gregory received Baptism and developed an inclination for monastic life: solitude as well as philosophical and spiritual meditation fascinated him, as he wrote:

> Nothing seems to me greater than this: to silence one's senses, to emerge from the flesh of the world, to withdraw into oneself, no longer to be concerned with human things other than what is strictly necessary; to converse with oneself and with God, to lead a life that transcends the visible; to bear in one's soul divine images, ever pure, not mingled with earthly or erroneous forms; truly to be a perfect mirror of God and of divine things, and to become so more and more, taking light from light...; to enjoy, in the present hope, the future good, and to converse with angels; to have already left the earth even while continuing to dwell on it, borne aloft by the spirit.[38]

As he confides in his autobiography, he received priestly ordination with a certain reluctance for he knew that he could later have to be a bishop, to look after others and their affairs, hence, could no longer be absorbed in pure meditation.[39] However, he subsequently accepted this vocation and took on the pastoral ministry in full obedience, accepting, as often happened to him in his life, to be carried by Providence where he did not wish to go (cf. Jn 21:18). In 371, his friend Basil, Bishop of Caesarea, against Gregory's own wishes, desired to ordain him Bishop of Sasima, a strategically important locality in Cappadocia. Because of various problems, however, he never took possession of this see and instead stayed on in the city of Nazianzus.

In about 379, Gregory was called to Constantinople, the capital, to head the small Catholic community faithful to the Council of Nicea and to belief in the Holy Trinity. The majority adhered instead to Arianism, which was "politically correct" and viewed by emperors as politically useful.[40] Thus, he found himself in a condition of minority, surrounded by hostility. He delivered five *Theological Orations* in the little church of the Anastasis precisely in order to defend the Trinitarian faith and to make it intelligible.[41] These discourses became famous because of the soundness of his doctrine and his ability to reason, which truly made clear that this was the divine logic. And the splendour of their form also makes them fascinating today. It was because of these orations that Gregory acquired the nickname: *The Theologian*. His way of elaborating theology was not merely human reflection or even less, only a fruit of complicated speculation, but rather sprang from a life of prayer and holiness, from a persevering dialogue with God. In the silence of contemplation, interspersed with wonder at the marvels of the mystery revealed, his soul was engrossed in beauty and divine glory.

While Gregory was taking part in the Second Ecumenical Council in 381, he was elected Bishop of Constantinople and presided over the Council; but he was challenged straightaway by strong opposition, to the point that the situation became untenable. These hostilities must have been unbearable to such a sensitive soul. What Gregory had previously lamented with heartfelt words was repeated: "We have divided Christ, we who so loved God and Christ! We have lied to one another because of the Truth, we have harboured sentiments of hatred because of Love, we are separated from one another."[42] Thus, in a tense atmosphere, the time came for him to resign. In the packed cathedral, Gregory delivered a farewell discourse of great effectiveness and dignity. He ended his heartrending speech with these words: "Farewell, great city, beloved by Christ... My children, I beg you, jealously guard the deposit of faith that has been entrusted to you (see 1 Tm 6:20), remember my suffering (see Col 4:18). May the grace of Our Lord Jesus Christ be with you all."[43]

Gregory returned to Nazianzus and for about two years devoted himself to the pastoral care of this Christian community. He then withdrew definitively to solitude in nearby Arianzum, his birthplace, and dedicated himself to studies and the ascetic life, and to his garden. It was in this period that he wrote the majority of his poetic works and especially his autobiography: the *De Vita Sua*, a reinterpretation in verse of his own human and spiritual journey, an exemplary journey of a suffering Christian, of a man of profound interiority in a world full of conflicts. He is a man who makes us aware of God's primacy, hence, also speaks to us, to this world of ours: without God, man loses his grandeur; without God, there is no true humanism.[44]

Gregory was a mild man and always sought in his life to bring peace to the Church of his time, torn apart by discord and heresy. He strove with Gospel daring to overcome his own timidity in order to proclaim the truth of the faith. He felt deeply the yearning to draw close to God, to be united with him. He expressed it in one of his poems in which he writes: "Among the great billows of the sea of life, here and there whipped up by wild winds... one thing alone is dear to me, my only treasure, comfort and oblivion in my struggle, the light of the Blessed Trinity."[45] Gregory wrote how Mary, who gave Christ His human nature, is the true Mother of God, or *Theotokos*.[46] With a view to her most exalted mission she was "purified in advance" which is already a distant prelude to the Dogma of the Immaculate Conception.[47] Mary is proposed to Christians, and especially to virgins, as a model and a help to call upon in times of need.[48]

Gregory teaches that human persons must show solidarity with one another. He writes: "We are all one in the Lord (cf. Rm 12:5), rich and poor, slaves and free, healthy and sick alike; and one is the Head from which all derive: Jesus Christ. And as with the members of one body, each is concerned with the other, and all with all." He emphasizes that man must imitate God's goodness and love:

> If you are healthy and rich, alleviate the need of whoever is sick and poor; if you have not fallen, go to the aid of whoever has fallen and lives in suffering; if you are glad, comfort whoever is sad; if you are fortunate, help whoever is smitten with misfortune. Give God proof of your gratitude for you are one who can benefit and not one who needs to be benefited... Be rich not only in possessions but also in piety; not only in gold but in virtue, or rather, in virtue alone. Outdo your neighbour's reputation by showing yourself to be kinder than all; make yourself God for the unfortunate, imitating God's mercy.[49]

Gregory teaches first and foremost the importance and necessity of prayer: "It is necessary to remember God more often than one breathes", because prayer is the encounter of God's thirst with our thirst.[50] God is thirsting for us to thirst for Him.[51] In a poem which is at the same time a meditation on the purpose of life and an implicit invocation to God, Gregory wrote:

> You have a task, my soul, a great task if you so desire. Scrutinize yourself seriously, your being, your destiny; where you come from and where you must rest; seek to know whether it is life that you are living or if it is something more. You have a task, my soul, so purify your life: Please consider God and his mysteries, investigate what existed before this universe and what it is for you, where you come from and what your destiny will be. This is your task, my soul; therefore, purify your life.[52]

In 390, God welcomed into His arms this faithful servant who had defended Him in his writings with keen intelligence and had praised Him in his poetry with such great love.

6.4 The Syriac Fathers

6.4.1 Origins of Syriac

Syriac is a form of Aramaic, a language whose many dialects have been in continuous use since the eleventh century BC. Originally the language of the Aramean people, Aramaic became the lingua franca of the Near East by the sixth century BC. It was the native tongue of the ancient Chaldeans, a second language to the Assyro-Babylonians, an official language of the Persian Achaemenians, and a common language of the Jews replacing Hebrew. Jesus and the Apostles spoke and preached in Aramaic. Syriac is the Aramaic dialect of Edessa (present-day Urfa in southeast Turkey), a centre of early intellectual activity. It became an important literary language around the second and third centuries. The earliest dated Syriac inscription is from AD 6, and the earliest parchment, a deed of sale, is from 243. The earliest dated manuscript was produced in November 411, probably the earliest dated manuscript in any language.

The oldest of the Syriac scripts, known as Estrangelo "rounded", was fully developed by the fifth century. Later, two geographic scripts would derive from it: West Syriac, whose proper name is Serto, and East Syriac. The Syriac writing system lent its vocalization system to Hebrew and Arabic in the seventh century, before which Semitic languages were written using consonants only. Syriac is written from right to left. It is a cursive script where some, but not all, letters connect within a word. The alphabet consists of 22 letters, all of which are consonants.

The spread of Syriac was based on at least two factors: the spread of Christianity in the Semitic-speaking world, and commerce on the Silk Road; both activities sometimes overlapped. A testimony of this rather remarkable expansion is the bilingual Chinese and Syriac text from Sian in China. Today, a few million Christians in India of various denominations follow the Syriac tradition. Within a few centuries from its origin, Syriac produced a wealth of literature in all sorts of fields, literary, philosophical, liturgical, scientific, historical, and linguistic, to name but a few.

The fourth century witnessed the first major writings that survived till this day. The oldest Syrian Church Father Aphraates (or Aphrahat), called the Persian sage, was an ascetic and probably also a bishop (in the monastery of St Matthew near Mosul). Twenty-three treatises are extant, which were written in the years 337–345; they give a kind of survey of the whole body of Christian doctrine. The most celebrated writer of this period, however, is Ephrem the Syrian (c. 306–373), the "lyre of the Holy Spirit". He is the theologian-poet par excellence, and perhaps, the only theologian-poet to rank beside Dante. Ephrem produced a wealth of theological works in prose and artistic poetry. His fame resulted in many writings of later centuries to be attributed to him. Of his genuine works, however, we have received many commentaries, expositions, refutations, letters, and, above all, poetry.

Another Syriac Father is Jacob of Sarug, Bishop of Batnae near Edessa (d. 521). We are informed about his life and work by no less than three different bio-bibliographical accounts.[53] He wrote many prose letters and sermons, also funeral orations and edifying biographies ; he translated the six *Centuria* of Evagrius Ponticus. There are further long metrical Homilies (e.g. 3300 lines on the Passion of our Lord), partly of a high poetical standard, and religious hymns, some of which have been incorporated in the liturgy. Several Liturgies or Anaphora as well as an Order of Baptism and Confirmation are also attributed to him. We now take a closer look at St Ephrem.

6.4.2 St Ephrem the Syrian

St Ephrem the Syrian was born into a Christian family in Nisibis in about 306 AD. He was educated and grew up beside James, Bishop of Nisibis (303–338), and with him founded the theological school in his city. He was ordained a deacon and was intensely active in local Christian community life until 363, the year when Nisibis fell into Persian hands. Ephrem then emigrated to Edessa, where he continued his activity as a preacher. He died in this city in 373, a victim of the disease he contracted while caring for those infected with the plague. It is not known for certain whether he was a monk, but we can be sure in any case that he remained a deacon throughout his life and embraced virginity and poverty. Thus, the common and fundamental Christian identity appears in the specificity of his own cultural expression: faith, hope—the hope which makes it possible to live poor and chaste in this world, placing every expectation in the Lord—and lastly, charity, to the point of giving his life through nursing those sick with the plague.

St Ephrem has left an important theological inheritance. His substantial corpus can be divided into four categories: works written in ordinary prose (his polemic works or biblical commentaries); works written in poetic prose; homilies in verse; and lastly, hymns, undoubtedly Ephrem's most abundant production. He is a rich and interesting author in many ways, but especially from the theological point of view. It is the fact that theology and poetry converge in his work which makes it so special. If we desire to approach his doctrine, we must insist on this from the outset: namely, on the fact that he produces theology in poetical form. Poetry enabled him to deepen his theological reflection through paradoxes and images. At the same time, his theology became liturgy, became music; indeed, he was a great composer, a musician. Theology, reflection on the faith, poetry, song and praise of God go together; and it is precisely in this liturgical character that the divine truth emerges clearly in Ephrem's theology. In his search for God, in his theological activity, he employed the way of paradoxes and symbols. He made ample use of contrasting images because they served to emphasize the mystery of God. On the Nativity of Christ. Ephrem expressed his wonder before the Virgin Mary in inspired tones:

> The Lord entered her and became a servant; the Word entered her, and became silent within her; thunder entered her and his

voice was still; the Shepherd of all entered her; he became a Lamb in her, and came forth bleating.

He that gives food to all went in, and knew hunger. He who gives drink to all went in, and knew thirst. Naked and bare came forth from her the Clother of all things in beauty[54]

To express the mystery of Christ, Ephrem uses a broad range of topics, expressions and images. In one of his hymns he effectively links Adam (in Paradise) to Christ in the Eucharist:

It was by closing with the sword of the cherub that the path to the tree of life was closed. But for the peoples, the Lord of this tree gave himself as food in his (Eucharistic) oblation.

The trees of the Garden of Eden were given as food to the first Adam. For us, the gardener of the Garden in person made himself food for our souls. Indeed, we had all left Paradise together with Adam, who left it behind him.[55]

To speak of the Eucharist, Ephrem adopted two images, embers or burning coal and the pearl.[56] The burning coal theme was taken from the Prophet Isaiah (cf. Is 6: 6). It is the image of one of the seraphim who picks up a burning coal with tongs and simply touches the lips of the Prophet with it in order to purify them; the Christian, on the other hand, touches and consumes the Burning Coal which is Christ himself:

In your bread hides the Spirit who cannot be consumed; in your wine is the fire that cannot be swallowed. The Spirit in your bread, fire in your wine: behold a wonder heard from our lips.

The seraph could not bring himself to touch the glowing coal with his fingers, it was Isaiah's mouth alone that it touched; neither did the fingers grasp it nor the mouth swallow it; but the Lord has granted us to do both these things.

The fire came down with anger to destroy sinners, but the fire of grace descends on the bread and settles in it. Instead of the fire that destroyed man, we have consumed the fire in the bread and have been invigorated.[57]

St Ephrem also speaks of the pearl, both as a Eucharistic image and as a symbol of the riches and beauty of faith:

I placed the pearl, my brothers, on the palm of my hand, to be able to examine it. I began to look at it from one side and from the other: it looked the same from all sides. Thus is the search for the Son inscrutable, because it is all light. In its clarity I saw the Clear One who does not grow opaque; and in his purity, the great symbol of the Body of Our Lord, which is pure. In his indivisibility I saw the truth which is indivisible.[58]

Ephrem is a theologian who reflects poetically, on the basis of Holy Scripture, on the mystery of man's redemption brought about by Christ, the Word of God incarnate. His is a theological reflection expressed in images and symbols taken from nature, daily life and the Bible. Ephrem gives his poetry and liturgical hymns a didactic and catechetical character: they are theological hymns yet at the same time suitable for recitation or liturgical song. On the occasion of liturgical feasts, Ephrem made use of these hymns to spread Church doctrine. Time has proven them to be an extremely effective catechetical instrument for the Christian community.

Ephrem reflected on the theme of God the Creator: nothing in creation is isolated and the world, next to Sacred Scripture, is a Bible of God:

The keys of doctrine which unlock all of Scripture's books,
have opened up before my eyes the book of creation
the treasure house of the Ark, the crown of the Law.
This is a book which, above its companions, has in its narrative
made the Creator perceptible and transmitted His actions;
it has envisioned all His craftsmanship, made manifest His
works of art.[59]

By using his freedom wrongly, man upset the cosmic order, but Christ redeemed him:

Adam was heedless as guardian of Paradise,
for the crafty thief stealthily entered;
leaving aside the fruit—which most men would covet—
he stole instead the Gardens inhabitant!
Adam's Lord came out to seek him; He entered Sheol and found
him there,
then led and brought him out to set him once more in Paradise.[60]

The role of women was important to Ephrem. The way he spoke of them was always inspired with sensitivity and respect: the dwelling place of Jesus in Mary's womb greatly increased women's dignity. Ephrem held that just as there is no Redemption without Jesus, there is no Incarnation without Mary. The divine and human dimensions of the mystery of our redemption can already be found in Ephrem's texts; poetically and with fundamentally scriptural images, he anticipated the theological background and in some way the very language of the great Christological definitions of the fifth-century Councils.

Ephrem, honoured by Christian tradition with the title *Harp of the Holy Spirit*, remained a deacon of the Church throughout his life. It was a crucial and emblematic decision: he was a deacon, a servant, in his liturgical ministry, and more radically, in his love for Christ, whose praises he sang in an unparalleled way, and also in his love for his brethren, whom he introduced with rare skill to the knowledge of divine Revelation.

Notes

[1]   For a detailed description of the barbarians see chapter twelve below.

[2]   M. Aquilina, *The Fathers of the Church. An Introduction to the First Christian Teachers* (Huntington, IN: Our Sunday Visitor Press, 1999).

[3]   Possidius, *Life of Saint Augustine* 1,1. See also V. Pacioni, *Augustine of Hippo. His Philosophy in a Historical and Contemporary Perspective* (Leominster: Gracewing, 2010), p. 1.

[4]   St Augustine, *Confessions*, IX, 9, 19–22.

[5]   *Ibid.*, I, 11, 17.

[6]   *Ibid.*, I, 16, 26.

[7]   *Ibid.*, II, 2, 2.

[8]   *Ibid.,.,* III, I, 1.

[9]   *Ibid.*, IV, 2, 2.

[10]   *Ibid.*, III, 3, 6.

[11]   *Ibid.*, III 4, 7.

[12]   *Ibid.*, III, 4, 8.

[13]   *Ibid.*, III, 5,9.

[14]   St Augustine, *De beata vita, v*, 1, 4.

[15]   *Ibid., v.* 1, 4.

[16]   St Augustine, *Confessions,,* V, 3,3.

17   *Ibid.*, V, 8, 15.

18   *Ibid.* V, 9, 16.

19   *Ibid.*, VII, 5, 7.

20   *Ibid.*, VI, 1, 1.

21   *Ibid.*, V, 13, 23.

22   St Augustine, *De beata vita*, 1, 4.

23   St Augustine, *Confessions*, V, 14, 24; VI, 4, 6.

24   St Augustine, *De beata vita*, 1, 4.

25   See Pacioni, *Augustine of Hippo*, pp. 18–19, 24. He refers to two fundamental essays by N. Cipriani which appeared in the 1990s: *Le fonti cristiane della dottrina trinitaria nei primi dialoghi di S.Agostino*, «Augustinianum» XXXIV, 1994, pp. 253–312, and *L'ispirazione tertullianea nel «De libero arbitrio» di S. Agostino*, in *Il mistero del male e la libertà possibile: lettura dei dialoghi di S.Agostino*, Roma 1994, pp. 165–178.

26   St Augustine, *Confessions,*, VIII, 12, 29–30.

27   *Ibid.*, X, 27, 38.

28   See the *Rule of St Augustine*, which precedes that of St Benedict by about 120 years. See also chapter 11 below.

29   St Augustine, *Sermon*, 339, 4.

30   See chapter 9 below.

31   See K. Baus, *History of the Church* (eds. H. Jedin and J. Dolan), Volume 1, *From the Apostolic Community to Constantine* (New York: Herder, 1965), pp. 229–230.

32   *Ibid.*

33   See chapter 7, subsection 7.2.14 below.

34   Baus, *History of the Church*, Volume 1, p. 241f.

35   For the heresy of Arianism see chapter 7, subsection 7.2.9 below.

36   See J. Quasten *Patrology* (Utrecht: Spectrum, 1960), Vol. III, pp. 204, 236, 254.

37   St Gregory Nazianzen, *Orationes* 43: 16, 20.

38   *Ibid.*, 2: 7.

39   Cf. St Gregory Nazianzen, *Carmina historica*, 2: 1, 11, *De Vita Sua*, 340–349 in *PG* 37, 1053.

40   See Pope Benedict XVI, *Discourse at General Audience* (8 August 2007).

41   St Gregory Nazianzen, *Orationes*, 27–31 in *SC* 250, 70–343.

42   Idem, *Oratio* 6, 3 in *SC* 405, 128.

43   Idem, *Oratio* 42, 27 in *SC* 384, 112–114.

44   See Pope Benedict XVI, *Discourse at General Audience* (8 August 2007).

45   St Gregory Nazianzen, *Carmina historica*, 2, 1, 15 in *PG* 37, 1250ff.

46   Idem., *Epistle* 101, 16 in *SC* 208, 42.

47   Idem, *Oratio* 38, 13 in *SC* 358, 132.

[48]   Idem, *Oratio* 24, 11 in *SC* 282, 60–64.

[49]   Idem, *Oration,* 14, 26 *De Pauperum Amore* in PG 35, 892.

[50]   Idem, *Oratio* 27, 4 in *SC* 250, 78.

[51]   Cf. Idem, *Oratio* 40, 27 in *SC* 358, 260.

[52]   Idem, *Carmina historica* 2, 1, 78 in *PG* 37, 1425–1426.

[53]   According to the studies of P. Peeters, P. Krueger and C. Vona the letters betraying his Monophysite outlook have wrongly been foisted upon him; but this does not yet seem to have been conclusively proved.

[54]   St Ephrem, *Hymn on the Nativity,* 11:6–8.

[55]   Idem, *Hymn 49:* 9–11.

[56]   See Pope Benedict XVI, *Discourse at General Audience* (28 November 2007).

[57]   St Ephrem, Hymn *De Fide* 10: 8–10.

[58]   Idem, Hymn *On the Pearl* 1: 2–3.

[59]   Idem, Hymn *On Paradise,* 6:1.

[60]   *Ibid.,* 8:10.

7 COUNCILS AND HERESIES

Viewing the common public prosperity enjoyed at this moment, as the result of the great power of divine grace, I am desirous above all things that the blessed members of the Catholic Church should be preserved in one faith, in sincere love, and in one form of religion, towards Almighty God. But, since no firmer or more effective measure could be adopted to secure this end, than that of submitting everything relating to our most holy religion to the examination of all, or most of all, the bishops, I convened as many of them as possible, and took my seat among them as one of yourselves; for I would not deny that truth which is the source of my greatest joy, namely, that I am your fellow-servant.

Constantine the Great, *Letter on the Council of Nicaea*

7.1 Councils

ECUMENICAL COUNCILS ARE those to which the bishops, and others entitled to vote, are convoked from the whole world (*oikoumene*) under the presidency of the Pope or his legates, and the decrees of which, having received papal confirmation, bind all Christians. A council, ecumenical in its convocation, may fail to secure the approbation of the whole Church or of the Pope, and thus not rank in authority with Ecumenical councils. We consider here the first five Ecumenical councils in the beginnings of Christianity

7.1.1 The First Council of Nicaea

Though the Council of Jerusalem (Acts 15 and Galatians 2) was the first Church Council, attended by the Apostles, the first

Ecumenical (world-wide) Council was convened by the Roman Emperor Constantine the Great with Pope Saint Sylvester I sitting on the Throne of Peter as the thirty-third successor of Christ's appointed Apostle. The site was the city of Nicaea (now known as İznik, in modern-day Turkey), just south of Constantinople in Asia Minor, a place easily accessible to the majority of the bishops, particularly those from Asia Minor, Syria, Palestine, Egypt, Greece, and Thrace. A special importance was also attached to this Council because the persecution of Christians had just ended with the the Edict of Milan in February 313.

Emperor Constantine had invited all 1800 bishops of the Church (about 1000 in the east and 800 in the west), but a lesser and unknown number attended. Eusebius of Caesarea counted 250, Athanasius of Alexandria counted 318, and Eustathius of Antioch counted 270 (all three were present at the council). Later, Socrates Scholasticus recorded more than 300, and Evagrius, St Hilary, St Jerome and Rufinus recorded 318. Bishops attended from every region of the Empire except Britain. Each bishop had his assistants. Athanasius of Alexandria, a young deacon and companion of Bishop Alexander of Alexandria, was among these assistants. Athanasius eventually spent most of his life battling against Arianism. Saint Athanasius argued convincingly for condemning Arius and he was at the forefront in defining the *consubstantiality* of the Son with the Heavenly Father.

The following issues were among those discussed at the Council:

1. The Arian question;
2. The celebration of Easter;
3. The Meletian schism;

The Arian controversy was a Christological dispute that began in Alexandria between the followers of Arius (the Arians) and the followers of St Alexander of Alexandria (known as *Homoousians*). Alexander and his followers believed that the Son was of the same substance as the Father, co-eternal with him. The Arians believed that they were different and that the Son, though he may be the most perfect of creations, was only a creation. A third group (known as *Homoiousians*) attempted a compromise position, saying that the Father and the Son were of similar substance. The Council declared that the Father and the Son are of the same substance and are co-eternal, basing the declaration in the claim that this was a formulation of traditional Christian belief handed down from the Apostles. This belief was expressed in the Nicene Creed.

Then the question of the date of Easter was discussed at Nicaea.[1] The Council did not declare the Alexandrian or Roman calculations as normative. Instead, it gave the Bishop of Alexandria the privilege of announcing annually the date of Christian Passover to the Roman Curia. Although the synod undertook the regulation of the dating of Christian Passover, it communicated its decision to the various dioceses, rather than establishing a canon. There was subsequent conflict over this very matter.

The suppression of the Meletian schism was one of the three important matters that came before the Council of Nicaea. Meletius (bishop of Lycopolis in Egypt), it was decided, should remain in his own city of Lycopolis, but without exercising authority or the power to ordain new clergy; moreover he was forbidden to go into the environs of the town or to enter another diocese for the purpose of ordaining its subjects. Meletius retained his episcopal title, but the ecclesiastics ordained by him were to receive again the imposition of hands, the ordinations performed by Meletius being therefore regarded as invalid. Clergy ordained by Meletius were ordered to yield precedence to those ordained by Alexander, and they were not to do anything without the consent of Bishop Alexander. In the event of the death of a non-Meletian bishop or ecclesiastic, the vacant see might be given to a Meletian, provided he were worthy and the popular election were ratified by Alexander. As to Meletius himself, episcopal rights and prerogatives were taken from him. These mild measures, however, were in vain; the Meletians joined the Arians and caused more dissension than ever, being among the worst enemies of Athanasius. The Meletians ultimately died out around the middle of the fifth century. The status of the lapsed in the persecution under Licinius was also discussed, and it promulgated several new Church laws, called canons or fixed rules of discipline.

7.1.2 The First Council of Constantinople

Fifty-six years after Nicaea, in the year 381, the Roman Emperor of the East, Theodosius I, convened the second General Council. Pope Saint Damasus I sent his papal legates. Over 150 bishops attended, mainly from the East. Presiding over the council in succession were Timothy of Alexandria, Meletius of Antioch, Gregory Nazianzus, and Nectarius of Constantinople. The Council Fathers reaffirmed the doctrine of the First Council of Nicaea and defined the *consubstantiality* of the Holy Spirit with the Father and the Son, thereby condemning the heresy of Macedonius.

Seven canons, four of these being doctrinal and three disciplinary, are attributed to the Council. The first canon is an important dogmatic condemnation of all shades of Arianism, also of Macedonianism and Apollinarianism. In addition to affirming what had been said earlier at Nicaea and condemning the various semi-Arian attitudes, the council also expanded the statement on the Holy Spirit to combat the heresy of the *Pneumatomachi* or Macedonians. This group had affirmed Nicaea's simple statement that "We believe in the Holy Spirit", but denied that the Holy Spirit constituted the eternally existing Third Person of the Holy Trinity. The new creed defined the Holy Spirit as "the Lord, the Giver of Life, Who proceeds from the Father, With the Father and the Son He is worshipped and glorified". The statement regarding the Spirit's procession from the Father is particularly significant because it established that the Spirit, like the Son, must be of the same substance (*ousia*) as God the Father. The Council's decision regarding the Holy Spirit thus gave official endorsement to the concept of the Trinity as it came to be understood in mainstream Christian tradition.

The second canon renews the Nicene legislation imposing upon the bishops the observance of diocesan and patriarchal limits. The third canon reads: "The Bishop of Constantinople, however, shall have the prerogative of honour after the Bishop of Rome because Constantinople is New Rome." This canon expressed the rising importance of the new imperial capital, just fifty years old. The fourth canon declares invalid the consecration of Maximus of Constantinople, the Cynic philosopher and rival of Gregory of Nazianzus, as Bishop of Constantinople. The fifth canon accepts the churchmen of Antioch who affirm the Trinity. It was passed in response to the Tome of Pope Damasus I, The sixth canon limits the ability to accuse bishops of wrongdoing, stipulating that those who bring such charges must be prepared to have their own characters and orthodoxy examined. The seventh canon regards procedures for receiving certain heretics into the Church. Those guilty of Arianism, Novatianism, and some other heresies do not require new baptism, but Eunomians, Montanists, and Sabellians must be baptized again..

At the Council of Chalcedon (451) a new version of the Nicene Creed was published and attributed to this council of 381. However, earlier sources show no awareness of this, and attribute to the council simply a confirmation of the original version of the Creed, issued at Nicaea in 325.

7.1.3 The Council of Ephesus

Fifty years after the First Council of Constantinople, in the year 431, Theodosius' son Theodosius II ruled as emperor. He was much more in tune with the Church, influenced by his saintly sister Saint Pulcheria and, in harmony with Pope Saint Celestine I, a third General Council was called in Ephesus in the southern tip of Asia Minor. The Council of Ephesus, also known as the Third Ecumenical Council dealt with the Nestorian controversy. It was held over several sessions at the Church of Our Lady in Ephesus, Asia Minor (modern Turkey). The Council was called after Patriarch Cyril of Alexandria appealed to Pope Celestine I to condemn Patriarch Nestorius of Constantinople for heresy due to Nestorius' refusal to use the term *Theotokos* (Mother of God) in relation to the Blessed Virgin Mary. Thinking to defend himself from the charge, Nestorius convinced the Emperor Theodosius II to hold an empire-wide council to resolve the matter.

The council assembled on 22 June 431, with Cyril of Alexandria as president. Nestorius had been invited to attend but choose not to do so, sensing that he was badly outnumbered. Now officially summoned, he still did not comply, and his supporters also boycotted the meeting. The session proceeded, and Nestorius was solemnly condemned as a heretic by the majority. The sentence was worded as follows:

> Since in addition to the rest the most impious Nestorius has neither been willing to obey our citation, nor to receive the most holy and God-fearing bishops whom we sent to him, we have necessarily betaken ourselves to the examination of his impieties; and, having apprehended from his letters and from his writings, and from his recent sayings in this metropolis which have been reported, that his opinions and teachings are impious, we being necessarily impelled thereto both by the canons [for his contumacy] and by the letter [to Cyril] of our most holy father and colleague Celestine, Bishop of the Roman Church, with many tears have arrived at the following grievous sentence against him: Our Lord, Jesus Christ, Who has been blasphemed by him, has defined by this holy synod that the same Nestorius is excluded from all episcopal dignity and from every assembly of bishops.

At the Council of Ephesus, the Pope's decrees against the Pelagians were read and confirmed.

7.1.4 The Council of Chalcedon

Twenty years after Ephesus, in the year 451, Saint Pulcheria played a key role in the fourth General Council; this time influencing her husband Marcian, then the Roman Emperor of the East, to coordinate with Pope Saint Leo the Great in convening it at Chalcedon in Thessalonica just northwest of Constantinople. Attendance at this council was very high, with 500–600 bishops participating. Presiding over this assembly was Bishop

Paschasinus of Lilybaeum (Marsala, Sicily), the first of the papal legates. However, apart from the papal delegation and two African bishops, practically all the bishops belonged to the Eastern Church. Once again a false teaching needed to be corrected. This time *Monophysitism* (the false teaching that Christ had only one nature) was at the forefront of controversy. It had been taught by the Abbot Eutyches who also aroused discord, causing confusion so that the Council asserted that Constantinople should be on an equal basis with Rome ecclesiastically. Vigorously opposing this and Eutyches, Pope Leo determined in his Dogmatic Epistle of 10 October 451 that the See of Peter in Rome is and always shall enjoy primacy with no equal, and that Eutyches was to be considered a heretic. Leo was proclaimed the "Soul of Chalcedon" and the Council agreed unanimously that through Pope Leo, Peter had spoken and Eutyches was condemned.

Following the lead of Pope Leo I, the Council sought a middle path between the extremes known as Nestorianism and Monophysitism, ultimately settling on a formula that ran as follows:

Following the holy Fathers, we unanimously teach and confess one and the same Son, our Lord Jesus Christ: the same perfect in divinity and perfect in humanity, the same truly God and truly man, composed of rational soul and body; consubstantial with the Father as to his divinity and consubstantial with us as to his humanity; like us in all things but sin. He was begotten from the Father before all ages as to his divinity and in these last days, for us and for our salvation, was born as to his humanity of the virgin Mary, the Mother of God. We confess that one and the same Christ, Lord, and only-begotten Son, is to be acknowledged in two natures without confusion, change, division, or separation. The distinction between natures was never abolished by their union, but rather the character proper to each of the two natures was preserved as they came together in one person (*prosopon*) and one hypostasis.[2]

In addition to its theological decrees, the council issued a large number of disciplinary rules governing Church administration and authority.

7.1.5 The Second Council of Constantinople

The Second Council of Constantinople, also known as the Fifth Ecumenical Council was a meeting of mostly Eastern Church leaders convened by Emperor Justinian I from 5 May to 2 June 553. Presided over by Patriarch Eutychius of Constantinople, the council dealt mainly with the emperor's wish to produce a formal condemnation of the heretical Three Chapters, which was a collection of statements by three deceased disciples of the deposed Nestorius, Theodore of Mopsuestia, Theodoret of Cyrrhus, and Ibas of Edessa. Justinian hoped that the public rejection of these supposedly Nestorian writings and their authors would help reconcile the empire's Monophysites with the Council of Chalcedon, which had determined that Christ had two natures, divine and human. The council was resisted by Pope Vigilius, who had been brought to Constantinople against his will several years previously, after he refused to condemn the Three Chapters. Vigilius questioned whether the writers in question were truly heretics and feared that their condemnation would weaken Chalcedon and encourage Monophysitism. Vigilius had long resisted the emperor's policy, but after the council concluded, he finally acquiesced, endorsing the its findings and formally condemning the Three Chapters. This Council also affirmed the condemnations declared at the Council of Carthage in 416 and previous condemnations by Popes of various heresies.

7.2 Heresies

Heresies have been with us from the Church's beginning. They even have been started by Church leaders, who were then corrected by councils and popes. Fortunately, we have Christ's promise that heresies will never prevail against the Church, for

He told Peter, "You are Peter, and on this rock I will build my Church, and the gates of hell will not prevail against it" (Mt 16:18). The Church is truly, in Paul's words, "the pillar and foundation of the truth" (1 Tm 3:15).

Heresy, in the sense of falling away from the Faith, became possible only after the Faith had been promulgated by Christ. Its advent is clearly foretold by Christ: "Many false prophets will arise; they will deceive many" (Mt 24:11). Already in New Testament times, St Peter warned against the presence of heretics:

> As there were false prophets in the past history of our people, so you too will have your false teachers, who will insinuate their own disruptive views and, by disowning the Lord who bought them freedom, will bring upon themselves speedy destruction... People like this are dried-up springs, fogs swirling in the wind, and the gloom of darkness is stored up for them. (2 Pt 2:1, 17)

St Paul also noted the existence of heresies: "For there must be also heresies: that they also, who are approved, may be made manifest among you" (1 Co 11:19). St Thomas Aquinas defined heresy as "a species of infidelity in men who, having professed the faith of Christ, corrupt its dogmas".[3] God allows His faithful to be exposed to heresy in order to test their faith, their docility, and obedience to Catholic authority. Heresy (from Greek αἵρεσῃ, which originally meant "choice") is a controversial or novel change to a system of beliefs, especially a religion, that conflicts with established dogma. It is distinct from apostasy, which is the formal denunciation of one's religion, principles or cause, and blasphemy, which is irreverence toward God or religion. The founder or leader of a heretical movement is called a *heresiarch*, while individuals who espouse heresy or commit heresy, are known as heretics.

The Catechism of the Catholic Church states

> Incredulity is the neglect of revealed truth or the wilful refusal to assent to it. Heresy is the obstinate post-baptismal denial of some truth which must be believed with divine and Catholic faith, or it is likewise an obstinate

> doubt concerning the same; apostasy is the total repudiation of the Christian faith; schism is the refusal of submission to the Roman Pontiff or of communion with the members of the Church subject to him.[4]

To commit heresy, one must refuse to be corrected. A person who is ready to be corrected or who is unaware that what he has been saying is against Church teaching is not a heretic. A person must be baptized to commit heresy. This means that movements that have split off from or been influenced by Christianity, but that do not practice baptism (or do not practice valid baptism), are not heresies, but separate religions. Examples include Muslims, who do not practice baptism, and Jehovah's Witnesses, who do not practice valid baptism. Finally, the doubt or denial involved in heresy must concern a matter that has been revealed by God and solemnly defined by the Church (for example, the Trinity, the Incarnation, the Real Presence of Christ in the Eucharist, the Sacrifice of the Mass, the Pope's infallibility, or the Immaculate Conception and Assumption of Mary). It is important to distinguish heresy from schism and apostasy. In schism, one separates from the Catholic Church without repudiating a defined doctrine. Apostasy (from the Greek ἀποστασία — apostasia) is the formal disaffiliation from or abandonment or renunciation of the Christian religion by a person. We now consider some examples of heresies which circulated in the early centuries of the Church.

7.2.1 Gnosticism (First and second centuries)

Gnosticism has its roots just after the beginning of the Christian Church. Some researchers state that evidence of its existence even predates Christianity. Whichever the case, the error of gnosticism had affected the culture and Church of the time and possibly even earned a mention in 1 John 4. The word "gnosticism" derives from the Greek word "gnosis" which means "knowledge". There were many groups that were Gnostic and it isn't possible to easily describe the nuances of each variant of Gnostic doctrines. However, generally speaking, Gnosticism taught that salvation is achieved through special knowledge (gnosis). This knowledge usually dealt with the individual's relationship to the transcendent Being.

The unknowable God was far too pure and perfect to have anything to do with the material universe which was considered evil. Therefore, God generated lesser divinities, or emanations. One of these emanations, Wisdom desired to know the unknowable God. Out of this erring desire the demiurge, an evil god, was formed and it was this evil god that created the universe. A characteristic feature of the Gnostic conception of the universe is the role played in almost all Gnostic systems by the seven world-creating *archons*.[5] The demiurge along with *archons* kept the mortals in bondage in material matter and tried to prevent the pure spirit souls from ascending back to god after the death of the physical bodies. Since, according to the Gnostics, matter is evil, deliverance from material form was attainable only through special knowledge revealed by special Gnostic teachers. Christ was the divine Redeemer who descended from the spiritual realm to reveal the knowledge necessary for this redemption. In conclusion, Gnosticism is dualistic. That is, it teaches there is a good and evil, spirit and matter, light and dark, dualism in the universe.

What we know about Gnosticism is gleaned from the writings of Irenaeus, Hippolytus, Tertullian, Origen, and some later manuscripts discovered in the eighteenth century such as the Codex Askew, Codex Bruce, the Berlin Gnostic Codes and, most recently, the Nag Hammadi collection. Nag Hammadi is a town in Upper Egypt near ancient Chenoboskion and thirteen codices were discovered there about 1945. St Irenaeus of Lyons (130–202) refuted the Gnostic heresy, which was perhaps the first error concerning reason and faith in the history of the Church. St Irenaeus declared that God should not be sought after by means of numbers, syllables, and letters, as did the Gnostics. For a system does not spring out of numbers, but numbers from a system; nor does God derive His being from things made, but things made derive their being from God. For all things originate from one and the same God.

The danger of Gnosticism is very clear. It denies the Incarnation of God as the Son. In so doing, it denies the true efficacy of the atonement since, if Jesus is not God, He could not atone for all of mankind and we would still be lost in our sins.

> The fact that the Gnostics belittled matter meant that they could not accept the Incarnation. Thus their knowledge of God was based on what they could acquire through their secret and elitist understanding of things rather than through revelation received from Christ. In contrast to the Gnostics the Church dismantled barriers of race, social status and gender, and proclaimed from the first the equality of all men and women before God. One important implication of this touched the realm of truth. The elitism which had hallmarked the ancients' search for truth was clearly abandoned. Since access to the truth enables access to God, it must be denied to none.[6]

7.2.2 Marcionism (Second Century)

Marcionism is the dualist belief system that originated from the teachings of Marcion of Sinope around the year 144. Marcion was son of the Bishop of Sinope in Pontus, born around 110 AD, evidently from wealthy parents. He is described as a ship owner by Tertullian, who wrote about a generation after his death. Marcion affirmed Jesus Christ as the Saviour sent by God and Paul as His chief apostle, but he rejected the Hebrew Bible and Yahweh. Marcionism in some ways anticipated the dualism of Manichaeism. As Marcionism arose in the very beginning of the Christian era and from the very start had adopted a strong ecclesiastical organization that paralleled that of the Orthodox Christian Church, the movement was a dangerous foe of Christianity. Early on, Marcionism was denounced by its opponents as heresy. These opponents also wrote against it, notably by Tertullian in a five-book treatise titled *Adversus Marcionem* that was written about 208. Marcion's writings are lost, though they were widely read and numerous manuscripts must have existed. Even so, many scholars claim it is possible to reconstruct and deduce a large part of ancient Marcionism through what later critics, especially Tertullian, said concerning Marcion.

Marcion declared that Christianity was totally distinct from and in opposition to Judaism. He rejected the Hebrew Bible entirely and declared that the God of the Hebrew Bible was a lesser demiurge, who had created the earth, but was the source of evil. Focusing on the Pauline traditions of the Gospel, Marcion felt that all other concepts of the Gospel, and especially any association with the Old Testament religion, were opposed to, and a backsliding from the truth. He further regarded the arguments of Paul regarding law and gospel, wrath and grace, works and faith, flesh and spirit, sin and righteousness, and death and life as the essence of religious truth. He ascribed these aspects and characteristics to two principles, the righteous and wrathful god of the Old Testament, who is at the same time identical with the Creator of the world, and a second God of the Gospel, quite unknown before Christ, who is only love and mercy.

7.2.3 Manichaeism (Second century onwards)

Manichaeism was one of the most influential heresies of the early centuries and its remnants survived well into the Middle Ages in the forms of Catharism and Albigentianism. Its Persian founder Mani (216?–276 A.D.) created a religion that was a curious blend of Gnosticism, Christianity, and the teachings of Persian thinkers. Among the characteristics of Manichaeism was the error that all religions are equally valid. Manichaeism proposed a dualist view of creation, with two cosmic kingdoms, which included a Kingdom of Light (the Primal God) and the Kingdom of Darkness (Satan). God was seen as the Creator of the spiritual world and Satan that of the material world. Manichaeism accepted as prophets: Adam, Noah, Abraham, Zoroaster, Buddha, Jesus, Paul, and Mani. The system had a Docetic view of Christ "a divine being clothed in the semblance of man". Manichaeism had five grades or levels of believers who held the notion of cycles of life with reincarnation. They preached strict and stoical asceticism.

The most famous convert from Manichaeism was St Augustine, who repudiated the heresy in 384 AD, and later stated:

> Through the assisting mercy of God, the snares of the Manichaeans having been broken to pieces and left behind, having been restored at length to the bosom of the Catholic Church, I am disposed now at least to consider and to deplore my recent wretchedness. For there were many things that I ought to have done to prevent the seeds of the most true religion wholesomely implanted in me from boyhood, from being banished from my mind, having been uprooted by the error and fraud of false and deceitful men.[7]

7.2.4 Docetism (Second century)

Docetism was an error with several variations concerning the nature of Christ. Generally, it taught that Jesus only appeared to have a body, that he was not really incarnate, (from the Greek δοκέω—dokeo meaning to seem). This is the heresy that Jesus' physical body was an illusion, as was His crucifixion; that is, Jesus only seemed to have a physical body and to physically die, but in reality He was incorporeal, a pure spirit, and hence could not physically die. This error evolved from the dualistic philosophy which viewed matter as inherently evil, that God could not be associated with matter, and that God, being perfect and infinite, could not suffer. Therefore, God as the Word, could not have become flesh as in John 1:1,14, "In the beginning was the Word, and the Word was with God, and the Word was God... And the Word became flesh, and dwelt among us." This denial of a true Incarnation meant that Jesus did not truly suffer on the Cross and that He did not rise from the dead.

The basic principle of Docetism was refuted by the Apostle John in 1 John 4:2–3: "By this you know the Spirit of God: every spirit that confesses that Jesus Christ has come in the flesh is from God; and every spirit that does not confess Jesus is not from God; and this is the spirit of the antichrist, of which you have heard that it is coming, and now it is already in the world."[8]

Ignatius of Antioch (died 98 or 117), Irenaeus (115–190), and Hippolytus (170–235) wrote against the error in the early part of the second century. Docetism was condemned at the Council of Chalcedon in 451.

7.2.5 Adoptionism (Second century)

Adoptionism is an error concerning Christ that first appeared in the second century. Those who held it denied the preexistence of Christ and, therefore, His divinity. Adoptionists taught that Jesus was tested by God and after passing this test and upon His baptism, He was granted supernatural powers by God and adopted as the Son. As a reward for His great accomplishments and perfect character Jesus was raised from the dead and adopted into the Godhead. This error arose out of an attempt by people to understand the two natures of Jesus. The scriptures tell us that Jesus is both God and man: "In Him, in bodily form, lives divinity in all its fullness" (Col 2:9). This is known as the doctrine of the Hypostatic Union where in the one Person of Christ, there are two natures: God and man. According to Epiphanius's account of the Ebionites, the group believed that Jesus was chosen because of his sinless devotion to the will of God.[9] Theodotus of Byzantium was the most prominent adherent to this error. Adoptionism was condemned as a heresy by Pope Victor (190–198 AD). The heresy was rejected by the First Council of Nicaea, which held to the orthodox doctrine of the Trinity, identifying Jesus as eternally begotten of the Father.

7.2.6 Montanism (Late second Century)

Montanus lived in the Phrygian area of Asia Minor at the back end of the second Century AD. He declared that the Holy Spirit was giving new revelations to the Church, and named himself and two women, Priscilla and Maximilla, as prophets, although there were others as well. The heresy originated at Hierapolis and flourished throughout the region of Phrygia, leading to the movement being referred to as *Cataphrygian* (meaning it was "from Phrygia"). It spread rapidly to other regions of the Roman Empire at a time before Christianity was generally tolerated or legal and was referred to as the New Prophecy. In the West, among the Montanist leaders was Proclus, with whom the Roman priest Gaius published a debate. The emphases of the New Prophecy seem to have been on resisting persecution, fasting, and avoiding remarriage, together with hostility to any compromise with sin. Few of these points were controversial when judged against the asceticism of the time. The most widely known defender of Montanism was undoubtedly Tertullian, onetime champion of orthodox belief, who believed that the new prophecy was genuine and he began to fall out of step with the Church. Some people have drawn parallels between Montanism and modern Pentecostalism (which some call Neo-Montanism).

The fundamental differences between Montanism and Orthodox Christianity began to emerge. First the Montanists held the notion that their own prophecies superseded and fulfilled the doctrines proclaimed by the Apostles. They encouraged ecstatic prophesying, contrasting with the more sober and disciplined approach to theology dominant in orthodox Christianity at the time and since. The Montanists subscribed to the erroneous view that Christians who fell from grace could not be redeemed, also in contrast to the orthodox Christian view that contrition would lead to a sinner's restoration to the Church. They held a stronger emphasis on the avoidance of sin and Church discipline than in orthodox Christianity. The Montanists emphasized chastity, but in a wrong-headed way, including forbidding remarriage, and even the dissolution of some marriages; in particular, their prophetesses abandoned their husbands. Their prophets dyed their hair, stained their eyelids, and were allowed to play with tables and dice and lend on usury.

A letter of St Jerome to Marcella, written in 385, refutes the claims of Montanists who had been troubling her:

> In the first place we differ from the Montanists regarding the rule of faith. We distinguish the Father, the Son, and the Holy Spirit as three persons, but unite them as one

substance. They, on the other hand, following the doctrine of Sabellius force the Trinity into the narrow limits of a single personality. We, while we do not encourage them, yet allow second marriages, since Paul bids the younger widows to marry (1 Tim 5:14). They suppose a repetition of marriage a sin so awful that he who has committed it is to be regarded as an adulterer. We, according to the apostolic tradition (in which the whole world is at one with us), fast through one Lent yearly; whereas they keep three in the year as though three saviours had suffered.[10]

7.2.7 Sabellianism or Modalism (Early third Century)

Sabellius was a third century priest and theologian who most likely taught in Rome, but may have been an African from Libya. Basil and others regard him as a Libyan from Pentapolis, but this seems to rest on the fact that Pentapolis was a place where the teachings of Sabellius thrived, according to Dionysius of Alexandria. What is known of Sabellius is drawn mostly from the polemical writings of his opponents like Hippolytus. Sabellius, was excommunicated by Pope Callixtus I in 220. Sabellius taught that God was indivisible, with Father, Son, and Holy Spirit being only three modes or manifestations of one divine Person.

The Sabellianists therefore erroneously taught that Jesus Christ and God the Father were not distinct persons, but two aspects or offices of one person. According to them, the three persons of the Trinity exist only in God's relation to man, not in objective reality. Modalism, which states that God is a single person, is a denial of the Holy Trinity, and proposed that God, throughout biblical history, has revealed Himself only in three modes, or forms. A Sabellian modalist would say that the One God successively revealed Himself to man throughout time as the Father in Creation; the Son in Redemption; and the Spirit in Sanctification and Regeneration.

Thus, God is a single person who first manifested himself in the mode of the Father in Old Testament times. At the Incarnation, the mode was the Son. After Jesus' Ascension, the mode is the Holy Spirit. These modes are consecutive and never simultaneous. In other words, the Father, the Son, and the Holy Spirit never all exist at the same time, only one after another. Modalism denies the distinctiveness of the three persons in the Trinity even though it retains the divinity of Christ.

7.2.8 Patripassianism (Third Century)

Patripassianism is the error that God the Father suffers (from Latin, *Pater* "Father" and *passio* "suffering"). Its adherents held that God the Father was incarnate and suffered on the Cross and that whatever happened to the Son happened to the Father and so the Father co-suffered with the human Jesus on the Cross. Patripassionism began in the third century AD. Patripassionism developed in the waters of Sabellianism, especially because of the lack of distinction between God the father and God the Son. Sabellius had advanced the doctrine of one God sometimes referred to as "economic Trinity" and he opposed the Orthodox doctrine of the "essential Trinity". Noetus was truly a Patripassian and taught that the Father and the Son were one and the same and suffered on the Cross. Hippolytus condemned this error:

> The Scriptures speak what is right; but Noetus is of a different mind from them... See, brethren, what a rash and audacious dogma they have introduced, when they say without shame, the Father is Himself Christ, Himself the Son, Himself was born, Himself suffered, Himself raised Himself. But it is not so. The Scriptures speak what is right; but Noetus is of a different mind from them.[11]

A further exponent of Patripassianism was Praxeas, condemned by Tertullian:

> He [Praxeas] maintains that there is one only Lord, the Almighty Creator of the world, in order that out of this doctrine of the unity he may fabricate a heresy. He says that the Father Himself came down into the Virgin, was

Himself born of her, Himself suffered, indeed was Himself Jesus Christ.[12]

7.2.9 Arianism (Fourth Century)

Arianism developed around 320, in Alexandria, Egypt, concerning the person of Christ and is named after Arius of Alexandria. For his doctrinal teaching he was exiled to Illyria in 325 after the first ecumenical council at Nicaea condemned his teaching as heresy. It was one of the worst heresies within the early Church that developed a significant following. Arius taught that only God the Father was eternal and too pure and infinite to appear on the earth. Therefore, God produced Christ the Son out of nothing as the first and greatest creation. The Son is then the one who created the universe. Because the Son relationship of the Son to the Father is not one of nature, it is, therefore, adoptive. God adopted Christ as the Son. Though Christ was a creation, because of his great position and authority, he was to be worshipped and even looked upon as God. Some Arians even held that the Holy Spirit was the first and greatest creation of the Son. At Jesus' Incarnation the Arians asserted that the divine quality of the Son, the Logos, took the place of the human and spiritual aspect of Jesus, thereby denying the full and complete Incarnation of God the Son, second Person of the Holy Trinity.

Arianism was solemnly condemned in 325 at the First Council of Nicaea, which defined the divinity of Christ, and in 381 at the First Council of Constantinople, which defined the divinity of the Holy Spirit. These two councils gave us the Nicene creed, which Christians recite at Mass every Sunday.

7.2.10 Apollinarianism (Fourth century)

Apollinarianism was the heresy taught by Apollinaris the Younger, bishop of Laodicea in Syria about 361. He taught that the Logos of God, which became the divine nature of Christ, took the place of the rational human soul of Jesus and that the body of Christ was a glorified form of human nature. In other words, though Jesus was a man, He did not have a human mind but that the mind of Christ was solely divine. Apollinaris taught that the two natures of Christ could not coexist within one person. His solution was to lessen the human nature of Christ.

Apollinarianism was condemned by the Second General Council at Constantinople in 381. This heresy denies the true and complete humanity in the person of Jesus which in turn, can jeopardize the value of the atonement since Jesus is declared to be both God and man to atone. He needed to be God to offer a pure and holy sacrifice of sufficient value and He needed to be a man in order to die for men. Jesus is completely both God and man, "for in Him dwells all the fullness of deity in bodily form" (Col 2:9). This is known as the Hypostatic Union. The basis for the true doctrine is found in Scripture: "In the beginning was the Word, and the Word was with God, and the Word was God... and the Word became flesh and dwelt among us" (Jn 1:1,14).

7.2.11 Donatism (Fourth century)

Donatism was the error taught by Donatus, bishop of Casae Nigrae (North Africa), that the effectiveness of the sacraments depends on the moral character of the minister. In other words, if a minister who was involved in a serious enough sin were to baptize a person, that baptism would be considered invalid. Donatism developed as a result of the persecution of Christians ordered by Diocletian in 303, in which all churches and sacred scriptures of the Christians were to be destroyed.[13] In 304 another edict was issued ordering the burning of incense to the idol gods of the Roman empire. Of course, Christians refused, but it did not curtail the increased persecution. Many Christians gave up the sacred texts to the persecutors and even betrayed other Christians to the Romans. These people became known as *traditores*, Christians who betrayed their faith and also other Christians.

At the consecration of bishop Caecilian of Carthage in 311, one of the three bishops, Felix, bishop of Aptunga, who consecrated Caecilian, had given copies of the Bible to the Roman persecutors. A group of about 70 bishops formed a synod and declared the consecration of the bishop to be invalid. Great debate arose concerning the validity of the sacraments (baptism, the Eucharist) by one who had sinned so greatly against other Christians.

After the death of Caecilian, Aelius Donatus the Great became bishop of Carthage and it is from his name that the movement is called. The Donatists were gaining "converts" to their cause and a division was arising in the Catholic church. They began to practice rebaptism which was particularly troublesome to the church at the time and was condemned at the Synod of Arles in 314 since it basically said the authority in the Catholic church was lost. The Donatist issue was raised at several ecumenical councils and finally submitted to Emperor Constantine in 316. In each case the consecration of bishop Caecilian was upheld. However, persecution fuels emotions and by 350 the Donatists had gained many converts and outnumbered the Orthodox in Africa. But it was the apologetic by Augustine that turned the tide against the Donatist movement which eventually died out in the next century.

The problem with Donatism is that no person is morally pure. The effectiveness of the baptism or administration of the Eucharist does not cease to be effective if the moral character of the minister is in question or even demonstrated to be faulty. Rather, the sacraments are powerful because of what they are, outward signs of inward grace, which signify what they contain and contain what they signify. God is the one who works in and through them and He is not restricted by the moral state of the administrant.

7.2.12 Pelagianism (Fifth century)

In the early fifth century a debate arose between Pelagius (c. 354–420), a British monk, and Augustine, the Bishop of Hippo in North Africa. They disagreed over the relationship between human nature after the Fall and saving, divine grace in Jesus Christ. When Pelagius arrived in Rome and saw the city's lack of morality, he developed a reputation for being a spiritual director who urged people to reform their behaviour and live lives as upstanding, moral citizens. Pelagius rejected the doctrines of original sin and justification by faith. He emphasized unconditional free will and the ability to better oneself spiritually without grace. This was in direct contrast to Augustine, who believed that humanity was completely helpless in Adam's sin and in desperate need of grace. Specifically, Pelagius took issue with Augustine's prayer in his Confessions, which asked God to grant humans grace to act in accordance with his divine commands: "Grant what you command and command what you will."[14] Pelagius denied that we inherit original sin from Adam and claimed that we become sinful only through the bad example of the sinful community into which we are born. According to Pelagius, Adam's sin in no way made humans corrupt, but instead "over the years our sin gradually corrupts us, building an addiction and then holding us bound with what seems like the force of nature itself."[15] Humans by nature have a clean slate, and it is only through voluntary sin that humans are made wicked. Potentially, then, one could live a sinless life and merit heaven without grace. Conversely, he denied that we inherit righteousness as a result of Christ's death on the Cross and said that we become personally righteous by instruction and imitation in the Christian community, following the example of Christ. Pelagius stated that man is born morally neutral and can achieve heaven under his own powers. According to him, God's grace is not truly necessary, but merely makes easier an otherwise difficult task.

The controversy came to a head when Augustine opposed Pelagian teaching. Augustine did not deny that man had a will and that he could make choices. However, Augustine asserted that the effects of original sin were passed to the children of Adam and Eve and that man's nature was thereby wounded. Man could choose what he desired, but those desires were influenced by his sinful nature and he was unable to refrain from sinning. Pelagius cleared himself of charges, primarily by hiding his real beliefs; however, at the Council of Carthage in 418 AD, his teachings were branded as heresy. The Council of Ephesus in 431 AD, again condemned Pelagian doctrine and it was banished in the Greek portion of the Church. However, in the West, the teachings held on, primarily in Britain and Gaul.

7.2.13 Semi-Pelagianism (Fifth century)

Semi-Pelagianism is a weaker form of Pelagianism proposed by the monks of Southern Gaul on the island of Lérins and at Marseilles, in particular Abbot John Cassian.[16] This approach did not deny original sin and its effects upon the human soul and will. It taught that God and man cooperate to achieve man's salvation. This cooperation is not by human effort as in keeping the law, but rather in the ability of a person to make a choice according to free will. The semi-Pelagian teaches that man can make the first move toward God by seeking God out of his own free will and that man can cooperate with God's grace even to the keeping of his faith through human effort. This would mean that God responds to the initial effort of person and that God's grace is not absolutely necessary to maintain faith.

The problem with this system is that it undervalues grace, as the completely unmerited and freely-given gift of God upon the sinner. However, if man is the one who first seeks God, then God is responding to the good effort of seeking him. This would mean that God is offering a proper response to the initial effort of man. This is not grace, but what is due the person who chooses to believe in God apart from God's initiative. Semi-Pelagianism was condemned at the Council of Orange in 529.

7.2.14 Nestorianism (Fifth Century)

This heresy concerning the person of Christ was initiated by Nestorius, bishop of Constantinople, who denied Mary the title of *Theotokos* (Greek: "God-bearer" or "Mother of God"). Nestorius claimed that she only bore Christ's human nature in her womb, and proposed the alternative title *Christotokos* ("Christ-bearer" or "Mother of Christ"). Nestorius was deposed as Patriarch and sent to Antioch, then Arabia, and then Egypt.

Orthodox Catholic theologians recognized that Nestorius' theory would fracture Christ into two separate persons (one human and one divine, joined in a sort of loose unity), only one of whom was in her womb. The Church reacted in 431 with the Council of Ephesus, defining that Mary can be properly referred to as the Mother of God, not in the sense that she is older than God or the source of God, but in the sense that the person she carried in her womb was, in fact, God incarnate ("in the flesh"). Late last century, the Assyrian Church of the East, historically regarded as a Nestorian Church, signed a joint declaration on Christology with the Catholic Church and rejects Nestorianism.[17] It is now in the process of coming into full ecclesial communion with the Catholic Church.

7.2.15 Monophysitism (Fifth century)

Monophysitism is an error concerning the nature of Christ that asserts Jesus had only one nature, not two as is taught in the correct doctrine of the hypostatic union: Jesus is both God and man in one person. In monophysitism, the single nature was divine, not human. It is sometimes referred to as Eutychianism, after Eutyches 378–452, but there are slight differences. Monophysitism arose out of a reaction against Nestorianism which taught Jesus was two distinct persons instead of one. They went to the other extreme, claiming that Christ was one person with only one nature (a fusion of human and divine elements). They are thus known as Monophysites because of their erroneous claim that Christ had only one nature (Greek: *mono* = one; *physis* = nature). Its roots can even be traced back to Apollinarianism which taught that the divine nature of Christ overtook and replaced the human one.

Monophysitism was confined mainly to the Eastern church and had little influence in the West. In 451, the Council of Chalcedon attempted to establish a common ground between the monophysites and the orthodox, but it did not work and divisions arose in the Eastern church which eventually excommunicated the monophysites in the sixth century. The denial of the human nature of Christ is a denial of the true Incarnation of the Word as a man. Without a true Incarnation there can be no atonement of sin for mankind since it was not then a true man who died for our sins. Monophysitism was condemned as heresy at the Sixth Ecumenical Council in 680–681. Orthodox Catholic theologians recognized that Monophysitism was as bad as Nestorianism because it denied Christ's full humanity and full divinity. If Christ did not have a fully human nature, then He would not be fully human, and if He did not have a fully divine nature then He was not fully divine.

Notes

1   See chapter 4, subsection 4.10.2 above.
2   Council of Chalcedon, *Definition of the faith*.
3   See St Thomas Aquinas, *Summa Theologiae*, II–II°, q. 11, a. 1.
4   CCC 2089.
5   *Archon* (Greek ἄρχων, plural ἄρχοντες) is a Greek term that means "ruler" or "lord", frequently used as the title of a specific public office.
6   See Pope St John Paul II, *Fides et Ratio*, 19.
7   St Augustine, *On Two Souls, Against the Manichaeans*.
8   See also 2 John 7: "There are many deceivers at large in the world, refusing to acknowledge Jesus Christ as coming in human nature. They are the Deceiver; they are the Antichrist."
9   St Epiphanius, *Panarion* 30:3 & 30:13: "They too accept Matthew's gospel, and like the followers of Cerinthus and Merinthus, they use it alone. They call it the Gospel of the Hebrews, for in truth Matthew alone in the New Testament expounded and declared the Gospel in Hebrew using Hebrew script. After saying many things, this Gospel continues: "After the people were baptized, Jesus also came and was baptized by John. And as Jesus came up from the water, Heaven was opened, and He saw the Holy Spirit descend in the form of a dove and enter into Him. And a voice from Heaven said, 'You are my beloved Son; with You I am well pleased.' And again, 'Today I have begotten You.' "Immediately a great light shone around the place; and John, seeing it, said to Him, 'Who are you, Lord? And again a voice from Heaven said, 'This is my beloved Son, with whom I am well pleased.' Then John, falling down before Him, said, 'I beseech You, Lord, baptize me!' But He forbade him saying, 'Let it be so; for thus it is fitting that all things be fulfilled.'"
10 St Jerome, *Letter 41*.

11   Hippolytus, *Against Noetus*, 3.

12   Tertullian, *Against Praxeas*, 1.

13   See chapter 5 above, subsection 5.2.14 and section 5.3.

14   St Augustine, *Confessions*, X,

15   Pelagius, *Letter to Demetrias*, VIII.

16   St John Cassian was born around 360, most likely in the region of Scythia Minor, now Dobruja in modern-day Romania and Bulgaria. As a young adult he and an older friend, Germanus, traveled to Palestine, where they entered a hermitage near Bethlehem. After remaining in that community for about three years, they journeyed to the desert of Scetes in Egypt, where they visited a number of monastic foundations. While he was in Rome, Cassian accepted the invitation to found an Egyptian-style monastery in southern Gaul, near Marseilles. He may also have spent time as a priest in Antioch between 404 and 415. In any case, he arrived in Marseilles around 415. His foundation, the Abbey of St Victor, was a complex of monasteries for both men and women, one of the first such institutes in the West, and served as a model for later monastic development.

17   See *Common Christological Declaration between the Catholic Church and the Assyrian Church of the East* (11 November 1994).

8 THE NEW TESTAMENT CANON

Since some have taken in hand to set in order for themselves the so-called apocrypha and to mingle them with the God-inspired Scripture, according to what the original eye-witness and ministers of the word have delivered unto our fathers, I also, having been urged by true brethren and having investigated the matter from the beginning, have decided to set forth in order the writings that have been put in the canon, that have been handed down and confirmed as divine, in order that every one who has been led astray may condemn his seducers, and that every one who has remained stainless may rejoice.

St Athanasius, *Festal Letter 39*

8.1 The arrangement of the books

A S A PRELUDE to discussing the important question of the Canon on the New Testament, we need to mention some ideas about the arrangement of the books. First, the twenty-seven books of the New Testament are not listed in chronological order, or the order in which they were written historically; several other principles were operative. In fact, the overall order begins with the life of Jesus (the four Gospels), then deals with the growth of the Christian Church (Acts, Letters, Epistles), and finally focuses on the *Eschaton* (the end of time, as described symbolically in the Book of Revelation). In this way, a chronological and theological structure of past, present, and future can be discerned. The four Gospels are listed in what was traditionally regarded as their chronological order (namely Matthew was thought to be the oldest Gospel); most scholars today, however, believe that Mark was the first written Gospel (or at least the oldest of the four canonical Gospels in their full versions, as we know them today).

The Acts of the Apostles was originally the second volume of Luke's two-volume work; however, when the four Gospels were grouped together, Acts was placed after John. The letters written by Paul (or at least attributed to him) are divided into two sub-groups: those written to communities and those addressed to individuals; within each sub-group, the letters are arranged not in chronological order, but rather in decreasing order of length (more or less, although Galatians is slightly shorter than Ephesians). The anonymous Letter to the Hebrews comes immediately after the Pauline letters because some people attribute it to Paul. The Catholic or General Epistles are also listed in decreasing order of length, although letters attributed to the same apostle are grouped together. The Book of Revelation closes out the New Testament canon, since it concludes with a description of the end of time (New Heavens, New Earth, New Jerusalem, and so forth).

The word *Canon* comes from the Greek expression *kanōn* which is derived from a Semitic word (*qaneh* in Hebrew) meaning a reed. Classically it meant a measuring stick or metaphorically a rule or standard of excellence, a benchmark. In ecclesiastical usage it denoted a rule of faith. Most of us take it for granted to have a copy of Bible and do not ask how we received it. The question why the New Testament has twenty-seven books, not more and not less, hardly comes to our mind. While all of us are unlikely to think that they just simply dropped from the sky, we may not realize the long process which took place before those twenty-seven books were finally selected. The New Testament, as defined by the Council of Trent, does not differ, as regards the books contained, from that of all Christian bodies at present.

In the first place, Jesus wrote no book, and neither He nor His apostles (including Paul) directly gave us the list of the twenty-seven New Testament books. They neither used nor introduced the terms Old and New Testaments. Those terms were first used by Tertullian (around 170 AD). In fact Our Lord's and the later apostolic teachings were first transmitted and taught orally. One should bear in mind that the first Christians did not consider this oral transmission as inferior; the problem was simply that writing things down was time-consuming and costly. In Galatians 4:20, Paul wrote that he wished to be with the Galatians, so they could hear his tone. At that time, his personal presence was impossible and therefore a letter from him would be sufficient. On other occasions, Paul judged that a written communication would be more effective than anything he could say (2 Co 1:23–2:4). In short both oral and written forms were considered authoritative by the first Christians and are known to them as tradition (the Greek word translated as "tradition" comes from the verb which means "to deliver"). When Paul and others mentioned Scripture what they meant exactly is the Old Testament books. For example, the scripture known to Timothy (2 Tm 3:15) since his childhood definitely refers to Old Testament books. The first Christians did regard Jesus' unwritten words as authoritative as Scripture. Thus, in his First Letter to Timothy (1 Tm 5:18), Paul quoted as Scripture, both Deuteronomy 25:4 and Jesus' words, which are now recorded in Luke 10:7 (noting that the Gospel of Luke was probably written after Paul's epistles). In the same way, early Christian writers like Pope Clement of Rome (circa 96 AD), Ignatius, bishop of Antioch (circa 110 AD), Polycarp, bishop of Smyrna (circa 110–120 AD) considered Jesus' words as equal to those of Scriptures (Old Testament).

There are a number of surviving manuscripts of early New Testament books. The *Codex Sinaiticus* (4th Century) has all 27 books of our present New Testament, but also includes the *Epistle of Barnabas* and the *Shepherd of Hermas*. The *Codex Vaticanus* (4th century) was torn at the end, so does not reveal the whole list; the existing part consists of 21 books and part of Hebrews of our present New Testament. On the other hand *Codex Alexandrinus* (5th century) has the 27 books plus 1 and 2 Clement. The *Codex Claromontanus* (6th century) has no Philippians, 1 and 2 Thessalonians and Hebrews but includes the *Epistle of Barnabas*, the *Shepherd of Hermas*, the *Acts of Paul* and the *Revelation of Peter*. Another fourth century list, now known as Cheltenham list has only 4 Gospels, 13 Pauline epistles (minus Hebrews), Acts, Revelation, 1 John and 1 Peter.

Like the Old Testament, the New has books whose canonicity was formerly a subject of some discussion in the Church. There was discussion about entire books: the Epistle to the Hebrews, that of James, the Second of St Peter, the Second and Third of John, Jude, and Apocalypse; giving seven in all as the number of the New Testament contested books. There was discussion about three disputed passages: the closing section of St Mark's Gospel, 16: 9–20 about the apparitions of Christ after the Resurrection; the verses in Luke about the bloody sweat of Jesus, 22:43, 44; the narrative of the woman taken in adultery, St John, 7:53 to 8:11. Since the Council of Trent it is not permitted for a Catholic to question the inspiration of these passages.

8.2 The formation of the New Testament Canon

The idea of a complete and clear-cut Canon of the New Testament existing from the beginning, that is from Apostolic times, has no foundation in history. The Canon of the New Testament, like that of the Old, is the result of a development, of a process at once stimulated by disputes with doubters, both within and without the Church, and retarded by certain obscurities and natural hesitations, and which did not reach its final term until the dogmatic definition of the Council of Trent.

8.2.1 The early period (AD 100–220)

Those writings which possessed the unmistakable stamp and guarantee of Apostolic origin must from the very first have been specially prized and venerated, and their copies eagerly sought by local Churches and individual Christians of means, in preference to the narratives and *Logia*, or Sayings of Christ, coming from less authorized sources. Already in the New Testament itself there is some evidence of a certain diffusion of canonical books: 2 Peter 3:15–16, supposes its readers to be acquainted with some of St Paul's Epistles; St John's Gospel implicitly presupposes the existence of the Synoptics (Matthew, Mark, and Luke).

We may well presume that each of the leading Churches- Rome, Antioch, Thessalonica, Alexandria, Corinth, and others- would have possessed authoritative writings, although at this stage their lists may vary. Each community sought, by exchanging with other Christian communities, to add to its special treasure, and have publicly read in its religious assemblies all Apostolic writings which came under its knowledge. It was doubtless in this way that the collections grew, and reached completeness within certain limits, but a considerable number of years must have elapsed (counting from the composition of the latest book) before all the widely dispersed Churches of early Christendom possessed the new sacred literature in full. Since distribution was not easy, this meant that the Canon was not fixed very early, and this left room for variations which lasted a few centuries. However, evidence shows that from days touching on those of the last Apostles there were two well defined bodies of sacred writings of the New Testament, which constituted the firm, irreducible, universal minimum, and the nucleus of its complete Canon: these were the Four Gospels, as the Church now has them, and thirteen Letters of St Paul, and these two collections were known as the *Evangelium* and the *Apostolicum*. For example, Pope St Clement of Rome, writing to the Corinthians just before 100 AD stated:

> Take into your hands the epistle of Blessed Paul the Apostle. What did he write to you when the Gospel was first preached? Truly, under divine inspiration he wrote to you concerning himself, and Cephas, and Apollo, because even then you had formed factions among yourselves.[1]

Around the year 110 AD, St Ignatius of Antioch remarked to the Ephesians that St Paul mentioned them in "every letter", an expression which implies a collection of Pauline letters of acknowledged authority.[2] Indeed, the word Gospel seems to have been first used by the same St Ignatius, in his letter to the Smyrnaeans.[3] Papias, bishop of Hierapolis (around 125 AD) was known to have identified at least two Gospels (Matthew and Mark). A generation after Papias, St Justin Martyr mentioned the memoirs of Peter (possible the Gospel of Mark) and memoirs of the apostles, both of which he called Gospels: "For the Apostles, in the memoirs composed by them, which are called Gospels, have handed down to us what Jesus had thus enjoined upon them."[4] His disciple, Tatian, introduced the Diatessaron, which are the four Gospels combined into one in a chronological order with the Gospel of John as a framework.

One early collection of New Testament books was made by the heretic Marcion (around 150 AD). His "canon" consisted of the Gospel of Luke and ten of Paul's epistles which he referred to as Gospel and Apostle. However, he mutilated many of them to suit his error, in which he declared that the God of the Old Testament was different from the One whom Jesus spoke about. For this reason he rejected all Old Testament books. He broke away from Rome and established his own sect. The error of Marcion and other heretics was an occasion for the Church to define what belonged to written apostolic teaching, in terms of the collection of New Testament books.

By the end of the second century, all of the New Testament books were generally known, and the divine character of most of them was generally admitted. At that time, St Irenaeus, who was familiar with the traditions of many regions, and connected through his teachers with the close of the Apostolic era, explicitly names and accepts the four canonical Gospels, quotes twelve letters of St Paul as Scripture, mentions the letter to the Hebrews, and accepts the Apocalypse as Johannine.[5] Thus, Irenaeus testified to the existence of a Tetramorph, or Quadriform Gospel, given by the Word and unified by one Spirit. It seems clear, from Patristic testimonies, that an inviolable fourfold Gospel existed in the closing years of the Apostolic Era. Just how the

Tetramorph was welded into unity and given to the Church, is a matter of conjecture.

Another known collection of New Testament books is the second century Muratorian canon, named after L. A. Muratori who published the list, copied from a seventh century codex, discovered in the Ambrosian Library in Milan in 1740. The manuscript is mutilated at the beginning, but we can conclude that it has four Gospels, Acts, thirteen of St Paul's epistles, the letter of Jude, two of St John's letters, the Apocalypse of John (Revelation) and of Peter, and the Wisdom of Solomon. The Apocalypse of Peter does not belong to our New Testament, while the Wisdom of Solomon is now part of (Catholic) Old Testament. The compiler of this Canon mentioned the *Shepherd of Hermas* which could be read, but was not to be published for the people. He also included Paul's epistle to the Laodiceans.

Parallel to the chain of evidence we have traced for the canonical standing of the Gospels, a similar chain exists for the thirteen Epistles of St Paul, forming the other half of the irreducible kernel of the complete New Testament canon. All the authorities cited for the Gospel Canon show acquaintance with, and recognize, the sacred quality of these letters. St Irenaeus employs all the Pauline writings, except the short Philemon, as sacred and canonical. In this formative period, the Letter to the Hebrews did not obtain a firm footing in the Canon of the Universal Church. At Rome it was not yet recognized as canonical, as shown by the Muratorian catalogue of Roman origin; Irenaeus cited it, but makes no reference to a Pauline origin. Yet it was known at Rome as early as St Clement, as the latter's epistle attests. The Alexandrian Church admitted it as the work of St Paul, and canonical.

The question of the principle that dominated the practical canonization of the New Testament Scriptures is significant. The faithful must have had from the beginning some realization that in the writings of the Apostles and Evangelists they had acquired a new body of Divine Scriptures, a New written Testament destined to stand side by side with the Old. That the Gospel and

Epistles were the written Word of God, was fully realized as soon as the fixed collections were formed; but to seize the relation of this new treasure to the old was possible only when the faithful acquired a better knowledge of the faith. For Tertullian (circa 200) the body of the New Scripture is an *instrumentum* on at least an equal footing and in the same specific class as the *instrumentum* formed by the Law and the Prophets.

8.2.2 The period of discussion (AD 220–367)

In this stage of the historical development of the Canon of the New Testament we encounter for the first time a consciousness reflected in certain ecclesiastical writers, of the differences between the sacred collections in various sections of Christendom. This variation is witnessed to, and the discussion stimulated by, two of the most learned men of Christian antiquity, Origen, and Eusebius of Cæsarea, the ecclesiastical historian. Origen's travels gave him special opportunities to know the traditions of widely separated portions of the Church and made him very conversant with the discrepant attitudes toward certain parts of the New Testament He divided books with Biblical claims into three classes. First, those universally received, namely the four Gospels, the thirteen Pauline Epistles, Acts, Apocalypse, 1 Peter, and 1 John. Then, he listed those works whose Apostolicity was questioned, and these comprised Hebrews, 2 Peter, 2 and 3 John, James, Jude, Barnabas, the Shepherd of Hermas, the Didache, and probably the Gospel of the Hebrews. Personally, Origen accepted all of these as divinely inspired, though he tolerated contrary opinions. Origen's authority seems to have given to Hebrews and the disputed Catholic Epistles a firm place in the Alexandrian Canon. Finally, Origen listed some apocryphal works. Eusebius, Bishop of Cæsarea in Palestine, was one of Origen's most eminent disciples, a man of great learning. In emulation of his master, he also divided religious literature into three classes. However, Eusebius diverged from Origen in personally rejecting Apocalypse as an non-Biblical, though he was compelled to acknowledge its almost universal acceptance.

During this period, there was discussion about the Canon in the African, or Carthaginian Church. St Cyprian, whose Scriptural Canon certainly reflects the contents of the first Latin Bible, received all the books of the New Testament except Hebrews, 2 Peter, James, and Jude; however, there was already a strong inclination in his environment to admit 2 Peter as authentic.

8.2.3 The period of fixation (AD 367–405)

Around the year 363 AD, the Council of Laodicea published a list of 26 New Testament books, in which the book of Revelation was not included. The same list of 26 books was given by St Cyril of Jerusalem (died 386 AD) and by St Gregory of Nazianzen. The influence of St Athanasius on the Canon of the New Testament was most constructive. In 367, Athanasius, bishop of Alexandria gave the list of 27 New Testament books, for the first time without making any distinction between them and which now becomes our New Testament.[6]

8.3 The Criteria for Canonicity

In the light of the definition of the Canon of the New Testament by the Church, we may wish to summarize the conditions for acceptance into this Canon. The first criterion is Apostolic authority, in other words that the book was written by an apostle or under his influence: the writers were direct or indirect eyewitnesses of Christ. Second, the book must be within orthodoxy, that is its contents held to the rule of faith and did not contain heresy. The book fits into the tradition of faith, and is mutually complementary and related to other accepted Christian writings. The third condition is catholicity, or universal acceptance as canonical within the Greek, Latin, and Eastern churches by the end of the fourth century. The fourth criterion is antiquity, namely that the book must have been written between birth of Christ and the death of last apostle. A fifth condition is that of inspiration, which is the internal witness of the Holy Spirit in the text to the Church's authority defining the book as canonical and inspired. Finally, the liturgical use, or its acceptance as a reading in public liturgical worship, bears witness to its canonicity.

By itself, none of New Testament books can prove its canonicity and if we rely on the testimony of the Christians in the first and second century, they too may have different opinions on a particular book. As mentioned earlier, some (7 books) were accepted as canonical after some dispute. Thus we need other and final criteria, the authority of the Church which has the final say regarding which book belongs to our Old and New Testaments. Catholics have no problem to accept this criteria, which is a historical fact and is even supported by a testimony of Paul himself, recorded in 1 Timothy 3:15 which says: the Church is the foundation and pillar of truth. It was by the apostolic Tradition that the Church discerned which writings are to be included in the list of the sacred books.[7]

Even those Catholic theologians who defend Apostolicity as a test for the inspiration of the New Testament admit that it is not exclusive of another criterion, namely Catholic tradition as manifested in the universal reception of compositions as Divinely inspired, or the ordinary teaching of the Church, or the infallible pronouncements of ecumenical councils. This external guarantee is the sufficient, universal, and ordinary proof of inspiration. The unique quality of the Sacred Books is a revealed dogma. Moreover, by its very nature inspiration eludes human observation and is not self-evident, being essentially superphysical and supernatural. Its sole absolute criterion, therefore, is the Holy inspiring Spirit, witnessing decisively to Himself, not in the subjective experience of individual souls, as Calvin maintained, neither in the doctrinal and spiritual tenor of Holy Writ itself, according to Luther, but through the constituted organ and custodian of His revelations, the Church. All other evidences fall short of the certainty and finality necessary to evoke the absolute assent of faith.

8.4 Examples of non-canonical books

Our example is the Epistle to the Laodiceans, estimated to have been written at the close of the 3rd century AD. How it came to be held in high regard can be seen from the end of St Paul's Letter to the Colossians, where this request is made of its recipients: "When this epistle has been read among you, have it read also in the church of the Laodiceans; and see that you read the epistle from Laodicea" (Col 4:16). This tantalizing reference, though somewhat ambiguous as to who wrote whom, offered a tempting invitation to some unknown author to provide the text of an Epistle of Paul to the Laodiceans, who were the neighbours of the congregation at Colossae. By the fourth century, St Jerome reported that "some read the Epistle to the Laodiceans, but it is rejected by everyone".[8] It commanded a certain respect in the Western Church for period of 1000 years. Comprising only 20 verses, the epistle is a collection of phrases and sentences taken from the genuine Pauline Epistles, particularly Philippians. After the author has expressed his joy at the faith and virtue of the Laodiceans, he warns them against heretics, and exhorts them to remain faithful to Christian doctrines and the Christian pattern of life. The epistle purports to have been written from prison.

There is no evidence of a Greek text. The epistle appears in more than 100 manuscripts of the Latin Vulgate (including the oldest, the celebrated Codex Fuldensis, 546 AD), as well as in manuscripts of early Albigensian, Bohemian, English, and Flemish versions. At the close of the 10th century Aelfric, a monk in Dorset, wrote a treatise in Anglo-Saxon on the Old and New Testaments, in which he stated that the apostle Paul wrote 15 Epistles. In his enumeration of them he placed Laodiceans after Philemon. About 1165 AD, John of Salisbury, writing about the Canon of Scripture to Henry, Count of Champagne, acknowledges that "it is the common, indeed almost universal, opinion that there are only 14 Epistles of Paul ... But the 15th is that which is written to the church of the Laodiceans."[9] The Epistle to the

Laodiceans is included in all 18 German Bibles printed prior to Luther's translation, beginning with the first German Bible, issued by Johann Mental at Strasburg in 1488. In these the Pauline Epistles, with the Epistle to the Hebrews, immediately follow the Gospels, with Laodiceans standing between Galatians and Ephesians. In the first Czech (Bohemian) Bible, published at Prague in 1488 and reprinted several times in the 16th and 17th centuries, Laodiceans follows Colossians and precedes I Thessalonians. Thus, as Bishop Lightfoot phrased it: "for more than nine centuries this forged epistle hovered about the doors of the sacred Canon, without either finding admission or being peremptorily excluded."[10] It was not until the Council of Florence (1439–43) that the See of Rome delivered for the first time a categorical opinion on the Scriptural canon. In the list of 27 books of the New Testament there are 14 Pauline Epistles, that to the Hebrews being last, with the book of Acts coming immediately before the Revelation of John. The Epistle to the Laodiceans is not even mentioned. It is clear that the reason for the exclusion of this book is that it is too late, namely not Apostolic. We give here the text of the Epistle to the Laodiceans:

> Paul, an apostle not of men and not through man, but through Jesus Christ, to the brethren who are in Laodicea: 2. Grace to you and peace from God the Father and the Lord Jesus Christ. 3. I thank Christ in all my prayer that you are steadfast in him and persevering in his works, in expectation of the promise for the day of judgment. 4. And may you not be deceived by the vain talk of some people who tell (you) tales that they may lead you away from the truth of the gospel which is proclaimed by me. 5. And now may God grant that those who come from me for the furtherance of the truth of the gospel (...) may be able to serve and to do good works for the well-being of eternal life. 6. And now my bonds are manifest, which I suffer in Christ, on account of which I am glad and rejoice. 7. This ministers to me unto eternal salvation, which (itself) is effected through your prayers and by the help of the Holy Spirit, whether it be through life or through

death. 8. For my life is in Christ and to die is joy (to me). 9. And this will his mercy work in you, that you may have the same love and be of one mind. 10. Therefore, beloved, as you have heard my presence, so hold fast and do in the fear of God, and eternal life will be your portion. 11. For it is God who works in you. 12. And do without hesitation what you do. 13. And for the rest, beloved, rejoice in Christ and beware of those who are out for sordid gain. 14. May all your requests be manifest before God, and be steadfast in the mind of Christ. 15. And what is pure, true, proper, just and lovely, do. 16. And what you have heard and received, hold in your heart and peace will be with you. 17. Salute all the brethren with the holy kiss. 18. The Saints salute you. 19. The grace of the Lord Jesus Christ be with your spirit. 20. And see that this epistle is read to the Colossians and that of the Colossians among you.[11]

A further example of a non-canonical book is the so-called *Gospel of Judas*. While the Epistle to the Laodiceans is excluded from the Canon of the New Testament because it was probably composed outside the Apostolic era, the Gospel of Judas is plainly a heretical work. The National Geographic Society has announced its intentions to publish an English translation of this text. The 31-page manuscript, written in Coptic, purportedly surfaced in Geneva in 1983 and has only now been translated. Though the manuscript still must be authenticated, it likely represents a fourth- or fifth-century text, and is a copy of an earlier document produced by a Gnostic sect called the Cainites. The document paints Judas Iscariot in a positive light, and describes him as obeying a divine ordinance in handing over Jesus to the authorities for the salvation of the world. It may well be a copy of the *Gospel of Judas* referred to by St Irenaeus of Lyons in his work *Against the Heresies*, written around 180 AD.

Indeed, Gnosticism is responsible for a number of non-canonical writings. The roots of Gnosticism are an esoteric collection of Eastern religious philosophies which are parasitic and dualistic in nature. Gnosticism, derived from the Greek word *gnosis* (knowledge) claimed a superior secret understanding of things. It was a system based on an elitist human striving for philosophical knowledge rather than on faith; in Gnosticism, the distinction between the eternal uncreated Supreme Being and all other beings was blurred or erased. In its widely various mythological forms, Gnosticism espouses a pantheon of divine beings anywhere from two to thirty. The production of matter was conceived of in terms of a downward emanation from God. Its basic myth attributes the creation of the material world to a lesser, evil god or demiurge while Jesus' heavenly father is the good god beyond all knowledge. Matter, on this account, is evil, and along with it, the human body as well. In man's creation a "spark of divinity" got trapped in some human bodies. Salvation consists in liberating this divine spark from its material prison, and the only path to salvation is secret knowledge of the Gnostic myth imparted to an elect. In this system Jesus could not have really become man because such an incarnation would imply that a good divine being mixed with evil matter. Therefore, he only appeared to be human. The ancients called this theological approach to Christ *doceticism*, meaning a question simply of appearance, not reality. The canonical Scriptures portray a very human Jesus who hungers, thirsts, suffers temptation and weeps. The Gnostic gospels, on the other hand, depict a phantom-like Jesus that is, when they depict the life of Jesus at all. The Gnostic writings generally lack historical narrative, and are often simply a compilation of abstract sayings. It is little wonder that they appeal to the adherents of contemporary New Age philosophies. Gnosticism invaded other religious systems and exploited their symbols to its own end. So, even though a Gnostic might speak of Jesus, he would use the historical figure of Christ to convey his own mythological agenda.

8.5 *The* Da Vinci Code

It is out of these false sources that fantasy like the *Da Vinci Code* is concocted.[12] This blasphemous book is an attack on the basic beliefs of Christianity as remains clear from Dan Brown's statement: "... almost everything our fathers taught us about Christ is false."[13] The *Da Vinci Code* presents a mistaken theory that Christianity is a lie, that Christian rituals are taken from pagan religions and that the New Testament of the Bible is a forgery. The *Da Vinci Code* denies the authority and veracity of the Gospels: "More than eighty gospels were considered for the New Testament, and yet only a relative few were chosen for inclusion... The Bible as we know it today was collated by the pagan Roman Emperor Constantine the Great... From this sprang the most profound moment in Christian history. Constantine commissioned and financed a new Bible, which omitted those gospels that spoke of Christ's human traits and embellished those gospels that made him godlike. The other gospels were outlawed, gathered up, and burned."[14]

Instead, there are four New Testament Gospels, which are named Matthew, Mark, Luke and John. Bible scholars believe that these were written during the first century in which Jesus lived. On the other hand, the Gnostic writings are generally believed to have been written later—about 100 to 300 years later. These Gnostic texts borrowed some elements from Christianity, including the names of Jesus and his apostles, but these writings are not Christian. In response to these new, false writings the regional churches drew up lists of the authentic books that had been handed down from the apostles. There were relatively very few "gospels" and other documents with any confirmed link to apostolic times, not 80 gospels as claimed by Dan Brown. By the middle of the second century, Christian writers regularly cited only the gospels of Matthew, Mark, Luke and John, as well as Paul's letters, as the most reliable sources of information about Jesus' life and the faith of the apostles. On the question of "mass burning of texts deemed heretical," there is no evidence to support that claim. Books rejected by the Church simply disappeared because people stopped using them, and nobody bothered to make new copies in that age, long before the invention of the printing press.

The process by which the Bible formed was one that took time as we have described above. Constantine did not have anything to do with this process, either before or after he converted to Christianity. The process by which the canon of Scripture was formed was largely complete by the time of Constantine which was the early fourth century. *The Da Vinci Code* also asserts that the canon of Scripture was altered at the order of Constantine, at the Council of Nicaea in 325, to support his "new" doctrine of the divinity of Christ.[15] Brown asserts this myth in order to deny the evidence that exists against his position. He cannot back up this claim, for there is no evidence for it whatsoever. No Scripture scholar supports this position. On the contrary, the writings of the Church Fathers (and even non-Christian historians) before the time of Constantine show that Christians regarded Jesus as God. Actually St John's Gospel describes St Thomas calling Jesus "my Lord and my God' (John 20:28). Even before John's Gospel was finished, St Paul's letters repeatedly affirmed faith in Christ as divine. The Council of Nicaea in 325 did not invent faith in the divinity of Christ, but reaffirmed it once again in the Creed that we still use every Sunday.[16]

The *Da Vinci Code* also teems with historical misinformation. The claim that the Emperor Constantine shifted the Christian day of worship to Sunday is simply false. We know from St Paul and other New Testament writers that, soon after Jesus rose from the dead, Christians replaced Saturday with Sunday as their central day of worship. What Constantine did in March 321 was to decree Sunday to be a day of rest from work. He did not make Sunday the day of worship for Christians; it already was that from the first century.[17]

When putting his case for goddess worship, Brown belittles the Jewish roots of Christianity. He assures us that "virtually all the elements of Catholic ritual—the altar, communion were taken directly from earlier pagan mystery religions". Doesn't Brown know about the use of altars in ancient Jewish worship, in which much of the Christian ritual had its roots? Communion originated in the Jewish Passover, celebrated by Jesus and His disciples on the night before He died. Brown introduces some stunning falsehoods about ritualistic sex in the Jerusalem Temple. Israelite men did not come to the Temple to enjoy a "spiritual" experience by engaging in sacred sex with priest-esses. That is a sheer fabrication. There were no priestesses offering sacred sex in the Temple. According to Brown, the Holy of Holies housed not only God but also his "powerful female consort, Shekinah". Now "Shekinah" is a word not found in the Bible but in later Rabbinic writings. It denotes the closeness of God to His people, not to His (alleged) female consort.[18]

According to Dan Brown, in the most dramatic cover-up in history, the official Church suppressed the truth about Mary's relationship with Jesus and did its best to discredit Mary Magdalene. *The Da Vinci Code* makes the utterly false claim Jesus was married to Mary Magdalene. The novelist misuses Leonardo Da Vinci's painting of the Last Supper to support his false thesis.

Instead of unveiling the real Mary Magdalene, Brown dis-guises and belittles her. In all four Gospels she is the prominent figure in the stories of Jesus' Resurrection. She stands by the cross at His death, witnesses His burial, returns to the tomb on Easter Sunday, discovers it to be open and empty, meets Jesus himself now gloriously alive, and then announces to the male disciples the wonderful news of the Resurrection. Early Popes like Leo the Great and Gregory the Great called her the apostle to the apostles and the new Eve proclaiming not death but life to the men. Brown's idea that the official Church ran a smear campaign against Mary Magdalene remains nonsense.[19]

> To sum up. Brown added no fresh evidence to previously discredited attempts to establish that Jesus was married to Mary Magdalene and fathered one or more children by her. Brown did not unveil any astonishing new truth. But he did reveal enormous gaps in his own education, and a willingness to endorse historical lies and errors. The truth did not matter to him. What mattered was creating the most successful fiction for the market.[20]

The reason that Brown and a handful of mainly New Age authors have tried to identify Mary Magdalene as the wife of Jesus is obvious. She is one of the few women disciplines of Christ who is prominent, whose name we know. Other female disciples of Jesus are known to be married to others (for example, Joanna the wife of Chuza in Luke 8:3) or are too insignificant ("the other Mary" in Matthew 28:1) or we don't know their names (the Syro-Phoenecian woman in Matthew 15:28). If one wants to force Jesus into the role of being married, Mary Magdalene is one of the few prominent and (seemingly) available women to be pushed into that role. There is nothing whatever in the New Testament that states or implies that Jesus was married to Mary Magdalene. According to the New Testament, Mary of Magdala was a devout follower of Christ and one of the first witnesses of His Resurrection (cf. Mt 28:1), but not His wife. There is no evidence in the writings of the Church Fathers that she was married to Jesus. Jesus also made affirmations that indicated that He wasn't married to anyone. He explained that some voluntarily refrain from marrying in order to be fully consecrated to God. He says that there are some disciples who "have made themselves eunuchs for the kingdom of heaven's sake" (Mt 19:12). He portrays voluntary abstention from marriage as the highest form of consecration, and as the Founder of the Church, it would be strange for Him to hold up such a standard if He Himself did not meet it.

Jesus' celibacy is a historical fact with important theological ramifications. His celibacy is connected with His divine nature in a like manner that the perpetual virginity of Our Lady points to Christ's divinity. The fact that Jesus has no blood descendants is also important theologically since it means that a relationship to Him can only be by adoption; in the Gospels, in fact, He says: "Whoever does the will of My Father in heaven is My brother and sister and mother" (Mt 12:50). This is to steer people away from the blood relationship to Him and towards the adoptive relationship. Moreover, the early Church was unanimous in regarding Jesus as unmarried. This is not a later doctrine of the Church

Fathers but something found in the New Testament itself. The authors of the New Testament regularly depict the Church as "the bride of Christ" (2 Co 11:2; Ep 5:21–33; cf. Rev 21:9–10). This metaphor would never have developed if a flesh-and-blood wife existed. Only if Christ was celibate would the Church have come to be depicted metaphorically as His bride.

Notes

1   Pope St Clement I, *Letter to the Corinthians*, 47, 1 in *PG* 1, 305.

2   St Ignatius of Antioch, *Letter to the Ephesians*, 12,2 in *Sources Chrétiennes*, 10 (Paris: Cerf, 1945), pp. 58–59.

3   Idem, *Letter to the Smyrnaeans*, 5,1 and 7,2 in *Sources Chrétiennes*, 10, pp. 124–127.

4   St Justin Martyr, *First Apology*, 1, 66 in *PG* 6, 429.

5   St Irenaeus, *Against the heresies*, 3, 11 in *PG* 7, 885.

6   See St Athanasius, *Letter* 39 in *PG* 26, 1438.

7   Cf. Vatican II, *Dei Verbum*, 8.

8   St Jerome, De viris illustribus, 5.

9   John of Salisbury, *Epistle 209*.

10   J. B. Lightfoot, *Saint Paul's Epistles to the Colossians and to Philemon* (London: 1890[9]), p. 297.

11   Text from W. Schneemelcher (ed.), *New Testament Apocrypha* (Louisville: Westminster/John Knox Press, 1989[6]), Volume 2, pp. 43–44. The Latin text runs as follows: 1:1 Paulus apostolus non ab hominibus neque per hominem sed per Iesum Christum, fratribus qui sunt Laodiciae. 1:2 gratia vobis et pax a Deo Patre et Domino Iesu Christo. 1:3 gratias ago Christo per omnem orationem meam, quod permanentes estis in eo et perseverantes in operibus eius, promissum expectantes in diem iudicii. 1:4 neque destituant vos quorundam vaniloquia insinuantium, ut vos evertant a veritate evangelii quod a me praedicatur. 1:5 et nunc faciet Deus, ut qui sunt ex me ad profectum veritatis evangelii deservientes et facientes benignitatem operum quae salutis vitae aeternae 1:6 et nunc palam sunt vincula mea quae patior in Christo; quibus laetor et gaudeo. 1:7 et hoc mihi est ad salutem perpe-tuam; quod ipsum factum orationibus vestris et administrantem Spiritum Sanctum, sive per vitam sive per mortem. 1:8 est enim mihi vere vita in Christo et mori gaudium. 1:9 et in ipsum in vobis faciet misericordiam suam, ut eandem dilectionem habeatis et sitis unianimes. 1:10 ergo, dilectissimi, ut audistis praesentia mei, ita retinete et facite in timore Dei, et erit vobis vita in aeternum; 1:11 est enim Deus qui operatur in vos. 1:12 et facite sine retractu quaecumque facitis. 1:13 et quod est, dilectissimi, gaudete in Christo. et praecavete sordidos in lucro. 1:14 omnes sint

petitiones vestrae palam apud Deum. et estote firmi in sensu Christi. 1:15 et quae integra et vera et pudica et iusta et amabilia facite. 1:16 et quae audistis et accepistis, in corde retinete, et erit vobis pax. 1:17 salutate omnes fratres in osculo sancto. 1:18 salutant vos sancti. 1:19 gratia Domini Iesu cum spiritu vestro. 1:20 et facite legi Colosensium vobis.

[12]   The *Da Vinci Code* is a novel by Dan Brown, a former English teacher and writer of three other books. This blasphemous and evil book is a piece of escapism, which produces a cocktail that mixes religion, conspiracy, sex, murder and mystery. In Brown's novel, the term *Da Vinci Code* refers to cryptic messages supposedly incorporated by Leonardo Da Vinci into his famous artwork, *The Last Supper*. According to the novel, Leonardo was a member of an ancient secret society called the "Priory of Sion" dedicated to preserving the "truths" that Jesus designated Mary Magdalene as his successor, that His message was about the celebration of the "sacred feminine," that Jesus and Mary Magdalene were married and they had a daughter, that the Holy Grail of legend and lore is really Mary Magdalene - the "sacred feminine," - the vessel who carried Jesus' blood or His child. A full refutation of *The Da Vinci Code* will not be undertaken here. There are many excellent books which have done this, like C. E. Olsen & S. Miesel, *The Da Vinci Hoax: Exposing the Errors in The Da Vinci Code* (San Francisco: Ignatius Press, 2004) and A. Welborn, *De-coding Da Vinci. The facts behind the fiction of The Da Vinci Code* (Huntington, IN: Our Sunday Visitor, 2004). Welborn also points out many blatant mistakes in Brown's art history concerning Leonardo da Vinci, on almost every aspect of the artist's life and work. Brown presents himself as some sort of devotee and expert in art history. However, he also consistently refers to the artist in question as "da Vinci", as if this were his name. It's not. It's the indicator of his home town. The artist's name was "Leonardo," and that is the name by which he is called in any art book you might pick up. Anyone who claims to be an art expert and refers to the artist as "da Vinci" is as credible as a person claiming to be a Church historian who refers to Jesus as "of Nazareth".

[13]   D. Brown, *The Da Vinci Code* (New York: Doubleday, 2003), p. 235.

[14]   *Ibid.*, pp. 231, 234.

[15]   See Brown, *The Da Vinci Code*, p. 234.

[16]   See G. O'Collins, *From Rome to Royal Park* (Leominster: Gracewing, 2016), p. 19.

[17]   See *ibid*.

[18]   See *ibid.*, p. 20.

[19]   See *ibid.*, pp. 21–22.

[20]   *Ibid.*, p. 21.

9 FAITH AND REASON

For as the pomegranate, with the rind containing it, has within it many cells and compartments which are separated by tissues, and has also many seeds dwelling in it, so the whole creation is contained by the spirit of God, and the containing spirit is along with the creation contained by the hand of God. As, therefore, the seed of the pomegranate, dwelling inside, cannot see what is outside the rind, itself being within; so neither can man, who along with the whole creation is enclosed by the hand of God, behold God.

Theophilus of Antioch, *To Autolycus*

And since no one can scale a precipice unless there be jutting ledges to aid his progress to the summit, I have here set down in order the primary outlines of our ascent leading our difficult course of argument up the easiest path; not cutting steps in the face of the rock, but levelling it to a gentle slope, that so the traveller, almost without a sense of effort may reach the heights.

St Hilary of Poitiers, *On the Trinity*

VERY EARLY ON in Christian tradition, the place of reason and philosophy in relation to God began to be developed. A certain dividing line between a positive and a negative approach to philosophy is to be found in many Christian thinkers, since in several authors two tendencies live together as it were: the Christian, full of reservations about a philosophy permeated with paganism, and the Greek, which instead is dominated by it. Christian reflection made use of ancient Greek philosophy, in which Aristotelian thought was perhaps the most compatible with Christian doctrine, but which had nevertheless to be purified in order to be adopted in some aspects by Christian thinkers. As regards Platonic notions, these underwent profound changes, especially with regard to concepts such as the immortality of the soul, the divinization of man and the origin of evil.[1]

In the anonymous *Epistle to Diognetus*, sometimes attributed to Mathetes, and composed around the year 130 AD, one finds a clear idea of the relationship between Christians and the surrounding world, which also indicates, on the one hand, that their way of life has not been humanly devised and, on the other, manifests an openness to philosophy. "For the Christians are distinguished from other men neither by country, nor language, nor the customs which they observe. For they neither inhabit cities of their own, nor employ a peculiar form of speech, nor lead a life which is marked out by any singularity. The course of conduct which they follow has not been devised by any speculation or deliberation of inquisitive men; nor do they, like some, proclaim themselves the advocates of any merely human doctrines. But, inhabiting Greek as well as barbarian cities, according as the lot of each of them has determined, and following the customs of the natives in respect to clothing, food, and the rest of their ordinary conduct, they display to us their wonderful and confessedly striking method of life."[2] This document clearly indicates that faith must be reasonable and represents an important testimony since the author was in direct contact with the Apostles: "I do not speak of things strange to me, nor do I aim at anything inconsistent with right reason; but having been a disciple of the Apostles, I am become a teacher of the Gentiles."[3] A profound insight is offered regarding the two trees in the garden of Eden, the one being of knowledge and the other of life. The fact that God from the beginning planted both trees in the midst of paradise indicates that knowledge is the way to life, but our first parents did not use this knowledge properly, they were, through the fraud of the Serpent, stripped naked. For neither can life exist without knowledge, nor is knowledge secure without life. Hence both trees were planted close together. The Christian by his rebirth has become a paradise of delight, being in himself a tree bearing all kinds of produce and flourishing well, being adorned with various fruits; thus knowledge and life must be linked.[4]

9.1 The Christian West

9.1.1 St Irenaeus

St Irenaeus of Lyons (130–202) refuted the Gnostic heresy, which was perhaps the first one concerning reason and faith in the history of the Church. Gnosticism, derived from the Greek word *gnosis* (knowledge) claimed a superior secret understanding of things. It was a system based on philosophical knowledge rather than on faith, where the distinction between the eternal uncreated Supreme Being and all other beings was blurred or erased. The production of matter was conceived of in terms of a downward emanation from God or as the work of a demiurge. The fact that the Gnostics belittled matter meant that they could not accept the Incarnation. Thus their knowledge of God was based on what they could acquire through their secret and elitist understanding of things rather than through revelation received from Christ. In contrast to the Gnostics the Church dismantled barriers of race, social status and gender, and proclaimed from the first the equality of all men and women before God. One important implication of this touched the realm of truth. The elitism which had hallmarked the ancients' search for truth was clearly abandoned. Since access to the truth enables access to God, it must be denied to none.[5]

St Irenaeus declared that God should not be sought after by means of numbers, syllables, and letters, as did the Gnostics. For a system does not spring out of numbers, but numbers from a system; nor does God derive His being from things made, but things made derive their being from God. For all things originate from one and the same God.[6] St Irenaeus reminded his readers that man is infinitely inferior to God and cannot have experience or form a conception of all things like God. Thus a due humility is required in the search for knowledge concerning God.[7] Therefore, truth and the testimony concerning God should be the criteria in the search for knowledge about God; this attitude towards investigation of the mystery of the living God should lead to an increase in the love of Him who has done, and still does, such great marvels. St Irenaeus pointed out that even with respect to creation, the knowledge of some things belongs only to God, while others which come within the range of human knowledge; similarly, in regard to the mysteries in the Scriptures, some can be explained by the grace of God, while others must be left in the hands of God. In this way, not only in the present world, but also in that which is to come, God should for ever teach, and man should for ever learn the things taught him by God. Thus, perfect knowledge cannot be attained in the present life: many questions must be submissively left in the hands of God.[8] St Irenaeus declared in a well-known passage that the Word of God was made Man, born of the Virgin Mary, recapitulating in Himself His own handiwork, and bringing salvation to it.[9] This recapitulation of the human being by Christ, must also include a redemption of the human mind, enabling it to receive knowledge of God.

9.1.2 Tertullian

An apparently total rejection of Greek philosophy was most vividly exemplified in Tertullian's exclamations: "What does Athens have in common with Jerusalem? What concord is there between the Academy and the Church? What between heretics and Christians? Our instruction comes from 'the porch of Solomon,' who had himself taught that 'the Lord should be sought in simplicity of heart.' Away with all attempts to produce a mottled Christianity of Stoic, Platonic, and dialectic composition!"[10] Tertullian's apparent distrust of reason could be a factor in the formation of the rigorist stance which he took in later life, and his joining of the Montanist sect. On the other hand, in Tertullian's *Apology*, addressed to the supreme authorities of the

Empire about the year 200, his attitude to the question of the use of reason is more nuanced, and he indicates ways of arriving at the existence of God through the use of reason:

> The object of our worship is the One God, He who by His commanding word, His arranging wisdom, His mighty power, brought forth from nothing this entire mass of our world, with all its array of elements, bodies, spirits, for the glory of His majesty; whence also the Greeks have bestowed on it the name of cosmos. The eye cannot see Him, though He is spiritually visible. He is incomprehensible, though in grace He is manifested. He is beyond our utmost thought, though our human faculties conceive of Him. He is therefore equally real and great... This it is which gives some notion of God, while yet beyond all our conceptions; our very incapacity of fully grasping Him affords us the idea of what He really is. He is presented to our minds in His transcendent greatness, as at once known and unknown. And this is the crowning guilt of men, that they will not recognise One, of whom they cannot possibly be ignorant. Would you have the proof from the works of His hands, so numerous and so great, which both contain you and sustain you, which minister at once to your enjoyment, and strike you with awe; or would you rather have it from the testimony of the soul itself? Though under the oppressive bondage of the body, though led astray by depraving customs, though enervated by lusts and passions, though in slavery to false gods; yet, whenever the soul comes to itself, as out of a surfeit, or a sleep, or a sickness, and attains something of its natural soundness, it speaks of God... O noble testimony of the soul by nature Christian![11]

The interesting element in Tertullian's standpoint is that he considers both an interior way of discussion to arrive at the existence of God and also an exterior way. These two ways are complementary and will be a keynote in all subsequent thought both in the Christian West and in the Christian East. In general, as regards demonstrations of God's existence, the Greek Fathers preferred the cosmological proofs of God which proceed from external experience: the Latin Fathers preferred the psychological proofs which flow from inner experience.

9.1.3 Lactantius

Around 305 AD, Lactantius wrote the tract *On the Workmanship of God*, addressed to his pupil Demetrianus. According to Lactantius, God the Creator has endowed man with perception and reason, so that it might be evident that the human person derives from Him, because He Himself is intelligence, He Himself is perception and reason. God did not bestow that power of reason upon the other animals. However, God created the human being without those defences imparted to other animals, because wisdom was able to supply those things which the condition of nature had denied to him. He made him naked and defenceless, because he could be armed by his talent, and clothed by his reason. It is wonderful how the absence of those things which are given to the brutes contributes to the beauty of man. For if He had given to man the teeth of wild beasts, or horns, or claws, or hoofs, or a tail, or hairs of various colours, the human being would have been a misshapen animal. Man was formed to be an eternal and immortal being; God did not arm him, as the others, without, but within; nor did He place his protection in the body, but in the soul: since it would have been superfluous, when He had given him that which was of the greatest value, to cover him with bodily defences, especially when they hindered the beauty of the human body.[12]

9.1.4 St Hilary of Poitiers

St Hilary of Poitiers (315–367), a great Western Church Father also dealt with the relationship between faith and reason. His argument for a natural affirmation of the existence of God lies in the recognition of beauty in the cosmos. The Creator of great things is supreme in greatness, the Maker of beautiful things is supreme in beauty. Since the work transcends our thoughts, all thought must be transcended by the Maker. Thus heaven and air and earth and seas are beautiful: the whole universe is beautiful, hence the Greek expression *cosmos* which signifies order. However, if human thought can appraise this beauty of the universe by a natural instinct, must not the Lord of this universal beauty be recognised as Himself most beautiful amid all the beauty that surrounds Him? For although the splendour of His eternal glory overtax our mind's best powers, it cannot fail to see that He is beautiful. We must in truth confess that God is most beautiful, with a beauty which, though it transcend our comprehension, evokes our perception.[13] At the same time, Hilary is very definite about the obedience of steadfast faith which "rejects the vain subtleties of philosophic enquiry" and embraces a truth lying beyond the grasp of reason which "refuses to be vanquished by treacherous devices of human folly, and enslaved by falsehood."[14] Faith will not confine God within the limits which enclosed our common reason. The deeds of God, carried out in a manner beyond our comprehension, cannot be understood by our natural faculties, for the work of the Infinite and Eternal can only be grasped by an infinite intelligence. Hence, just as the truths that God became man, that the Immortal died, that the Eternal was buried, do not belong to the rational order but are an unique work of power, so on the other hand it is an effect not of intellect but of omnipotence that He Who is man is also God, that He Who died is immortal, that He Who was buried is eternal.[15]

St Hilary accepts the use of analogical expressions when speaking about God, but stresses that these are neither perfect nor complete. There can be no comparison between God and earthly things, yet the weakness of our understanding forces us to seek for illustrations from a lower sphere to explain our meaning about loftier themes. The course of daily life indicates how our experience in ordinary matters enables us to form conclusions on unfamiliar subjects. St Hilary thus regards any comparison as helpful to man rather than as descriptive of God, since it suggests, rather than exhausts, the sense that we seek.[16] Considering Christ's expression concerning His Father: "the

Father is in me and I am in the Father" (Jn 10:38), Hilary affirms
that here God's power brings within the range of faith's understanding an expression which is in itself beyond our comprehension. "Thus truth beyond the dull wit of man is the prize of faith
equipped with reason and knowledge; for neither may we doubt
God's Word concerning Himself, nor can we suppose that the
devout reason is incapable of apprehending His might."[17] When
St Hilary tried to defend the true faith concerning the Holy
Trinity, he admitted:

> my brain whirls, my intellect is stunned, my very words
> must be a confession, not that I am weak of utterance, but
> that I am dumb. Yet a wish to undertake the task forces
> itself upon me; it means withstanding the proud, guiding
> the wanderer, warning the ignorant. But the subject is
> inexhaustible; I can see no limit to my venture of speaking
> concerning God in terms more precise than He Himself
> has used. He has assigned the Names Father, Son and
> Holy Spirit, which are our information of the Divine
> nature... All is ineffable, unattainable, incomprehensible.
> Language is exhausted by the magnitude of the theme,
> the splendour of its brightness blinds the gazing eye, the
> intellect cannot compass its boundless extent. Still, under
> the necessity that is laid upon us, with a prayer for pardon
> to Him Whose attributes these are, we will venture,
> enquire and speak.[18]

9.1.5 St Augustine

The most famous Doctor of the patristic period in the Western
Church was St Augustine (354–430), who in his own life had
experienced various philosophies first hand, before he finally
came to Christian faith. His encounter with different currents of
thought left him unsatisfied and his reason found its true home
only in the Catholic Church: "From this time on, I gave my
preference to the Catholic faith. I thought it more modest and not
in the least misleading to be told by the Church to believe what
could not be demonstrated — whether that was because a demonstration existed but could not be understood by all or whether the

matter was not one open to rational proof—rather than to have a rash promise (from the Manichaeans) of knowledge with mockery of mere belief, and then afterwards to be ordered to believe many fabulous and absurd myths impossible to prove true."[19] St Augustine was the first to formulate concisely the mutual relations between reason and faith: "I believe in order to understand; and I understand, the better to believe."[20] At the same time, he elucidated the place which authority held in faith: "What we believe we owe to authority, what we know we owe to reason."[21]

St Augustine developed the interior way of seeking God, which did however depend on a reflection on exterior created reality:

> I asked the heavens, the sun, moon, and stars; and they answered, "Neither are we the God whom you seek." And I replied to all these things which stand around the door of my flesh: "You have told me about my God, that you are not He. Tell me something about Him." And with a loud voice they all cried out, "He made us." My question had come from my observation of them, and their reply came from their beauty of order. And I turned my thoughts into myself and said, "Who are you?" And I answered, "A man." For see, there is in me both a body and a soul; the one without, the other within. In which of these should I have sought my God, whom I had already sought with my body from earth to heaven... But the inner part is the better part; for to it, as both ruler and judge, all these messengers of the senses report the answers of heaven and earth and all the things therein, who said, "We are not God, but He made us." My inner man knew these things through the ministry of the outer man, and I, the inner man, knew all this—I, the soul, through the senses of my body.[22]

St Augustine also suggested how the Holy Trinity leaves an image impressed upon the human person, who if he reflects upon himself realises that he is, he knows, and he wills.[23] To be, to know and to will are dim analogies, but valid ones which can be used to illustrate the mystery of the Father, the Son and the

Holy Spirit. The very fact that St Augustine hazards such an analogy, indicates his desire to underline a rational approach to faith. He pointed out that faith is reasonable, by using an analogy between human faith and divine faith. In human relationships people accept on trust, by human faith, certain things which are unseen. Why is it therefore not possible also to accept by divine faith what God reveals? St Augustine refutes the attitude of those unbelievers who seem through prudence to be unwilling to believe what they cannot see, since in their human activities they believe even those things which are not seen.[24] He shows how absurd is the attitude of those who will only believe what they see; they seem almost to be precursors of modern empiricists or positivists. Citing the example of friendship, St Augustine argues that one cannot see the will and affections of a friend, but one still believes in them. One's own will and the will of the friend are instead perceived by the mind, by the power of reason. He retorts to the precursors of the positivists: "You discern your friend's face with the faculties of your own body, you discern your own faith through the powers of your own mind; but you do not love your friend's faith, unless there exists in you that faith, through which you believe that which is in him but which you do not see."[25] He remarks that if faith be taken away from human affairs, great disorder and fearful confusion must follow. If people cease to believe what they do not see, who will love anyone with mutual affection, since love itself is invisible?[26] St Augustine concludes that we certainly ought to believe certain temporal things, which we do not see not, in order that we may merit to see eternal things also, which we believe. He adopts the analogy of human faith within friendship and thus applies it to supernatural faith. The wills of friends, which are not seen, are believed through symbols which are seen. In a similar way, the Church, which is now seen, is a guarantee of the past things unseen, and a herald of the future things which have not yet been revealed. St Augustine proposed that if we believe lesser authorities in our everyday life, should be not accept the higher authority of God?[27]

According to this great Doctor of the Church, it is the authority of God revealing Himself in Christ which provides a healing and a purification of the intellect. This authority raises the mind from dwelling merely on the earth, and helps it to turn from the love of this world to love of the True God. There exists a happy conspiracy between the outward form of all things, which assuredly flows from some fountain of truest beauty, and the inward conscience which both exhort the mind to seek God, and to serve God. The same God Himself appointed some authority, whereby, as on a safe staircase, we may be lifted up unto God. One external proof of this authority is through the visible miracles which Christ performed: The sick were healed, the lepers were cleansed; walking was restored to the lame, sight to the blind, hearing to the deaf. The men of that time saw water turned into wine, five thousand filled with five loaves, seas passed on foot, the dead rising again. Some of these wonders provided more for the good of the body, others more for the good of the soul but all were carried out for the good of men by their witness to God's authority.[28] St Augustine also mentioned that faith also in a certain sense "prepares for reason"[29] namely it grants wisdom and health to the intellect and brings the reasoning power to a greater perfection.

9.1.6 Boethius

Boethius (480–524) was a Latin Christian philosopher who was distinctly optimistic concerning the capabilities of human reason in its quest for God. His basis was that the universe is rational because it has been created by God who is supremely rational, as exemplified in the following verse:

> O you who rule the universe by perpetual reason,
> sower of earth and heaven,
> you who from eternity order time to pass
> and remaining stabile permit all things to be moved,
> whom no external causes pushed to form
> a true work of flowing material by an innate form
> of the highest good free of envy, by a celestial example

you lead all, the most beautiful itself managing by mind
a beautiful universe and shaping it in a similar image;
and ordering the perfect to finish the perfect parts,
you bind the elements with numbers, as winters with flames,
the dry lands harmonise with waters, purer fire
may not fly off nor do weights bring down sunken lands.[30]

Boethius also anticipated the thought of St Anselm in his ontological argument for the existence of God when he declared: "The common conception of the human spirit proves that God, the principle of all things, is good; for since nothing better than God can be thought of, who may doubt that what nothing is better than is good?"[31] Boethius opposed chance explanations of the universe, which were in vogue during his time, much as they are today. "If chance is defined as an outcome of random influence, produced by no sequence of causes, I am sure that there is no such thing as chance, and I consider that it is but an empty word…. For what place can be left for anything happening at random, so long as God controls everything in order? It is a true saying that nothing can come out of nothing."[32] Boethius was also most famous for his affirmation, in a classical passage, that the eternity of God also lies within reach of human reason:

Then that God is eternal
is the judgement by the common reason of all peoples.
Then let us consider what eternity may be;
for this will make clear to us at once
divine nature and knowledge.
Then eternity is at once
the total and perfect possession of interminable life.
This is more clearly evident
from comparison of the temporal.
For whatever lives in time
proceeds from the past through the present into the future
and there is nothing established in time
which can grasp at once the entire space of its life,
but in fact it does not yet apprehend tomorrow
while it has already lost yesterday;
And in this time of today

your life is no more than a changing, passing moment.
So what comprehends and so possesses at once
the entire fullness of interminable life,
to whom nothing of the future may be absent
nor has anything of the past vanished,
is rightly asserted to be eternal
and it must be both present in control of itself
to always stand by itself
and have present the infinity of passing time. [33]

9.1.7 St Isidore of Seville

St Isidore of Seville (560–636) marked the end of the Fathers of
the Church, and in many ways represented a bridge between
the patristic epoch and the Middle Ages. He warned against
laziness of the intellect in relation to faith and encouraged study,
reading and prayer to arrive at a deeper understanding of what
God has revealed:

> Some people are naturally endowed with intelligence but
> they neglect the pursuit of reading and they despise by
> their neglect the things which they might have been able
> to know by reading. On the other hand, some people have
> a love of knowledge, but are hindered through a slowness
> of understanding; but they do manage through constant
> reading to acquire the wisdom which the cleverer people
> in their idleness do not. Just as the one who is slow at
> understanding, nevertheless gains the prize for good study
> because of his application, so the one who neglects the
> natural ability to understand, which he has been given by
> God, stands as a culprit to be condemned, since he despises
> the gift he has received, and sins through idleness.[34]

An episode is recounted whereby he once noticed water drip-
ping on a rock near where he sat. The drops of water that fell
repeatedly carried no force and seemed to have no effect on the
solid stone. And yet he saw that over time, the water drops had
worn holes in the rock. Isidore realised that if he kept working
at his studies, his seemingly small efforts would eventually pay
off in great learning. His encyclopaedia of knowledge, the

Etymologies, contained all the knowledge that was available at the time and was a popular textbook for nine centuries. Isidore was therefore called "The Schoolmaster of the Middle Ages." He also wrote books on grammar, astronomy, geography, history, and biography as well as theology. When the Arabs brought study of Aristotle back to Europe, this was nothing new to Spain because Isidore's open mind had already reintroduced the philosopher to students there. He stated that "The more conscientious one is in becoming familiar with the sacred writings, the richer an understanding one will draw from them: just as when the earth is cultivated to a greater extent, the more abundant is its harvest."[35] St Isidore is now the patron saint of information technology.

9.2 The Christian East

9.2.1 St Justin

An openly constructive dialogue with Greek philosophy was undertaken by St Justin (100–165). He based his discourse upon the creation of the universe out of nothing by God: "For as in the beginning He created us when we were not, so do we consider that, in like manner, those who choose what is pleasing to Him are, on account of their choice, deemed worthy of incorruption and of fellowship with Him. For the coming into being at first was not in our own power; and in order that we may follow those things which please Him, choosing them by means of the rational faculties He has Himself endowed us with, He both persuades us and leads us to faith."[36] Reason therefore plays an important part in the process of coming to faith in Justin's vision. Justin also proposed a theory of the seeds of the Word. In this perspective, the eternal Word of God manifested Himself prophetically and in figure to the Jews, also showed Himself partially to the Greeks in the form of seeds of truth. "We worship and love the Word who is from the unbegotten and ineffable God, since also He became man for our sakes, that, becoming a partaker of our sufferings, He might also bring us healing. For all the writers were able to see realities darkly through the sowing of the implanted word that was in them. For the seed and imitation imparted according to capacity is one thing, and quite another is the thing itself, of which there is the participation and imitation according to the grace which is from Him." Justin concludes that, since Christianity is the historical and personal manifestation of the Word in His totality, it follows that "everything beautiful that was said by anyone belongs to us Christians."[37] St Justin continued to hold Greek philosophy in high esteem after his conversion, but insisted that he had found in Christianity "the only sure and profitable philosophy."[38] The worship offered to Christ must be reasonable, since the Christian has learned that He is the Son of the true God Himself.[39]

St Justin's approach was developed by the school of Alexandria, and in the first instance by Clement (160–215). Here not only is Greek philosophy not rejected, but it is actually seen as a help in defending the faith: "Greek philosophy, with its contribution, does not strengthen truth; but, in rendering the attack of sophistry impotent and in disarming those who betray truth and wage war upon it, Greek philosophy is rightly called the hedge and the protective wall around the vineyard."[40] Clement, in a magnificent manner distinguishes and explains the various characteristics of faith, knowledge and wisdom. Knowledge is a perfecting of man as man, and is further elevated "by acquaintance with divine things" conformable to itself and to the divine Word. Faith is perfected by knowledge, and this faith, without searching for God, confesses His existence, and glorifies Him. It is from this faith and in accordance with the faith that the knowledge regarding God, is through His grace, to be acquired as far as possible. Knowledge (*gnosis*) differs from the wisdom (*sophia*), which is the result of teaching. It is undoubtedly belief in God which is the basis of knowledge. "Faith is then, so to speak, a comprehensive knowledge of the essentials; and knowledge is the strong and sure demonstration of what is received by faith, built upon faith by the Lord's teaching, carrying the soul on to certainty, knowledge, and comprehension. And, in my view, the first saving change is that from heathenism to faith... and the second, that from faith to knowledge. And the latter terminating in love, thereafter gives the loving to the loved, that which knows to that which is known."[41]

9.2.2 Origen

Origen (185–253) carried forward the thought of the Alexandrian school in regard to the rôle of reason. He underlined the importance of reason in access to the Scriptures, in which the accounts related in the Gospels concerning Jesus, invites thinking people to more than a "simple and unreasoning faith"; what is required is insight into the meaning of the writers, so that the purpose with which each event has been recorded may be discovered.[42] Origen observed that it is much more consonant with the spirit of Christianity to give assent to doctrines upon grounds of reason and wisdom than on that of faith alone, and that it was only in certain circumstances that the approach of naked faith was desired by Christianity, in order not to leave men altogether without help, as is shown by St Paul when he wrote: "Since in the wisdom of God the world was unable to recognise God through wisdom, it was God's own pleasure to save believers through the folly of the gospel (1 Co 1:21)."[43] In one of his most beautiful passages from the *Commentary on the Song of Songs*, Origen links reason and love describing how God wounds the soul which loves Him with His arrow of love, His own Word. Here are linked a reflection upon the beauty of creation, leading to the Word, through Whom all things were made, as well as a love which perfects reason:

> And the soul is moved by heavenly love and longing when, having clearly beheld the beauty and the fairness of the Word of God, it falls deeply in love with His loveliness and receives from the Word Himself a certain arrow and wound of love... If, then, a man can so extend his thinking as to ponder and consider the beauty and the grace of all the things that have been created in the Word,

the very charm of them will so smite him, the grandeur of their brightness will so pierce him as with *a chosen arrow*—as says the prophet—that he will suffer from the arrow Himself a saving wound, and will be kindled with the blessed fire of His love.[44]

Origen then proposes the analogy between Solomon and Christ, and the Queen of Sheba and the Church. The Queen, like the Church is chosen from the nations. The Queen came to hear the wisdom of Solomon; the Church also comes to hear the wisdom of the true Solomon, and of the true Peace-Lover, Our Lord Jesus Christ. "She too at first comes *trying Him with riddles and with questions,* which had seemed to her insoluble before; and He resolves all her perplexity concerning the knowledge of the true God, and concerning the created things of the world, the immortality of the soul, and the future judgement, all of which ever remained doubtful and uncertain for her and for her teachers, at least for the Gentile philosophers."[45] Origen eluci-dated how the Wisdom of Christ transcends all the thought of pagan philosophers. For when the Queen, as type of the Church, spoke to Solomon (as a type of Christ) she was amazed and exclaimed: "The report is true which I heard in my own country concerning Your word and concerning Your prudence. For because of Your word, which I recognised as the true word, I came to You. For all the words that were said to me, and which I heard while I was in my own country, from worldly teachers and philosophers were not true words. That only is the true word, which is in You."[46]

9.2.3 Theophilus of Antioch

One of the most outstanding exponents of the Antiochene school of theology regarding reason and faith was Theophilus of Antioch , active during the second half of the second century. In his reply to Autolycus, an idolater who scorned Christians, he formulated many rational demonstrations of God's existence. In reply to the retort of his opponent, "Show me your God," Theophilus replied: "Show me yourself as a man, and I will show you my God." The eyes of the soul are capable of seeing, and the ears of the heart are able to hear; for as those who look with the eyes of the body perceive earthly objects and what concerns this life, and discriminate at the same time between things that differ, whether light or darkness, white or black, deformed or beautiful, well-proportioned and symmetrical or dispropor-tioned and awkward, or monstrous or mutilated; and as in like manner also, by the sense of hearing, we discriminate either sharp, or deep, or sweet sounds; so the same holds good regarding the eyes of the soul and the ears of the heart, that it is by them we are able to behold God. For God is seen by those who are enabled to see Him when they have the eyes of their soul opened: for all have eyes; but in some they are covered, and do not see the light of the sun. Yet it does not follow, because the blind do not see, that the light of the sun does not shine; but let the blind blame themselves and their own eyes. Theophilus linked with sin the incapacity for seeing God with the eyes of the soul. When there is rust on the mirror, it is not possible that a man's face be seen in the mirror; so also when there is sin in a man, such a man cannot behold God. As when a film of impurity on the eyes prevents one from beholding the light of the sun: so also do iniquities involve man in darkness, so that he cannot see God.[47] For Theophilus, "the appearance of God is ineffable and indescribable, and cannot be seen by eyes of flesh. For in glory He is incomprehensible, in greatness unfathomable, in height inconceivable, in power incomparable, in wisdom unrivalled, in goodness inimitable, in kindness unutterable."[48] At the same time, he outlined how God may be known through His creation.

Theophilus drew the analogy between the human soul and God. For just as the soul in man is invisible to men, but is perceived through the motion of the body, so God cannot indeed be seen by human eyes, but is beheld and perceived through His providence and works. Just as any person, when he sees a ship on the sea rigged and in sail, and making for the harbour, will clearly deduce that there is a captain in her who is steering her; so also we must perceive that God is the governor of the whole universe, though He be not visible to the eyes of the flesh, since He is incomprehensible. For if a man cannot look upon the sun, though it be a very small heavenly body, on account of its exceeding heat and power, how shall not a mortal man be much more unable to face the glory of God, which is unutterable?[49] However, in order to make the deduction from the creation to its Creator, the human person needs a healing of the intellect because of the blindness of the soul, and the hardness of the heart. However if there is a desire at least for healing, the Physician, will soothe the eyes of the soul and of the heart. God is the Physician who heals through His word and wisdom.[50] Finally, Theophilus provides some examples to indicate that the Christian doctrine of the resurrection of the body is reasonable. Through His creation God illustrates many analogies of resurrection, so that we may see that the resurrection is indeed reasonable. One example is seen in the "dying" of seasons, and days, and nights, and how these also "rise again". A further picture is found in the seed of wheat which, when it is cast into the earth, first dies and rots away, then is raised, and becomes a stalk of corn. The work of resurrection is going on in man, even though he be unaware of it. For when someone has fallen sick, and lost flesh, and strength, and beauty; but then received again from God mercy and healing, and recovered also physical strength, that person has in a sense experienced a prefiguration of the resurrection. In all these things the wisdom of God shows that He is able to effect the general resurrection of all men.[51]

9.2.4 St Athanasius of Alexandria

St Athanasius of Alexandria (296–373) was another Eastern Father who was a staunch defender of reasoned faith. He demonstrated the illogical nature of idol worship, indicating that no part of the creation can be a god because of the mutual dependence of those parts. For if a man take the parts of creation separately, and consider each by itself, for example the sun by itself alone, and the moon apart, and again earth and air, and heat and cold, separating them from their mutual conjunction, he will certainly find that not one is sufficient for itself, but all are in need of one another's assistance, and subsist by their mutual help. For the Sun is carried round along with, and is contained in, the whole heaven, and can never go beyond its own orbit, while the moon and other stars testify to the assistance given them by the Sun: while the earth again evidently does not yield its crops without rains, which in their turn would not descend to earth without the assistance of the clouds; but not even would the clouds ever appear of themselves and subsist, without the air.[52] Neither can the cosmic totality be God, for that would make God consist of dissimilar parts, and subject Him to possible dissolution. For if the combination of the parts makes up the whole, and the whole is combined out of the parts, then the whole consists of the parts, and each of them is a portion of the whole. However this is very far removed from the conception of God. For God is a whole and not a number of parts, and does not consist of various elements, but is Himself the Maker of the system of the universe.[53]

Athanasius asserted that "the soul of man, being intellectual, can know God of itself, if it be true to its own nature."[54] By affirming the existence of the rational human soul, Athanasius proposed a stepping stone to the contemplation of the Creator. The existence of the human soul is proved by the essential difference between man and the animals. The human person alone thinks of things external to himself, and reasons about things not actually present, and exercises reflection, and chooses by judgement the better of alternative reasonings. For the irrational animals see only what is present, and are impelled solely by what meets their eye, even if the consequences to them are injurious, while man is not impelled toward what he sees merely, but judges by thought what he sees with his eyes. In order to illustrate his point, Athanasius adopts the example of a lyre in the hands of a skilled musician. For each string of this musical instrument delivers its proper note, high, low, or intermediate, sharp or otherwise, yet their scale is indistinguishable and their time not to be recognised, without the artist. For only then is the scale evident and the time right, when the player holding the lyre plucks the strings and touches each in tune. In like manner, the senses are deployed in the body like the strings in a lyre; when the skilled intelligence presides over them, then too the soul distinguishes and knows what it is doing and how it is acting. This characteristic is specific to mankind, and this is what is rational in the soul of man and of woman, and shows that it is truly distinct from what is to be seen in the body.[55]

For Athanasius, only when the soul gets rid of the stains of sin is it able to know God directly, and then its own rational nature is once more the image of the Word of God, in whose likeness it was created. However, he pointed out that even if the soul cannot pierce the cloud which sin draws over its vision, it nevertheless can attain to the knowledge of God from the things which are seen, since creation, as though in written characters, declares in a loud voice, by its order and harmony, its own Lord and Creator.[56] St Athanasius proclaims that creation a revelation of God, especially because of the order and harmony which pervades it. Anyone seeing the circle of heaven and the course of the sun and the moon, and the positions and movements of the other stars, as they take place in opposite and different directions, while yet in their difference all with one accord observe a consistent order, should be able to come to the conclusion that these are not ordered by themselves, but have a Maker distinct from themselves who orders them.[57] The great Eastern Doctor applies a similar musical analogy once again to illustrate that the harmony in nature is a reflection of the unity of God. If one were to hear from a distance a lyre, composed of many different strings, and marvel at the concord of its symphony, in that its sound is composed neither of low notes exclusively, nor high nor intermediate only, but all combine their sounds in equal balance; one would not fail to perceive from this that the lyre was not playing itself, nor even being struck by more persons than one, but that there was one musician, even if he did not see him, who by his skill combined the sound of each string into the tuneful symphony. In a similar manner, since the order of the whole universe is perfectly harmonious, without discord of the higher against the lower or the lower against the higher, and all things making up one order, it is consistent to think that the Ruler and King of all Creation is one and not many, Who by His own light illumines and gives movement to all.[58]

Finally, St Athanasius showed that the rationality and order of the Universe indicates that it is the work of the Reason or Word of God. Three similes illustrate the power of the Word who guarantees rationality to the Universe. The first picture is that of a choir composed of different people, children, women, and old men, and those who are still young, and, when one, namely the conductor, gives the sign, each utters sound according to his nature and power, the man as a man, the child as a child, the old man as an old man, and the young man as a young man, while all make up a single harmony. The second image is that of the human soul which at one time moves our several senses in a rational way according to the proper function of each, so that when some one object is present all alike are put in motion, and the eye sees, the ear hears, the hand touches, the smell takes in odour, and the palate tastes. The third example is that of a very great city, administered under the presence of the king who has built it; for when he is present and gives orders, and has his eye upon everything, all obey; some busy themselves with agriculture, others hasten for water to the aqueducts, another goes forth to procure provisions, one goes to senate, another enters the assembly, the judge goes to the bench, and the magistrate to his court. The workman likewise settles to his craft, the sailor goes down to the sea, the carpenter to his workshop, the physician to his treatment, the architect to his building; and while one is going to the country, another is returning from the country, and while some walk about the town others are going out of the town and returning to it again: but all this is going on and is organised by the presence of the one Ruler, and by his management. These similes show how we must conceive of the whole of creation: for by the power of the Word of God, all things simultaneously fall into order, and each discharge their proper functions, and a single order is made up by them all together.[59] The similes apply to the whole Universe, seen and unseen. By the power of the Divine Word of the Father that governs and presides over all, the heaven revolves, the stars move, the sun shines, the moon goes her circuit, and the air receives the sun's light and the winds blow: the mountains are reared on high, the sea is rough with waves, and the living things in it grow the earth abides fixed, and bears fruit, and man is formed and lives and dies again, and all things whatever have their life and movement; fire burns, water cools, fountains spring forth, rivers flow, seasons and hours come round, rains descend, clouds are filled, hail is formed. snow and ice congeal, birds fly, creeping things move along, water-animals swim, the sea is navigated, the earth is sown and grows crops in due season, plants grow, and some are young, some ripening, others in their growth become old and decay, and while some things are vanishing others are being generated and are coming to light.[60]

9.2.5 St John Damascene

St John Damascene (676–770) wrote beautifully about the natural knowledge of God. The knowledge of God's existence has been implanted by Him in all human beings by nature. This creation, too, and its maintenance, and its government, proclaim the majesty of the Divine nature.[61] Despite this fact that the knowledge of the existence of God is implanted in the human being by nature, the wickedness of the Evil One has prevailed so mightily against man's nature as even to drive some into the pit of destruction whereby they deny the existence of God.[62] St John Damascene indicated that the Apostles convinced by means of miracles, but since he claimed not to have that gift, he proposed instead some rational demonstrations of God's existence. An example of his proofs is one which was a precursor of one of St Thomas Aquinas' proofs. It runs like this. All things, that exist, are either created or uncreated. If, then, things are created, it follows that they are also wholly mutable. For things, whose existence originated in change, must also be subject to change, whether it be that they perish or that they become other than they are by act of wills. However, if things are uncreated they must, for consistency, be also wholly immutable. For things which are opposed in the nature of their existence must also be opposed in the mode of their existence, that is to say, must have opposite properties: who, then, will refuse to grant that all existing things, not only such as come within the province of the senses, but even the angels, are subject to change and transformation and movement of various kinds? For the things belonging to the rational world, namely angels and spirits and demons, are subject to changes of will, whether it is a progression or a retrogression in goodness, whether a struggle or a surrender; while the others suffer changes of generation and destruction, of increase and decrease, of quality and of movement in space. Things then that are mutable are also wholly created. However, things that are created must be the work of some Maker, and the Maker cannot have been created. For if He had been created, He also must surely have been created by some one, and so on till we arrive at something uncreated. The Creator, then, being uncreated, is also wholly immutable. And who could this be other than Deity?[63]

The Fathers both of Eastern and of Western Christendom showed how reason, freed from the bondage of paganism, could find its way out of the blind alley of myth and superstition and be enlightened by the liberating force of the Gospel. Purified and rightly tuned, therefore, reason could rise to the higher planes of thought, providing a solid foundation for the perception of being, of the transcendent and of the absolute.[64]

Notes

1   See Pope St John Paul II, *Fides et ratio* 39.
2   *Epistle to Diognetus*, c.5 in *PG* 2, 1173–1174.
3   *Ibid.*, c.11 in *PG* 2, 1183–1184.
4   Cf. *ibid.*, c.12 in *PG* 2, 1185–1186.
5   See Pope St John Paul II, *Fides et ratio* 19.
6   See St Irenaeus, *Adversus haereses* Book II, chapter 25, 1 in *PG* 7, 798.
7   See *ibid.*, chapter 25, 3 and 4 in *PG* 7, 799.
8   See *ibid.*, chapter 28, 1–3 in *PG* 7, 804–806.
9   See *ibid.*, Book III, chapter 22, 1–2 in *PG* 7, 955–958.
10   Tertullian, *De Praescriptione Haereticorum*, chapter 7 in *PL* 2, 20.
11   Idem, *Apology*, 17 in *PL* 1, 375–377.
12   Lactantius, *On the Workmanship of God*, chapter 2 in *PL* 7, 14–16.
13   See St Hilary of Poitiers, *On the Trinity*, Book I, n.7 in *PL* 10, 30.
14   *Ibid.*, n.13 in *PL* 10, 34.
15   See *ibid.*, in *PL* 10, 35.
16   See *ibid.* n.19. in *PL* 10, 38–39.
17   *Ibid.*, n.22 in *PL* 10, 39.
18   *Ibid*, Book II, n.5 in *PL* 10, 54.
19   Saint Augustine, *Confessions*, Book 6, chapter 5, 7 in *PL* 32, 722.
20   Idem, *Sermon* 43, chapter 7, 9 in *PL* 38, 257–258. The Latin is "Intellige, ut credas, verbum meum; crede, ut intelligas, verbum Dei."
21   Idem, *De utilitate credendi* (On the profit of believing), 11, 25 in *PL* 42, 83. The Latin is "Quod intelligimus igitur, debemus rationi: quod credimus, auctoritati."
22   Idem, *Confessions*, Book 10, chapter 6, n. 9 in *PL* 32, 783.
23   *Ibid*, Book 13, Chapter 11, n. 12 in *PL* 32, 849.
24   See St Augustine, *De fide rerum quae non videntur* (Concerning faith in things not seen), chapter 1 in *PL* 40, 171.
25   *Ibid.*, chapter 3 in *PL* 40, 174.
26   Cf. *Ibid.*, chapter 4 in *PL* 40, 176.
27   Cf. *Ibid.*.
28   See St Augustine, *De utilitate credendi*, Book I, chapter 16, n.34 in *PL* 42, 89–90.
29   *Ibid.*, chapter 17, n.35 in *PL* 42, 91. The Latin text runs: "Nam si nulla certa ad sapientiam salutemque animis via est, nisi cum eos rationi praecolit fides; quid est aliud ingratum esse opi atque auxilio divino, quam tanto labore praedictae auctoritati velle resistere?"
30   Boethius, *Consolation of Philosophy*, Book 3, verse 9 in *PL* 63, 758–760.
31   *Ibid.*, Book 3, prose 9 in *PL* 63, 765.

[32]   *Ibid.*, Book 5, prose 1 in *PL* 63, 830–831.

[33]   *Ibid.*, Book 5, prose 6 in *PL* 63, 858–859.

[34]   Saint Isidore, *Book 3 of the Sentences* , chapter 9, 5–8 in *PL* 83, 681–682.

[35]   Idem, *Book 3 of the Sentences* , chapter 9, 2 in *PL* 83, 681. The Latin is
       "Quanto quisque magis in sacris eloquiis assiduus fuerit, tanto ex eis
       uberiorem intelligentiam capit; sicut terra, quae quanto amplius excolitur,
       tanto uberius fructificat."

[36]   St Justin Martyr, *The First Apology*, 10 in *PG* 6, 341–342.

[37]   St Justin Martyr, *The Second Apology*, 13 in *PG* 6, 465–466.

[38]   Idem. *Dialogue with Trypho*, 8 in *PG* 6, 491–492.

[39]   Cf. Idem, *The First Apology*, 13 in *PG* 6, 345–348.

[40]   Clement of Alexandria, *Stromata*, Book I, c. 20 in *PG* 8, 817–818.

[41]   *Ibid.*, Book VII, c. 10 in *PG* 9, 481–482.

[42]   See Origen, *Contra Celsum*, Book 1, n. 42 in *PG* 11, 737–738.

[43]   See Origen, *Contra Celsum*, Book 1, n. 13 in *PG* 11, 679–680.

[44]   See Origen, *Commentary on the Song of Songs*, Prologue 2 in *Ancient
       Christian Writers* vol. 26, Origen. *The Song of Songs Commentary and
       Homilies*, translated and annotated by R. P. Lawson (New York: Newman
       Press, 1956) pp. 29–30. See also the passage from the song of Songs to
       which Origen refers, namely Ct 2:5, which in the Greek Septuagint reads:
       τετρωμένη ἀγάπης ἐγώ or "I am wounded by love." The New Jerusalem
       Bible translation "I am sick with love" is rather weaker. This passage has
       inspired many generations of Christian mystics besides Origen, including
       St Gregory of Nyssa, St Augustine, St Theresa of Avila and St John of the
       Cross to consider the wound of love. See also Is 49:2 "He made me into
       a sharpened arrow and concealed me in his quiver."

[45]   Origen, *Commentary on the Song of Songs*, Book 2, 1 in *The Song of Songs
       Commentary and Homilies*, p. 98.

[46]   *Ibid.*, p.100. 1 K 10:6–8; 2 Ch 9:5–7.

[47]   See Theophilus of Antioch, *To Autolycus* Book I, n. 2 in *PG* 6, 1025–1028.

[48]   *Ibid.*, n. 3 in *PG* 6, 1027–1028.

[49]   See *ibid.*, n. 5 in *PG* 6, 1031–1032.

[50]   See *ibid.*, n. 7 in *PG* 6, 1033–1036.

[51]   See *ibid.*, n. 13 in *PG* 6, 1041–1044.

[52]   See St Athanasius, *Against the Heathen* Part I, n. 27 in *PG* 25, 51–56.

[53]   See *ibid.*, n.28 in *PG* 25, 55–58.

[54]   *Ibid.*, n.30 in *PG* 25, 61–62.

[55]   See *ibid.*, n.31 in *PG* 25, 61–64.

[56]   See *ibid.*, n.34 in *PG* 25, 67–70.

[57]   See *ibid.*, n.35 in *PG* 25, 69–72.

[58]   See *ibid.*, n.38 in *PG* 25, 75–78.

[59]   See *ibid.*, n.43 in *PG* 25, 85–88.

60   See *ibid.*, n.44 in *PG* 25, 87–88.
61   See St John Damascene, *An Exposition of the Orthodox Faith* Book I, chapter 1, in *PG* 94, 789–790.
62   *Ibid.*, Book I, chapter 3, in *PG* 94, 793–798.
63   See St John Damascene, *An Exposition of the Orthodox Faith* Book I, chapter 3, in *PG* 94, 793–798.
64   See Pope St John Paul II, *Fides et ratio* 41.

10 THE ROLE OF WOMEN

The Church gives thanks for each and every woman...
The Church gives thanks for all the manifestations of the
feminine 'genius' which have appeared in the course of
history, in the midst of all peoples and nations; she gives
thanks for all the charisms which the Holy Spirit distrib-
utes to women in the history of the People of God, for all
the victories which she owes to their faith, hope and
charity: she gives thanks for all the fruits of feminine
holiness"

Pope John Paul II, *Mulieris Dignitatem*, 31.

WE HAVE ALREADY illustrated the central role of Our Blessed Lady at the beginning of this book. She is the most important woman at the beginnings of Christianity. Virginity and motherhood are two particular dimensions of the fulfilment of the female personality. In the light of the Gospel, they acquire their full meaning and value in Mary, who as a Virgin became the Mother of the Son of God.

10.1 New Testament Times

The New Testament Gospels, written toward the last quarter of the first century, acknowledge that women were among Jesus' earliest followers. From the beginning, Jewish women disciples, including Mary Magdalene, Joanna, and Susanna, had accompanied Jesus during his ministry and supported him out of their private means (Luke 8:1–3). Jesus spoke to women both in public and private. According to one account, an unnamed Gentile woman (Canaanite, by birth a Syro-Phoenician) was the occasion for Jesus to teach that the ministry of God is not limited to particular groups and persons, but belongs to all who have faith (Mark 7:24–30; Matthew 15:21–28). Jesus was a frequent visitor at the home of Mary and Martha, and was in the habit of teaching and eating meals with women as well as men. When Jesus was arrested, women remained firm, even when his male disciples are said to have fled, and they accompanied him to the foot of the cross. It was women who were reported as the first witnesses to the Resurrection, chief among them again Mary Magdalene.

In addition to the Twelve, pillars of the Church and fathers of the new People of God, many women were also chosen to number among the disciples. We can only mention very briefly those who followed Jesus himself, beginning with the Prophetess Anna (cf. Lk 2:36–38), the Samaritan woman (cf. Jn 4:1–39), the Syro-Phoenician woman (cf. Mk 7:24–30), the woman with the haemorrhage (cf. Mt 9:20–22) and the woman whose sins were forgiven (cf. Lk 7:36–50). Sometimes women appear in the parables which Jesus of Nazareth used to illustrate for his listeners the truth about the Kingdom of God. This is the case in the parables of the lost coin (cf. Lk 15:8–10), the leaven (cf. Mt 13:33), and the wise and foolish virgins (cf. Mt 25:1–13).

Particularly eloquent is the story of the widow's mite. While "the rich were putting their gifts into the treasury... a poor widow put in two copper coins". Then Jesus said: "This poor widow has put in more than all of them... she out of her poverty put in all the living that she had" (Lk 21:1–4). In this way Jesus presents her as a model for everyone and defends her, for in the socio-juridical system of the time widows were totally defenceless people (cf. also Lk 18:1–7).[1]

10.1.1 The Anointing of Jesus

The anointing of Jesus is an event reported by the Synoptic Gospels and the Gospel of John, in which a woman pours the entire contents of an *alabastron* of very expensive perfume over the head of Jesus. This event is a subject of considerable debate, as many scholars hold that it is actually two separate events: one occurring at the beginning of Jesus' ministry in which He offered forgiveness to a repentant woman, and the other in which He is anointed in preparation for His burial.

Luke's Gospel speaks of Jesus' feet being anointed by a woman had been sinful all her life, and who was crying; and when her tears started landing on the feet of Jesus, she wiped His feet with her hair (Lk 7:36–50). In conformity with what Jesus Himself said of the woman who anointed His head shortly before the Passion: "Truly, I say to you, wherever this Gospel is preached in the whole world, what she has done will be told in memory of her" (Mt 26: 13; Mk 14: 9), their testimony cannot be forgotten.

Many biblical historians hold that this episode could not have occurred only a few days prior to the crucifixion, due to the numerous events that followed in Luke's Gospel. John 12:1–8 names her Mary, and the text assumes her to be Mary, a sister to Lazarus, as it also identifies her sister Martha. Although the woman's act has traditionally been associated with Mary Magdalene, there is no biblical text identifying her as such. According to the Gospel of Mark 14:3, the perfume in his account was the purest of spikenard oil.

The passage in Luke is similar to another episode of Jesus being anointed by a woman, and is often confused with it. So if we are to understand the story of Jesus anointed by a sinful woman, we need to disentangle it from the story of Jesus' anointing at Bethany near the end of His ministry (Mt 26:6–13; Mk 14:1–11; Jn 12:1–10). The two events are confused easily enough because of several similarities: Jesus is anointed with expensive perfume, He is anointed by a woman, and the anointing takes place in the house of a man named Simon. However, the differences between the accounts show that the passage in Luke 7:36–50 is really a different incident from that found in Matthew 26:6–13; Mark 14:1–11; John 12:1–10. The anointing at Bethany differs in that it takes place at the home of Simon the Leper, not Simon the Pharisee. The woman doing the anointing at Bethany is not spoken of as sinful, but actually appears to be Mary, Lazarus' sister. Furthermore, the meaning of the anointing at Bethany is to prefigure Jesus' burial. Also, the anointing is on the head in Matthew and Mark, although on the feet in John. The criticism is by disciples, especially Judas, over the value of the perfume that is "wasted", rather than a criticism of the morals of the woman doing the anointing.

In John the use of the word "dinner" refers exclusively to Jesus' Last Supper with His disciples. This dinner has echoes of that meal. John's version of the story combines elements from both Luke and Mark, namely Mary anoints Jesus' feet (Luke) but this is linked with Jesus' burial (Mark). In John the verb 'to wipe' is the same verb used to describe Jesus' wiping of His disciples' feet at the foot–washing in John 13:5. Mary's anointing and wiping of Jesus' feet thus point toward Jesus' foot–washing at the Last Supper. A possible conclusion is that the four Gospels represent two anointing incidents:

A) The first chronologically is seen in Luke 7:36–50.
B) The second chronologically is represented by Mark 14:1–11, upon which Matthew 26:6–13 is totally dependent.

The episode in John 12:1–8 is an amalgamated story, incorporating details from both incidents and adding details from Luke 10:38–42. It is significant that by actually replacing the original location of the pouring of the "costly ointment of pure nard" from Jesus' Head (Mk 14:3=Mt 26:7), originally understood as a prophetic act of messianic character, parallel to St Peter's confession at Caesarea Philippi (Mk 8:27ff and parallels), to Jesus' feet (Jn 12:3), John made a woman proleptically anticipate the incident of the washing by Jesus Himself of His disciples' feet. By so doing, John changed even an act of "witness" into an act of *diakonia*.

The mystical significance of St John's account of the anointing is further underlined by the mention of Mary's action in John 11:2. This verse constitutes a prolepsis—a rhetorical figure consisting in the anticipation of a future event.[2] From the Synoptic Gospels, Christians of John's day already knew about Martha and Mary from Luke 10:38–42. Therefore John's reference in John 11:2 to Mary's anointing of Jesus in John 12:2 is clearly understandable as underlining the mystical importance of Mary's action in John chapter 12, by anticipating it in John chapter 11. Moreover, the context of John chapter 11 is the raising of Lazarus which itself prefigures the

The Gospels then tell us that the women, unlike the Twelve, did not abandon Jesus in the hour of His Passion (cf. Mt 27: 56, 61; Mk 15: 40). Among them, Mary Magdalene stands out in particular. Not only was she present at the Passion, but she was also the first witness and herald of the Risen One (cf. Jn 20: 1, 11–18).

10.1.2 Mary of Bethany

No fewer than six women in the New Testament are named Mary: the Mother of God; Mary Magdalene; Mary of Bethany; Mary, wife of Cleophas; Mary, mother of John Mark; and a Christian woman in Rome. Often, the way the biblical authors distinguished them was by using place names or patriarchal family names associated with them. Mary of Bethany was the sister of Martha and Lazarus, the followers of Jesus who lived in Bethany. The Gospel of John is the only gospel account that makes an explicit reference to Mary (sister of Lazarus) as the unidentified sinner who anoints Jesus' feet at the house of Simon the Pharisee, as we have seen above (see also Jn 11:1–3, 21).

Traditionally, the sinful woman (Lk 7:36–50) who anointed Jesus with costly spikenard from her alabaster jar in Luke 7:37 became associated early on with both Mary Magdalene and Mary of Bethany. However, these figures have now been distinguished.

10.1.3 Mary Magdalene

In the four Gospels, Mary Magdalene seems to be distinguished from other women named Mary by adding "Magdalene" to her name.[3] Traditionally, this has been interpreted to mean that she was from Magdala, a town thought to have been on the western shore of the Sea of Galilee. Luke 8:2 says that she was actually called Magdalene. In Hebrew *Migdal* means tower or fortress;[4] in Aramaic, *Magdala* means tower or "elevated, great, magnificent".

According to Luke 8:2 and Mark 16:9, Jesus cleansed her of "seven demons". At the time of the Crucifixion and Resurrection, Mary Magdalene comes to the fore in the gospels. Uniquely among the followers of Jesus, she is specified by name (though not consistently by any one Gospel) as a witness to three key events: Jesus' Crucifixion, his burial, and the discovery of his tomb to be empty. Mark 15:40, Matthew 27:56 and John 19:25 mention Mary Magdalene as a witness to the Crucifixion, along with various other women. Luke does not name any witnesses, but mentions "women who had followed him from Galilee" standing at a distance" (Lk 23:49). In listing witnesses who saw where Jesus was buried by Joseph of Aramathea, Mark 15:47 and Matthew 27:61 both name only two people: Mary Magdalene and "the other Mary", who in Mark is "the mother of James". Luke 23:55 describes the witnesses merely as "the women who had come with Jesus from Galilee". John 19:39–42 mentions no other witness to Joseph's burial of Jesus except for Joseph's assistant Nicodemus. However, John 20:1 then names Mary Magdalene in describing who discovered the tomb to be empty. Mark 16:1 says she was accompanied by Salome and Mary the mother of James, while Matthew 28:1 omits Salome. Luke 24:10 says the group who found the empty tomb consisted of "Mary Magdalene, Joanna, Mary the mother of James, and the others with them".

In Mark, Matthew, and John, Mary Magdalene is first witness to the Resurrection. John 20:16 and Mark 16:9 both straightforwardly say that Jesus' first post-resurrection appearance was to Mary Magdalene alone. Mary Magdalene is thus the first to meet the Risen Christ. At first she thinks He is the gardener; she recognizes Him only when he calls her by name: "Jesus said to her, 'Mary'. She turned and said to Him in Hebrew, 'Rabbuni' (which means Teacher). Jesus said to her, 'Do not hold me, for I have not yet ascended to the Father, but go to my brethren and say to them, I am ascending to my Father and to your Father, to my God and your God.' Mary Magdalene went and said to the disciples, 'I have seen the Lord'; and she told them that He had said these things to her" (Jn 20:16–18).

Pope Gregory the Great's homily on Luke's gospel dated 14 September 591 first suggested that Mary Magdalene was a prostitute:

> She whom Luke calls the sinful woman, whom John calls Mary, we believe to be the Mary from whom seven devils were ejected according to Mark. And what did these seven devils signify, if not all the vices?… It is clear, brothers, that the woman previously used the unguent to perfume her flesh in forbidden acts.[5]

It was because of this association of Mary as a prostitute that she became the patroness of "wayward women", and "Magdalene houses" became established to help save women from prostitution. Ecclesial tradition in the West, especially since the time of Gregory the Great, has identified St Mary Magdalene, and the woman who anointed Christ's feet with perfume in the house of Simon the Pharisee, and the sister of Lazarus and Martha, as one and the same person.[6]

Rabanus Maurus (died 856) affirms on various occasions the relevance of this woman "who so loved Christ and was so greatly loved by Christ".[7] Saint Anselm of Canterbury (died 1109) wrote of her as "chosen because you are beloved and beloved because you are chosen of God".[8] From the twelfth century Abbot Hugh of Semur (died 1109), Peter Abelard (died 1142), and Geoffrey of Vendome (died 1132) all referred to Mary Magdalene as the sinner who merited the title *apostolorum apostola*, with the title becoming commonplace during the twelfth and thirteenth centuries. It was precisely to Mary Magdalene that St Thomas Aquinas reserved the special title, "Apostle of the Apostles" (*apostolorum apostola*), dedicating to her this beautiful comment: "Just as a woman had announced the words of death to the first man, so also a woman was the first to announce to the Apostles the words of life."[9] It was with good reason that the Angelic Doctor applied this term to Mary of Magdala, for she is the witness to the risen Christ and announces the message of the Lord's resurrection just like the rest of the Apostles.[10]

In tradition, Mary of Bethany had been identified as Mary Magdalene. The French legend of *Saint Lazare of Bethany* is that Mary, her sister Martha, her brother Lazarus, Maximinus, one of the Seventy Disciples, and some companions, expelled by persecutions from the Holy Land, crossed the Mediterranean in a frail boat with neither rudder nor mast and landed in Provence at the place called Saintes-Maries-de-la-Mer near Arles. Mary Magdalene came to Marseille and converted the whole of Provence. She is said to have retired to a cave on a hill by Marseille, La Sainte-Baume (holy cave or *baumo* in Provençal), where she gave herself up to a life of penance for thirty years. When the time of her death arrived, around 75 AD, she was carried by angels to Aix and into the oratory of Saint Maximinus, where she received the Viaticum; her body was then laid in an oratory constructed by St Maximinus at Villa Lata, afterwards called St Maximin. Between the third and fourth century, her body was placed in a magnificent white marble tomb, and remained therein until the year 710. The Cassian Monks had founded their Monastery in St Maximin in 415 and were the guardians of the Magdalene relics. However, when the Saracens invaded France, destroying all Christian symbols, the monks transferred the relics to a more modest tomb for safety reasons. Before fleeing, they completely buried the tomb and their chapel. When the invaders left in 973, nothing could be found of the relics, though many searches were made. In 1279, when Charles II, King of Naples (nephew of King Louis IX of France, who was canonized as St Louis), erected a Dominican convent at La Sainte-Baume, the shrine was found intact, with an explanatory inscription stating why the relics had been hidden. The transfer of the remains was made to the crypt on 5 May 1280.

10.1.4 Martha

Jesus often visited Martha, Mary, and their brother Lazarus at their house in Bethany, near Jerusalem. The gospels mention members of this family several times, but in one account, Jesus and His disciples visited them in Bethany (Luke 10:38–42). While Martha worked in the kitchen preparing a meal for the guests,

Mary, her sister, sat at the feet of Jesus and listened to Him discoursing. Martha, annoyed that her sister wasn't helping with the meal preparation, complained to Jesus. Jesus made the point succinctly: Martha could spend all of her time worrying about the concrete things of the world (food preparation, entertaining the guests), but Mary had chosen to learn about things not of this world. The nourishment Mary sought was not for the body, but for the soul; she had chosen the better part, and it would never be taken from her (see Lk 10:40–42).

When their brother Lazarus died, Martha and Mary sent for Jesus. When she was told he was approaching the town, Martha went to meet the Lord. Mary remained inside the house until her presence was requested. That day, Jesus gave the grieving Martha words of hope after she told him that she believed Lazarus would rise again at the resurrection on the last day. Jesus told Martha that she would see Lazarus before then (Jn 11:25–27).

10.1.5 Mary, Wife of Cleophas

This biblical Mary was the mother of James the Less and Joseph (Mk 15:40, Mt 27:56). She has also been called Mary the mother of James (Mk 16:1, Lk 24:10), but her relationship, if any, to the Mother of Jesus is not clear. Some biblical historians have called Cleophas the brother of Joseph (Jesus' foster father), meaning that Mary, wife of Cleophas would be the Blessed Virgin Mary's sister-in-law: "Now there stood by the cross of Jesus his mother, and his mother's sister, Mary the wife of Cleophas, and Mary Magdalene" (Jn 19:25). The Gospel of John certainly states that Mary of Cleophas was among those women who stood by the Cross, but the text doesn't make clear if the Gospel writer was identifying the Mary, wife of Cleophas, as the sister-in-law of the Blessed Virgin. Tradition does not mention the Virgin Mary as having any brothers or sisters.

10.1.6 Salome, Wife of Zebedee

Salome, like Mary, wife of Cleophas, may have been related to Jesus' family. Certainly, she was a faithful follower of the Lord. The Hebrew form of her name may be *Shulamit* or *Shulamith*, with the Hellenized form being Salome. She is named in the Gospels of Mark and Matthew among the women present at the crucifixion (Mt 27:56; Mk 15:40–41). Matthew 27:56 says that the mother of Zebedee's children was there as well; he refers to Salome not by her name but as "the mother of Zebedee's children" (Matthew 27:56). Her sons were James the Great and John the Evangelist. Jesus gave called them "Boanerges" or "the Sons of Thunder" (Mk 3:17).

The Gospel of Mark reveals that Salome was with the women who went to the tomb to anoint Jesus' Body with oils and spices. "When the Sabbath was over, Mary of Magdala, Mary the mother of James, and Salome, bought spices with which to go and anoint him. And very early in the morning on the first day of the week they went to the tomb when the sun had risen" (Mk 16:1–2).

10.1.7 St Veronica

Saint Veronica or Berenice, was a pious woman of Jerusalem who, according to tradition, moved with pity as Jesus carried His cross to Golgotha, gave Him her veil that he might wipe his forehead. Jesus accepted the offering and after using it handed it back to her, the image of His face miraculously impressed upon it. The name Veronica derives from the (Latin: *vera*) meaning true or truthful, and (Greek: *eikon*) meaning image; The name *Veronica* is also a latinization of Berenice, a Macedonian name, meaning "bearer of victory" (corresponding to Greek: phere-nikē). There is no reference to the story of St Veronica and her veil in the canonical Gospels. The closest is the miracle of the woman who was healed by touching the hem of Jesus' garment (Lk 8:43–48); her name is later identified as Veronica by the apocryphal *Acts of Pilate*.[11]

These pious traditions cannot be documented, but there is no reason why the belief that such an act of compassion did occur should not find expression in the veneration paid to one called Veronica. Saint Veronica was mentioned in the reported visions of Jesus by Sister Marie of St Peter, a Carmelite nun who lived in Tours, France, and started the devotion to the Holy Face of Jesus. In 1844, Sister Marie reported that in a vision, she saw Saint Veronica wiping away the spit and mud from the face of Jesus with her veil on the way to Calvary. She said that sacrilegious and blasphemous acts today are adding to the spit and mud that Saint Veronica wiped away that day. According to Sr Marie of St Peter, in her visions Jesus told her that He desired devotion to His Holy Face in reparation for sacrilege and blasphemy. Acts of Reparation to Jesus Christ are thus compared to Saint Veronica wiping the face of Jesus.

Blessed Anne Catherine Emmerich, depicts a long and touching description of the St Veronica episode and she identifies the true name of St Veronica also as Seraphia, a cousin of St John the Baptist:

> While the procession was passing through a long street, an incident took place which made a strong impression upon Simon. But when the procession had advanced about two hundred steps from the spot where Simon began to assist our Lord in carrying his cross, the door of a beautiful house on the left opened, and a woman of majestic appearance, holding a young girl by the hand, came out, and walked up to the very head of the procession. Seraphia was the name of the brave woman who thus dared to confront the enraged multitude; she was the wife of Sirach, one of the councillors belonging to the Temple, and was afterwards known by the name of Veronica, which name was given from the words vera icon (true portrait), to commemorate her brave conduct on this day.

> Seraphia had prepared some excellent aromatic wine, which she piously intended to present to our Lord to refresh him on his dolorous way to Calvary. She had been

standing in the street for some time, and at last went back into the house to wait. She was, when I first saw her, enveloped in a long veil, and holding a little girl of nine years of age whom she had adopted, by the hand; a large veil was likewise hanging on her arm, and the little girl endeavoured to hide the jar of wine when the procession approached. Those who were marching at the head of the procession tried to push her back; but she made her way through the mob, the soldiers, and the archers, reached Jesus, fell on her knees before him, and presented the veil, saying at the same time, "Permit me to wipe the face of my Lord." Jesus took the veil in his left hand, wiped his bleeding face, and returned it with thanks. Seraphia kissed it, and put it under her cloak. The girl then timidly offered the wine, but the brutal soldiers would not allow Jesus to drink it. The suddenness of this courageous act of Seraphia had surprised the guards, and caused a momentary although unintentional halt, of which she had taken advantage to present the veil to her Divine Master. Both the Pharisees and the guards were greatly exasperated, not only by the sudden halt, but much more by the public testimony of veneration which was thus paid to Jesus, and they revenged themselves by striking and abusing him, while Seraphia returned in haste to her house.

No sooner did she reach her room than she placed the woollen veil on a table, and fell almost senseless on her knees. A friend who entered the room a short time after, found her thus kneeling, with the child weeping by her side, and saw, to his astonishment, the bloody countenance of our Lord imprinted upon the veil, a perfect likeness, although heartrending and painful to look upon. He roused Seraphia, and pointed to the veil. She again knelt down before it, and exclaimed through her tears, 'Now I shall indeed leave all with a happy heart, for my Lord has given me a remembrance of himself.' The texture of this veil was a species of very fine wool; it was three times the length of its width, and was generally worn on the shoulders. It was customary to present these veils to persons who were in affliction, or over-fatigued, or ill, that they might wipe their faces with them, and it was done in order to express sympathy or compassion. Veronica kept this veil until her death, and hung it at the head of her bed; it was then given to the Blessed Virgin, who left it to the Apostles, and they afterwards passed it on to the Church.[12]

The episode of Veronica is celebrated in the sixth Station of the Cross. St Veronica is commemorated on 12 July.

10.1.8 St Thecla

Thecla (Ancient Greek: Θέκλα) was a saint of the early Christian Church, and a follower of Paul the Apostle. St Methodius of Olympus wrote in *The Banquet of the Virgins* that she had great knowledge in profane philosophy as well as literature.[13] He also stated that she expressed herself with strength and eloquence as well as sweetness and affability. She was converted by St Paul and became knowledgeable in our religion. He praised her love for Jesus Christ, which she demonstrated on countless occasions, principally in her combats for the Faith. She was a native of Isauria or Lycaonia. St Thecla was considered as one of the most beautiful ornaments of the century of the Apostles. St Augustine, St Epiphanius, St Ambrose, and other Fathers mention, that around the year 45, St Paul converted her to the faith by his preaching at Iconium; his discourses kindled in her a great love of holy virginity, which she eagerly embraced, in an age which seemed very tender for so great a resolution. Thecla's mother, and her fiancé Thamyris (who was a nobleman), became concerned that Thecla would follow Paul's demand that one must fear only one God and live in chastity, and punished both Paul and Thecla. She was denounced as a Christian to the authorities by her mother. She was tied to a stake to be burned, but the flames were put out by rains from Heaven before she was even touched by them. She was released by the embarrassed governor with orders to leave Iconium. She left father and mother, and a house abounding in gold and riches where she lived in state and plenty: she left her companions, friends, and country, desiring to possess only the treasure of the love and grace of God, and to find Jesus Christ, who was all things to her.

Thecla travelled with Paul to Pisidian Antioch. There a nobleman named Alexander desired Thecla and attempted to take her by force. Thecla fought him off, assaulting him in the process, and was put on trial for assaulting a nobleman. She was sentenced to be eaten by wild beasts and was exposed naked in the amphitheatre, but clothed with her innocence; and this ignominy enhanced her glory and her crown. Her heart was undaunted, her holy soul exulted and triumphed with joy in the midst of lions, leopards, and tigers: and she waited with a holy impatience the onset of those furious beasts, whose roaring filled even the spectators with terror. However, the lions suddenly forgot their natural ferocity, and the rage of their hunger, walked gently up to the holy virgin, and laying themselves down at her feet, licked them respectfully as if to kiss them: and, at length, despite all the keepers could do to arouse and provoke them, they meekly retired like lambs, without hurting the servant of Christ.[14]

Although some authorities say that she died a martyr's death, it is likely she spent the latter part of her life she spent in devout retirement in Isauria, where she died, and was buried at Seleucia, the metropolis of that country.[15] There she lived a life of asceticism for a long time and, by healing the sick with wonderworking power, she converted many to Christianity. The doctors and soothsayers in Seleucia were envious of her, and sent some young men to defile her, hoping that the loss of her virginity would also mean the loss of her miraculous power. Thecla fled from these arrogant young men, but as they were about to catch her, she prayed to God for help. A large rock opened up and hid this holy virgin and bride of Christ. This rock was her refuge and her tomb. Over her tomb, a magnificent church was built under the first Christian emperors, which bore her name; it was visited by crowds of pilgrims and was rendered famous by many miracles.[16] In Ma'loula, Syria, there is a Greek Orthodox nunnery of St Thecla, *Deir Mar Takla*, built near what is said to be her cave tomb, reached by stairs in the mountainside, a pilgrimage site with a holy well.

In June 2010, on a wall of the fourth-century Catacombs of St Thecla in Rome, Vatican archaeologists of the Pontifical Commission for Sacred Archaeology, using laser technology to remove layers of clay and lime rind, discovered a frescoed portrait of St Paul the Apostle, "recognizable by his thin face and dark pointed beard... with small eyes and furrowed brow", which they believe is the oldest image in existence of St Paul, dating from the late fourth century.[17] Above the colonnade in St Peter's Square, there is a statue in honour of St Thecla installed in 1666. He feast day is kept on 23rd September in the Roman Catholic Church. The Eastern Orthodox Churches commemorate her on 24 September.

10.2 Early Christian community

After the death and Resurrection of Jesus, women continued to play prominent roles in early Christianity. The letters of Paul — dated to the middle of the first century — and his greetings to acquaintances offer fascinating and solid information about many Jewish and Gentile women who were prominent in early Christianity. His letters provide vivid clues about the kind of activities in which women engaged more generally. He greets Prisca, Junia, Julia, and Nereus' sister, who worked and travelled as missionaries in pairs with their husbands or brothers (Romans 16:3, 7, 15).

Paul recounts that Prisca and her husband risked their lives to save his. He praises Junia as a prominent Christian, who had been imprisoned for her labor. Mary and Persis are commended for their hard work (Rm 16:6, 12). Euodia and Syntyche are called his fellow-workers in the gospel (Ph 4:2–3). Here is clear evidence of women active in the earliest work of spreading the Christian message.

It is not surprising then to see women taking leadership roles in house churches. Paul tells of women who were the leaders of such house churches (Apphia in Philemon 2; Prisca in 1 Co 16:19). This practice is confirmed by other texts that also mention women who headed churches in their homes, such as Lydia of Thyatira (Ac 16:15) and Nympha of Laodicea (Col 4:15). Women held offices and played significant roles in group worship. Paul, for example, greets a deaconess named Phoebe (Rm 16:1) and mentions women are praying and prophesying during worship (1 Co 11). Philip the evangelist had four virgin daughters who were prophetesses (Ac 21:8–9).[18]

10.3 Women martyrs

Women were also prominent as martyrs, as we have seen, and suffered violently from torture and painful execution by wild animals and paid gladiators. In fact, the earliest writing definitely by a woman is the prison diary of Perpetua, a relatively wealthy matron and nursing mother who was put to death in Carthage at the beginning of the third century on the charge of being a Christian. In it, she records her testimony before the local Roman ruler and her defiance of her father's pleas that she recant. She tells of the support and fellowship among the confessors in prison, including other women. But above all, she records her prophetic visions. Through them, she was not merely reconciled passively to her fate, but claimed the power to define the meaning of her own death.

In a situation where Romans sought to use their violence against her body as a witness to their power, and where the Christian editor of her story sought to turn her death into a witness to the truth of Christianity, her own writing lets us see the human being caught up in these struggles. She actively relinquishes her female roles as mother, daughter, and sister in favour of defining her identity solely in spiritual terms. However horrifying or heroic her suffering may seem, her brief diary offers an intimate look at one early Christian woman's spiritual journey.

10.3.1 St Cecilia

St Cecilia (*Caecilia*), a Roman lady, one of the four principal virgins and martyrs of the Western Church, is commemorated in both the Latin and Greek churches on 22 November. The veneration paid to her can be traced to a very early period. At the time of pope Symmachus (498 AD) there was a church of St Cecilia at Rome, in which he held a council.

According to tradition, Cecilia was born at Rome of a noble family. She resolved, out of love for her Lord, to devote herself to Him by a vow of perpetual virginity. Her parents wished her to marry Valerian, a young Roman, who at that time was not a Christian. She went through the marriage ceremonies; but when alone with her young husband, told him of her vow, and Valerian allowed her to keep it. At her entreaty, he sought out Pope Urban I, at the third milestone on the Via Appia, and received baptism at his hands. On returning to his spouse, wearing the white robe of a neophyte, he found her praying in her chamber, and an angel of God at her side. The angel then crowned them with roses and lilies. In answer to Valerian's prayer, the angel promised that his brother, Tiburtius, should become a Christian, and foretold that both brothers should receive the crown of martyrdom. In 230 AD Turcius Almachius, prefect of the city, took advantage of the emperor Alexander Severus' absence to give free vent to his hatred of the Christians, and daily put many to death. Valerian and Tiburtius were soon brought before his tribunal. After being scourged, the two brothers were commanded to offer incense to the gods. On refusing, they were condemned to be beheaded and given in charge to an officer of the prefect, Maximus. So moved was Maximus by their exhortations that in the night he and all his family, together with the lictors, believed and were baptized.[19]

On the next morning, his prisoners were beheaded at the place called Pagus Triopius on the Via Appia at the fourth mile from Rome. When the news reached the prefect that Maximus also had become a Christian, he ordered him to be scourged to death with leaden balls. Soon afterwards he sent his officers to Cecilia and bade her sacrifice to the gods. She retorted:

> You call gods, these objects which we all see are but useless stones. Touch them yourself, and you will feel what they are. Why thus expose yourself to the ridicule

of the people ? Every one knows that God is in heaven.
These stone statues would be of more service if they were
cast into a furnace and converted into lime. They decay
in their idleness, and are incapable of either protecting
themselves from the flames, or of delivering you from
them. Christ alone can save from death, and deliver the
guilty from eternal fire.[20]

The prefect commanded her to be shut up in her bath, and that the
furnace should be heated with wood seven times hotter than it
normally was. But a heavenly dew falling upon the spouse of
Christ refreshed and cooled her body, and preserved her from
harm. A day and a night the prefect waited for news of her death.
Then he sent one of his soldiers to behead her; but though the
sword smote her neck thrice, the executioner could not cut off her
head, and he departed, leaving her on the floor of her bath covered
in blood. For three days longer she lived, never ceasing to exhort
the people whom she loved to continue steadfast in the Lord, and
watching over the distribution of her last alms. As Cecilia was
dying she received the visit of Pope Urban I and declared:

Father, I asked this delay of three days, from our Lord,
that I might place in the hands of your Holiness, my last
treasure, the poor whom I feed and who will miss me. I
also bequeath to you this house in which I have lived, that
you may consecrate it as a church, and that it may become
the temple of the Lord forever.[21]

Having given her house to the Church, she gave up her spirit
into the hands of the living God:

After these words, the virgin thought only of preparing her
soul to meet its Spouse. She thanked Christ, that He had
deigned to associate her to the glory of the athletes, and
had crowned her with a wreath composed of the roses of
martyrdom, twined with the lilies of virginity. The heavens
were already opened to her eyes, and a moment of faint-
ness announced that her last hour was approaching. She
was lying upon her right side, in an attitude of virginal
modesty. At the last moment, her arms fell by her side, and,
turning her face against the ground so that none could

witness the last secret communings of her departing soul
with the divine object of all her love, she tranquilly expired.[22]

Urban I and his deacons buried her in the cemetery of Callixtus
on the Via Appia near the third milestone. Her house he
consecrated to God as a church for ever. It is alleged that her
body was found at Rome by Pope Paschal I in 821 AD, in the
cemetery of Praetextatus, adjoining that of Callixtus on the Via
Appia, and that it was removed by him to the church of St
Cecilia, which he was then rebuilding, and which stands on the
site of her house, in Trastevere.[23] The relics of St Cecilia with
those of Valerian, Tiburtius, and Maximus, also those of Popes
Urban and Lucius, were taken up by Pope Paschal, and reburied
under the high altar of St Cecilia in Trastevere.

10.4 Women scholars

10.4.1 St Marcella of Rome

Not all women were martyrs though. One example is St Marcella,
who was descended from the illustrious Roman family of the
Marcelli, and had great wealth. Her mother Albina was a widow
when Athanasius came as an exile to Rome in 340. As a small girl
Marcella heard Saint Athanasius speak; his stories of the Desert
Fathers of Egypt enthralled her, planting deep in her heart the
seeds of a future marked by asceticism and devoted to the Word
of God. She married, but her husband died after seven months,
and she refused a second marriage offered her by the wealthy
Cerealis, a man of consular rank but advanced in years. When this
elderly Roman consul proposed to leave her all his money if she
would marry him, Marcella replied, "If I wished to marry, I should
look for a husband, not an inheritance." Her ascetic tendency was
confirmed by the arrival in Rome of the Egyptian monk Peter in
374. She was the first in the city to make the monastic profession.
She continued to live with her mother in their palatial residence
on the Aventine hill, but with the utmost simplicity. She was not

immoderate in her asceticism, and followed the counsels of her mother, from whose company she never departed.

When Jerome came to Rome in 382, she sought him out because of his repute for Biblical learning, and made him, at first against his will, her constant companion. A circle of ladies gathered round her, and her house became a kind of academy dedicated to the study of the Scriptures, and to psalmody and prayer. Marcella frequently visited the shrines of the Roman martyrs, seeking their intercession. She distributed her considerable wealth, "preferring to store her money in the stomachs of the needy rather than hide it in a purse".

Marcella was eager for learning, and would not accept any doubtful explanation, so that Jerome found himself in the presence of a judge rather than a disciple. At times she took her teacher to task for his severity and quarrelsomeness.[24] He wrote for her some 15 different treatises on difficult passages of Scripture and Church history; it was for Marcella that Saint Jerome wrote his explanation of the Hebrew words Amen and Alleluia. On his departure in 385, Jerome hoped that she might have accompanied her close friends Paula and Eustochium to Palestine. A letter written by those two ladies on their settlement at Bethlehem invites her in glowing terms to come and enjoy with them the Holy Land; but she remained at Rome. After her mother's death in 387 she retired to a little house outside the city with her young friend Principia and devoted her whole time to good works. She still had a keen interest in Jerome's theological pursuits, and when Rufinus came to Rome and disputes arose as to his translation of Origen's *On the principles*, she threw herself eagerly into the controversy. Having, in conjunction with Pammachius and Oceanus, ascertained Jerome's view of the matter, she urged Pope Anastasius I (399–403) to condemn Origen and his defenders; and, when he hesitated, went to him and pointed out the passages which, she contended, though veiled in Rufinus' translation, demanded the Pope's condemnation. Pope Anastasius completely yielded, and like Theophilus of Alexandria condemned Origen and his upholders.

In a letter to the Roman lady Principia, Saint Jerome compares Marcella to the prophetess Anna in Saint Luke's Gospel. "Let us then compare her case with that of Marcella," he says, "and we shall see that the latter has every way the advantage. Anna lived with her husband seven years; Marcella seven months. Anna only hoped for Christ; Marcella held Him fast. Anna confessed Him at His birth; Marcella believed in Him crucified. Anna did not deny the Child; Marcella rejoiced in the Man as king".[25] This is Jerome's spiritual portrait of Marcella: she clung to Christ, believed in Him crucified, and rejoiced in Him as King. Several of Saint Jerome's letters to Marcella survive and are well worth reading.

Marcella lived till the sack of Rome by Alaric. The Goths, supposing her to be affecting poverty to conceal her wealth, used personal violence, but at her entreaty spared Principia, and at last allowed them to take sanctuary in St Paul's church. Among the sayings of Saint Marcella, a favourite comes from this period in her life when a humiliated Rome was in the throes of a famine and Marcella herself was languishing after having been turned out of her own home. She was eighty-five at the time, and she said: "By heaven's grace, captivity has found me a poor woman, not made me one. Now, I shall go in want of daily bread, but I shall not feel hunger since I am full of Christ." A few months later, St Marcella died in the arms of Principia, leaving all she had to the poor. Her feast day is 31 January.

10.4.2 St Paula

Paula, a noble and wealthy Roman lady, accompanied Jerome to Palestine in 385, and lived the rest of her life at Bethlehem, dying in 404. The chief details of her life were given in Jerome's Epitaph of her addressed to Eustochium.[26] She was born in 347, and while quite young was married to the senator Toxotius, of the Julian family, which traced its descent from Aeneas. Through her mother Blaesilla she was connected with the Scipios and the Gracchi, through her father Rogatus, linked with a Greek family, which traced its descent from Agamemnon. Her family was connected with the *Aemilian gens*, and her name taken from that of the illustrious Paulus. Jerome records these ancestral glories in her epitaph:

> Who was sired by Scipio, fathered by the Pauli,
> The Gracchi's offspring, Agamemnon's famous descendant,
> Lies in this tomb. Once upon a time called Paula,
> Mother of Eustochium, first of the Roman senatorial class,
> She followed Christ's penury and rural Bethlehem.[27]

Paula was possessed of great wealth, owning, amongst other properties, the town of Nicopolis or Actium. During her early married life, though always without reproach in her character, she lived in the usual luxury of Roman patricians. She gave birth to four daughters, Blaesilla, who married, but lost her husband and died early in 384; Paulina, wife of Pammachius; Julia, called Eustochium, and Ruffina, who died early, probably in 386; and one son, called after his father Toxotius. After the birth of a son she appears to have adopted the practice of continence, but to have still lived with her husband, whose death (probably in 380) she deeply lamented.[28] In 382, during the synod held at Rome (following on the council of Constantinople), she entertained the bishops Epiphanius of Salamis and Paulinus of Antioch, and through them her ascetic tendencies, already considerable, were heightened. Through these bishops, she met St Jerome, who had come to Rome with them, and he became her friend. She imbibed through Jerome her love for the study of Scripture, and, with her daughter Eustochium, attended his readings at the palace of Marcella. She gave vast sums to the poor, spending her own fortune and that of her children in charity. She assumed a coarse dress and a menial appearance, and undertook all sorts of menial duties in the relief of distress.

Her mind was set upon the monastic life and upon the country of the Eastern hermits. After the death of Blaesilla she determined to leave Rome, and, early in 385, disregarding the tears of her son, Toxotius, then a child, who was left to the wardship of the *praetor*, and the entreaties of Ruffina, then a girl of marriageable age, who begged her mother to wait till she was married, she sailed for the East.[29] After visiting Epiphanius in

Cyprus, she rejoined Jerome and his friends at Antioch. With him she braved the winter's journey through Lebanon to Palestine and Egypt, from whence returning the whole party settled in Bethlehem in the autumn of 386. Her letter to Marcella inviting her to come to Palestine shows her enthusiastic delight in every sacred place and association in the Holy Land.[30] Paula and Eustochium lived at first in a cottage till their convent and hospice were built. They then founded a monastery for men, and a convent of three degrees for women, who lived separately, though having the same dress, and met for the services. Paula's capacity of management, her patience and tact, are warmly praised by Jerome.[31] She is said by Palladius to have had the care of Jerome and to have found it a difficult task.[32] Her scriptural studies, begun in Rome, were carried on earnestly at Bethlehem. She had (through her father's family) a good knowledge of Greek, and she learnt Hebrew to be able to repeat and sing the Psalms in the original. She was remarkably teachable, and when doubts were suggested to her by Origenistic teachers, she was able at once, with Jerome's help, to refute them. Her charities were so incessant that Jerome states that she left Eustochium with a great debt, which she could only trust the mercy of Christ would enable her to pay. It is believed that Jerome, who had in vain counselled prudence and moderation, gave her pecuniary help in her later years. Her health was weak; her body slight; her mortifications, against many of which Jerome remonstrated and which gave occasion to some scandals, and her frequent illnesses had worn her away; and in her 57th year (404) she sank under a severe attack of illness. Jerome describes with deep feeling the scene at her death, the personal attention of her daughter to all her wants, the concern of the whole Christian community. The bishops of the surrounding cities were present. John of Jerusalem, who only four years before had been at strife with the convents of Bethlehem, was there. Her funeral was a kind of triumph, the whole Church being gathered together to carry her to her resting-place in the centre of the cave of the Nativity. Her feast day, that of her death, is 26 January.[33]

10.5 Mother of an emperor: St Helena

Flavia Julia Helena Augusta, first wife of Constantius Chlorus, and mother of Constantine the Great, was born around 248, died around 330. Helena's birthplace is not known with certainty. The sixth-century historian Procopius is the earliest authority for the statement that Helena was a native of Drepanum, in the province of Bithynia in Asia Minor. Her son Constantine renamed the city Helenopolis after her death in 330, which supports the belief that the city was her birthplace.[34] She was probably of humble parentage, being, according to one account, the daughter of an innkeeper. Saint Ambrose was the first to call her a stabularia, a term translated as "stable-maid" or "innkeeper". He makes this fact a virtue, calling Helena a bona stabularia, a "good stable-maid".[35] In Great Britain, later legend, mentioned by Henry of Huntingdon but made popular by Geoffrey of Monmouth, claimed that Helena was a daughter of the King of Britain, Cole of Camulodunum, who allied with Constantius to avoid more war between the Britons and Rome.[36]

Constantius, when he made her acquaintance, was a young officer in the army, of good family and position, nearly related, by the female line, to the emperor Claudius, and appears to have at first united her to himself by the looser tie then customary between persons of such different conditions This looser tie did not differ in outward appearance from the ordinary civil marriage by mutual consent, and was sometimes called conjugium inaequale. Her son Constantine, apparently her only child, was born probably in 274, at Naissus in Dardania (now Niš in Serbia), the country where his father's family had for some time been settled. After his birth Constantius probably advanced Helena to the position of a lawful wife.

After living with Constantius some twenty years Helena was divorced on the occasion of his elevation to the dignity of Caesar in 292; the Augustus Maximian, in choosing him for his colleague, requiring this, as a matter of policy, in order that Constantius might marry his own step-daughter, Theodora.[37]

When Constantine succeeded in 306, he probably recalled his mother to the court, but direct proof of this is wanting. We have a coin stamped HELENA. N. F. (nobilissima femina), with a head on one side and a star in a laurel crown upon the other, perhaps struck in her honour whilst Constantine was still Caesar. Eusebius stated that Constantine paid his mother great honours, and caused her to be proclaimed Augusta to all the troops, and struck her image on gold coins.[38] Eusebius also tells us that through Constantine she became a Christian.[39]

Eusebius speaks strongly of her youthful spirit when she, in fulfilment of a vow, made her pilgrimage to the Holy Land, despite her great age, nearly 80 years.[40] Constantine appointed his mother Helena as Augusta Imperatrix, and gave her unlimited access to the imperial treasury in order to locate the relics of Judeo-Christian tradition. In 326–28 Helena undertook a trip to the Holy Places in Palestine. She was responsible for the construction or improvement of two churches, the Church of the Nativity, Bethlehem, and the Church on the Mount of Olives, sites of Christ's birth and ascension. Local founding legend attributes to Helena's orders the construction of a church in Egypt to identify the Burning Bush of Sinai. The chapel at St Catherine's Monastery—often referred to as the Chapel of Saint Helena—is dated to the year AD 330.

Jerusalem was still rebuilding from the destruction of Emperor Hadrian, who had built a temple dedicated, according to conflicting accounts, to Venus or Jupiter over the site of Jesus' tomb near Calvary and renamed the city Aelia Capitolina. According to tradition, Helena ordered the temple torn down and, chose a site to begin excavating, which led to the recovery of three different crosses. Then, refusing to be swayed by anything but solid proof, the empress (perhaps through Bishop Macarius of Jerusalem) had a woman who was already at the point of death brought from Jerusalem. When the woman touched the first and second crosses, her condition did not change, but when she touched the third and final cross she suddenly recovered, and Helena declared the cross with which the woman had been touched to be the True Cross.[41] On the site of discovery, Constantine ordered built the Church of the Holy Sepulchre as well as those on other sites detected by Helena.

She also found the nails of the crucifixion. To use their miraculous power to aid her son, Helena allegedly had one placed in Constantine's helmet, and another in the bridle of his horse. St Gregory of Tours (d. 595) adds that the discovery was made on 3 May 326; that, during a great storm which occurred soon after, Helena put one of the nails into the sea, which was at once calmed; that two more were used for the emperor's bridle, and the fourth placed on the head of his statue; that the lance, crown of thorns, and pillar of scourging were preserved and worked miracles.[42] Helena left Jerusalem and the eastern provinces in 327 to return to Rome, bringing with her large parts of the True Cross and other relics, which were then stored in her palace's private chapel, where they can be still seen today. Her palace was later converted into the Basilica of the Holy Cross in Jerusalem. Tradition also has it that the site of the Vatican Gardens was spread with earth brought from Golgotha by Helena to symbolically unite the blood of Christ with that shed by thousands of early Christians, who died in the persecutions of Nero.

Helena received almost unlimited supplies of money from her son and spent it in royal charities to the poor and bounties to the soldiery; as well as using her power to free prisoners and criminals condemned to the mines and to recall persons from exile.[43] She was a frequent attendant at the church services, and adorned the buildings with costly offerings.[44] St Helena died in 330 with her son at her side. She was buried in the Mausoleum of Helena, outside Rome on the Via Labicana. Her sarcophagus is on display in the Pio-Clementine Vatican Museum. Her feast day is kept on 18 August. She is the patron saint of new discoveries.

10.6 Sister of Church Fathers: St Macrina

The eldest child of her parents Basil and Emmelia, by her position in the family and still more by her force of character, high intellectual gifts, and earnest piety, Macrina proved the well-spring of good to the whole household, and so contributed largely to form the characters of her brothers. To her brother St Basil in particular she was ever a wise and loving counsellor. Basil was born around 329, and Macrina probably around 327. She received her name from her paternal grandmother. She was very carefully educated by her mother, who was more anxious that she should be familiar with the sacred writers than with heathen poets. Macrina committed to memory the moral and ethical portion of the books of Solomon and the whole of the Psalter. Before her twelfth year she was ready at each hour of the day with the Psalm liturgically belonging to it.[45]

Her personal beauty, which, according to her brother Saint Gregory of Nyssa, surpassed that of all of her age and country, and her large fortune, attracted many suitors. Of these her father selected a young advocate, of good birth and position, and when he was cut off by a premature death, Macrina resolutely refused any further proposals of marriage.[46] After her father's death (around 349) she devoted herself to the care of her widowed mother, the bringing up of her infant brother Peter, and the supervision of the interests of her family. Emmelia was left burdened with a large and extensive property, and the maintenance of and provision for nine children. Of the greater part of this load Macrina relieved her. They resided then, or soon afterwards, on the paternal estate near the village of Annesi, on the banks of the Iris, near Neocaesarea (now in northern Turkey), which Macrina never left.

Her brother Basil returned from Athens around 355 elated with his university successes. Macrina taught him the enthusiastic love for an ascetic life which she herself felt.[47] Brother and sister settled on their paternal estate on opposite banks of the Iris. The premature death of her most dearly loved brother Naucratius, on a hunting expedition, 357, strengthened her resolution to separate from the world, and she persuaded her mother also, who was nearly broken-hearted at their loss, to

embrace the ascetic life. The nucleus of the sisterhood was
formed by their female servants and slaves.

Devout women, some of high rank, soon gathered round
them, while the birth and high connexions of Macrina and her
mother attracted the daughters of the most aristocratic families
in Pontus and Cappadocia to the community.[48] Macrina took to
her retreat her youngest brother Peter.[49] The elevation of her
brother Basil to the see of Caesarea in 370 became a stimulus to
a higher pitch of asceticism. Peter was ordained priest by his
brother, probably in 371.[50] In 373 Emmelia died, holding the
hands of Macrina and Peter and offering them to God with her
dying breath, as the first-fruits and tithes of her womb, and was
buried by them in her husband's grave at the chapel of the Forty
Martyrs. Macrina sustained her third great sorrow in the death
(on 1 January 379) of her brother St Basil, whom she had long
regarded with reverential affection.

Nine months after, her brother Gregory of Nyssa (now a
bishop) paid her a visit. Owing to his banishment under Valens
and other persecutions it was eight or nine years since they had
met. He found her sister an aged invalid, parched with fever,
stretched on planks on the ground, the wood barely covered with
a bit of sackcloth. The pallet was carefully arranged to face the
east. On her brother's approach she made a vain effort to rise to
do him honour as a bishop; Gregory prevented her, and had her
placed on her bed.[51] With great self-restraint Macrina restrained
her groans, checked her asthmatic pantings, and putting on a
cheerful countenance endeavoured to divert him from the present
sorrow. She ventured to speak of Basil's death; Gregory completely broke down; and when her consolations proved unavail-
ing, she rebuked him for sorrowing like those who had no hope
for one who had fallen asleep in Christ. Gregory defending
himself, she bid him argue out the point with her.

After a somewhat prolix controversy, Macrina, as though
under divine inspiration—her words pouring out without stay,
like water from a fountain,[52] delivered the long discourse on the
resurrection and immortality of the soul which Gregory has

recorded—more probably in his own rather than his dying sister's words—in the *Dialogue on the Soul and Resurrection*, entitled τὰ Μακρίνια to commemorate Macrina.[53] On the conclusion of this remarkable discourse (in which the purificatory nature of the fire of hell is unmistakably set forth, the anguish being in exact proportion to the rootedness of the sinful habits), she noticed that her brother was weary and sent him to rest awhile in an arbour in the garden. Towards the close of the same day he revisited her bedside. She began a thankful review of her past life, recounting God's mercies to her.[54] At last her voice failed, and only by the motion of her lips and her outspread hands—was she known to be praying. She signed her eyes, mouth, and breast with the cross. Dusk came on; lights were brought in; she immediately attempted to chant the a hymn of thanksgiving—but silently with her hands and with her heart. She once more signed her self on the face with the cross, gave a deep sigh, and finished her life and her prayers together.[55] Round her neck was found an iron cross, and a ring containing a particle of the true cross.[56] She was buried by her brother in the grave of her parents in the chapel of the Forty Martyrs, about a mile from her monastery. Gregory was assisted in carrying the bier by Araxius the bishop of the diocese (probably Ibora), and two of the leading clergy. After her death many miracles said to have been performed by her were reported to Gregory.[57] Her feast day is kept on 19 July.

10.7 Christian wives: Elpis

Among interesting female figures in early Christianity, were many wives and mothers like Elpis, the wife of Boethius, the philosopher. Elpis is a Greek word meaning hope. Anicius Manlius Torquatus Severinus Boethius, the most learned philosopher of his time, was born at Rome about AD 480, and was put to death ad 524. Boethius's first wife was Elpis, daughter of Festus. Elpis was a Sicilian lady and the authoress of two hymns in the Breviary, and she bore two sons to Boethius, Patricius and Hypatius, Greek consuls around AD 500. Elpis died about 493.

The importance of Elpis is that she composed a special hymn in honour of St Peter and St Paul, *Decora lux*.

> Decora lux æternitatis, auream
> Diem beatis irrigavit ignibus,
> Apostolorum quæ coronat Principes,
> Reisque in astra liberam pandit viam.
>
> Mundi Magister, atque cœli Janitor,
> Romæ parentes, arbitrique Gentium,
> Per ensis ille, hic per crucis victor necem
> Vitæ senatum laureati possident.
>
> O Roma felix, quæ duorum Principum
> Es consecrata glorioso ceteras
> Horum cruore purpurata ceteras
> Excellis orbis una pulchritudines.
>
> Sit Trinitati sempiterna gloria,
> Honor, potestas, atque jubilatio,
> In unitate gubernat omnia,
> Per universa sæculorum sæcula.

The English version of this hymn runs as follows:

> What fairer light is this than time itself doth own,
> The golden day with beams more radiant brightening?
> The princes of God's Church this feast day doth enthrone,
> To sinners heavenward bound their burden lightening.
> One taught mankind its creed, one guards the heavenly gate,
> Founders of Rome, they bind the world in loyalty;
> One by the sword achieved, one by the cross his fate;
> With laurelled brows they hold eternal royalty.
>
> Rejoice, O Rome, this day; thy walls they once did sign
> With princely blood, who now their glory share with thee.
> What city's vesture glows with crimson deep as thine?
> What beauty else has earth that may compare with thee?
> To God the three in one eternal homage be,
> All honour, all renown, all songs victorious,

Who rules both heaven and earth by one divine decree
To everlasting years in empire glorious.

The following epitaph has been handed down as that of Elpis, and has been said by some to have been written by Boethius himself:

Hope was my name, and Sicily my home,
Where I was nursed, until I came from thence
An exile for the love I bore my lord:
Apart from him my time was full of tears,
Heavy the day, laden with care the night,
(But with him all was joy and peace and love)
And now, my pilgrim's journey o'er, I rest
Within this sacred place, and witness bear
Before the throne of the Eternal Judge on high.

The catacombs in Rome bear witness to many married women. The epitaphs present marriage as a communion of souls and bodies. They underline the harmony of husband and wife as perennial companions and the joys of life together. The early Christians thought of marriage as an exclusive union, as is evidenced by the eulogies paid to a departed wife. Her utter faithfulness and upright and chaste conduct were remembered, which witnessed a unique love.[58]

Celsus Eutropius had lost his young wife when she was barely thirty, after eleven years of happy marriage. He expressed on her tombstone his happiness during the time he had spent with her.

CELSUS EUTROPIUS TO HIS WIFE
WHO LIVED ALWAYS WITH ME
WITHOUT CAUSING ME ANY DETRIMENT
TO MY SOUL AND LIFE.
SHE LIVED FOR 31 YEARS, 9 MONTHS AND
15 DAYS.
SHE DIED ON A THURSDAY.
WITH LOVING MEMORY IN PEACE.

Love and tenderness also figure in Flavius Crispinus' epitaph for his dear Aurelia. The wish that she may be at peace 'with the holy souls' means that the husband believes her to be in heaven, with God, in full possession of happiness. The very fact of being among the just is considered as part of the state of beatitude. The company of other holy ones makes the soul rejoice; it contributes to the delight of each and the happiness of all. Blessedness, therefore, means to be with God and the Saints, to enjoy their presence and know that one is welcome among them.[59]

> FLAVIUS CRISPINUS TO AURELIA ANIANE,
> MOST WORTHY WIFE,
> WHO LIVED 28 YEARS.
> WE WERE MARRIED FOR 9 YEARS WITH LOVE,
> AND SHE NEVER GAVE ME CAUSE FOR PAIN.
> FAREWELL, MY DEAR.
> BE AT PEACE
> WITH THE HOLY SOULS.
> FAREWELL IN CHRIST!

Notes

1   Pope Benedict XVI, *Discourse at General Audience* (14 February 2007).
2   See G. Van Belle, 'Prolepsis in the Gospel of John' in *Novum Testamentum* 43/4 (2001), pp. 334–347.
3   In Greek η Μαγδαληνή.
4   In Hebrew לדגמ.
5   Pope St Gregory the Great, *Homily 33*.
6   See Archbishop A. Roche, "Apostle of the Apostles" in *L'Osservatore Romano* (11 June 2016).
7   See Rabanus Maurus, *De vita Mariae Magdalenae, Prologus*: "dilectrix Christi et a Christo plurimum dilecta".
8   See St Anselm, *Oratio LXXIII ad sanctam Mariam Magdalenam*, "electa dilectrix et dilecta electrix Dei".
9   St Thomas Aquinas, *In Ioannem Evangelistam Expositio*, c. XX, L. III, 6.

10   See Archbishop A. Roche, "Apostle of the Apostles" in *L'Osservatore Romano* (11 June 2016).

11   The *Acts of Pilate*, also called the Gospel of Pilate, is a book of New Testament apocrypha. The dates of its accreted sections are uncertain, but scholars agree in assigning the resulting work to the middle of the fourth century. The text is found in the Greek *Acts of Peter and Paul* and as an appendix to the medieval Latin Gospel of Nicodemus rumoured to be written by a member of the Order of Nicodemus, although there is no intrinsic relation between the independent texts.

12   Bl Anne Catherine Emmerich, *The Dolorous Passion of Our Lord Jesus Christ*, chapter 34, "The Veil of Veronica".

13   St Methodius of Olympus, *The Banquet of the Virgins*Discourse 7, chapter 9.

14   St Ambrose, *Concerning virginity*, Book II, chapter 3, 20.

15   She is styled by Saints Gregory Nazianzen, Chrysostom, Augustine, a virgin and martyr.

16   See S. Davis, *The Cult of Saint Thecla: A Tradition of Women's Piety in Late Antiquity* (Oxford: OUP, 2001), pp. 35–39.

17   See *Biblical Archaeology Review* (36/1) Jan/Feb 2010, p. 18.

18   A ministry of deaconesses did indeed exist thereafter, and developed unevenly in the various parts of the Church. It seems clear that this ministry was not perceived as simply the feminine equivalent of the masculine diaconate. It was an ecclesial function, exercised by women, sometimes mentioned together with that of subdeacon in the lists of Church ministries. This sequence has encouraged the conclusion that the order of deaconess enjoyed the status of a sacramental rather than a sacrament. Some scholars also regard the deaconesses of Christian antiquity as an early expression of religious life. In any case, when the Church ceased to administer adult baptism, the office of deaconess gradually fell into disuse, and had disappeared by the eleventh century. It was very evident that the deaconess did not enjoy a participation in the ministerial priesthood. See P. Haffner, *The Sacramental Mystery* (Leominster: Gracewing, 2016), pp. 247–249.

19   The *lictor* (possibly from Latin: ligare, to bind) was a member of a special class of Roman civil servant, with special tasks of attending and guarding magistrates of the Roman Republic and Empire who held *imperium*, the right and power to command; essentially, a bodyguard.

20   P. Guéranger, *Life of St Cecilia Virgin and Martyr* (Philadelphia: Peter F. Cunningham, 1866), p. 123.

21   *Ibid.*, p. 129.

22   *Ibid.*

23   *Ibid.*, pp. 198–209.

24   See St Jerome, *Letter 37*, 2.

25   St Jerome, *Letter 127*.

26   See St Jerome, *Letter 108*.

27   This poem was originally inscribed at the tomb of Paula in the Church of the Nativity at Bethlehem. They were composed by St Jerome, and they survive, not on stone, but as mentions in a long epitaph to commemorate Jerome's long-time fellow researcher:
Scipio quam genuit, Pauli fudere parentes
Gracchorum suboles, Agamemnonis inclita proles,
hoc iacet in tumulo. Paulam dixere priores
Eustochiae genetrix Romani prima senatus
pauperiem Christi et Bethlemitica rura secuta est.
English translation of the poem by Peter Kruschwitz on https://thepetrifiedmuse.wordpress.com/2014/12/17/seasons-greetings/.

28   See St Jerome, *Letter 108*, 4.

29   The *praetor* in ancient Rome was a judicial officer who had broad authority in cases of equity, was responsible for the production of the public games, and, in the absence of consuls, exercised extensive authority in the government.

30   See St Jerome, *Letter 46*.

31   See St Jerome, *Letter 108*, 19.

32   Palladius, *The Lausiac History*, chapter 79.

33   See H. Wace, *A Dictionary of Christian Biography and Literature to the End of the Sixth Century AD, with an Account of the Principal Sects and Heresies* (Grand Rapids, MI: Christian Classics Ethereal Library, 2000), pp. 1284–1285.

34   A. Harbus, *Helena of Britain in Medieval Legend* (Rochester, NY: D.S. Brewer, 2002), p. 12.

35   St Ambrose, *De obitu Theodosii*, 42.

36   See Harbus, *Helena of Britain in Medieval Legend*.

37   Eutropius, *Brev.* 9, 22, 1.

38   Eusebius, *Life of Constantine*, 3, 47. Silver and copper coins are found with the name Flavia Helena Augusta, struck in her lifetime. Others with the remarkable epigraph Flavia Julia Helenae Augusta were struck at Constantinople and Treves as memorials after her death, and Theodora was also similarly commemorated, to mark the reconciliation of the two branches of the family. Helena is styled Augusta in inscriptions.

39   Eusebius, *Life of Constantine*, 3, 57.

40   *Ibid.*, 3, 42 & 46.

41   See Socrates, *Church History*, Book I, Chapter 13. St Ambrose, writing in 395 (*de Obitu Theodosii*, c. 41 ff), says that Helena was inspired by the Holy Spirit with the desire to search for the cross, that she distinguished the true Cross by its title, that two of the nails were used by the emperor, one being fixed in his crown and the other employed as a bit for his bridle.

42   St Gregory of Tours, *Liber Miraculorum*, I, 5 in *PL 71*, 709.

43   Eusebius, *Life of Constantine*, 3, 44.
44   Eusebius, *Life of Constantine*, 3, 45.
45   St Gregory of Nyssa, *Life of St Macrina*, 2, 179.
46   *Ibid.*, 2, 180.
47   *Ibid.*, 2, 181.
48   *Ibid.*, 2, 184, 186.
49   *Ibid.*, 2, 186.
50   *Ibid.*, 2, 187.
51   *Ibid.*, 2, 189.
52   *Ibid.*
53   St Gregory of Nyssa, *Peri psyches kai anastaseos* in *PG* 46, 12f.
54   *Ibid.*, 2, 191, 192.
55   *Ibid.*, 2, 195.
56   *Ibid.*, 2, 198.
57   *Ibid.*,199, 202–204.
58   See A. Baruffa, *The Catacombs of St Callixtus. History–Archeology–Faith* (Vatican City: LEV, third English Edition 2006), pp. 125–131.
59   See *ibid.*

11 MONKS AND MISSIONARIES

Let the monks' food be poor and taken in the evening, such as to avoid repletion, and their drink such as to avoid intoxication, so that it may both maintain life and not harm; vegetables, beans, flour mixed with water, together with the small bread of a loaf, lest the stomach be burdened and the mind confused. For indeed those who desire eternal rewards must only consider usefulness and use. Use of life must be moderated just as toil must be moderated, since this is true discretion, that the possibility of spiritual progress may be kept with a temperance that punishes the flesh. For if temperance exceeds measure, it will be a vice and not a virtue; for virtue maintains and retains many goods. Therefore we must fast daily, just as we must feed daily; and while we must eat daily, we must gratify the body more poorly and sparingly; since we must eat daily for the reason that we must go forward daily, pray daily, toil daily, and daily read.

St Columbanus, *Monks' Rules, Of Food and Drink*

MONASTICISM IS THE ancient Christian practice (from Greek: μοναχός, a solitary person) of withdrawal from the world in order to dedicate oneself fully and intensely to the life of the Gospel, seeking union with Jesus Christ. The focus of monasticism is the process of perfection to which every Christian is called. This ideal is expressed everywhere that the things of God are sought above all other things. In other words, a monk or nun is a person who has vowed to follow not only the commandments of the Church, but also the counsels (namely the vows of poverty, chastity, stability, and obedience).

The words of Jesus Christ which are the cornerstone for this ideal are "be perfect as your heavenly Father is perfect" (Mt 5:48).

11.1 Role models

The ancient models of the modern Christian monastic ideal are the Nazarites and the prophets of Israel. A Nazarite was a person voluntarily separated to the Lord, under a special vow, as found in Numbers 6:2–5:

> If a man or a woman wishes to make a vow, the Nazirite vow, to vow himself to the Lord, he will abstain from wine and fermented liquor, he will not drink vinegar derived from one or the other, he will not drink grape-juice or eat grapes, be they fresh or dried. For the duration of his vow he will eat nothing that comes from the vine, not even juice of unripe grapes or skins of grapes. As long as he is bound by his vow, no razor will touch his head; until the time for which he has vowed himself to the Lord is completed, he remains consecrated and will let his hair grow freely.

The prophets of Israel were set apart to the Lord for the sake of a message of repentance. Some of them lived under extreme conditions, voluntarily separated or forced into seclusion because of the burden of their message.

The most frequently cited "role-model" for the life of a hermit separated to the Lord, in whom the Nazarite and the prophet are believed to be combined in one person, is John the Baptist. John also had disciples who stayed with him and, as may be supposed, were taught by him and lived in a manner similar to his own:

> In due course John the Baptist appeared; he proclaimed this message in the desert of Judaea, "Repent, for the kingdom of Heaven is close at hand." This was the man spoken of by the prophet Isaiah when he said: A voice of one that cries in the desert, "Prepare a way for the Lord, make his paths straight." This man John wore a garment made of camel-hair with a leather loin-cloth round his waist, and his food was locusts and wild honey. (Mt 3:1–4)

The female role models for monasticism are the Most Holy Mother of God and the four virgin daughters of the deacon Philip:

> The end of our voyage from Tyre came when we landed at Ptolemais, where we greeted the brothers and stayed one day with them. The next day we left and came to Caesarea. Here we called on Philip the evangelist, one of the Seven, and stayed with him. He had four unmarried daughters who were prophets. (Ac 21:7–9)

The monastic ideal is also modelled upon the Apostle Paul, who was celibate: "I should still like everyone to be as I am myself; but everyone has his own gift from God, one this kind and the next something different. To the unmarried and to widows I say: it is good for them to stay as they are, like me" (1 Co 7:7–8).

However, the supreme Prototype of all Christian monasticism, communal and solitary, is Jesus Christ Himself: "Then Jesus was led by the Spirit out into the desert to be put to the test by the devil. He fasted for forty days and forty nights, after which He was hungry" (Mt 4:1–2).

Additionally, the earliest Church was a model for monasticism. The first Christian communities lived in common, sharing everything, according to the Acts of the Apostles:

> These remained faithful to the teaching of the apostles, to the brotherhood, to the breaking of bread and to the prayers. And everyone was filled with awe; the apostles worked many signs and miracles. And all who shared the faith owned everything in common; they sold their goods and possessions and distributed the proceeds among themselves according to what each one needed. (Ac 2:42–45)

11.2 St Paul of Thebes

Paul of Thebes or Paul the Hermit was born around 230 and died 15 January 341. He is the very first Christian historically known to have lived as a monk. As a young man, Paul fled to the Theban desert during the persecution of Decius and Valerian in around 250. He lived in the mountains of this desert in a cave near a clear spring and a palm tree, the leaves of which provided him with raiment and the fruit of which provided him with his only source of food till he was 43 years old, when a raven started bringing him half a loaf of bread daily. He would remain in that cave for the rest of his life, almost a hundred years later.

St Jerome relates the meeting of Saint Anthony and Paul, when the latter was aged 113.[1] When he was ninety St Anthony was tempted to pride, thinking he was the first to dwell in the desert. The Lord wanted to reveal the holiness of St Paul and his righteousness, and He sent His angel to St Anthony the Great, who had thought that he was the first to dwell in the wilderness. The angel told St Anthony, "There is a man who lives in the inner wilderness; the world is not worthy of his footsteps. By his prayers, the Lord brings rain and dew to fall on the Earth, and brings the flood of the Nile in its due season." When St Anthony heard this, he rose right away and went to the inner wilderness, a distance of one day's walk. God guided him to the cave of St Paul. He entered, and they bowed to each other, and sat down talking about the greatness of the Lord.

In the evening, the raven came bringing a whole loaf of bread. The two hermits conversed with each other for one day and one night. St Paul said to St Anthony, "Now, I know that you are one of the children of God. For seventy years, the Lord has been sending to me everyday, half a loaf of bread, but today, the Lord is sending your food also. Now, go and bring me back in a hurry the tunic that Emperor Constantine had given to St Athanasius." St Anthony went to St Athanasius, and brought the tunic from him and returned to St Paul. On his way back, he saw the soul of St Paul carried by the angels up to heaven. When he arrived to the cave, he found that St Paul had departed from this world. He kissed him, weeping, and clothed him in the tunic that he asked for, and he took his fibre tunic.

When St Anthony wanted to bury St Paul, he wondered how could he dig the grave. Two lions entered the cave, bowed their heads before the body of St Paul, and shook their heads as if they were asking St Anthony what to do. St Anthony knew that they were sent from God. He marked the length and width of the body on the ground, and they dug the grave with their claws, according to St Anthony's directions. St Anthony then buried the holy body, and went back to St Athanasius and told him what had happened. St Athanasius sent men to bring St Paul's body to him. They spent several days searching in the mountains, but they could not find the place of his grave. St Paul appeared to St Athanasius in a vision and told him that the Lord would not allow the revelation of the location of his body. He asked the St Athanasius not to trouble the men, but to have them brought back.

St Athanasius used to wear the palm fibre tunic three times a year during the Divine Liturgy. One time, he wanted to let the people know about the holiness of the owner of that tunic. He put it over a dead man, and the dead man rose up instantly. The news of this miracle spread all around the land of Egypt.

11.3 St Anthony the Great

He was born in to a wealthy family in upper Egypt about 254 AD. Also known as Anthony of Egypt, Anthony of the Desert, and Anthony the Anchorite. One day after a teaching on Jesus saying to the people: "If you want to be perfect, go, sell what you have and give to the poor, and you will have treasures in heaven; and come, follow Me" (Mt 19:21), St Anthony sold everything he owned, gave the proceeds to the poor, and left the city behind to live in the desert. In this first stage where Anthony gave himself to asceticism he lived in or quite near his village. He had a Master, an old man of a neighbouring village, and he tried to imitate him. He watched those round him who acted well and, like a bee, he nourished himself on the good things he found among them. For the rest, he prayed, he read the Bible which fed his prayer, and he worked for his daily bread and to give alms. These are the three occupations by which a novice is formed in the monastic life: prayer, reading and work.

In the second stage. Anthony goes to live in a tomb. This refers to an old custom of the East: the tombs are one or two kilometres from the village, each one is in a little house; on one side there is the tomb and on the other a small place where from time to time, on the anniversaries of the dead the relatives meet and eat together. The text tells us that there is a roof and a door. There one is well-protected and alone. The demons come, and are found throughout the life of Anthony. St Anthony was tempted by the devil, as St Athanasius recounts:

> But the devil, who hates and envies what is good, could not endure to see such a resolution in a youth, but endeavoured to carry out against him what he had been wont to effect against others. First of all he tried to lead him away from the discipline, whispering to him the remembrance of his wealth, care for his sister, claims of kindred, love of money, love of glory, the various pleasures of the table and the other relaxations of life, and at last the difficulty of virtue and the labour of it; he suggested also the infirmity of the body and the length of the time. In a word he raised in his mind a great dust of debate, wishing to debar him from his settled purpose.[2]

In the third stage, after his combat he goes out with an even greater desire to serve God. After the formation he received from a senior person and the combats against the demon, Anthony has become a monk, and he went to a fortress. It was nothing very grand; it was simply a guard post in the desert against thieves and enemy armies, a solid building in a dry land which commanded a pass or a strategic place and which was only occupied by soldiers when necessary. At the third stage, Anthony had learnt the secrets of God, and was full of the Holy Spirit. We have several lessons on the effects of the ascetic life. First of all, the ascetic life does not destroy a person, but restores him; Anthony is the same as before: "he looked the same as before he went into the desert".[3] Then the ascetic path enables the soul to recover its purity of heart and leads to equanimity, which the monastic tradition calls *apatheia*, a state in which a person has controlled his passions and subjected them to reason.

It is not that he no longer has any passion, which would be impossible, but that he is no longer dominated by them, he is the master.

Many people came and disturbed Anthony's quiet life. He was not able to be alone as he wished; the Lord used Anthony to work wonders. So Anthony was afraid. He said to himself: "I shall become full of pride or others will think I am better than I am." He thought this over carefully and decided: "I shall go to the Upper Thebaïd. Nobody will know me there." He came to a very high mountain. A stream, very clear and pure, ran at the foot of the mountain. Further away, some trees grew on the plain. Anthony liked the place, or rather, God made it pleasing to him.[4]

> So Anthony was alone in the inner mountain engaged in prayer and ascesis. The brothers who served him asked permission to come and see him each month and bring him some olives, vegetables and oil, for he was now an old man. Those who visited him have told us how many struggles he endured there, not against flesh and blood, but against the demons, as St Paul wrote. They heard the noise of many voices and of fighting. At night they saw the mountain filled with beasts and they watched Anthony struggling against these enemies and praying against them. He encouraged those who came. He fought on his knees, praying to the Lord.[5]

Vigilance and asceticism are necessary, they slowly transform even the body. Anthony is optimistic, he knows that we have nothing to fear from the devil if we resist him to his face. He has no real power, for Christ has conquered him. In order to overcome him, first we must unmask him, which is why discernment of spirits is so important:

> One can easily tell the difference between good angels and bad, if God gives the grace. A vision of the good ones brings no disturbance. They do not cry out, one does not hear their voice, but their presence is so gentle that the soul is suddenly filled with joy, delight and courage. The Lord who is our joy and the power of God the Father accompanies them. The thoughts of the soul remain calm

and untroubled so that, shining brightly, it sees those who appear by its own light. The soul is overcome by a desire for future realities, it longs to be united with them and follow them to heaven. If, being human, some are frightened by the vision of good spirits, they remove their fear with love. The coming and appearance of evil angels brings trouble with noise and shouting, as one might expect from unruly boys or brigands. This produces terror in the soul, confusion and trouble in the thoughts, depression, disgust for ascesis, listlessness, memory of relatives, fear of death and evil desires.[6]

Although he held no titles or position, his holiness marked him as one whose wisdom commanded respect. When the Synod of Nicaea was convened, he was invited to participate. His eloquent defence of the Orthodox doctrine concerning the person of Jesus Christ was instrumental in weakening the position of Arianism. His witness led to the eventual and complete elimination of Arianism.

Anthony went to see the monks on the outer mountain as he commonly did. God had given him knowledge of his approaching death. In his talk to the brothers he said: "I have come for the last time to see how you are. We shall not meet again in this life if I am not mistaken. It is time for my departure, I am nearly 105 years old."[7] The brothers begged him to stay with them till he died, but he refused. Anthony hurried away from the monks on the outer mountain, and took the road to the inner mountain where he had been living. Some months later he fell ill. Two brothers were living with him on the inner mountain. For fifteen years they had been practising ascesis with him and helping him in his old age. Anthony called to them and said:

I am going the way of my fathers, as the Bible says. I see that the Lord is calling me. Be vigilant. You have been ascetics for some time, do not stop now. Be zealous, as though you were just beginning, be whole-hearted. You know about the evil spirits and their tricks. They are strong and evil, but they cannot do much, so have no fear of them. Look at Christ at all times and have faith in him. Let your life be as though each day is the day of your

> death. Watch yourselves and remember my words. Join
> yourselves to Christ first of all and then to his saints. At
> your death they will welcome you as friends in the house
> of God where we will live for ever. Think about these
> things, and if you love me, keep me in mind as a father.[8]

He had instructed his followers to bury his body in an
unmarked, secret grave, lest his body become an object of
veneration. The monastic rules of Saint Anthony, the patriarch
of monastic life, have served as the basis for countless monasteries. After St Anthony, there were villages or colonies of
hermits of the eremitic type; and monasteries in which a
community life was led, of the cenobitic type.

11.4 St Macarius

Macarius of Egypt was born in Upper Egypt, in the village of
Shabsheer (Shanshour), in Al Minufiyah Governorate, around
300 AD. His father's name was Abraham and his mother's name
was Sarah and they had no son. In a vision one night, his father
saw the angel of the Lord, who told him that God was about to
give him a son, and his name would be known all over the earth,
and he would have a multitude of spiritual sons. Shortly after
this vision, they had a son and called him Macarius, which
means "Blessed". At some point before his pursuit of asceticism,
Macarius made his living smuggling nitre in the vicinity of
Nitria, a vocation which taught him how to survive in and travel
across the wastes in that area.[9] At a young age, Macarius was
forced to get married against his will. He pretended to be sick
and ask for his parents' permission to go to the wilderness to
relax. At his return, he found that his future wife had died a
virgin, and shortly after, his parents departed as well. Macarius
subsequently distributed all his money among the poor and
needy. Seeing his virtues, the people of his village brought him
to the bishop of Ashmoun who ordained him priest. A while
later, a pregnant woman accused him of having defiled her.
Macarius did not attempt to defend himself, and accepted the

accusation in silence. However, when the woman's delivery drew near, her labour became exceedingly difficult. She did not manage to give birth until she confessed Macarius's innocence. A multitude of people then came asking for his forgiveness, but he fled to the Nitrian Desert to escape all mundane glory.

St Macarius dwelt in the place that is now called the Coptic Orthodox Monastery of Parameos (El-Baramous). He founded this monastery around 335 AD; he first dug a hole in the rock for himself in the desert, and started to worship the Lord with great austerity. Soon, his fame spread and many visitors came to see him and loved him a great deal because they sensed his fatherliness, wisdom and the grace that was in him. St Macarius stayed in that place for twenty years until the Monastery of Parameos was completed and filled with monks who lived in holes around the main church, which did not yet have walls. During that period, St Macarius visited St Anthony twice, once in the year 343 AD and the other in the year 352 AD. He learned from St Anthony all his virtues and teachings. In 360 AD, St Macarius founded what is now the Coptic Orthodox Monastery of St. Macarius the Great, which lies in Wadi Natrun, the ancient Scetis, 92 kilometers from Cairo on the western side of the desert road to Alexandria. During his lifetime Macarius was spiritual father to more than four thousand monks of different nationalities: Egyptians, Greeks, Ethiopians, Armenians, Nubians, Asians, Palestinians, Italians, Gauls and Spaniards. During the years of the reign of the Arian emperor Valens (364-378), St Macarius the Great fought Arianism and was exiled around 374 AD, to an island in the Nile Delta, because of his support for the Orthodox teachings of St Athanasius. While he was there with St Macarius of Alexandria, a pagan leader's daughter began to have terrible fits, and everyone agreed she was possessed by a demon. The two monks were able to heal her, and in gratitude, the people tore down their pagan shrine and replaced it with a church. Hearing of this, the authorities were quick to send both monks back to their respective monasteries. On their return they were met by a multitude of fifty thousand monks of the Nitrian Desert.

Macarius died in the year 391, aged over ninety. After his death, the natives of his village of Shabsheer stole the body and built a great church for him in their village. The Coptic Patriarch Michael V of Alexandria brought the relics of Saint Macarius back to the Nitrian Desert. Today, the body of Saint Macarius is found in his monastery, the Monastery of Saint Macarius the Great in Scetis, Egypt.

11.5 *The eremitic life*

The eremitic life preceded the coenobitic one. We find out about monastic life of the eremitic kind from Palladius, a monk from Palestine who, in 388, went to Egypt to drink in the spirit of monasticism at the fountainhead. Christians continued to suffer under the authority of Rome and its emperors. The reign of Diocletian proved to be catastrophic for them. Empire-wide edicts were issued by Diocletian proclaiming that all churches and sacred books were to be destroyed. Most Christians who held an official position were stripped of their jobs and civil rights, while others were sold into slavery. In Egypt, Diocletian's army destroyed parts of Alexandria in 292 AD. Many died as martyrs and, by the turn of the century, tens of thousands of Christians were living in the desert.

On landing at Alexandria, Palladius put himself in the hands of a priest named Isidore, who in early life had been a hermit at Nitria and now apparently presided over a hospice at Alexandria without in any way abating the austerity of his life. The monks of Nitria were five thousand men strong; six hundred hermits also lived in the area. Palladius describes the monastery as having seven bakeries, three date palms, a church, a guest-house, and many gardens. Doctors, cooks, and winemakers lived there, but most of the monks made linen. On the advice of Isidore, Palladius placed himself under the direction of a hermit named Dorotheus who lived six miles outside Alexandria, with whom he was to pass three years learning to subdue his passions and then to return to Isidore to receive higher spiritual knowledge. This Dorotheus spent the whole day collecting stones to build cells for other hermits, and the whole night weaving ropes out of palm leaves. He never lay down to sleep, though slumber sometimes overtook him while working or eating.

Palladius who seems to have lived in his cell, ascertained from other solitaries that this had been their custom from youth upwards. Palladius' health broke down before he completed his time with Dorotheus, but he spent three years in Alexandria and its neighbourhood visiting the hermitages and becoming acquainted with about 2000 monks. From Alexandria he went to Nitria, where there was a monastic village containing about 5000 solitaries. There was no kind of monastic rule. Some of the solitaries lived alone, sometimes two or more lived together. They assembled at the church on Saturdays and Sundays. The church was served by eight priests of whom the oldest always celebrated, preached, and judged, the others only assisting.

Strangers were entertained in a guest-house:

> Next to the church is a guest-house, where they receive the stranger who has arrived, until he goes away of his own accord, without limit of time, even if he remains two or three years. Having allowed him to spend one week in idleness, the rest of his stay they occupy with work either in the garden, or bakery, or kitchen. If he should be an important person, they give him a book, not allowing him to talk to any one before the hour.[10]

If at the ninth hour a man stood and listened to the sound of psalmody issuing from the different cells, he would imagine, says Palladius, that he was caught up into paradise. Further into the desert was a place called cells, or *Cellia*, whither the more perfect withdrew. Here the solitaries lived in cells so far apart that that they were out of sight and out of hearing from one another. Like those of Nitria, they met only on Saturdays and Sundays at church,whither some of them had to travel a distance of three or four miles. Often their death was only discovered by their absence from church.

Women were also known to live as hermits in the desert. Many wealthy women freed their slaves and ran away to live a monastic life because they hated their decadent lifestyles and were sick of staying in loveless marriages. St Jerome is said to have convinced numerous women from the Roman nobility to enter a life of monasticism. In *The Lausiac History*, Palladius has a large number of anecdotes about women monks. An ascetic named Elias built a large monastery for women and provided them with all the necessities. Pachomius founded a monastery at Tabennisi for men and later built one across the river for women that housed four hundred. The men supplied them with food and other staples. Palladius mentions some women saints by name, including the Roman matrons Paula, Veneria, Theodora, Hosia, Adolia, and Basianilla, among others. Much is said of a woman named Melania. She was Spanish by birth and later became a Roman citizen. At twenty-two, she found herself a wealthy widow with a son. After finding her son a trustee, she sold her possessions and went to Mount Nitria. Melania travelled around Egypt and met many of the holy men, learning everything she could from them. Later, she built a monastery in Jerusalem and lived there for twenty-seven years with fifty other women.[11]

11.5.1 Stylites

Stylites (from Greek *stylos*, "pillar") or Pillar-Saints are a type of Christian ascetic who in the early days of the Byzantine Empire stood on pillars preaching, fasting and praying. They believed that the mortification of their bodies would help ensure the salvation of their souls. The first stylite was probably Simeon Stylites the Elder who climbed on a pillar in Syria in 423 and did not come down until his death 37 years later. Palladius recounts the story of a hermit in Palestine who dwelt in a cave on the top of a mountain and who for the space of twenty-five years never turned his face to the west (presumably the direction of the cave's entrance). St Gregory of Nazianzus speaks of a solitary who stood upright for many years together, absorbed in contemplation, without ever lying down.[12] Theodoret affirms that he had seen a hermit who had passed ten years in a tub suspended in midair from poles.[13]

11.6 The cenobitic life

11.6.1 St Pachomius

An Egyptian like Anthony, Pachomius was born in 292 of a pagan family of well-to-do peasants at Sne on the borders of the Nile a little higher up than Thebes. At that time Egypt was under Roman domination. In 312, the Emperor Maximin needed soldiers to make war against Licinius. At that time, when one had no soldiers, one took them; people were conscripted by force. Some soldiers came to Pachomius' village and took him away with other young men. He was about twenty years old and so ready for military service whether he liked it or not. So he was taken to Alexandria. As prisoners, he and his companions were shipped down the Nile to Thebes, the first large town, where they stopped for the night. The soldiers took the con-scripts to the prison in the town, and there, the Christians brought them food and assistance. Pachomius the pagan was moved by the charity of these Christians. It remained with him all his life; for him, a Christian does good to everyone. This conviction then influenced his conception of the monastic life in which the idea of the service of God and the brethren was central. After the war, Pachomius was set free at Antinoe. He went back up the Nile but he did not go home; he wanted to serve God and, like Anthony, he settled near a village (Seneset) where he was baptised about 313. In accordance with the promise he had made to serve mankind, he helped the people round about in any way he could. Then, like Anthony, he too became a disciple of an ascetic who lived nearby, and again like Anthony, he underwent many temptations.

Around 323 Pachomius left Palamon to live in an abandoned village called Tabennesi, always with the intention of being a hermit. One night Pachomius had a vision in which he was told:

"The will of God is that you should serve mankind in order to call them to Him." Pachomius, after his vision felt moved to build a monastery. Pachomius also acquired a following; he chose to mould them into a community in which the monks lived in individual huts or rooms—cells (from the Greek κελλια)—but worked, ate, and worshipped in shared space. This method of monastic organization is called *cenobitic* (community-based). Most monastic life is nowadays cenobitic in nature. The head of a monastery came to be known by the word for Father: in Syriac, *Abba*—in English, Abbot.

The birth of a cenobitic Order among hermits gives a glimpse of two contrary aspirations at the root of Pachomianism which had to be brought into harmony: on the one hand, the concern for individual perfection as found in the desert Fathers where each one sought his own way according to temperament and the call of grace; and on the other the aspect of common life required by cenobitism. The solution found by Pachomius, faithful to his intuition, was that each one should find his own perfection in serving others. He was convinced that personal individual perfection cannot be realised on this earth; this ideal of perfection can only be found in a community of brothers, the holy *Koinônia*, where all help each other in the spiritual combat.[14]

That the Pachomian monastery was a like a little village protected from relations with the outside by a huge wall with only one door and a porter checking arrivals: this put a distance between it and the outside world. Thus it was a little world in itself. Yet this little world was remarkably organised. In each house of this small village there lived about forty brothers all exercising the same craft; there was the house of bakers, the house of cooks, the house of cobblers; the house of scribes, and so forth. In each house the brothers lived under the authority of a housemaster, a "superior" helped by a "second in command". Three or four houses formed a "tribe". A monastery was composed of 10 tribes; thus 30 or 40 houses each with 40 brothers adds up to more than a thousand monks in a monastery (1200–1400). At the head of each monastery there was an abbot and one or two stewards. There were 9 monasteries of men and 3 of women. Pachomius' sister Maria had founded a monastery for virgins near Tabennisi under his direction. Two others followed, one near Tsmine and the other near Phbew. Everything was well organised there too; a chaplain was there to give them spiritual help. These 12 monasteries formed an Order governed by an Abbot General, Pachomius, and a head steward who lived at Phbew. Each year, all the monks gathered at Phbew to celebrate Easter, and in August to hold a sort of chapter of faults and reconciliation. On Saturdays and Sundays all the monks assembled in the church for Mass; on other days the Office and other spiritual exercises were celebrated in the houses. St Jerome translated the rule of St Pachomius into Latin in 404, and only this translation survives. The rule of St Pachomius influenced St Benedict, the most influential figure in Western monasticism, in preparing his own rule.

11.6.2 St Basil the Great

Basil was born about 330 at Caesarea in Cappadocia. He came from a wealthy and pious family which gave a number of saints, including his mother Saint Emily (also styled Emilia or Emmelia), grandmother Saint Macrina the Elder, sister Saint Macrina the Younger and brothers Saints Gregory of Nyssa and Peter of Sebaste. It is also a widely held tradition that Saint Theosebia was his youngest sister, who is also a saint in the Church.

Their father wanted his sons to do higher studies. He sent Basil first to Caesarea and then to Athens, the intellectual capital at the time, where he made friends with another Gregory who later was bishop of Nazianzus. With his studies finished, Basil returned to Caesarea and began to teach rhetoric. His eldest sister found that he was not living earnestly enough as a Christian and she strongly reproached him. Basil was touched by grace (he would call this his "conversion"), took what she said seriously and retired to a family property at Annesi where, with his family and some friends, he lived of retired life apart from the world: "One day, like a man roused from deep sleep,

I turned my eyes to the marvellous light of the truth of the Gospel, and I wept many tears over my miserable life."[15]

Basil's first monastic writing is found in his second letter, addressed to his friend Gregory of Nazianzus. It is the letter of a young man; Basil writes with the fervour of a young novice overflowing with consolations, no doubt profound ones. Besides his friend, who did not need to be convinced, his enthusiasm was openly addressed to their cultured friends who were scandalized to see him and his companions adopt a way of life fit for slaves. Basil clothed his ascetic ideal in philosophical language and concepts taken from rhetoric on purpose, very rarely quoting Scripture. He wanted to show that this ascetic ideal which seemed barbaric to his scandalized friends had its precedents in the wise men of Greece and corresponded to what they called *paideia*.[16] In this letter we find a beautiful description of prayer:

> The best prayer is one which imprints upon the soul a keen sense of God. This what it means to become a house of God: to have God dwelling within through our remembrance of him. We become a temple of God when earthly cares do not sever this continual remembrance of God and unforeseen emotions do not trouble the spirit. Fleeing all things, the one who loves God will draw near to him, chasing away the desires which lead to evil and holding to those things which lead to virtue.[17]

Unfortunately, Basil could not enjoy his solitude for long. Eusebius, his bishop, had noticed him; he ordained him priest and after three years he made him his coadjutor bishop. Five years later, Eusebius died and Basil succeeded him as bishop of Caesarea. It was a heavy burden, and he found himself up against many difficulties due to the religious and political climate.

With a wise balance, he was able to combine service to souls with dedication to prayer and meditation in solitude. Availing himself of his personal experience, he encouraged the foundation of numerous communities of Christians consecrated to God, which he visited frequently. Basil the Great, before embracing the monastic life, had made a careful study of monasticism in Egypt,

Palestine, Coelesyria, and Mesopotamia. The result was a decided
preference for the cenobitic life. He founded several monasteries
in Pontus, over one of which he himself for a time presided, and
very soon monasteries, modelled after his, spread over the East.
Basil created a very special monasticism: it was not closed to the
community of the local Church but instead was open to it. His
monks belonged to the particular Church; they were her life-
giving nucleus and, going before the other faithful in the following of Christ and not only in faith, showed a strong attachment
to him—love for him—especially through charitable acts. These
monks, who ran schools and hospitals, were at the service of the
poor and thus demonstrated the integrity of Christian life.[18]
Various founders of ancient monasticism drew on his works,
including St Benedict, who considered Basil his teacher.[19]

His monks assembled together for the psalms and genuflections seven times a day, in accordance with the Psalmist's words:
"Seven times a day I praise you for your just decrees." (Ps
119:164). There was prayer at midnight as in the psalm: "At
midnight I will rise and thank you for your just decrees" (Ps
119:62), at evening, morning and midday "Evening, morning
and at noon I will cry and lament" (Ps 55:18), at the third hour,
the hour of Pentecost, and at the ninth, the sacred hour of the
Passion. To complete the tale of seven, the midday prayer was
divided into two parts separated by the community meal.

Basil's monastic ideal is set forth in a collection of his writings
known as the *Asceticon*, the most important of which are the
Regulae fusius tractatae, a series of answers to questions, fifty-five
in number, and the *Regulae brevius tractatae*, in which three
hundred and thirteen questions are briefly answered. It must
not be supposed that the *Regulae* form a rule in the modern sense,
though it would be possible to go a good way towards consti-
tuting one out of them. They are answers to questions which
would naturally arise among persons already in possession of
a framework of customs or traditions. Sometimes they treat of
practical questions, but as often as not they deal with matters
concerning the spiritual life.

11.6.3 St Martin of Tours

We know about St Martin from the *Life of Martin* by Sulpicius
Severus. The date of Martin's birth is disputed; it was probably
around 316 AD. St Anthony was then 55 years old. He was born
in Savaria, in Pannonia, (present-day Hungary), where his
father, a military tribune and a pagan was on garrison duty
before being sent to Pavia in Italy. It was there that Martin was
brought up and probably met Christianity. His father wanted
him to become a soldier like himself and enter the army; Martin
did so reluctantly, for he was already a follower of Christ. He
was at Amiens when, in mid-winter, he shared his cloak with a
poor man who was very cold. Legend tells us that this poor man
was Jesus Christ. Martin, who was then a catechumen, was
baptised at Easter in 354. Two years later, in 356, he left the army,
and went to his parents, converting his mother but not his father.
It is possible that he met Hilary of Poitiers around 356. Between
357 and 360 he may have had some experience of the ascetic life
in Italy. It is certain that after Hilary's return from exile (360) he
founded a monastery at Ligugé, near Poitiers. There he lived the
life of a monk for 10 years and attracted many disciples.

However in 372 he was elected bishop of Tours. He wanted
to remain a monk and built himself a wooden cell outside the
cathedral. Disciples gathered round him, and then he founded
the monastery of Marmoutiers, which means "the great monastery". It was in fact a group of hermitages rather than a large
monastery. Life at Marmoutiers was poor, with community of
goods, a fairly flexible cenobitic life compared to the Pachomi-
ans—the sons of Gallo-roman families were not like the young
Egyptian peasants; much time was given to contemplation, to
the extent that there was no official work apart from copying
books. Marmoutiers was thus the forerunner of the medieval
monasteries with their workshops for copying manuscripts.

We have no personal document from Martin on his interior life.
It is not easy to form an exact idea of his spirituality from the
apologetic biography of Sulpicius Severus. It seems that Martin's

chief characteristic was that he remained a soldier at heart. In his community he insisted on obedience. For him the monk was the successor of the martyrs and he must demonstrate this by his patience and humility in following Christ. As a soldier, he must engage in combat against the devil. An interior combat, certainly, for Martin was visited by the devil like Anthony; but also an exterior combat in the destruction of pagan sanctuaries (for he believed that paganism was the work of the devil), and in healing those who were possessed. Finally, Martin was a pastor formed by Hilary. His spirituality, both active and exacting, was pastorally oriented; his asceticism was subordinated to preaching the Word. St Martin died at Candes-Saint-Martin on 11 November 397; his shrine became a famous stopping-point for pilgrims on the road to Santiago de Compostela. He is considered a spiritual bridge across Europe, given his association with both France and Hungary. His influence will also be seen on St Patrick and St Ninian.

11.6.4 Lérins Abbey

Lérins Abbey is a Cistercian monastery on the island of Saint-Honorat, one of the Lérins Islands, on the French Riviera, with an active monastic community. There has been a monastic community there since the fifth century. The construction of the current monastery buildings began around 1073. Today the monks cultivate vineyards and produce wine and liqueur. The island, known to the Romans as *Lerina*, was uninhabited until Saint Honoratus, a disciple of a local hermit named Caprasius of Lérins, founded a monastery on it at some time around the year 410. According to tradition, Honoratus made his home on the island intending to live as a hermit, but found himself joined by disciples who formed a monastic community around him. This had become "an immense monastery" by 427, according to the contemporary writings of John Cassian.

Several notable people have made Lérins famous; in the first place, its founder, Honoratus. In 395, Saint Honoratus (Honorat), a Roman nobleman, or according to some accounts, the son of King Andrioch and Queen Helenbore of Hungary deserted the court in order to lead a group of devoted disciples in search of the ascetic life. He withdrew to Cannes where he led the life of a solitary ascetic. After several pilgrimages to Greece, he ended by withdrawing to a cave in Esterel, and then, about 410, to the island of Lérins, which was full of snakes, which he drove into the sea. Since then, the island has been free of these reptiles. He welcomed many disciples there, one of whom was a close relative, Hilary of Arles, who would later write his life. Elected bishop of Arles in 428, Honoratus only stayed there for two years, dying in 430. He founded another monastery on an island in the Rhone. After entering Lérins, Hilary accompanied Honoratus to Arles, where he was elected as bishop to succeed him. Arles was then a metropolitan see whose jurisdiction included more than twenty-five bishoprics in Provence. Hilary gave the funeral oration for Honoratus, describing monastic life. Hilary was noted for his great generosity. He died in 449, aged 48.

Eucherius of Lyons came from a distinguished and cultivated family. He married and had two sons. He and his wife became Christians, handed their sons over to the monks of Lérins and built themselves hermitages on an island near Lérins. Eucherius became bishop of Lyons shortly after 432 and died about 450. His two sons also became bishops. A little later, Cesarius of Arles was born in 470 near Châlon-sur-Saône. When very young, he set out for Egypt, attracted by the fame of the land of monks. When he got to Marseilles, he boarded the ship and then disembarked at Lérins. He was about 20 years old and stayed there a dozen years. When he became ill, he was sent for treatment to Arles. There he was ordained deacon and then priest and was sent as abbot to the monastery of Trinquetaille. He then became bishop of Arles where he founded the monastery of Saint John for nuns. He then drew up a rule for this monastery; the first edition drew on the Eastern rules, the second on Augustine. Finally, there was Vincent of Lérins, a great theologian who wrote several works, in particular the *Commonitorium* (hand-book), in which he emphasized the importance of consulting both Scripture and the Fathers.

There is also a tradition that Saint Patrick, patron saint of Ireland, spent nine years here in the fifth century, preparing for the "great task of his life".[20] Many subscribe to the theory that Patrick studied under St Vincent de Lérins in the monastery on the Isle of Lérins around AD 412. In his *Confessio*, Patrick referred to the saintly brethren on the Isle of Lérins. Patrick regarded the Isle of Lérins as "an earthly paradise". A plaque near the entrance to the present buildings commemorates Patrick's years on the island.

11.6.5 St Benedict

Widely venerated as the Father of Western Monasticism, St Benedict of Nursia (470–543) wrote a monastic rule that has been followed continuously by monks in the West since the sixth century. St Benedict was born at Nursia, in Italy, around 470 AD Sent to school in Rome, he soon fled the worldliness of life in the city, abandoning his secular studies to become a monk. Although he first lived with a company of virtuous men, soon a miracle the holy man performed, fixing a broken vessel, attracted attention. He fled once again and took up residence in a mountain cave at Subiaco, near the site of a villa built by Nero. Here St Benedict lived in continual prayer and asceticism for three years. Eventually, God allowed his fame to spread once again, and he was asked by a nearby community of monks to become their abbot. The saint reluctantly agreed.

However, the men rebelled against his ascetic directions and attempted to poison him. St Benedict was unharmed, because as he made the sign of the cross over the poisoned drink, the cup shattered. He returned to his cave. Gradually individuals began to come to live near him at Subiaco, and in the end St Benedict built twelve monasteries for these spiritual children, living himself at a thirteenth. St Gregory notes a tradition that St Benedict had a sister, St Scholastica, who became a nun at one of his communities, and a famous story has her praying for a rainstorm on one occasion so as to enjoy more time in spiritual fellowship with her brother. Three days later, she died. St

Benedict saw her soul rising to heaven "in the likeness of a dove", and had her buried in his own tomb. (St Scholastica is remembered on February 10.) After receiving the Eucharist, St Benedict reposed in the oratory of his monastery, his arms lifted in prayer, in the year 543.

11.7 Britain and Ireland

Monks and missionaries played a special role in the spread and development of Christianity in the British Isles during the early centuries.

11.7.1 England

The first evidence of Christianity in England is from the late second century AD, although there may have been Christians in Britain before then. Roman Britain was a cosmopolitan place and people from all over the empire settled there; soldiers from many countries served there so we do not know who first introduced Christianity to England. At that time the Romans were not tolerant of Christianity, and waves of persecution crossed the empire. St Alban, the first British Christian martyr, was killed in a town called Verulamium in 304 AD. Much later an abbey was built there dedicated to St Alban and gave its name to the town of St Albans.

In 313 the Emperor Constantine granted Christians freedom of worship. So persecution ended and during the fourth century Christianity became widespread in England. In 314 three British bishops attended a church council in Arles in France, Eborius bishop of York, Restitutus bishop of London and Adelius bishop of Caerleon (Gwent). Therefore, by that time the Church was flourishing and organised in England.

The Hinton St Mary Mosaic is the earliest known image of Christ in England and dates from the fourth century. This magnificent mosaic was discovered buried beneath a field in the village of Hinton St Mary, Dorset, in 1963. The artwork was designed as a continuous floor in two panels for one large room divided by a pair of short cross-walls. In the central roundel is what is thought to be one of the earliest representations of Christ and, if so, the only such portrait on a mosaic floor from anywhere in the Roman Empire. He is portrayed as a clean-shaven man. The bust is placed before the Greek letters *chi* and *rho*, the first two letters of Christ's name. Placed together as a monogram they formed the normal symbol for Christianity at this time.

In 407, the last Roman soldiers left Britain. In 410, the Roman Emperor Honorius replied to a request for assistance with his Rescript, telling the Roman Britons to manage their own defence. Over the following decades Roman civilisation broke down. In the fifth and sixth centuries Saxons, Angles and Jutes from Germany and Denmark invaded southern and eastern England and gradually conquered most of the country.

In 429 the bishops of Britain sent an appeal to the continent for help against the Pelagians who were corrupting the faith of the island. Agricola, the son of Severinus, who, after the birth of this son, was chosen bishop and became a Pelagian, spread the poison of this heresy in Britain.[21] St Prosper, who was in Rome in 431, tells us in his Chronicle that Pope Celestine commissioned the Church in Gaul to send help, and St Germanus (Germain) of Auxerre and St Lupus of Troyes were deputed to cross over to Britain. On his way Germanus stopped at Nanterre, where he met a young child, Genevieve, destined to become the patroness of Paris. The crossing to England was endangered by a terrible storm:

> There on a sudden they were obstructed by the malevolence of demons, who were jealous that men of such eminence and piety should be sent to bring back the people to salvation. They raised storms, and darkened the sky with clouds. The sails could not support the fury of the winds, the sailors' skill was forced to give way, the ship was sustained by prayer, not by strength, and as it happened, their spiritual leader and bishop, being spent with weariness, had fallen asleep. Then, as if because resistance flagged, the tempest gathered strength, and the ship, overwhelmed by the waves, was ready to sink. Then

the blessed Lupus and all the rest, greatly troubled, awakened their elder, that he might oppose the raging elements. He, showing himself the more resolute in proportion to the greatness of the danger, called upon Christ, and having, in the name of the Holy Trinity, taken and sprinkled a little water, quelled the raging waves, admonished his companion, encouraged all, and all with one consent uplifted their voices in prayer. Divine help was granted, the enemies were put to flight, a cloudless calm ensued, the winds veering about set themselves again to forward their voyage, the sea was soon traversed, and they reached the quiet of the wished-for shore.[22]

Germanus and Lupus confronted the British clergy at a public meeting before a huge crowd in Britain. The Pelagians were described as being conspicuous for riches, brilliant in dress and surrounded by a fawning multitude. The bishops debated and, despite having no popular support, Germanus was able to defeat the Pelagians using his superior rhetoric. Tradition tells us that the main discussion with the representatives of Pelagianism took place at St. Alban's, and resulted in the complete defaet of the heretics. The miraculous healing of the blindness of a ten-year-old girl convinced everyone of the doctrine of Germanus and Lupus who then promoted the cult of Saint Alban in his shrine. Germanus remained in Britain for some time preaching, and established several schools for the training of the clergy.

Germanus also led the native Britons to a victory against a Pictish and Saxon army, at a mountainous site near a river, of which Mold in North Wales is the traditional location. After baptising his troops he ordered them all to cry "Alleluia!" The sound apparently so terrified the invaders that they fled before battle could be brought.[23]

Later, Pope St Gregory the Great decided on a mission to the English. In the year 596, some 40 monks set out from Rome to evangelize the Anglo-Saxons in England. Leading the group was Augustine, the prior of their monastery in Rome. Hardly had he and his men reached Gaul when they heard stories of the ferocity of the Anglo-Saxons and of the treacherous waters of the English

Channel. Augustine returned to Rome and to St Gregory the Great who had sent them only to be assured by the pope that their fears were groundless.

Augustine again set out. This time the group crossed the English Channel and landed in the territory of Kent, ruled by King Ethelbert, a pagan married to a Christian princess named Bertha. Ethelbert received them kindly, set up a residence for them in Canterbury and within the year, on Pentecost Sunday, 597, was himself baptized. Soon after his arrival, Augustine founded the monastery of Saints Peter and Paul, which later became St Augustine's Abbey, on land donated by the king.

After being consecrated a bishop in Arles, France, at the command of Pope Gregory, Augustine returned to Canterbury, where he founded his see.[24] He constructed a church and monastery near where the present cathedral, begun in 1070, now stands. As the faith spread, additional sees were established at London and Rochester. In a letter Gregory wrote to the patriarch of Alexandria in 598, he claimed that more than 10,000 Christians had been baptised. Work was sometimes slow and Augustine did not always meet with success.

Labouring patiently, Augustine wisely heeded the missionary principles—quite enlightened for the times—suggested by Pope Gregory the Great: purify rather than destroy pagan temples and customs; let pagan rites and festivals be transformed into Christian feasts; retain local customs as far as possible.[25] The success Augustine achieved in England before his death in 605, a short eight years after he arrived in England, would eventually bear fruit long after in the conversion of England. Augustine of Canterbury can truly be called the "Apostle of England".

11.7.2 St Ninian

The only written evidence about St Ninian, the Apostle of Scotland, comes from the accounts of the Venerable Bede, writing 300 years later,[26] and St Aelred, writing approximately 700 years later.[27] However, Aelred claims to rely on an earlier account "written by a barbarian" which suggests he may have copied from an ancient source; and extensive details imply that source could have been written by a member of Ninian's community in Galloway.

St Ninian's exact year of birth is unknown, but is believed to be some time around 360 AD. Some traditions say his place of birth is Galloway, others say Strathclyde, other accounts say he was born in Brythonic Cumbria, probably Rheged. Since Rheged is believed to have extended into Dumfries and Galloway, and since Strathclyde was sometimes called Cumbria or Cumberland, these accounts are not necessarily in conflict. Ninian's father was said to have been a Christian king.[28]

Ninian travelled to Rome as a young man to study Christianity, where his eagerness to learn brought him to the notice of Pope Damasus, who decided to train the young man personally.

> The most blessed youth having arrived at Rome, when he shed tears, proofs of his devotion, before the sacred relics of the apostles, and had with many prayers commended the desire of his heart to their patronage, betook himself to the Bishop of the Supreme See, and when he had explained to him the cause of his journey, the Pope accepted his devotion, and treated him with the greatest affection as his son. Presently he handed him over to the teachers of truth to be imbued with the disciplines of faith and the sound meanings of Scripture.[29]

After St Damasus died, his successor, Pope Siricius, consecrated St Ninian a bishop and commissioned him to return to Britain to preach the Christian faith. Travelling from Italy back to Britain through France, Ninian heard of the great work being done by St Martin of Tours at his abbey in Marmoutiers, and went to visit him. St Ninian stayed at the abbey for some time and was encouraged and helped in his work by St Martin who became his friend and left a lasting impression on him.[30]

When St Ninian returned to Scotland to begin an evangelical mission there, masons from St Martin's Monastery in Tours helped with the construction of his first church. It was a whitewashed stone building at a time when most churches were wooden, and its colour made it easy to see from great distances away. Ninian named his church *Candida Casa* (the White House), and in the language of that time it became known as Whithorn (which means "shining house"). St Aelred states that news of St Martin's death reached Ninian while he was building *Candida Casa*, and as a result Ninian decided to dedicate the building to Martin.[31] Whithorn's lasting fame rests on its claim to be the location of the first Christian church in Scotland and the first Christian settlement north of Hadrian's wall. Although over-shadowed in popular imagination by Columba and his church at Iona, Whithorn's claim to be the first church in Scotland was substantiated by the Venerable Bede in approximately 730 AD. During archaeological excavations in the late twentieth century, remnants of a white plastered wall were found which some believe could be ruins from this first church. This church became Ninian's base and from it he and his monks evangelized the neighbouring area.

At the time of St Ninian, the Picts were divided into two main groups, the Northern Picts and the Southern Picts. According to Bede, the Southern Picts were converted by St Ninian while the Northern Picts were later converted by St Columba.[32] The Southern Picts are those south of the mountains known as the Mounth, which cross Scotland north of the Firths of Clyde and Forth. Placename evidence and local tradition suggest that St Ninian in his mission travels worked his way up the east coast of Scotland, possibly reaching as far as the Shetland Islands. As a result, St Ninian is referred to as the apostle of the northern Britons and Picts.

Unfortunately, his work among the southern Picts seems to have had but a short lived success. Later references indicate that after St Ninian the Picts abandoned Christianity and returned to their old beliefs. St Patrick, in his epistle to Coroticus, terms the Picts "apostates", and references to Ninian's converts having abandoned Christianity are found in writings of St Columba and St Kentigern, the first Bishop of Glasgow. As St Columba and others had to start afresh converting the Picts in the late 500s, it would seem that either St Ninian's Pictish converts returned to paganism after his departure, or possibly that Bede did indeed get his dates and identities confused, and St Ninian and St.Columba were indeed operating at much the same time.

Ninian was known for his miracles, among them curing a Chieftain of blindness. Other stories of healing and miraculous deeds include his punishment and cure of King Tudvael, the acquittal of a priest accused of fornication, the providential growth of leeks, the miraculous umbrella which saved his book from the rain, cures of the blind, leprous and malformed and, after his death, many cures associated with a visit to his grave. Reports of these miracles led to many conversions. St Ninian died around the year 432. Although the body of St Ninian was buried in the church at Whithorn (Wigtownshire), no relics are now known to exist.

The monastery Ninian founded at Whithorn became famous as a school of monasticism within a century of his death. It is also known as The Great Monastery, maintaining the flame of St Martin of Tours' spiritual lineage with its ascetical training and mystical aspirations. His missionary foundation helped Christianity to grow in strength, therefore he is called the first Apostle of Christianity in Scotland. His church and shrine at Whithorn became a centre of pilgrimage, and King James IV of Scotland was said to be a regular visitor. Today the Cathedral is in ruins, but pilgrimages are still made to Whithorn and St Ninian's cave, to which it is said he retired when he needed peace to meditate and pray. St Ninian's feast day is celebrated on 16 September.

11.7.3 St Patrick

The historical Patrick is much more attractive than the Patrick of legend. It is unclear exactly where Patricius Magonus Sucatus (Patrick; Irish: Naomh Pádraig) was born—somewhere in the west between the mouth of the Severn and the Clyde. He was the son of Calphurnius and Conchessa. His mother was related to great patron of Gaul, St Martin of Tours. Before he became

Patricius (meaning "Father of the Citizens"), which later evolved into Patrick, the boy went by his birth name—Maewyn Succat. About 405, when Patrick was in his teens (14–16), he was captured by Irish raiders and became a slave in Ireland. There in Ballymena (or Slemish) in Antrim (or Mayo), Patrick first learned to pray intensely while tending his master's sheep in contrast with his early years in Britain when he "knew not the true God" and did not heed clerical "admonitions for our salvation". After six years, he was told in a dream that he should be ready for a courageous effort that would take him back to his homeland.

He ran away from his owner and travelled 200 miles to the coast. His initial request for free passage on a ship was turned down, but he prayed, and the sailors called him back. The ship on which he escaped was taking dogs to Gaul (France). At some point he returned to his family in Britain, then seems to have studied at the monastery of He received some kind of training for the priesthood in Gaul, possibly in Auxerre, including study of the Latin Bible, but his learning was not of a high standard, and he was to regret this always. He spent the next 15 years at Auxerre where he became a disciple of Saint Germanus of Auxerre; he spent time in the Abbey of Lérins from 412 and was possibly ordained about 417. Saint Germanus consecrated him bishop around 432, and sent him to Ireland to succeed Saint Palladius, the first bishop, who had died earlier that year. Patrick made his way to Ireland about 435.

In his *Confessio* Patrick wrote: "It was not by my own grace, but God who overcame it in me, and resisted them all so that I could come to the peoples of Ireland to preach the Gospel. I bore insults from unbelievers, so that I would hear the hatred directed at me for travelling here."[33] He set up his see at Armagh and organized the Church into territorial sees, as elsewhere in the West and East. St Patrick stipulated that "that clerics should be ordained everywhere for this people who have lately come to believe, and who the Lord has taken from the ends of the earth".[34] While Patrick encouraged the Irish to become monks and nuns, it is not certain that he was a monk himself; it is even less likely that in his time the monastery became the principal unit of the Irish Church, although it was in later periods. The choice of Armagh may have been determined by the presence of a powerful king. There Patrick had a school and presumably a small *familia* in residence; from this base he made his missionary journeys.

Saint Patrick established the Catholic Church throughout Ireland on lasting foundations: he travelled throughout the country preaching, teaching, building churches, opening schools and monasteries, converting chiefs and bards, and everywhere supporting his preaching with miracles. In 433 AD St Patrick determined to strike a blow at the very centre of Celtic paganism, and directed his course towards Tara. He sailed to the mouth of the Boyne, where, he laid up his boats, as to this day it is impossible for the smallest boats to sail up the Boyne between Drogheda and Navan. Patrick proceeded along the North bank of the river to the hill of Slane, the loftiest elevation in the country, dominating the vast plain of Meath. Being determined to celebrate Easter on the hill of Slane, Patrick lit his Paschal fire on Easter Eve (the fire of Christ never to be extinguished in Ireland), a custom which we know from other sources was universal at that time. This fire was at once seen on Tara, where the pagan king of Ireland, Laoghaire, was holding a convention of the chiefs of Ireland. The ritual of the convention demanded that no fire should be lit in his dominions on this night till the king's fire was lit on Tara. St Patrick's act directly challenged the edict of the king, who proceeded to Slane to punish the bold aggressor. The narrative of the conflict between St Patrick and king Laoghaire and his priests is marked by a series of miracles terminating with the defeat of paganism and the baptism of great numbers of the Irish, including Laoghaire himself, who yielded a nominal adhesion to the truth. He converted the king's daughters Saints Ethenea and Fidelmia. He threw down the idol of Crom Cruach in Leitrim. Patrick wrote that he daily expected to be violently killed or enslaved again.

He gathered many followers, including Saint Benignus, who would become his successor. That was one of his chief concerns, as it always is for the missionary Church: the raising up of native clergy. He wrote:

> It was most needful that we should spread our nets, so that a great multitude and a throng should be taken for God. Also that there should be clerics to baptise and encourage a people in need and want. This is what the Lord says in the gospel: he warns and teaches in these words: "Go therefore and teach all nations, baptising them in the name of the Father and of the Son and of the Holy Spirit, teaching them to observe all that I have commanded you; and behold I am with you all days, even to the end of the age."[35]

Patrick visited Rome in 442 and 444, and had contact with the Pope. As the first real organizer of the Irish Church, Patrick is called the Apostle of Ireland. According to the Annals of Ulster, the Cathedral Church of Armagh was founded in 444, and the see became a centre of education and administration. Patrick organized the Church into territorial sees, raised the standard of scholarship (encouraging the teaching of Latin), and worked to bring Ireland into a closer relationship with the Western Church.

Towards the end of his life, Patrick made his now famous retreat of forty days on Cruachan Aigli in Mayo from which the age-long Croagh Patrick pilgrimage derives. He longed to retire for a while to refresh his soul in solitude, and for that purpose on the Saturday before Ash Wednesday in the year 441, he took himself to the mountain top. Here he spent the days of Lent, chastising his body with fasts, pouring out his heart to God, and entreating Him with prolonged importunity and with tears that the Faith may not fail in the land of Erin. The *Book of Armagh* mentions that God summoned all the saints of Ireland, past, present and future, to appear before their father in the Faith to comfort him with a vision of the teeming harvest his labours would produce, and to join him in blessing their kinsmen and their country. From that sacred spot on Holy Saturday, Patrick with outstretched hands solemnly blessed the people of Ireland that they might cling to the Faith, and the land of Erin that no poisonous reptile might infest it. Then, refreshed with divine grace and comforted with the assurance that his labours would fructify forever, he came down from the mountain to celebrate Easter with the little flock he had left at Aughagower. Patrick may have died at Saul on Strangford Lough, Downpatrick, where he had built his first church. Glastonbury claims his alleged relics. The National Museum at Dublin has his bell and tooth, presumably from the shrine at Downpatrick, where he was originally entombed with Saints Brigid and Columba. According to the latest reconstruction of the old Irish annals, Patrick died in 493 AD on March 17, which is his feast day.

St Patrick's Breastplate is contained in the ancient Book of Armagh, from the early ninth century, along with Patrick's Confession. St Patrick is said to have written this prayer to strengthen himself with God's protection as he prepared to confront and convert Laoghaire, high king of Ireland. There are some similarities to Paul's exhortation to "put on the whole armour of God" (Ep 6:10–18), except that it is much more detailed.

> I bind unto myself today
> The strong Name of the Trinity,
> By invocation of the same
> The Three in One and One in Three.
>
> I bind this today to me forever
> By power of faith, Christ's Incarnation;
> His baptism in Jordan river,
> His death on Cross for my salvation;
> His bursting from the spicèd tomb,
> His riding up the heavenly way,
> His coming at the day of doom
> I bind unto myself today.
>
> I bind unto myself the power
> Of the great love of cherubim;
> The sweet "Well done" in judgment hour,
> The service of the seraphim,
> Confessors' faith, Apostles' word,
> The Patriarchs' prayers, the prophets' scrolls,

All good deeds done unto the Lord
And purity of virgin souls.

I bind unto myself today
The virtues of the star lit heaven,
The glorious sun's life giving ray,
The whiteness of the moon at even,
The flashing of the lightning free,
The whirling wind's tempestuous shocks,
The stable earth, the deep salt sea
Around the old eternal rocks.

I bind unto myself today
The power of God to hold and lead,
His eye to watch, His might to stay,
His ear to hearken to my need.
The wisdom of my God to teach,
His hand to guide, His shield to ward;
The word of God to give me speech,
His heavenly host to be my guard.

Against the demon snares of sin,
The vice that gives temptation force,
The natural lusts that war within,
The hostile men that mar my course;
Or few or many, far or nigh,
In every place and in all hours,
Against their fierce hostility
I bind to me these holy powers.

Against all Satan's spells and wiles,
Against false words of heresy,
Against the knowledge that defiles,
Against the heart's idolatry,
Against the wizard's evil craft,
Against the death wound and the burning,
The choking wave, the poisoned shaft,
Protect me, Christ, till Thy returning.

Christ be with me, Christ within me,
Christ behind me, Christ before me,
Christ beside me, Christ to win me,
Christ to comfort and restore me.

Christ beneath me, Christ above me,
Christ in quiet, Christ in danger,
Christ in hearts of all that love me,
Christ in mouth of friend and stranger.

I bind unto myself the Name,
The strong Name of the Trinity,
By invocation of the same,
The Three in One and One in Three.
By Whom all nature hath creation,
Eternal Father, Spirit, Word:
Praise to the Lord of my salvation,
Salvation is of Christ the Lord.

11.7.4 St Brigid

The first non-Roman area to adopt monasticism was Ireland, which developed a unique form closely linked to traditional clan relations, a system that later spread to other parts of Europe, especially France. The earliest monastic settlements in Ireland emerged at the end of the fifth century. The first identifiable founder of a monastery was Saint Brigit, a saint who ranked with Saint Patrick as a major figure of the Irish church. The monastery at Kildare was a double monastery, with both men and women ruled by the Abbess, a pattern found in other monastic foundations.

Saint Brigid of Kildare or Brigid of Ireland (Brigit, Bridget, Bridgit, Bríd or Bride) (Irish: *Naomh Bhríde*) (467–525) was a founder of several convents who is venerated as a saint. She is considered one of Ireland's patron saints along with Saints Patrick and Columba. Her feast day is February 1, the traditional first day of spring in Ireland.

According to tradition, Brigid was born at Faughart near Dundalk, County Louth, Ireland. According to her biographers her parents were Dubhthach, a pagan chieftain of Leinster, and Brocca, a Christian Pict who had been baptized by Saint Patrick. Some accounts of her life suggested that Brigid's mother was in fact Portuguese, kidnapped by Irish pirates and brought to Ireland to work as a slave in much the same way as Patrick.

She grew up marked by her high spirits and tender heart, and as a child, she heard Saint Patrick preach, which she never forgot. Brigid received the veil from Saint Mel and professed vows dedicating her life to Christ. She is believed to have founded a convent in Clara, County Offaly—her first: other foundations followed. But it was to be in Kildare that her major foundation would emerge. Around 470 she founded Kildare Abbey, a double monastery, for nuns and monks, on the plains of Cill-Dara, "the church of the oak", her cell being constructed under a large oak tree. As Abbess of this foundation she wielded considerable power. Brigid and her successor Abbesses at Kildare had an administrative authority equal to that of a Bishop until the Synod of Kells in 1152.

11.7.5 St Enda

Enda was an Irish prince born around 450 AD, and when his father died, he succeeded him as king and went off to fight his enemies. The soldier Enda was converted by his sister, Saint Fanchea, an abbess. He visited Fanchea, who tried to persuade him to lay down his arms. He agreed, if only she would give him a young girl in the convent for a wife. He renounced his dreams of conquest and decided to marry. The girl she promised turned out to have just died, and Fanchea forced him to view the girl's corpse, to teach him that he too, would one day face death and judgment. Faced with the reality of death, and by his sister's persuasion, Enda decided to study for the priesthood, and Fanchea sent him to *Candida Casa* in southwestern Scotland, a great centre of monasticism in England. There he took monastic vows and was ordained.

Enda's monks imitated the asceticism and simplicity of the earliest Egyptian desert hermits. It is said that Enda learned the principles of monastic life at Rosnat in Britain, which was Saint Ninian's hermitage in Galloway. About 484 he was given land in the Aran Islands by his brother-in-law, the King of Cashel. Three limestone islands make up the Aran Islands: Inishmore, Inishmaan and Inisheer. The three islands of Aran stretch across the mouth of Galway Bay, forming a kind of natural breakwater against the Atlantic Ocean.

Inishmore was at that time a lovely island with wooded valleys, green fields, and fair sheltered nooks bright with wild flowers, and the peaceful island was surrounded by the blue water of the sea, which sometimes made music in the dark caves, but more often dashed with the sound of thunder against its lofty cliffs. These cliffs rose out of the water to the height of 300 feet on the western side of the island, and from there the land fell in gentle slopes towards the eastern sea-shore. Enda built his monastery and church near the sea or the north-east corner of the island, where the land was most fertile, and he there led a life of great holiness. St Enda died in the year 530 and is regarded as the father of Irish monasticism.

11.7.6 St David

Saint Patrick was inspired by an angel to prophesy David's birth thirty years before the event.[36] This took place in 497 AD at Henvynyw that is identified as the site of the former Roman garrison of Loventium in what is now Cardiganshire.

David's father was Sant, a prince of the line of Cunedda, who is sometimes called Sandda or Xanthus, all three names meaning 'saint'. Sant's own father Ceredig gave his name to Cardiganshire, and his mother was the daughter of Brychan from whom Breconshire originates. Sant had been told in a dream that his son would be blessed with three gifts: a stag to reflect his lordship over the Serpent who deceived our First Parents in the Garden of Eden, a fish to indicate his life-long abstinence from meat, and a swarm of bees whose honey would be sweet testament to his holiness.[37]

> These gifts foretell his life, for the honeycomb proclaims his wisdom, for as honey lies in wax, so he held a spiritual mind in a temporal body. And the fish declares his aquatic life, for as a fish lives in water, so he, rejecting wine and beer and everything that can intoxicate, led a blessed life in God on bread and water only. The stag signifies his

power over the Old Serpent, for as a stag, having deprived serpents of their food, seeks a fountain of water and is refreshed as in youth with the strength received, so he, borne on high as on stags' feet, deprived the Old Serpent of the human race of his power of hurting him and fled to the fountain of life with constant flowings of tears, and, being renewed from day to day, so brought it to pass that in the name of the Holy Trinity, by the frugality of moderate repasts, he began to have saving knowledge and the power of governing demons.[38]

There are no doubts about the sanctity of David's mother Saint Non, or Nonnita, who was the daughter of Gynyr of Caergawch, a Pembrokeshire chieftain. She gave birth to her illustrious son during some unusually stormy weather in a place now commemorated by the ruined Chapel of Saint Non. David was baptised by Saint Ailbe who wrote a monastic Rule, was famed as a travelling evangelist and founder-Bishop of the Tipperary diocese of Imlech in the province of Munster, "and was led by Divine Providence from Ireland to Henvynyw at this time". Not only did a miraculous spring of water suddenly appear to facilitate the administration of the Sacrament, but an elderly monk who had been blind from birth "took some of the water in which the infant David had been thrice dipped, and sprinkled it thrice on his own face, whereupon he received sight for the first time."[39] After the death of her husband Sant, David's mother Non became a nun renowned for her holiness, and as the spiritual mother of many religious women.

At Henvynyw, the holy David walked to school every day to learn the alphabet, the Psalms, the lessons for the whole year, and attend Mass. We do not know to whom Sant and Non entrusted their son's early education but, one can reasonably surmise that, thanks to Saint Patrick, there were still monks in the area who provided tuition for the children. Later, David embraced the monastic life and studied for the Priesthood at Ty Gwyn, Saint Patrick's 'White House' Seminary, under the benign direction of Saint Illtyd (Illtud).[40]

After his ordination, David went to Whitland in Carmarthen-shire where he studied the Scriptures for ten years with academic guidance from Illtyd and Paulinus. It did not take Paulinus long to recognise that David possessed outstanding qualities, and he nominated him to be his eventual successor as Abbot of Whitland. However, having been so informed in an angelic visitation, he told him that he must first undertake a mission of evangelisation. In a spirit of obedience, David prepared by immersing himself in a period of solitary prayer in the Vale of Ewias, where Llantony Abbey was later built. He then set out to take the Gospel to other territories some of which were alien or hostile, occasionally on horseback, often on foot, and always with a total disregard for distance, hardship and danger. He proclaimed the Good News of the Kingdom of God and was successful in recruiting to the religious life many generous souls who would teach and demonstrate the life of Faith that has been handed down from the Apostles. Meanwhile, Saint Paulinus lived to the great age of one hundred and four but, in his later years became afflicted with blindness, which David is reported as having "cured by his prayers and making the Sign of the Cross over his beloved master".[41]

Having returned from his apostolic journeys, Abbot David built his principal monastery on the Ty Gwyn site in the Vallis Rosina of Menevia, and placed it under the protective patronage of Saint Andrew the Apostle and Patron of Scotland.Like all Celtic monks, David and his community rigorously observed the austere rule and ascetic practices of the Desert Fathers that had been adopted in Gaul and transmitted to Britain. They fashioned their own habits from animal skins, and followed a demanding schedule of manual labour that required pulling the plough themselves without the help of oxen. They drank only water, certainly never beer, abstained from meat, and ate only bread with salt, herbs, watercress and, maybe, the occasional leek. Saint Benedict's experiences at Subiaco were replicated when maidservants, at the behest of the resentful wife of a local chieftain called Boia, made obscene and futile attempts to seduce the monks of Ty-Dewi.[42]

Then, as happened in Benedict's case, some of David's community who recoiled from his demanding standards poisoned his bread, and he was saved only by the timely arrival from Ireland of Saint Scuthyn who alerted him to the deadly loaf which he blessed and ate himself without any ill effects.[43]

The monks' life of prayer included fidelity to the Divine Office, evenings spent in meditation, reading and writing, and the observance of a strict vigil of prayer from Friday evening to Sunday morning with only one hour's rest after midnight on Saturday. They were devoted to evangelical poverty, and declined any personal possessions to the extent that they would never lay claim for example to "my book", but only to its use for which they had permission. David himself earned the epithet *Aquaticus* (The Waterman) a reference perhaps to the number of baptisms he conducted, or the only drink that ever passed his lips, or his favourite penance of totally immersing himself in cold water while reciting the Psalms that he loved as the prayers of his Lord Jesus.[44] He took to heart Saint Paul's recommendation to Saint Timothy that became an inspiring charisma for his brethren and a wider flock.

> As one dedicated to God, you must aim to be saintly and religious, filled with faith and love, patient and gentle. Fight the good fight of the Faith, and win for yourself the eternal life to which you were called when you made your profession and spoke up for the truth in front of many witnesses, following Jesus who spoke up for the truth in front of Pontius Pilate (1 Tm 6:11–13).

In the confused world of those times, Celtic monasteries like David's became beacons of stability and purpose. For his part, David won universal acclaim for his selfless devotion to works of charity and mercy, and his evident personal holiness and pious practice that included frequent genuflections to remind himself and others of God's abiding presence.

In addition to evangelising and instructing the people, the monastic orders increasingly disseminated the arts of music, painting, architecture, carving and sculpture. They copied books, wrote and embellished manuscripts, and opened libraries. They built schools, hospitals, dormitories, kitchens, dairies, butteries, bakeries, laundries, and guest houses where they extended hospitality as though they were greeting Christ Himself. They developed systems of farming and land management, and used water-pipes, filter-tanks and drains in the construction of lavatories, washing troughs, and the bath-houses they provided for the sick and infirm. As their international character grew, monasteries became communication channels of news, and temporal rulers and their subjects appreciated the wise advice of monks who were trained in regular habits of routine, business, accountancy and, above all, who were motivated by the ideals of service to the people.

David later made significant missionary journeys to Ireland, Brittany and Cornwall, and in these endeavours his faithful companions were Saints Teilo and Padern, otherwise called Paternus of Wales. On the occasion of their journey to Jerusalem, the three saintly pilgrims had reached Gaul when an Angel endowed Father David with the gift of tongues just like the Apostolic gathering of old, so that he was able to communicate with and inspire those who lived in that country. The Patriarch and highest ranking Bishop of Jerusalem was prepared for their arrival because he, too, had been favoured with a visit from an Angel. The heavenly messenger told him that "three Catholic men are coming from the limits of the West. You are to receive them with joy and the grace of hospitality, and consecrate them to the episcopate."[45] With great joy, the Patriarch duly anointed David as Archbishop, and Teilo and Padern as Bishops:

> When it was time for them to return home, he presented David with four gifts: a consecrated altar, a remarkable bell, a crozier, and a vestment woven with gold. To save them being burdened with such impediments on their journey home, he sent them to Wales by way of angels.[46]

Archbishop David had not long returned from Jerusalem with Bishops Teilo and Padern when the Synod of Brevi in Cardiganshire was convened by Saint Dyfrig, the Archbishop of Caerleon-on-Usk. Originally from Madley near Hereford, he was also known as Dubricius or Devereux and had also been a disciple of Saint Germanus. Dyfrig's intention was to quell some further interest in the heresy of Pelagius that had arisen, but the impressive assembly of bishops, abbots, monks, princes, delegated clergy and eminent laity did not make much progress until Saint Paulinus suggested that David should take charge as the Synod's President. Despite his humble misgivings and protests, he accepted the responsibility in obedience and duly won great approval for his eloquence and positive approach to ensuring the efficiency of the Synod's decision-making process.

Because this ecclesiastical council was held in the open air, some of those at the back of the assembly found it difficult to see David let alone hear him. When they drew attention to this, "the ground on which he stood rose miraculously as he was preaching so that standing on this hill he might be seen and heard by all, lifting his voice like a trumpet, and a white dove settled on his shoulder, a sign of God's approving grace and blessing".[47] The village of Llandewi Brefi, meaning David's church at the River Brevi, marks the Synod's location.

Rhygyfarch reports that David's consecration as Archbishop by the Patriarch of Jerusalem was warmly welcomed at the Synod and confirmed by popular acclaim:

> He had made such an impression that, with the consent of all the Bishops, Kings, princes, nobles, and all grades of the entire Britannic race, he was made Archbishop, and his monastery, too, is declared the metropolis, the principle church, of the whole country, so that whoever ruled it would be accounted Archbishop.[48]

At first, David's sense of unworthiness prompted him to decline the appointment but, again, obedience to God's will prevailed over his humility. In his ministry to all, he kept in mind the words of Saint James: "The wisdom that comes from above is essentially something pure; it also makes for peace, and is kindly and considerate, full of compassion and shows itself by doing good" (Jm 3:16–18).

It is unlikely that David and his successors would have enjoyed the type of Archiepiscopal and Metropolitan authority that carried responsibility for associated dioceses as it is understood today. Abbots in the Celtic Church were often consecrated bishops, but this did not mean that they were invested with diocesan responsibility in the canonical sense. It is probable, therefore, that David's was one of the monastery-bishoprics that coincided with the period of a particular Abbot's tenure. Nevertheless, even if the title of Archbishop may have been honorary, it was certainly an indication of popular, personal pre-eminence, and such was the regard in which David was held.

It is a measure of his authority, influence and acceptability that David took it upon himself to convene the Synod of Victory at Caerleon-on Usk in order to erase the remaining vestiges of Pelagianism once and for all.

> A crowd of bishops, priests and Abbots renewed what they had confirmed in the former Synod of Brevi, some useful matters being added. So, from these two synods, all the churches of our country take their standard and rule by Roman authority. The decrees which he had confirmed with his mouth, the Bishop David alone committed to writing with his own sacred hand, to be confirmed later by the Pope, Saint Felix IV, who had opposed the heresy with great determination.[49]

According to the *Book of Llandav*, when the time was right, Saint Dyfrig resigned from his See in David's favour and 'gave him the title of metropolitan Archbishop of Wales.' David then transferred the Seat of ecclesiastical government to Menevia where the future St David's became the Cathedral city of the Western See. David's efforts on behalf of God's People in Wales and beyond continued unabated and, despite the relentless physical demands with no diminution in his asceticism, he lived to a ripe old age. Received wisdom has it that 1st March 589 is the most probable date when he entered into the joy of the Lord whom he had served so valiantly. There is also an opinion that the year might have been 604. If this were the case, one might hope David had the joy of knowing that Saint Gregory the Great, who had been elected Pope in 590, had commissioned the conversion of England through Saint Augustine and his monks who arrived in 597.

At Mass on the Sunday prior to 1st March, David preached a particularly inspiring sermon to the large congregation, but he began to feel unwell shortly after the Consecration. When the celebration of Mass had been completed, he blessed the people with his customary warmth and asked them "to persevere in what you have learned from me and what you have seen with me. On 1st March I shall go the way of my fathers. Farewell in the Lord; never shall we be seen on this earth again". As 1st March dawned, an angel comforted him with the news that "the long desired day is at hand", and with great happiness and contentment he replied, "Lord, let your servant now depart in peace."[50] His last words to his sorrowing community were "Be joyful, and keep your faith and your creed. Do the little things in life that you have seen me do and what you have heard about. I am going to walk the path that our fathers have trod before us." The chronicler adds that "the monastery was filled with angels as Christ received his soul".[51]

11.7.7 Saint Columbanus

Saint Columbanus was an Irish missionary notable for founding a number of monasteries on the European continent from around 590 in the Frankish and Italian kingdoms, most notably Luxeuil (in present-day France) and Bobbio (Italy), and stands as an exemplar of Irish missionary activity in early medieval Europe. He spread among the Franks a Celtic monastic rule and Celtic penitential practices for those repenting of sins, which emphasized private confession to a priest, followed by penances levied by the priest in reparation for the sin. He is also one of the earliest identifiable Hiberno-Latin writers.

Columbanus was born in Nobber, County Meath, Ireland, in 540, the year Saint Benedict died, and from childhood was well instructed. His first master was Sinell, Abbot of Cluaninis in Lough Erne. The Irish words "Cluan Innish", which mean meadow and island, have been contracted to "Cleenish", where the remains of the monastery can be seen at Bellenaleck, County Fermanagh. He then moved to the celebrated monastery of Bangor on the coast of Down, which at that time had for its abbot St Comgall. There Columbanus embraced the monastic state, and for many years led a life conspicuous for fervour, regularity and learning. At about the age of 40 he seemed to hear incessantly the voice of God bidding him to preach the Gospel in foreign lands. At first his abbot declined to let him go, but at length he consented.

Columbanus set sail with twelve companions; their names are believed to be St Attala, Columbanus the Younger, Cummain, Domgal (Deicolus?), Eogain, Eunan, St Gall, Gurgano, Libran, Lua, Sigisbert and Waldoleno. This little band passed over to Britain, landing probably on the Scottish coast. Some contend they may have landed in and crossed Cornwall en route to Brittany. They remained only a short time in England and then crossed over to France, where they arrived probably in 585. The landing site of Columbanus is marked by a shrine at Carnac in Brittany. At once, they began their apostolic mission.

Wherever they went, the people were struck by their modesty, patience and humility. France at that period was in sore need of such a band of monks and preachers. Owing partly to the incursions of barbarians, and partly due to the remissness of the clergy, vice and impiety were prevalent. Here the abbot and his monks led the simplest of lives, their food often consisting of nothing but forest herbs, berries, and the bark of young trees. The fame of Columbanus' sanctity drew crowds to his monastery. Many, both nobles and rustics, asked to be admitted into the community. Sick persons came to be cured through their prayers. But Columbanus loved solitude. Often he would withdraw to a cave seven miles distant, with a single companion who acted as messenger between himself and his brethren.

After a few years, the ever-increasing number of his disciples obliged him to build another monastery. Columbanus accordingly obtained from King Gontram the Gallo-Roman castle named *Luxovium* (Luxeuil), some eight miles distant from

Annegray. It was in a wild district, thickly covered with pine forests and brushwood. This foundation of the celebrated Luxeuil Abbey took place in 590. But these two monasteries did not suffice for the numbers who came, and a third had to be erected at Fontaines. The superiors of these houses always remained subordinate to Columbanus. It is said that at this time he instituted a perpetual service of praise, known as *laus perennis*, by which choir succeeded choir, both day and night. He wrote his Rule for these flourishing communities, which embodied the customs of Bangor and other Celtic monasteries. For nearly 20 years Columbanus resided in France and, during that time, observed the unreformed computation of Easter. But a dispute arose. The Frankish bishops were not well disposed towards this stranger abbot, because of his ever-increasing influence, and at last they showed their hostility. They objected to his Celtic Easter and his exclusion of men as well as women from the precincts of his monasteries.[52]

With a famous work entitled: *De poenitentiarum misura taxanda*, also written at Luxeuil, Columbanus introduced Confession and private and frequent penance on the Continent. It was known as "tariffed" penance because of the proportion established between the gravity of the sin and the type of penance imposed by the confessor.[53] These innovations roused the suspicion of local Bishops, a suspicion that became hostile when Columbanus had the courage to rebuke them openly for the practices of some of them. The controversy over the date of Easter was an opportunity to demonstrate their opposition: Ireland, in fact, followed the Eastern rather than the Roman tradition. The Irish monk was convoked in 603 to account to a Synod at Chalon-sur-Saône for his practices regarding penance and Easter. Instead of presenting himself before the Synod, he sent a letter and at the same time he wrote to Pope Boniface IV asking him to defend the Irish tradition.[54]

Columbanus then came into conflict with the royal house for having harshly reprimanded King Theuderic for his adulterous relations. This created a whole network of personal, religious and political intrigues and manoeuvres which, in 610, culminated in a Decree of expulsion banishing Columbanus and all the monks of Irish origin from Luxeuil and condemning them to definitive exile. They were escorted to the sea and, at the expense of the court, boarded a ship bound for Ireland. However, not far from shore the ship ran aground and the captain, who saw this as a sign from Heaven, abandoned the voyage and, for fear of offending God, brought the monks back to dry land. Instead of returning to Luxeuil, they decided to begin a new work of evangelization and embarked on a boat on the Rhine and travelled up the river. After a first stop in Tuggen near Lake Zurich they went to the region of Bregenz, on Lake Constance, to evangelize the Alemanni.

Columbanus is reported to have performed a miracle in Bregenz, Austria. The townspeople had placed a large vessel in the town centre, filled with beer. They told Columbanus it was intended as a sacrifice to their god Wodan, whom they identified with Roman Mercury. Angrily, Columbanus breathed on the vessel, which broke asunder with a loud noise, spilling the beer. However, soon afterwards, because of political events unfavourable to his work, Columbanus decided to cross the Alps with the majority of his disciples. Only one monk whose name was Gall stayed behind; it was from his hermitage that the famous Abbey of St Gall in Switzerland subsequently developed.[55]

After about a year, in consequence of another rising against the community, Columbanus resolved to cross the Alps into Italy. On his arrival at Milan in 612, Columbanus met with a kindly welcome from Lombard King Agilulf and Queen Theodelinda. He immediately began to confute the Arians and wrote a treatise against their teaching, which has been lost.

Saint Columbanus went to see Pope St Gregory the Great in Rome whom he had addressed as follows:

> We Irish, though dwelling at the far ends of the earth, are all disciples of St Peter and St Paul... Just as the faith was first delivered to us by yourselves, the successors of the Apostles, it is held by us unchanged... We are bound to the Chair of Peter, and although Rome is great and

renowned, through that Chair alone is she looked on as
great and illustrious among us... On account of the two
Apostles of Christ, you [the Pope] are almost celestial, and
Rome is the head of the whole world, and of the Churches.[56]

It was necessary that, in Italy, Columbanus should have a settled
abode, so the king gave him a tract of land called Bobbio,
between Milan and Genoa, near the River Trebbia, situated in
the the Apennines. On his way there he taught the Faith in the
town of Mombrione, which is called San Colombano to this day.
At Bobbio the saint repaired the half-ruined church of St Peter,
and erected his celebrated abbey. He died at Bobbio on 23
November 615. His body has been preserved in the abbey church
at Bobbio, and many miracles are said to have been wrought
there through his intercession. His feast day is 23 November.

11.7.8 St Laserian

St Laserian was the son of Cairel, a nobleman of Ulster, and of
Gemma, daughter of Aidan, king of the British Scots. He lived the
life of a hermit on Holy Isle, off the Isle of Arran, on the West of
Scotland. As an adult, he is said to have travelled to Rome, and
to have remained there for fourteen years. There he was ordained
priest by Pope St Gregory the Great, and soon after returned to
Ireland. Coming to Old Leighlin, he was affectionately received
by St Cobban, who governed the monastery there. This saint
conceived such a high opinion of St Laserian that he gave up to
him his monastery and went to erect a monastery elsewhere.
Laserian is said to have had 1,500 monks under him at Leighlin.

St Laserian wrote one of the earliest vernacular pieces of
vision literature in Christian tradition. The existing fragment
shows him leaving the monastery of Clúain (possibly Clonmac-
nois or Cloyne) to purify the church of Clúain Cháin in Con-
naught. After a fast of three nights, his soul was taken up by two
angels, who escort him to Hell to show him the horrors that
await unrepentant sinners. The angels explain to one devil eager
to take Laserian from them that their guest is granted the vision
in order that "he will give warning before us to his friends".

> Thereupon the man's soul went into Hell itself, even a sea of fire with an unspeakable storm and unspeakable waves upon it. And he saw the souls aflame in that sea, and their heads all above it; and they were wailing and lamenting, crying woe without ceasing throughout the ages. Some of the souls had fiery nails through their tongues, which were sticking out of their heads; others through their ears, others through their eyes.[57]

The angel who had accompanied him to Hell said:

> Tell people to repent, for whoever shall make repentance and remain in it shall not be in this place, but will be in a place of comfort away from this evil. Tell people also that he who is under the displeasure of God should be repentant, since God accepts repentance if it be done from a pious heart, and God's mercy will help him.[58]

At this time there was controversy in Ireland as to the right time for celebrating Easter. Some were for adopting the new Roman method, but most of the clergy and nation were attached to the old computation, until the year 630, when, in consequence of an admonitory letter from Pope Honorius I, a synod was held at or near Leighlin, which was attended by a great number of persons, and amongst others by the heads of several of the greatest religious establishments in the South of Ireland. St Laserian spoke in favour of the Roman system.[59]

As there was disagreement, it was resolved by the elders that some wise and humble persons should be sent to Rome, as children to their mother. Among these was St Laserian, in all probability, for he certainly was at Rome the same year. These delegates saw at Rome how people from various countries celebrated Easter at one and the same time, and they returned to Ireland to announce to those who had deputed them, that the Roman method of keeping Easter was now accepted in the whole Christian world. Before his return to his native island, Laserian had been consecrated bishop by Pope Honorius I. He survived his return only a few years, and he died on 18 April 639. He was buried in his own church at Leighlin, and his memory is greatly revered in the province of Leinster.

Notes

1   St Jerome, *The Life of Paulus*, 7–18.
2   St Athanasius, *Life of Anthony*, 5.
3   *Ibid.*, 14.
4   *Ibid.*, 49–50.
5   *Ibid.*, 51.
6   *Ibid.*, 36.
7   *Ibid.*, 89.
8   *Ibid.*, 91.
9   W. Harmless, *Desert Christians: An Introduction to the Literature of Early Monasticism* (Oxford: Oxford University Press, 2004), p. 174.
10   Palladius, *The Lausiac History*, chapter 7.
11   *Ibid.*, chapter 46.
12   See St Gregory of Nazianzus, *Carminum* Liber II, *Historica* in *PG* 37, 1456.
13   See Theodoret, *Philotheus*, chapter 28.
14   *Koinônia* in Greek means communion, or more loosely, fellowship.
15   St Basil, *Letter 223* in *PG* 32, 824.
16   *Paedeia* or paideia (παιδεία) was a system of instruction in Classical Athens in which students were given a well-rounded cultural education. Subjects included rhetoric, grammar, mathematics, music, philosophy, geography, natural history, and gymnastics. Paedeia was the process of educating humans into their true form, the real and genuine human nature.
17   St Basil, *Letter 2*.
18   See Pope Benedict XVI, *Discourse at General Audience* (4 July 2007).
19   See St Benedict, *Rule*, 73, 5.
20   M. Mulhall, "St Patrick and the Monastery of Lérins" in *The Irish Monthly* 17/194(1889), p. 395.
21   For Pelagianism, see chapter seven, subsection 7.2.12 above.
22   St Bede, *Ecclesiaistical History*, Book I, chapter 17.
23   *Ibid.*, Book I, chapter 20.
24   See *ibid.*, Book I, chapter 27.
25   See *ibid.*, Book I, chapter 30.
26   St Bede, *Ecclesiastical History of the English People*, Book III, chapter 4.
27   St Aelred of Rievaulx, *The Life of St Ninian*.
28   *Ibid.*, chapter 1.

29   *Ibid.*, chapter 2.

30   *Ibid.*

31   *Ibid.*, chapter 3.

32   St Bede, *Ecclesiastical History of the English People*, Book III, chapter 4.

33   St Patrick, *Confession*, 37.

34   *Ibid.*, 38.

35   *Ibid.*, 40. See Mt 28:19–20.

36   Rhygyfarch, *Life of St David*, 3.

37   *Ibid.*, 2.

38   *Ibid.*

39   *Ibid.*, 7. See also L. Toke, "St. David" in *The Catholic Encyclopedia* (New York: Robert Appleton Company, 1908). Retrieved 26 January 2012 from *New Advent*: http://www.newadvent.org/cathen/04640b.htm.

40   See *The life of St Illtud* probably composed in Cemis, Pembrokeshire, in the twelfth century. Found in the British Museum Cotton MS Vespasian, A xiv.

41   See Rhygyfarch, *Life of St David*, 11.

42   See *ibid.*, 17.

43   *Ibid.*, 37–38.

44   See T. D. Griffen, Address to the Saint David's Society of Saint Louis, "Saint David Aquaticus" (3 March 1996), pp. 2–3.

45   Rhygyfarch, *Life of St David*, 46.

46   *Ibid.*, 48.

47   *Ibid.*, 52.

48   *Ibid.*, 53.

49   See *ibid.*, 55.

50   See Rhygyfarch, *Life of St David*, 59.

51   *Ibid.*, 63.

52   The Irish and British churches shared a method of dating Easter, that was different from the system used on the Continent. Calculating the proper date of Easter was a complicated process involving a lunisolar calendar. Various tables were produced in antiquity that attempted to calculate Easter for a series of years. Insular Christianity used a calculation table that was similar to one approved by Saint Jerome. However, by the sixth and seventh centuries it had become obsolete and had been replaced by those of Victorius of Aquitaine and, more accurately, those of Dionysius Exiguus. As the Celtic world established renewed contact with the Continent it became aware of the divergence; the first clash over the matter came in Gaul in 602, when Columbanus resisted pressure from the local bishops to conform. Most groups, like the southern Irish, accepted the updated tables with relatively little difficulty, with the last significant objectors being the monks from the monastery of Iona and its many satellite institutions. See also chapter 4, section 4.10 above.

53   See chapter 4, section 4.6 above.
54   See St Columbanus, *Epistula I.*
55   Pope Benedict XVI, *Discourse at General Audience* (1 June 2008).
56   St Columbanus, *Epistula X*, 2, 10.
57   *The Vision of St Laisrén*, edited and translated by K. Meyer, *Stories and Songs from Irish Manuscripts* (London, 1899). Reprint from *Otia Merseiana* 1 (1899), pp. 113–28.
58   *Ibid.*
59   See chapter 4, section 4.10 above.

12 THE FALL OF ROME

Meanwhile the poor are being robbed, widows groan, orphans are trodden down, so that many, even persons of good birth, who have enjoyed a liberal education, seek refuge with the enemy to escape death under the trials of the general persecution. They seek among the barbarians the Roman mercy, since they cannot endure the barbarous mercilessness they find among the Romans.

Salvian, *On the Government of God*, 5, 5.

AFTER NEARLY HALF a millennium of rule, the Romans finally lost their grip on Europe in the late 400s AD. This century left in its wake great devastation, political chaos and the difficult question of what caused the Fall of Rome. Though Roman government in the form of the Byzantine Empire survived in the East for almost another thousand years, so-called barbarian forces overran western Europe, spelling the end of an era. While Rome's absence in the West brought with it tremendous change—and none of it seemed very positive, at least at first—before we can even address the question of how and why Rome fell, one must understand how this transition happened and what exactly came to a close with Rome.

12.1 The barbarian invasions

The term "barbarian" (*barbarus*) derived from a Greek word descriptive of bearded foreigners (*barbaros* meaning "bearded"). The Romans used the term in describing peoples beyond the Empire's borders, particularly those not belonging to one of the great civilizations—namely Roman, Greek or (later) Christian. The Romans usually ignored these peoples, but in 9 AD, they lost a decisive battle against the tribes in the Teutoburg Forest. In response, the Romans constructed a wall between the the Rhine and Danube rivers to protect this part of the Empire from the "barbarians", a tactic which worked in Scotland a century later when Hadrian's Wall was built to keep out the Picts.[1]

12.1.1 The Vandals

The Vandals descended from Germanic tribes present in central Europe in the earliest days of the Roman Empire: the term "Vandilii" is used by Tacitus.[2] Some of these tribes had migrated from Scandinavian areas sometime after 1000 BC. They were warlike and largely illiterate. Many of the tribes were migratory by nature, staying in particular regions long enough to hunt and farm but leaving few lasting monuments or settlements. By 100 BC, a number of tribes had migrated southward to the Rhine and Danube rivers, then the northern frontiers of the Roman Empire. The Romans called the expansive foreign region north of the rivers *Germania*, after the Germani, one of the wandering tribes. The Vandals settled between the Elbe and Vistula. At the time of the Marcomannic War (166-81 AD) they lived in what is now Silesia. During the third century when the Roman Empire was in crisis with many powerful enemies at their borders, the Vandals and their allied Sarmatians invaded the Roman territory along upper Rhine river in 270 AD.[3] About 271 AD the Roman Emperor Aurelian was obliged to protect the middle course of the Danube against them. In AD 330 they were granted lands in Pannonia on the right bank of the Danube by Constantine the Great. The Vandals embraced Arian Christianity during the reign of Emperor Valens in the AD 360's. There were two branches of the Vandal Confederacy: the Siling Vandals in the northwest and the Asding Vandals in the south. By 400, they had begun to migrate westward in response to the threat of the Huns (a nomadic Asiatic people related to the Mongols). By the early fifth century, closely pursued by the Huns, the two branches of Vandals (Siling and Asding) and other Germanic tribes: Suebi,[4] Alemanni,[5] Burgundians and a clan of Alans[6] went on the move.

The Vandals burst onto the stage of European history in dramatic fashion one freezing night in December AD 406 when, together with other barbarians, the Alans, the Suebi, the Alemanni and the Burgundians, they crossed the ice-bound Rhine into the Roman Empire. They surprised the Romans and breached the frontier at Mainz. The border had already been weakened as, a year previous, the Roman General Flavius Stilicho (his background was Vandal) had been forced to collect some Roman soldiers posted along the Rhine, in order to defend Rome from the Visigoth King Alaric and his army. With the Roman frontier breached, many hundreds of thousands of barbarians settled in Gaul, and various barbarian bands roamed unchecked across large parts of Gaul for two and a half years. It was the worst ravaging of Gaul ever known. Finally the two branches of the Vandals (Siling and Asding), as well as the Suebi and Alans, crossed the Pyrenees into Spain after being defeated by the Franks in battle and being harassed by the Goths (Visigoths). Within two years of being in Spain, the various conquering tribes dividing up their spoils, apparently by lot, the Siling Vandals and Alans taking the richest area, Baetica in the south, while the Asdings and Suebi took the north of Galicia.

In 410 AD, a pivotal moment in Western history, the Visigoths, under the command of their king Alaric, captured the city of Rome. Rome was known as the Eternal City because the Romans thought that it would literally never fall, and the year 410 shook this belief to its foundations and ultimately led to the collapse of the Roman Empire. Alaric rushed on Rome, but Rome's towers and walls were too much for the wild men who marched with Alaric. The Goths blockaded the city and ravaged the neighbourhood. At last upon the payment of a large ransom, Alaric withdrew to Tuscany. However, the ambitious Visigoth was determined to have his way. He kept on demanding from Honorius Dalmatia, Venetia, and Noricum, plus tribute. To save Rome from another attack, Pope Innocent personally went with an embassy from Rome to the imperial court at Ravenna. Honorius, safe himself, would not budge. Once more Alaric attacked the city; once again he was baffled by Rome's lofty walls. However, on a third attempt, traitors opened the Salarian gate and the Goths poured into the helpless city. For five days the barbarians burned and plundered. The world was shocked by the fall of great Rome. Pope Innocent, still at Ravenna, must have been heartbroken. It was to a ravaged city that he returned.

St Jerome, in his cave at Bethlehem, wept on receiving the news of the sack of Rome, and in his commentary on Ezekiel, which he was writing when he heard the news, wrote: "Who could have believed that Rome, founded on triumphs over the world, could fall to ruin; and that she, the mother of nations, should also be their tomb?"[7] He also wrote to Principia these words: "The City which had taken the whole world was itself taken."[8] This event brought Christians to the point where they really thought the Lord would return, for Jerome again said, "The world sinks into ruin: yes! but shameful to say our sins still live and flourish. The renowned city, the capital of the Roman Empire, is swallowed up in one tremendous fire; and there is no part of the earth where Romans are not in exile."[9]

It is remarkable that the barbarians laboured with the same zeal in the destruction of idolatry as in the destruction of the empire, and really promoted the victory of the Christian religion. The Gothic king Alaric, on entering Rome, expressly ordered that the churches of the apostles Peter and Paul should be spared, as inviolable sanctuaries; and he showed a humanity, which Augustine justly attributes to the influence of Christianity (even heterodox Arian Christianity) on these barbarous people.[10]

The world itself seemed to have been destroyed, and everyone sought answers about what to do and what to believe in. Those who adhered to the waning pagan faith were quick to blame the Christians, claiming that the gods had abandoned Rome because many Romans had forsaken them and taken the new faith. These Romans claimed that Christians were not patriotic enough because they asked people to serve God rather than the state, and they advocated forgiveness toward enemies. More important, they said the Christian God had failed to protect Rome, as he should have done, since Constantine had declared him to be the one true God. The angry wrangling between the two communities prompted Augustine to begin writing *The City of God* in 413. The first ten books of this tome, which make up the first part of the work, refute the pagans' charges that Christians brought about the fall of Rome. The first five books deal with the pagan belief that people must worship the old gods to achieve material advantages in this world, including the continuation of the Roman Empire and the supremacy of the city of Rome.

The Vandals were invited into Africa by a rebellious Roman warlord, Bonifatius, who was keen to recruit their support. Two brothers, Guntheric and Gaiseric, responded by organising an expedition which proved to be the largest ever sea-borne movement of a barbarian peoples. Guntheric died before the plans came to fruition but in Gaiseric the Vandals were left with a leader of immense ability—one of the ablest of all barbarian leaders. So it was that in 428, some 80,000 Vandals and Alans, of whom probably 20,000 were combatants, landed near Tangiers. There was little opposition and within two years, only Carthage and a couple of other cities were still holding out. By this time, the Vandals had been joined by a number of Spaniards and Moors, and a land which had known nothing but peace and prosperity for centuries was given over to plunder and massacre. Carthage finally fell in 439, giving the Vandals a major naval base from which to raid the Western Mediterranean. This they did with their customary ferocity, culminating in the sack of Rome itself in 455.

But in the end, the Vandals amounted to nothing more than raiders and plunderers. Unlike the Goths and the Franks, they proved unable to put down roots and enjoy the fruits of the lands they had conquered. When, in 533, Justinian sent Belisarius to invade the Vandal Kingdom, the great general destroyed it utterly. It left barely a trace behind. "Vanity of vanities,"

Gelimer, the last King of the Vandals is said to have murmured, as he grovelled at Justinian's feet, "all is vanity".

12.1.2 The Goths

The Goths originated in a land called Gothiscandza, now identified as southern Scandinavia. They began to move to what would become their long-standing homeland between the Oder and the Vistula, in what is now Poland. There was a slow, steady drift from the Oder-Vistula region into the Ukraine, or Scythia as it was known to the ancients. This region already contained a very mixed population, and the Goths would very certainly have mixed with these to produce a population that was even less homogeneous. By the middle of the third century AD, the Goths were becoming a formidable power, of which the Romans were given notice when a Gothic army crossed the Danube in 238, extorting substantial bribes before withdrawing. It did not take long for Goths to find their way into the ranks of the Imperial Army, and there may even have existed a formal treaty with the Emperor Gordian III. This did not prevent a second invasion in 250, the Goths being led by their king, Kniva, who also commanded warriors of other tribes, including the Vandals, as well as a number of Roman deserters. Kniva led his army as far south as Philippopolis, which he sacked, then comprehensively defeated a Roman army at Abrittus in 251.

Further invasions followed, including sea-borne raids, culminating in the taking of no less a prize than Trebizond in 258 AD.[11] A massive invasion of Asia Minor followed, resulting in the acquisition of massive plunder and many slaves, who may have been instrumental in the conversion of the Goths to Christianity. The subsequent spread of the new religion was largely the work of Ulfila, a native Goth, born in about 311. It was Ulfila, also, who created the Gothic alphabet, which enabled his translation of the Bible into Gothic. The fact that the strand of Christianity which took hold amongst the Goths was Arianism, was to prove significant centuries later, when they came up against the Catholic Franks.

The Goths, were hit very hard and quickly by the invasion of the Huns from Asia, so that by 350 AD they were split into two groups: the Ostrogoths ("Eastern Goths") and the Visigoths ("Western Goths"). By 376 AD, the Ostrogoths had fallen completely in Hunnic hands, where they were victimized and enslaved for nearly a century.

The Visigoths, severed from their brethren but saved from the brunt of the Mongol assault by the mere fact that they lived further west than the Ostrogoths, desperately sought protection by appealing to Rome for asylum. There, they ran up against an impermeable shield of customs stations at the Roman border, a veritable wall of imperial protection which was by then standard policy when barbarians began complaining and waving their hands. Thus squeezed between scorn and the spear, the Visigoths panicked and not a few tried to push their way into Roman territory. Facing a surge of frantic immigrants, the Roman Emperor Valens had little choice but to relent and let them in.

Once inside the boundaries of Rome, the Visigoths found safety from the Huns but at the same time a new and in many ways more dangerous foe. As new-comers to Roman civilization, they were ill-equipped to live in a state run on taxes, mired in the complex language of legalities, and thus made easy prey for unscrupulous, greedy imperial bureaucrats who cheated and abused them. Very quickly, the Visigoths found themselves bound in something heavier and more constricting than chains— the gruesome coils of red tape—and they responded as any reasonable barbarian would: they demanded fair treatment and, when their pleas went unheard, they went on a rampage.

Valens called out his army, a threat meant to intimate the Visigoths into returning to their designated territory and tithes. But like the truant step-children they were, the barbarians remained disobedient. Left with no other recourse but corporal punishment, Valens met the Visigoths in combat at the Battle of Adrianople (378 AD) in northeastern Greece, and what happened was not only unexpected but unthinkable to any Romen living then or dead. Primed by the insults to their pride—or because they were simply scared out of their minds—the Visigoths defeated and massacred the Roman legions sent to keep them in their room. Worse yet, Valens himself was killed in the course of the conflict.

12.1.3 The Huns

The event which, more than any other, presaged the fall of the Roman Empire was the arrival of a group of the Huns in Eastern Europe, forcing many Germanic peoples to migrate southwards and westwards and setting off a chain reaction which could only end with the inundation of the Empire itself.

A tribe known as the Xiongnu existed in western China at the time of the Han Dynasty (the last two centuries BC). They divided into two groups, the smaller of which migrated southwards. The majority, however, went north-west in search of new homes. Traveling all the way from Mongolia in the Far East, the Huns began encroaching on Europe sometime after 350 AD. Toughened by decades of crossing the Russian steppes on small ponies, these marauding Asiatic nomads spread terror far and wide, developing a reputation for great ferocity. They found their way into the valley of the Volga and, in the second half of the Fourth Century, attacked the Alans (a people related to the Sarmatians, who lived between the Volga and the Don).

After routing the Alans, they then went on to conquer the Ostrogoths and drive the Visigoths westwards. Early in the Fifth Century, they seem to have been reinforced by fresh hordes, and had become so powerful that, by the time of the Emperor Theodosius the Great, the Romans felt obliged to pay them a substantial tribute. Still, the Hunnic Empire could not pose a serious threat to the Empire; its economy was too primitive, its internal divisions too great, and Hunnic skills in strategy and siege-craft too lacking to defeat a sophisticated, organised opponent.

By about 420 AD, however, a Hunnic Confederacy had been established, enriched by plunder and tribute, by the hiring out of mercenaries to the Romans, and by the extortion of what can only be called protection money. Their empire stretched from the Baltic to the Caspian when, in 445, one of their two joint-rulers murdered his colleague and seized control of the Confederacy. The murdered man was named Bleda and his murderer was his own younger brother, Attila.

It is said that Attila reinforced his position by digging up a rusty old sword and proclaiming it to be the Sword of Mars.[12] The Empire he inherited was built on and sustained by booty; without a continual flow of plunder and tribute it could not survive. So it was that the Attila launched an immediate invasion of Eastern Europe. This was in 447 AD, a time when the Empire was already suffering a series of natural catastrophes—earthquakes, pestilence and famine—and it is little wonder that the Christian Romans saw the Huns as the very Horsemen of the Apocalypse.

The victories of this period may have more to do with Roman demoralisation than any inherent military superiority of the invaders. The Huns fought as horse archers, though their forces were much bolstered by the heavy cavalry of their Germanic subjects. In fact, the composition of the opposing armies would have been remarkably similar, with large numbers of Germans and even Huns to be found on both sides. The Roman Army of the time was little more than an assembly of allied or mercenary tribes, with few native Romans amongst them.

During the next three years, Attila's men lived off the booty and tribute of the Eastern Empire before turning, in 450 AD, to the West. The Western Empire at this time was nominally ruled by the Emperor Valentinian III but was effectively controlled by the warlord, Aëtius. It was Aëtius who assembled a confederacy with which to confront the Hunnic threat. This was composed of Franks, Visigoths and his own Romano-Germanic army.

The two forces met in 451 at the great battle of the Catalaunian Fields, near Châlons-sur-Marne. It was a brutal battle of little tactical subtlety, barbarian against barbarian, and by the end of the day Aëtius had the upper hand. He could have finished Attila once and for all but he did not. Knowing that, with the Huns destroyed, his Visigothic allies would overrun the whole of Gaul, he let the Huns escape. It was a judgment which the citizens of Italy would bitterly rue.

Infuriated and apparently under-educated in military proto-col, Attila took the loss as an insult, a kind of challenge, and turned south heading for Italy. The Romans in panic fled at his approach. Even the Emperor Valentinian III abandoned the capital—but the great leader of the Church, Pope Leo I, not only courageously stood his ground but went to face down Attila in person. In one of the most remarkable moments in history (452 AD), they actually did meet and speak, but only in private. According to Prosper of Aquitaine, Attila was so impressed by Pope Leo that he withdrew.[13] In the wake of their discussion, Attila wheeled about yet again, this time leaving Italy never to return.

Pope Leo had persuaded Attila to spare the city and Attila, in terror of the Cross, retreated. He had planned to destroy Constantinople, and ensure that the Romans would remain in thrall to him forever. However in 453, lying in a drunken stupor, Attila suffered a nose bleed. The blood trickled down the back of his throat and choked him to death. For a man who had boasted that "where my horse has trodden, no grass grows" it was a curiously anti-climactic death. The Empire he had created did not survive him.

With Attila dead, the Huns ceased to be a mortal threat to the Roman Empire—though the West never recovered and soon passed into the hands of the barbarians. Yet such was the mark left on men's minds that every subsequent wave of Asiatic invaders in the centuries to come were known to westerners are "Huns" (even the Magyars, several centuries later, so that the realm they founded is known to this day as Hungary).

The remnants of Attila's Huns regrouped in south-eastern Europe, ruling over the Slavs of that region. These peoples were to found a new Empire which troubled the Byzantines for hundreds of years, and were known as the Bulgars.

12.1.4 The Franks

The Franks are first mentioned in the historical record in the middle of the third century but may have originated as early as the late second century. Their name means "courageous" or "bold", the kind of name that might have been used by war-bands to describe themselves. For that is the likeliest origin of the Franks—groups of adventurers banding together to attack the lower Rhine frontier of the Roman Empire.

The military power of the Franks developed rapidly after the middle of the Third Century and, along with the Alemanni and others, they began raiding the Western Empire freely between 250 and 275, sweeping across Gaul in 274–5. The Franks operated by sea as well as land, raiding the Channel coasts and using rivers to attack inland. According to one source, they invaded eastern Spain and seized ships with which to invade Africa.

The Romans stabilised the Rhine frontier during the reign of Diocletian (284–305) and groups of defeated Germans were settled in northern Gaul at the end of the third century, tilling the soil and providing unspecified military service to Rome. These settlers enjoyed a very humble status within the Empire, being only half-free and tied to the land. However, several regiments of Franks are listed in the early fifth century *Notitia Dignitatum* and some leading commanders of the fourth century Roman army were Frankish or part-Frankish by birth.[14]

There is no indication, at this time, of any unified Frankish power. Frankish kings are mentioned but none of these seems to have ruled effectively or for long, ambitious rulers preferring a more lucrative role in the service of the Empire. With the imperial frontier in ruins by 420, power passed into the hands of Frankish leaders between that date and about 440, though Roman authority was not yet wholly defunct, provided in the person of the patrician, Aëtius, who operated against them on several occasions, struck treaties with them and recruited aid from them, most notably against the Huns in 451.

After defeat by the Romans at Vicus Helena in 440, the Frankish king Chlodio was recognised as a federate leader and left in possession of the region around Tournai, from where he created a significant enclave of Frankish power. Similar enclaves may have been created elsewhere; around Trier, for example.

The Kingdom of Tournai made considerable progress between 450 and 480, first under Chlodio and then under Childeric, who maintained the Franks' federate status while expanding his influence in western Gaul as far as the Somme. His successor was Chlodovech or Clovis. The latter (c. 466–511) not only destroyed the power of his rivals, uniting the Franks under his rule, but extended his authority over other peoples, east and west. Clovis' victories over the Thuringians and Alemanni began the process of Frankish domination over the Germanic peoples east of the Rhine; his victory over Syagrius, the self-styled King of the Romans at Soissons in 486 established Frankish hegemony in northern Gaul; finally his defeat of Alaric II at Vouillé in 507, drove the Visigoths back into Spain (apart from their small toehold in Septimania). Before Clovis died, in accordance with Salian tradition, he divided his kingdom between his four sons. His eldest son, Theuderic ruled from Rheims, while Chlodomer, Childebert and Chlothar, ruled respectively from Orleans, Soissons and Paris. They, and his grandsons after them, extended Frankish rule as far as the middle Danube, conquered the Burgundians and drove the Ostrogoths from Provence. By the middle of the century, the initial period of expansion ended and Frankish kings had to reward followers and endow the Church by granting away their own estates and revenues, thus diminishing their resources so that, in time, power passed to the families which had most benefited from this largesse. The full consequences of this would not come to fruition, however, until the middle of the seventh century.

Frankish expansion was more a matter of conquest than colonisation and though some Franks did settle in northern Gaul, there was little upheaval of the native population. Government remained largely in the hands of bishops and counts drawn from the ranks of the Gallo-Roman aristocracy . Clovis' conversion to Orthodox Catholic Christianity contributed greatly to their acceptance of Frankish rule; the Burgundians and Visigoths had both converted to the heretical Arian form of Christianity.

12.2 The Sack of Rome in 455

In 454, the Emperor Valentinian III murdered Aëtius. The following year Valentinian was stabbed to death by Aëtius' followers. The story goes that Eudoxia, the widow of the emperor, was then forced to marry Maximus against her will. Petronius Maximus was generally believed to have been the grandson of the usurper Maximus who had been crushed by the Theodosius the Great. He had been Consul at age 38 and became Praetorian Prefect of Italy six years later. He became emperor of the West Empire after Valentinian's death.

The widow Eudoxia knew that an appeal to Constantinople would have little chance of being answered. So she decided to write to Gaiseric, inviting him to take possession of Rome. However no invitation was needed, since Gaiseric's peace treaty had been with Aëtius and Valentinian III. Now they were dead and so was the treaty. Emperor Maximus who hurried to get his son married to Eudoxia instead of Huneric, to whom she was long since promised, angered Gaiseric. The Vandal fleet had been built up for the last ten years and now awaited a major expedition.

A major Vandal fleet left Carthage for Rome. Gaiseric and his nobles expected to clash with the imperial fleet somewhere at sea. However, when they sailed along the coast of Italy they found themselves unopposed and sighted the port of Rome, Ostia, on 31 May 455. The Romans were already terrified, sending their wives and daughters away to safety. The gates of Rome could not cope with the number of people seeking to flee. Emperor Maximus had no chance to raise his army in defence of his capital and decided to ride out of Rome. Unfortunately for him, an angry Roman crowd recognised him and stoned him to death. This emperor had reigned for just 70 days. Three days after Maximus' death, unopposed, King Gaiseric stepped ashore at Ostia

For the fourth time in less than half a century, a barbarian stood at the gates of Rome. Fearing for the safety of Rome, Pope Leo I heroically decided to speak with the leader of the barbarians on the behalf of his city. He was met by King Gaiseric and persuaded him not to burn and slaughter. Gaiseric decided to give certain promises: there would be no killing, no torturing to discover the location of hidden treasure and no destruction of buildings, public or private. On these terms the gates of Rome were wide open to him allowing him to enter the city with no ressistance. The Vandals plundered for two weeks. While Gaiseric stayed at the Imperial palace, his men took all the treasures, statues, Solomon's Temple, even part of the gilded roof of the Temple of Jupiter Capitolinus was removed. Yet his greatest prize were Empress Eudoxia, her two daughters, Eudocia and Placidia, and Gaudentius, the son of Aëtius. Everything was carted to Ostia, loaded into the waiting ships, from where he and his men departed in good order and sailed back to their stronghold in North Africa. The people of Rome and its buildings were generally left unharmed.

12.3 The Fall of Rome in 476

All the provinces of the western empire, outside of Italy, had fallen into the hands of barbarians, infected for the greater part with idolatry or Arianism. The ten last emperors, over a period of twenty years, were rather shadows of power than sovereigns, and in the eighth year of the pontificate of Pope Simplicius (reigned 468 to 483), Rome itself fell a prey to foreigners. Salvian, a learned priest of Marseilles in 440, wrote an elegant book on Divine Providence, in which he shows that these calamities were a just chastisement of the sins of the Christians; saying, that if the Goths were perfidious, and the Saxons cruel, they were, however, both remarkable for their chastity; as the Franks were for humanity, though addicted to lying: and that though these barbarians were impious, they had not so perfect a knowledge of sin, nor consequently were so criminal as those whom God chastised by them.[15] The disorders of the Roman state paved the way for this revolution. Excessive taxes were levied in the most arbitrary ways. The governors oppressed the people at discretion, and many were obliged to take shelter among the barbarians: for the Bagaudes, Franks, Huns, Vandals, and Goths raised no taxes upon their subjects: on which account nations once conquered by them were afraid of falling again under the Roman yoke, preferring what was called slavery, to the empty name of liberty.

Italy, by oppressions, and the ravages of barbarians, was left almost a desert without inhabitants; and the imperial armies consisted chiefly of barbarians, hired under the name of auxiliaries, as the Suevi, Alans, Heruli, Goths, and others. These soon saw their masters were in their power. The Heruli demanded one third of the lands of Italy, and, upon refusal, chose for their leader Odoacer, someone of the lowest extraction, but a tall, resolute, and intrepid man, then an officer in the guards, and an Arian heretic, who was proclaimed king at Rome in 476. He put to death Orestes, who was regent of the empire for his son Augustulus, whom the senate had advanced to the imperial throne. The young prince had only reigned eight months, and his great beauty is the only thing mentioned of him. Odoacer spared his life, awarded him a salary of six thousand pounds of gold, and permitted him to live at full liberty near Naples. Pope Simplicius was wholly taken up in comforting and relieving the afflicted, and in sowing the seeds of the Catholic faith among the barbarians.

The fall of mighty Rome in AD 476 profoundly impacted the secular world and the Church. From that time on the Roman Empire in the West passed out of existence. This event plunged the western world into the Dark Ages in politics, economics and religion. The collapse of Rome, even though it was predicted by some, shocked the world. Fortunately for the true Church in the Roman Empire, many of the barbarian tribes were professing Christians. They were Arians and not orthodox, but at least they were somewhat sympathetic. Thus, many true Christians were spared death and Church property was not destroyed. The western section of the Roman Empire was then completely under barbarian dominion and broken up into various states. This was a difficult time, for now Catholics, Arians and pagans all tried to settle down side by side, and this did not make for harmonious relationships.

12.4 Why did Rome fall?

Many theories exist as to why Rome fell, but all beg the question *whether* Rome really fell. The first major historian to deal with the decline and Fall of Rome was the fifth century historian Zosimus, but since then many historians of ancient Rome have tackled the causes for the fall of this powerful empire. In 1984, German professor Alexander Demandt collected 210 different theories on why Rome fell, and new theories have emerged since then.[16] Some of the reasons supplied can be summarized as follows.

12.4.1 Antagonism between the Senate and the Emperor

The Roman Emperor had the legal power to rule Rome's religious, civil and military affairs with the Senate acting as an advisory body. The emperor had power over life and death, as in the old saying "Power corrupts and absolute power corrupts absolutely".[17] The powerful, wealthy Roman Emperors inevitably became corrupt and many lived a debauched and immoral lifestyle. The Roman Empire saw divisions between the Senate and the Emperors. Either the Senate did not like the Emperor or the Emperors was at odds with the Senate.

12.4.2 Decline in Morals

A decline in morals, especially in the rich upper classes and the emperors, had a devastating impact on the Romans. This included immoral and promiscuous sexual behaviour including adultery and orgies. Emperors such as Tiberius kept groups of young boys for his pleasure; Caligula was sexually perverse; Nero practised incest and also had a male slave castrated so he could sexually abuse him; Heliogabalus married and divorced five women, including a vestal virgin;[18] Commodus had harems of concubines and enraged the Romans by sitting in the theatre dressed in a woman's garments. The decline in morals also effected the lower classes and slaves. Pagan festivals took place, such as Saturnalia and Bacchanalia, where sacrifices, ribald songs, lewd acts and sexual promiscuity were practised. Bestiality and other lewd and sexually explicit acts were exhibited in the Colosseum arena to amuse the mob. Brothels and forced prostitution flourished. Widespread gambling occurred on the chariot races and gladiatorial combats. There was a considerable consumption of alcohol. Sadistic cruelty was inflicted upon both men and beasts in the arena.

Life became cheap: bloodshed led to more bloodshed and extreme cruelty. The values, the ideals, customs, traditions and institutions of the Romans declined. The basic principles, standards and judgments about what was valuable or important in life also declined. The total disregard for human life resulted in a lack of ethics—a perverted view of what was right and wrong, good and bad, desirable and undesirable. Any conformity to acceptable rules or standards of human behaviour were being lost.

Even after Constantine and the rise of Christianity, moral life was not always sound, as Salvian testified around 424 AD:

> If Christ said the people of Sodom are less to be condemned than all who neglect the Gospels, then we who in most of our actions show our neglect of the Gospel teachings are in graver danger, especially since we are not willing to be content with crimes long familiar, that seem a part of our daily life. Many are not satisfied with the customary vices, with litigation, slander and rapine, with drunkenness and gorging at feasts, with forgeries and perjury, with adultery and homicide. Finally, however inhuman the atrocities involved, all the crimes involving injury to their fellow men are not enough for

them, but they must needs turn the blasphemous violence
of their mad minds against the Lord also.[19]

12.4.3 Fast expansion of the Empire and constant warfare

The rapid growth of the Empire led to the need to defend the
borders and territories of Rome. The people of the conquered
lands, most of whom were referred to as barbarians, hated the
Romans. Taxes on the foreigners were high and constantly
increased and frequent rebellions arose. Constant warfare
required heavy military spending. The Roman army became
over-stretched. The barbarians, who had been conquered, and
other foreign mercenaries were allowed to join the Roman army.
The knowledge that the barbarians gained of Roman warfare
and military tactics by serving in the Roman army were eventually turned against the Empire and led to the sack of Rome by
the Visigoths led by an ex-army soldier Alaric.

12.4.4 Failing Economy

The Government was constantly threatened by bankruptcy. The
cost of defending the Empire, the failing economics, heavy
taxation and high inflation was another reason why the Roman
Empire fell. The majority of the inhabitants of the Roman Empire
failed to share in the incredible prosperity of Rome. The flow of
gold to the Orient to pay for luxury goods led to a shortage of
gold to put in Roman coins. Roman currency was devalued to
such an extent that a system of bartering returned to one of the
greatest civilisations the world had ever known.

12.4.5 Slave labour

The number of slaves increased dramatically during the first two
centuries of the Roman Empire. The Roman's dependency on
slave labour led not only to the decline in morals, values and
ethics but also to the stagnation of any new technology to
produce goods more efficiently. Romans could rely on slave
power for all their needs, and this reliance inhibited technolog-

ical change and growth. The terrible treatment of slaves led to rebellion and several Servile (Slave) Wars, the most famous being the revolt led by Spartacus. In the later centuries of the Empire and the advent of Christianity the attitudes towards slaves changed. With manumission (the act of freeing a slave) the number of slaves declined together with the manpower that Rome depended upon.

Cheap slave labour in turn resulted in the unemployment of the the people of Rome who became dependent on hand-outs from the state. The Romans attempted a policy of unrestricted trade but this led to working class Romans being unable to compete with foreign trade. The government were therefore forced to subsidize the working class Romans to make up the differences in prices. This resulted in thousands of Romans choosing just to live on the subsides sacrificing their standard of living with an idle life of ease. The massive divide between the rich and the poor increased still further.

If the thousands of unemployed Romans became bored this led to civil unrest and rioting in the streets. The Mob needed to be amused — the gladiatorial games had to be provided. The cost of the gladiatorial games was born by the Emperors, and therefore the state, and corrupt politicians who sponsored the games to curry favour and support with the Mob. The cost of the gladiatorial games eventually came to one third of the total income of the Empire.

12.4.6 The barbarian invasions

The barbarian invasions described above seem to be the immediate cause of the Fall of Rome in 476 AD.

12.4.7 Health issues

Plagues and lead poisoning may have played their part in the decline of Rome. The Roman Empire suffered the severe and protracted Antonine Plague starting around 165 AD.[20] For about twenty years, waves of one or more diseases, possibly the first epidemics of smallpox and measles, swept through the Empire, ultimately killing about half the population. Similar epidemics, such as the Plague of Cyprian, also occurred in the third century. The severe fall in population could have left the state apparatus and army too large for the population to support, leading to further economic and social decline that eventually killed the Western Empire. The Eastern half survived due to its larger population, which even after the plagues was sufficient for an effective state apparatus.

Human skeletal remains recovered from Pompeii indicate that the Romans were indeed exposed to high concentrations of lead. Jerome Nriagu, a geochemist, argued in 1983 that lead poisoning contributed to the decline of the Roman empire. His work centred on the level to which the ancient Romans, who had few sweeteners besides honey, would boil must in lead pots to produce a reduced sugar syrup called *defrutum*, concentrated again into *sapa*. This syrup was used to some degree to sweeten wine and food. Lead also leached from the glazes on amphorae and other pottery, from pewter drinking vessels and cookware, and from lead piping used for municipal water supplies and baths.[21] This theory has not received wide acceptance.

12.4.8 The role of Christianity

Edward Gibbon, an English Enlightenment classical historian in the later half of the eighteenth century argued in his book *The Decline and Fall of the Roman Empire* that the rise of Christianity emasculated the native vigour of Rome, leaving it open to more virile conquerors, namely the barbarians. Gibbon proposed that Christianity created a belief that a better life existed after death, which fostered an indifference to the present among Roman citizens, thus sapping their desire to sacrifice for the Empire.[22] This is a proposition full of holes and inconsistencies, saying in the end less about the Roman Empire than its British counterpart, the real target of Gibbon's book. If Christianity so weakened the Roman West in late antiquity, why didn't it weaken the other half, the staunchly orthodox East which survived nearly a millennium after the collapse of the West? Christianity redirected the attention of many Romans away from affairs of state, but it did not undermine their civilization. On the contrary, it was as natural an outgrowth of their culture, as Roman as anything else they created: theatre, epic poetry, gladiators, ship-building, all of which were imports. It must be remembered that Gibbon, as an Enlightenment thinker, was very hostile to organized religion in general, and to Christianity in particular.

12.5 Did Rome really fall?

The historical truth is that Rome did not really fall; rather, it evolved. Roman *coloni* (farmers tied to the land) gradually became Medieval serfs. The patron-and-client relationship, so central in Roman society, slowly assumed the name and nature of the lord-and-vassal bond, the social order underlying much of European society in the Middle Ages. So, if Rome fell, it was only in slow motion.

However change *did* come to Rome in the fifth century—as it has in every century of human history—and a particularly drastic change it was. Many of the conventions which had once ruled the ancient Romans' lives evaporated, never to re-emerge. Primarily, citizenship in Rome offered little or no protection to its denizens, like membership in a club that was now defunct. That, in turn, precipitated an even more serious casualty, the loss of pride in being Roman, and of all things *that* perhaps lies at the heart of the problem.

The popes in Rome more than once stood up to defend the state, when Emperors did not, as Pope Leo the Great did when he confronted and turned Attila from Italy. Churchmen like him were defending not only their homes but their home institution, both Mother Rome and Mother Church. Seen this way, Rome did not "fall" at all but passed its great cultural legacy, the very heart of its civilization, to the burgeoning Christian world.

Even after the barbarian invasions, the Roman way of doing things did not immediately change; barbarians came to Rome not to destroy it, but to share in its benefits, and thus they tried to preserve the Roman way of life. The rise of the Frankish realm in Europe can be seen as a continuation of the Roman Empire, and thus validates the crowning of Charlemagne as the first Holy Roman Emperor as a successor of the Roman Emperors.[23]

12.6 Impact upon Christianity

The effects of the changes in Rome upon Christianity were indeed manifold. First, a Christian Roman culture developed in the East. In AD 330 Constantine moved the capital of the Roman Empire from Rome to Byzantium for political and military reasons. He renamed this eastern city Constantinople which subsequently became a thriving centre. When the western section of the Empire fell (including Rome), the Latin-Greek-Christian culture moved completely to the east, and this section of the empire did not fall until 1453, when it was taken by the Turks and the Islamic religion. The Turks renamed it Istanbul. Most of the emperors and populace in the Byzantine Empire were at least Christian by profession.

Second, the Papacy became more prominent. The leading members of the Roman society fled the West and went East when they knew that the barbarians were coming. When Rome fell, there was no emperor left, but the bishop of Rome stayed and was respected by the local people and by the barbarian tribes because they were often professing Christians. This left the pope preeminent in the social life of the city, and his moral authority increased enormously as a result. In the East, the emperor would often have dispute with the bishop of Constantinople, and he would appeal to the bishop of Rome as an arbitrator. The bishop of Rome took the place of the emperor and became a political leader as well as a spiritual leader. His authority went almost unchallenged.

A third consequence of the fall of the Roman empire was that the Church was left to educate and evangelize the barbarian tribes. The Church not only sought the conversion of the pagan tribes, but it also had the task of educating and civilizing them.

Many of the tribes such as the Huns, Jutes, Anglos, Saxons, Franks, had little no Christian background. Most of the others were Arian in their theology. In the 500 years following the invasion of the Roman Empire by the barbarians (by the year 1000), all the new nations of Europe had become Christian. Some of these converted barbarians became excellent missionaries themselves. The British monk, Patrick, became the missionary to Ireland. Columba, an Irish monk, took the Christian message to the land of Scotland. Boniface took the Gospel to the Frisians, and Willibrord took the Faith to the Netherlands—both of these men were English.

A major milestone was the conversion of Clovis, the King of the Franks (AD 496). Clovis was the king of the barbarian tribe of the Franks, who settled in northern Gaul. Clovis saw a sign in the sky, and that this sign was from God to assure him he could win a battle in war. He won the battle, and he and three thousand of his warriors professed Christianity at once. Later, his whole tribe made their professions. This was the first case in history of a whole tribe of barbarians professing Christianity because their king did. Clovis accepted the Roman Catholic position over against the other barbarian tribes who were still Arian. Some 200 years after the wholesale profession of the Franks, this tribe would stop the onrushing Turks at the Battle of Tours in AD 732, when Charles Martel, the leader of the Franks, blocked the hosts of Islam.

A fourth by-product of the dissolution of the Roman Empire was that monasticism grew strongly. As we saw, monastic living began with Paul of the Desert in Egypt. Men and women became hermits who separated themselves from all worldly practices and congregated together in monasteries. Men and women desired to live holy lives, but could not because the pull of the world was too strong especially from outside of the Church. After the fall of Rome in AD 476, the desire for monastic living increased, for the world in general was in a mess. Many thousands of Christians, in all sincerity, gave themselves to an ascetic life in monastic orders, and the monks preserved learning and culture after the fall of Rome. Many texts remaining from the Roman and Greek cultures were preserved and recopied by the monks. Into the cauldron forged by the Fall of Rome many new cultures were fused, and the genius of Christianity was the leaven to civilize and develop these cultures for the glory of God.

Notes

[1]   The Picts occupied Britain north of the Antonine Wall, although in actual fact there never was a race or tribe called the Picts. The name was an adopted one, assumed in the same manner that the Britons of later Wales adopted Cymry as their name, and Cymru as their country (instead of Prydein, otherwise known as Britain). No Picts existed as any sort of separate people. The Latin word Picti first occurs in a panegyric written by Eumenius in AD 297 and is taken to mean "painted or tattooed people" (from Latin pingere "to paint", pictus, "painted", cf. Greek "πυκτίς" -pyktis, "picture"). See S. M. Foster, *Picts, Gaels, and Scots: Early Historic Scotland (London:* Batsford, 2004), p. 11: "Much ink has been spilt over what the ancient writers meant by Picts, but it seems to be a generic term for people living north of the Forth-Clyde isthmus who raided the Roman Empire."

[2]   Gaius Cornelius Tacitus, *De Origine et situ Germanorum,* 2.

[3]   The Sarmatians were a coalition of Iranian nomadic tribes, which moved gradually from the Caspian plains to eastern Europe and threatened the Roman empire.

[4]   The *Suebi* (Suevi) were a confederation of Germanic peoples who came into existence by the first century AD, and perhaps earlier, but they seem to have had origins as an individual tribe of the same name. Spelled Suevi or Suebi by various authors, the core tribe migrated southwards from the southern Baltic coast in concert with many other Germanic tribes. In fact, the Romans knew the sea as Mare Suebicum, so familiar were they with the Suebi presence there. In the first century BC the tribe arrived on the east bank of the Rhine, with the River Main on their southern flank. Settling here, they were neighboured to the north by the Cherusci, and their presence survives in the historic name of the region, Swabia.

[5]   The Alemanni settled south-western Germany, northern Switzerland, and the Alsace region. Just like the Suebi, they were not a single people but a confederation, their very fitting name meaning 'all men'. The largest of their tribes included the Bucinobantes, and probably the Hermunduri (broken during the Marcomannic Wars and later absorbed into both the Alemanni and Thuringians) and the Semnones. Until at least the sixth century, it is likely that each tribe in the confederation largely ruled itself,

with a possible over-king simply providing military leadership in times of trouble (a system very similar to that used by the Roman republic). As they were located on the eastern side of the upper Rhine, and were therefore close to the borders of the Roman empire, the Alemanni name survives today in the Romance terms for the German people as a whole, such as Allemagne.

6   The Alans were originally an Iranian steppe people who settled in Scythia in the fourth century BC, displacing the Scythians, a similar Iranian Steppe culture. Scythia consisted of the plains which stretch from the north of the Black Sea over to the Caspian Sea. The Alani are first mentioned in the west by the Roman historian, Josephus, in the first century AD. He calls them a Scythian tribe living near the Don (Tanais) and the Sea of Azov. They seem to be indivisible from the Samartians and the Geloni of the same region. Herodotus mentions the Geloni (Gilans), so they were either closely related, or more likely the same peoples. The fourth century Roman writer Ammianus Marcellinus considered them to be the direct descendants of the Massagetae. Conquered by the Huns, they became allies, and most travelled west with the Huns. Split by the Hunnic attacks, some Alani tribes remained behind, dispersed across the steppes. They were forced by further waves of invaders to migrate into the Caucuses where they eventually founded the regionally-powerful kingdom of Alania, only to be conquered by the Mongols in the thirteenth century. They re-emerged as the Ossetians, based in modern Georgia and southern Russia.

7   St Jerome, *Commentary on Ezekiel*, Preface to Book III.

8   St Jerome, *Letter 127 to Principia*, 12.

9   St Jerome, *Letter 128 to Gaudentius*, 4.

10 See P. Schaff, *History of the Christian Church, Volume III: Nicene and Post-Nicene Christianity* (CCEL: 2002), p. 51.

11 Trebizond, (Trabzon in Turkish) is a city on the Black Sea coast of north-eastern Turkey and the capital of Trabzon Province. Trabzon, located on the historical Silk Road, became a melting pot of religions, languages and culture for centuries and a trade gateway to Iran in the southeast and the Caucasus to the northeast.

12 See Jordanes, *The Origin and Deeds of the Goths*, chapter XXXV: "When a certain shepherd beheld one heifer of his flock limping and could find no cause for this wound, he anxiously followed the trail of blood and at length came to a sword it had unwittingly trampled while nibbling the grass. He dug it up and took it straight to Attila. He rejoiced at this gift and, being ambitious, thought he had been appointed ruler of the whole world, and that through the sword of Mars supremacy in all wars was assured to him."

13 St Prosper of Aquitaine, *Chronicon*, sub anno 452.

14 The *Notitia Dignitatum* is one of the very few surviving documents of

Roman government, and details the administrative organisation of the eastern and western empires, listing several thousand offices from the imperial court down to the provincial level. It is usually considered to be up to date for the Western empire in the 420s, and for the Eastern empire in 400s.

[15]   See Salvian, *On the Government of God*, 7, 15. Salvian's best known work, is essentially an exposition of this thesis: that the decline of the Roman power actually demonstrated God's government and judgment of human actions, since the sins of the Romans were such as had always, since the fall of Adam, been visited with instant punishment. Salvian (or Salvianus) was a Christian writer of the fifth century, born probably at Cologne, sometime between 400 and 405. He retired with his wife Palladia to the monastery of Lerins.

[16]   See A. Demandt, *Der Fall Roms: Die Auflösung des römischen Reiches im Urteil der Nachwelt* (München: Beck,1984), p. 695.

[17]   John Dalberg-Acton, First Baron Acton, *Letter to Bishop Mandell Creighton* (5 April 1887) published in *Historical Essays and Studies*, edited by J. N. Figgis and R. V. Laurence (London: Macmillan, 1907)

[18]   Vestal virgins were women priestesses to the goddess of Hearth, Vesta, in Ancient Rome. The main duty they must perform was to guard the fire of Vesta. With this they would be endowed with many honours and rights that a normal woman would not have at that time. Their vow of chastity and their vow of sustaining the fire, made them vital individuals in that ancient time in history.

[19]   Salvian, *On the Government of God*, 4, 9.

[20]   See W. H. McNeill, *Plagues and Peoples* (Garden City, NY: Anchor Press/Doubleday, 1976)

[21]   See J. O. Nriagu, "Saturnine gout among Roman aristocrats. Did lead poisoning contribute to the fall of the Empire?" in *New England Journal of Medicine* 308/11 (March 1983), pp. 660–663.

[22]   E. Gibbon, *The History of the Decline and Fall of the Roman Empire* (London: A. Strachan, 1788), chapter 38.

[23]   See H. Pirenne, *Medieval Cities: Their Origins and the Revival of Trade* (Princeton: Princeton University Press, 1974). Henri Pirenne published his theory in the 1920s, and it remains influential to this day.

BIBLIOGRAPHY

Adams, E., *The earliest Christian meeting places: Almost exclusively houses? Library of New Testament studies. Early Christianity in context: v. 450*. London: T & T Clark, 2013.

Aquilina, M., *The Fathers of the Church: An introduction to the first Christian teachers*. Huntington, IN: Our Sunday Visitor, 1999.

Aquilina, M., *The witness of early Christian women: Mothers of the Church*. Huntington, IN: Our Sunday Visitor, 2014.

Aravecchia, N., *Christians of the Western Desert in Late Antiquity: The fourth-century church complex of Ain el-Gedida, Upper Egypt*. Doctoral dissertation: University of Minnesota, 2009.

Barry, A., *Lives of Irish Saints* 3rd ed.). Dublin: Gill, 1908.

Baruffa, A., *The catacombs of St Callixtus: History, archaeology, faith*. Vatican City: LEV, 1993.

Baus, K., *From the Apostolic Community to Constantine. History of the Church: Vol. 1*. New York: Seabury Press, 1980.

Baus, K., *The Imperial Church from Constantine to the Early Middle Ages. History of the Church: Vol. 2*. New York: Seabury Press, 1980.

Carroll, D., *Mary's House: The Extraordinary Story Behind the Discovery of the House Where the Virgin Mary Lived and Died*. Texas: Christian Classics, 2000.

Chadwick, H., *The Early Church*. Harmondsworth: Penguin Books, 1967.

Corley, K. E., *Maranatha: Women's funerary rituals and Christian origins*. Minneapolis: Fortress Press, 2010.

Cusack, M. F., *The Trias Thanmaturga ; or, Three wonder-working saints of Ireland: St Patrick, St Bridget and St Columba*. London: Murdock, 1870.

Davis, S. J., *The cult of Saint Thecla: A tradition of women's piety in late antiquity. Oxford early Christian studies*. Oxford, New York: Oxford University Press, 2001.

Demandt, A., *Der Fall Roms: Die Auflösung des römischen Reiches im Urteil der Nachwelt*. München: Beck, 1984.

Dunbar, A. B. C., *A Dictionary of saintly women*. London: G. Bell, 1904–1905.

Eckenstein, L., & Roscoe, C., *The women of early Christianity*. London, Milwaukee: Faith Press; The Morehouse Publishing Company, 1935.

Ferguson, E., McHugh, M. P., & Norris, F. W., *Encyclopedia of early Christianity* (2nd ed.). *Garland reference library of the humanities: vol. 1839*. New York: Garland, 1997.

Grech, P., *What was from the Beginning: The Emergence of Orthodoxy in the Early Church*. Leominster: Gracewing, 2016.

Gregg, J. A. F., *The Decian persecution*. Edinburgh and London: W. Blackwood and sons, 1897.

Guéranger, P., *Life of St Cecilia, virgin and martyr*. Philadelphia: P. F. Cunningham, 1866.

Haffner, P., *The Mystery of Reason*. Leominster: Gracewing, 2001.

Haffner, P., *The Mystery of Mary*. Leominster, Herefordshire, Mundelein, IL: Gracewing; Hillenbrand Books, 2004.

Haffner, P., *The Sacramental Mystery* 3rd ed.). Leominster: Gracewing, 2016.

Harbus, A., *Helena of Britain in medieval legend*. Suffolk, UK; Rochester, NY: D. S. Brewer, 2002.

Harmless, W., *Desert Christians: An introduction to the literature of early monasticism*. Oxford: Oxford University Press, 2004.

Heine, S., *Women and early Christianity: A reappraisal*. Minneapolis: Augsburg Publishing House, 1988.

Kelly, J. N. D., & Walsh, M., *A Dictionary of Popes* 2nd ed.). Oxford: Oxford University Press, 2010.

Laporte, J., *The role of women in early Christianity. Studies in women and religion: v. 7*. New York: E. Mellen Press, 1982.

Marshall, T., *The Eternal City: Rome and the origins of Catholic Christianity. The origins of Catholicism*. Dallas, TX: Saint John Press, 2012.

Midgley, J. B., *Dewi Sant: Saint David : patron of Wales*. Leominster: Gracewing, 2012.

Miriam, Sr., *The Life of the Virgin Mary, the Theotokos. Lives of Saints: Vol. 4*. Buena Vista, CO: Holy Apostles Convent, 1989.

Mourret, F., & Thompson, N. W., *A history of the Catholic Church*. St Louis, MO., London: B. Herder Book Co, 1930-.

O'Collins, G., *From Rome to Royal Park*. Leominster: Gracewing, 2016.

Pacioni, V., *Augustine of Hippo: His philosophy in a historical and contemporary perspective*. Leominster: Gracewing, 2010.

Rainy, R., *The ancient Catholic Church*. Edinburgh Scotland: Clark, 1902.

Regnault, L., *The day-to-day life of the Desert Fathers in fourth-century Egypt* 1st English ed.). Petersham, Mass.: St Bede's Publications, 1999.

Rich, A. D., *Discernment in the Desert Fathers: Diákrisis in the life and thought of early Egyptian monasticism. Studies in Christian history and thought*. Milton Keynes: Paternoster, 2007.

Rivington, L., *The Primitive Church and the See of Peter*. London: Longmans, Green, and Co, 1894.

Schaff, P., *History of the Christian Church, Volume II: Ante-Nicene Christianity. A.D. 100–325*. Grand Rapids, MI: Christian Classics Ethereal Library, 2002.

Schaff, P., *History of the Christian Church, Volume III: Ante-Nicene Christianity. A.D. 311–600*. Grand Rapids, MI: Christian Classics Ethereal Library, 2002.

Scholer, D. M., *Women in early Christianity. Studies in early Christianity: v. 14*. New York: Garland Pub, 1993.

Schukte, C. G., *The Life of Sr. Marie de Mandat-Grancey & Mary's House in Ephesus*. Charlotte, NC: Tan Books, 2011.

Todd, J. H., *St Patrick Apostle of Ireland: A memoir of his life and mission*. Dublin: Hodges, Smith and Co., 1864.

Wace, H., *A dictionary of Christian biography and literature to the end of the sixth century AD: With an account of the principal sects and heresies*. Grand Rapids, MI:: Christian Classics Ethereal Library, 2000.

Waddell, H., *The desert fathers*. New York: Sheed & Ward, 1936.

White, L. M., *House churches in early Christianity*. Nashville, TN: Christian Communications Inc, 1985.

Wordsworth, C., *A Church History to the Council of Nicea, AD 325*. London: Rivingtons, 1881.

INDEX OF PERSONS

Lightning Source UK Ltd.
Milton Keynes UK
UKOW02f0711301016

286407UK00002B/49/P